BEYOND
EXOTICISM

Refiguring American Music

A Series Edited by Charles McGovern and Ronald Radano

Timothy D. Taylor

BEYOND
EXOTICISM

WESTERN MUSIC AND THE WORLD

DUKE UNIVERSITY PRESS   DURHAM AND LONDON   2007
OCM 71146383

© 2007 Duke University Press

All rights reserved.

Printed in the United States of America on acid-free paper ∞

Designed by Heather Hensley

Typeset in Monotype Garamond by Tseng Information Systems, Inc.

Library of Congress Cataloging-in-Publication Data and republication
acknowledgments appear on the last printed page of this book.

For Sherry, my number only

CONTENTS

LIST OF MUSIC EXAMPLES

LIST OF FIGURES AND TABLES

FIGURES

TABLES

ACKNOWLEDGMENTS

Since some of the chapters in this volume began life as articles, there is a wide range of people whose help proved indispensable.

Some ideas in the Introduction were first presented at a seminar in January 2005, and I would like to thank Giovanni Giuriati for inviting me. The ideas presented in chapters 1 and 2 have a genesis going back quite a time; some were first auditioned at "Convergence and Congruence: A Symposium in Honor of Judith Becker" in Ann Arbor, October 2001. Since then several colleagues have offered comments and critiques, for which I am very grateful, in particular Susan Boynton, Jean Howard, and especially Olivia Bloechl.

Many of the ideas presented in chapter 3 with respect to the history of twentieth-century music were first tried out in my survey courses on twentieth-century music, and I received helpful suggestions from students over the years who heard these lectures.

Chapter 4 made its début as a paper invited by Patrice Petro and Tasha Oren, who asked me to participate in the conference "Transmissions: Technology, Media, Globalization" at the University of Wisconsin, Milwaukee, on 27 April 2002, where some of these ideas were first presented. I would also like to thank Karin Bijsterveld and Trevor Pinch, who invited me to present this material at the Sound Matters workshop at the University of Maastricht in November 2002, and the audience at the Institute of Social Research, University of Salford, who also provided useful feedback when I visited there that month. A different version of this chapter was presented at SUNY, Stony Brook, in April 2003, and I am grateful to that audience for their insightful comments and questions. The most recent iteration of this chapter was presented to the Global Studies Fellows at the University of California, Los Angeles, in January 2006, and I thank those who participated for their comments.

Chapter 5 began life as a meetings paper for the American Studies Association in 1998, and had another airing before a particularly generous and inquisitive audience in the Music Department at the University of Pennsylvania early in 1999. Thanks are due to Aaron A. Fox, René T. A. Lysloff, Carol Muller, Irene Nexica, Guthrie P. Ramsey, Gary Tomlinson, and Deborah Wong for their help in formulating the ideas in this chapter.

Aaron A. Fox invited chapter 6 for his volume on global country music, and I am grateful for his insightful and valuable input along the way.

For chapter 7 I am indebted to many people in the corporate world who were enormously helpful with their time and expertise: Dan Tardella of Daimler-Chrysler; Andrea Marcaccio and Nancy Fisher of Bozell Worldwide; Maureen Parish of Royal Caribbean Cruise Lines; Ann Haugen and Danny Hulsizer of Elias Associates; Gabrielle Doré of Michael Boyd Music; Erin Brosnan of McKinney and Silver; and Erin Shoor of Saatchi and Saatchi. I would also like to acknowledge lively audiences in the Department of Music at the University of North Carolina, as well as the Institute of Social Anthropology at the University of Bergen, who heard a shortened version of this chapter. Last, a number of friends and colleagues offered invaluable advice along the way: Steven Feld, Brad Garton, Thomas Payne, and Nancy Tomes.

I had fellowship support in the process of writing this, a junior fellowship from the American Council of Learned Societies, the National Humanities Center, the Humanities Council at Columbia University, a Charles A. Ryskamp Fellowship from the American Council of Learned Societies, and an Academic Senate grant from the University of California, Los Angeles. Many thanks are due to all of these organizations.

Thanks also go to Aaron M. Bittel, who digitized some of the music examples.

A few others offered their friendship and insights: Carol Babiracki, Tara Browner, John Canaday, Sue-Ellen Case, Barbara Ching, Tia DeNora, Alessandro Duranti, Susan Foster, Ana María Ochoa Gautier, Tamara Levitz, Susan McClary, Louise Meintjes, Elinor Ochs, Tom Porcello, Ron Radano, Timothy Rice, Anthony Seeger, Emily Thompson, Robert Walser, Christopher Waterman, and Bob White.

At Duke University Press, Ken Wissoker and Courtney Berger have been tremendously helpful and encouraging. And patient. Thanks also go to Fred Kameny.

I would also like to thank my parents, Lee and Jane Taylor, for their continued support over the years, including expert gardening advice on demand.

Steve Feld's work on this subject helped inspire my own, and I have also benefited greatly from his friendship, support, and critiques over the years.

This book was written in a period of considerable upheaval in my life, and many good people helped me through it, some of whom I have already named: Steve Feld, Anne McClintock, Louise Meintjes, Ingrid Monson, Ana María Ochoa Gautier, Dr. Shawn Nasseri, Paul Rabinow, Ron Radano, T. M. Scruggs, Kay Kaufman Shelemay, and Deborah Wong. In addition, many people at UCLA helped make my transition there a smooth and happy one: Donna Armstrong, Tara Browner, Hannah Huang, Susan McClary and Rob Walser, Jennie Molina, Dan Neuman, Carol Pratt, Betty Price, Tim and Ann Rice, Martha Rider, Dianne Roberts, Lisa Rubin, Anthony Seeger, and Chris and Glennis Waterman.

Mine wasn't the only life in upheaval, and last, in recognition of her good humor, inspiration, critiques, support, and understanding, I thank, as ever, Sherry B. Ortner, to whom this book is lovingly dedicated.

I would also like to thank my parents, Lee and Jane Taylor, for their continued support over the years, including expert gardening advice on demand.

Steve Feld's work on this subject helped inspire my own, and I have also benefited greatly from his friendship, support, and critiques over the years.

This book was written in a period of considerable upheaval in my life, and many good people helped me through it, some of whom I have already named: Steve Feld, Anne McClintock, Louise Meintjes, Ingrid Monson, Ana María Ochoa Gautier, Dr. Shawn Nasseri, Paul Rabinow, Ron Radano, T. M. Scruggs, Kay Kaufman Shelemay, and Deborah Wong. In addition, many people at UCLA helped make my transition there a smooth and happy one: Donna Armstrong, Tara Browner, Hannah Huang, Susan McClary and Rob Walser, Jennie Molina, Dan Neuman, Carol Pratt, Betty Price, Tim and Ann Rice, Martha Rider, Dianne Roberts, Lisa Rubin, Anthony Seeger, and Chris and Glennis Waterman.

Mine wasn't the only life in upheaval, and last, in recognition of her good humor, inspiration, critiques, support, and understanding, I thank, as ever, Sherry B. Ortner, to whom this book is lovingly dedicated.

This is a book about power, about systems of domination and oppression, and about who has had the power of representation of Others in music, from the seventeenth century to the present. Admittedly, this is a wide swath of time. But this book is not a survey. It is, rather, a study of the three main systems of domination and exploitation—colonialism, imperialism, and what we now call globalization—and the ideologies produced by them that foster appropriations of music and representations of nonwestern Others.

Given this orientation, there is a natural division in the book between feudal, state, and later corporate modes of domination and representation. Before the rise of mass culture in the late nineteenth century and the early twentieth, it is social élites with court composers who possess the power of commissioning and the vehicles of prestige; two of the musicians I will study in the following chapters worked for kings. But after the advent of mass culture and its industrialization, this power shifts. Social élites still have money and influence, but their culture, high culture, loses prestige over the course of the twentieth century to popular culture, which is far more lucrative. Representations of otherness are still worked out in élite forms, though these have practically no audience today.

With this historical shift, from the dominance of feudal states to nation-states to multinational corporations, the focus of this book, and its methodologies, also shift; analysis goes where the power of representation is. The first few chapters are concerned with western European art music and its composers. Understanding how power and representation worked in this era with respect to music requires a mode of textual exegesis that will be familiar to musicologists, though it is combined in equal measure with analyses of society, culture, and history that will be less familiar but, I hope, instructive. With the rise of mass culture, the power of representation relocates largely to corporations, and so analysis will be of corporate practices, advertising, and marketing—how these shape representations and, of course, sounds. Again, significant attention will be paid to the underlying social, cultural, and historical issues surrounding musics and musical practices, relying on interviews, music industry publications, web sites, internet newsgroups, and the popular press.

To be sure, some of the western European art music terrain has been covered before; questions of music and difference have become much more salient topics in musicology and ethnomusicology than they once were, with a spate of recent writings on the subject.[1] So far, however, globalization as a long-term process has received more attention from ethnomusicologists than from musicologists, though there is no reason why this should be so, since composers of classical music are also subjects in social, cultural, and historical processes.

Musicology has, however, offered a fair number of writings that tackle the theme of "exoticism" in music—that is, manifestations of an awareness of racial, ethnic, and cultural Others captured in sound. Many of these studies, it seems to me, suffer from a well-worn approach that tends to fetishize form and style. For example, in the leading English-language encyclopedia of music, the article on "exoticism," by a well-known musicologist of the subject, ranges from the sixteenth century to the present, and includes figures such as Bob Dylan, whose interest in roots and African American musics is characterized as exotic.[2] This kind of work, while very learned, nonetheless shows some of the symptoms of what I would call the classical music ideology, which finds a home not only in music departments but also more generally among the concert-going public.

Let me spend some time with this concept, for it suffuses much of the prior work on the subjects in this book. I think it is important to deconstruct this ideology, for when one is studying works in which representations of peoples from other cultures are present, the stakes become higher. It is one thing to think and write and speak unquestioningly of geniuses and master-pieces in and of themselves, but quite another when these ideas, as well as, more importantly, conceptions of selfhood and otherness, are at play, when one social group claims to own the power of representation while denying it to others, who are then represented.

By "the classical music ideology," I refer to an ideology that has as its two foundational tenets the concepts of "genius" and "masterpiece," two concepts that arose in their present form in the first half of the nineteenth century.[3] They are neither "true" nor "false," but culturally and historically located. That is, they are concepts that emerged in a particular place and time because of a complex of reasons that are social, technological, cultural, historical, and economic, though they are nonetheless concepts that some people accept as true. The situatedness of these and other ideas is well known to historians and students of culture, yet the classical music ideology remains dominant in most music departments.

A great deal is invested in these concepts. Composers, composing, and compositions are reified in the classic Marxist sense; works are likewise fetishized. Even though the composer is dead and their works are texts, both composers and works are thought to speak directly to the listener. A work of music can evoke an extremely personal set of reactions, initiate an astonishingly personal interior journey. This is thought to be almost a magical process, so powerful—and mystified—that classical music is akin to a religion in which composers are gods and their works sacred texts, with performers and sometimes musicologists vying for the position of high priest, with the position of hagiographer the consolation prize.

Thus musicologists tend to focus on the twin pillars of form and style, as though these emanate solely out of composers' heads as the purest distillation of their individuality. Or Great Works—assumed to be full of Great Ideas (though these are seldom explicated)—are compared to thinkers contemporaneous with the composers as though there is a Zeitgeist at work, without examining where these ideas come from, how they were shaped by the time and place of their origin, how they traveled.

That musicology is primarily based on the study of individuals and their works betrays a usually unacknowledged Enlightenment notion of the individual—and the later idea of genius—so that musicians are not usually viewed as subjects inhabiting a particular historical moment and a particular place, but instead are viewed unproblematically as total agents: things happen in a musical work because composers make them happen. Accordingly, biographical information on composers is sometimes used as a point of departure for musicological analyses, which can produce some useful insights; but other times, some writings run the risk of reductionism or essentialism by attributing how pieces sound to composers' psyches and biographies, rather than asking more complex questions about composers as social actors in particular times and places.

I would argue instead that we usually know too much about composers, and that if we knew less, we would be forced to learn more about their time and place, view them as social, cultural, and historical subjects rather than autonomous individuals with well-known biographies. To the extent that it is used at all, the composer's biography ought to be the window into a time and place, the mediator between the "private" self of the composer and the wider world.

For the classical music ideology, and thus much musicology, what are seen as incidental or irrelevant matters—such as culture and history (in a particular sense that I will address in a moment)—are usually left unattended to, or presented as generally inconsequential background to composers' lives and works. The absence of attention to history as a material force speaks to another of the foundational concepts of the classical music ideology, the idea of transcendence. Since artworks are thought to speak directly to their listeners or viewers, whatever history, culture, or social conditions produced them are thought to be irrelevant. But as Raymond Williams writes, "we have to break from the common procedure of isolating the object and then discovering its components. On the contrary we have to discover the nature of a practice and then its conditions."[4]

Its conditions, its history. The classical music ideology cherishes this idea of transcending the time and place in which a work was written, which means that most scholars of music tend not to cultivate a concept of history as, say, a historian does. History is not perceived as a dynamic force that shapes peoples' lives, shapes the way things were, and are. History instead is usually construed as a collection of facts that may or may not be relevant in studying a piece of music. As in ethnomusicology and anthropology where one speaks of the "culture concept," it is just as possible to talk about a "history concept" in the historical fields, though I take these two to be pretty much the same thing, the one in the past and the other in the present, with the understanding that the past is never wholly past and the present is never wholly present.

In English studies, there is some textual work being done today that is attentive to culture and history. The major figure is Stephen Greenblatt, who was instrumental in founding a new approach in literary studies called the new historicism; it is no accident that Greenblatt frequently acknowledges his debt to the anthropologist Clifford Geertz.[5] The new historicism situates literary works in more than just their cultural and historical contexts; it attempts to uncover meanings in works that were contemporary at the time. Why is this text the way it is? What were people thinking about, talking about, doing, in a particular moment, and how do all these things leave traces in texts? This is more of a social science perspective; as Max Weber writes, the social sciences are primarily interested in knowing "on the one hand the relationships and the cultural significance of individual events in their contemporary manifestations and on the other the grounds of their being historically 'so' and not 'otherwise.' "[6] Another guiding idea comes from Michel Foucault: "How is it that one particular statement appeared rather than another?"[7] That is, what are the historical, cultural (and other) reasons that resulted in a particular statement, defined broadly as any text? There is no reason not to introduce these perspectives to the rest of the humanities, as I will attempt to do in the following pages.

In the late 1980s the emergence of "new musicology" mounted a powerful challenge to many of the long-held assumptions of older musicologies that I have been critiquing here. I was in graduate school at the time, and the publication in 1987 of *Music and Society*, edited by Richard Leppert and Susan McClary, was greeted with palpable excitement by many of us, opening our eyes to new approaches, and pointing to earlier publications such as Jacques Attali's *Noise: The Political Economy of Music* that most of us hadn't know of before. More new musicology works followed, influential books such as Rose Rosengard Subotnik's *Developing Variations* and McClary's *Feminine Endings*, both in 1991, as well as a spate of important writings on popular music, with Simon Frith's *Sound Effects* and Robert Walser's *Running with the Devil* among the early and significant books.[8] These and other works offered powerful critiques of the musicological business-as-usual in their theoretical sophistication and their engagement with fields beyond musicology such as literature, women's studies, philosophy, sociology, and anthropology.

Yet while the new musicology did much to destabilize the canon and permit more works to be included in scholarship and teaching, it has done less to change the way that music is studied.[9] The classical music ideology is still operative in many quarters. The dominant musicological interest in "works" as self-contained entities, and in their form and style—apart from the conditions of their making and hearing—continues. History and culture continue to be ignored or minimized while composers and their works are still privileged, as is, increasingly, the critic-musicologist.

In part, I think, because of the cultural studies boom, such approaches have become so hegemonic, so naturalized, that even outsiders to musicology have adopted them when they broach musical subjects. To pick just a recent example that also addresses some of the concerns of the present book, Georgina Born and David Hesmondhalgh write in the introduction to *Western Music and Its Others* that their edited volume attempts to "enhance the classification of different modes of appropriating and representing other musical cultures, different techniques of the musical imaginary."[10] While I might not disagree that there is such a thing as "the musical imaginary" (though, of course, it needs to be historicized and socially situated), I would take exception to the authors' apparent assumption that modes of appropriating and representing other musical cultures stem solely from this imaginary. The editors well know that musicians don't work in vacuums, but the momentum of decades of musicological scholarship that emphasizes style and form at the expense of everything else is very difficult to overcome, even for musicological outsiders. The underlying reasons why a particular musician interacts with musics from another culture in a certain way are cultural, historical, and social—not to mention situational and contingent—and cannot be easily grouped into ahistorical or transhistorical "modes."

Likewise for the editors' attachment to "modernism" and "postmodernism" as style categories, which replicates musicological practices. While I suppose it is possible to group musicians into these broad classes (which grow vaguer daily through overuse), the editors' use of these categories is based on what composers do: "We can now discern two basic, structural relations-of-difference to the musical Other at work in musical modernism and postmodernism. The first, as in those composers who drew on other musics, is one of recognition of difference yet attempted aesthetic incorporation or subsumption. The second, as with serialism and other high-modernist tendencies, is the attempt to construct a 'relation' of absolute difference, nonrecognition, and nonreference."[11] This kind of periodizing is common nowadays in musicology and beyond, standing in for more thorough examinations of particular histories. Apart from the murkiness of this passage (are they saying that serialism is "postmodernist"?), one could offer enough counterexamples that would put this formulation in doubt. Serialism, after all, is only the most rigid of stylistic modernisms—plural—and there were plenty of modernist composers (such as Igor Stravinsky) who freely made use of music of their Others and played with serial techniques in the course of their careers. Even if there were not such examples, the underlying problem remains: the problem of "music and difference" is seen as a musical problem first, perhaps solely. I would argue instead that there is no such thing as "the musical Other," that this is an essentialized concept. People in different historical situations have ways of constructing their Others in different ways, which they do in part with music; the music of the Other has not played much of a role in this process until comparatively recently.

Thus, despite a nod toward the new musicology, writers such as Born and Hesmondhalgh, who in other ways have much of value to offer, are trapped into simply continuing the trend of earlier musicologists (though the authors are respectively an anthropologist and sociologist) by tending to concentrate on composers, specific pieces, and styles, rather than on broader ideological and cultural shifts that have left deep traces in musical processes and genres that might not be accessible, or even discernible, with their narrower approach. The result is that there tends to be a good deal of historical blindness, and concomitant absence of insight, on historical, cultural, and social questions in studies of music.

Ethnomusicology has been more sensitive to the question of situating particular practices in their cultural contexts than either musicology or cultural studies, but since its main methodology is ethnography it tends to be presentist in orientation, which means that history is rarely taken into account, though there are some notable exceptions such as in the work of Veit Erlmann and Ronald Radano, who know how to be deeply ethnographic while conducting historical research. Erlmann, for example, in writing what he calls a "historical ethnography," conducted extensive archival and historical research on South African musics to make a compelling argument about modernity and globalization, while Radano similarly made extensive use of historical materials in writing a serious and much-needed deconstructive history of "black music" in America that calls into question many cherished clichés about this music and its practices.[12]

Ethnomusicological and anthropological models for my own work include Steven Feld, who was the first to put the problem of world music on the map for most of us in an early and prescient article entitled "Notes on World Beat."[13] Later work by Louise Meintjes, among others, including a detailed and thoughtful ethnography of a recording studio in South Africa, has helped to enrich and deepen our knowledge of the production of "world music" in an international market.[14] Another example is the anthropologist Sunaina Maira's ethnography of diasporic South Asians in New York City,

Desis in the House, one of the best studies of music and identity I know.[15] These and other scholars are helping to blaze the trail of a new (ethno)musicology, to which I hope to contribute with this book.

Following these and other scholars, it is clearly possible to take a more ethnomusicological and anthropological approach to the study of music in history, to attempt to understand the deeper social, cultural, and historical underpinnings of musics and musical practices. Colonialism, imperialism, and globalization have had far greater effects than merely offering inspiration to composers, effects that have left deep marks in the cultures and practices of both colonializer and colonialized.[16]

Like many existing (ethno)musicological works, this book is also concerned with the surface manifestations of "exoticism," and colonialism, imperialism, and globalization, but it attempts to explain them by examining the social, cultural, and historical processes that gave rise to them, as well as to less obvious tracings of the Other in music. In doing so, the less evident residues of western music's encounters with other cultures can be unearthed. Thus, this book takes Weber, Foucault, and Williams seriously on their assertions quoted above. It is not only about works, or style, or form, or composers: it is a book about history and culture—and music that attempts to be sensitive to historical periods and conceptions of difference in them.

While there are some discussions of premodern musicking and otherness, chapters in this book range mainly over musics from the early modern to the present, and consider the various ways that "the West"—including the United States—has confronted, represented, and appropriated those whom it has taken to be, or constructed as, its Others, at home and abroad, how these various interactions and practices sound musically, and how the people represented also attempt to represent themselves. What emerges is that while some of these representations and appropriations are heavy-handed and xenophobic, these and more subtle modes of musical interaction date back for centuries. It is also clear that Europe's experiences with its colonialized Others informed European attitudes to its internal Others and vice-versa, ideologies that also found their way to the United States.

Following Marshall Berman, I place selfhood, the ability to narrate one's own life, at the center of modernity.[17] But western European modernity is predicated on a conception of selfhood that was made in large part in reaction to Europe's Others, and is still strongly dependent on constructions and conceptions of otherness. The "discovery" of the New World prompted the construction of new modes of difference, of new forms of otherness, and this discovery played an important, even constitutive, role in making modern selfhood. A new conception of otherness was one result of the colonial encounter, and a crucial factor in the rise of modernity itself.[18] Others (gendered, racialized, and classed) were no longer construed as existing on some sort of continuum with western subjects, but were instead forced into the subordinate half of a binary opposition. It has become fashionable in some theoretical camps in the last couple of decades to deconstruct binary oppositions, but people still live by them, still construct discourses and practices around them. I would argue that binary oppositions are by far the most salient means by which modern western bourgeois subjects made, and continue to make, conceptions of racial, ethnic, and cultural difference. Simply put, it is because of difference that modern western people can know who they are. As Stuart Hall writes in a memorable passage, "the English are racist not because they hate the Blacks but because they don't know who they are without the Blacks."[19]

To address these and other issues of difference, selfhood, and music, it is essential to move beyond the usual musicological rubric of "exoticism," introduced above; it is pointless to talk about "exoticism" as a kind of singular practice — there are, now, exoticisms. The term "exoticism" in its standard musicological usage tends to cover up, gloss over, the varieties of treatments of otherness in the last few hundred years. The point of the chapters that follow is not only to historicize dominant conceptions of otherness but also to historicize the many ways that otherness has been represented in music by Europeans and Americans.

The book is thus organized around three clusters of the organized domination of other peoples by westerners — colonialism, imperialism, and globalization — and the ways these systems construct different forms of otherness, conceptualizations of modern European selfhoods, and music.

There is a concern that in focusing on western modes of domination and representation, I risk homogenizing those whom the West constructs as its Others. I hope this book is not read that way. I hope, rather, that deconstructing the workings of power and historicizing "exoticism," so that whatever utility it may have is forever qualified, is in itself a useful project.

I probably need to say a word about what is included, and what isn't. Like my earlier books, this one takes something of a case study approach, although there is at the same time a loose organizing chronology. Though my earlier books met with some criticism for employing such an approach, I make no apology for it. Musicology and ethnomusicology have plenty of detailed histories and ethnographies in print already, on which I will rely frequently in the following pages. What is more pressing now, I think, is to try bringing these fields not only into greater dialogue with each other, but into dialogue with other fields in the social sciences and humanities. There are big conversations going on in anthropology, sociology, history, literature, and other fields that this book hopes to partake in and contribute to, and I hope that fellow workers in my fields of ethnomusicology and musicology take this book as an entry in a common conversation across disciplinary boundaries on major intellectual questions.

This book is divided into two sections, the first considering the historical systems of colonialism and imperialism, the second globalization as a cultural system. This division does not imply that ideologies of colonialism and imperialism are gone (there is, for example, a substantial literature on neo-colonialism and imperialism). On the contrary, much of the second part of the book demonstrates how earlier conceptions of difference are alive and well in our own era and the recent past.

Chapter 1 examines the rise of European colonialism, especially the impact of the "discovery" of the New World, and how changing conceptions of selfhood are intertwined with the origins of tonality (the musical system of functional harmony that is still used in most western musics), which arose around the beginning of the seventeenth century, and opera, which arose around the same time. Most musicologists have examined these histories strictly from a musical and technical vantage point, overlooking other aspects of European history that might have shaped the rise of these important developments in western European music. Tonality as a musical language creates centers and margins, effecting a kind of spatializing musical system in which Others can be managed at a distance. Opera was a powerful new dramatic representational form that was also used to manage Others. There is an extended discussion of a seventeenth-century English masque by Williams Lawes (baptized 1602, d. 1645) exemplifying the new attitudes toward music and space that are the subject of this chapter.

Chapter 2 considers how musical signs signifying nonwestern Others, particularly peoples from Africa and the Middle East, entered the western European musical vocabulary. By the early eighteenth century musical representation practices are set in place that remained for the better part of a century: "misplaced" downbeats, unexpected modulations, dissonances, and disjunct melodies. In other words, musical innovations were smuggled into works through their representations of otherness. Works considered include Jean-Philippe Rameau's *opéra-ballet Les Indes galantes* (1735), Mozart's *Die Entführung aus dem Serail* (1782), and Beethoven's Symphony no. 9 (1823).

Chapter 3 examines the "age of empire," roughly 1875–1914, in which Darwinian thought heavily influenced conceptions of difference. Other peoples were not seen as different, or even inferior as in the past, but further down the evolutionary scale, far behind their western counterparts in terms of cultural development. At the same time, urbanization and changes in consumption patterns gave rise to new forms of desire of the Other, with musicians and other artists writing of their fantasies of the exotic. The well-established ideology of the aesthetic, the notion of art for art's sake, found a new valence as a way to appropriate and represent Others while still keeping them at bay. The musical subjects of this chapter are Maurice Ravel and the American composers Charles Ives and Henry Cowell.

In some ways, *Beyond Exoticism* is a distant sequel to my *Global Pop: World Music, World Markets* in its concern for western treatments of otherness.[20] This kinship is clearest in part II, which is broadly organized around today's global corporate capitalism, and examines the acceleration of discourses of otherness and modes of representation of otherness since the Second World War, an acceleration that has come about as a result of new communication technologies, new regimes of consumerism, and new approaches in advertising and marketing. Now modes of representation can change in an instant, so quickly that it seems as though one day the music industry believes its Others to be one thing, and the next day something else—but that something else may well be a representation that has a history of hundreds of years. The rate of change of representations today is so rapid in large part because there are so many tropes of Otherness now available. As the following chapters will show, newer ideas about Others did not eclipse older ones, but instead complicated the notions of the Other and otherness. So in the last few decades, the Other, the exotic, have become extremely complex and powerful tropes in western culture that can change on a dime.

After some preliminaries to part II that introduce globalization and other key themes, chapter 4 examines the rise of the discourse of multiculturalism, signifying a new attitude toward difference. This attitude is explored in the music and discourse of the American bassist and producer Bill Laswell, who thoughtfully collaborates with other musicians and attempts to minimize the exploitative role that a western musician can play in relation to nonwestern musicians. This chapter argues that "collaboration" has become an important trope to signify how western and nonwestern musicians work together, but that at the same time market pressures force musicians to emphasize their individuality. Laswell provides a good example of how a musician manages these two ideologies, and how he traverses the complex terrain of production and consumption.

Chapter 5 fleshes out the question of hybridity in world music; if "collaboration" is the key sign of interpersonal relations in world music, then hybridity is the key metaphor of the resulting sound, a term applied both to musical sound and to the diasporic peoples who make such sounds, caught between their ancestral cultures and the dominant culture in which they live. The success of the discourses of hybridity has meant that older discourses of authenticity are no longer the only ways for western listeners to apprehend musics from other places. Listeners to world music are now less likely to criticize music that doesn't seem to be authentic, and are more likely to welcome it as a hybrid. This chapter traces the success of the hybridity concept and how the use of hybridity as a marketing term and productive category all too frequently collapses musics by Others—and the peoples themselves—into merely new forms of difference. As such, these musics continue to occupy the subordinate slot in global cultural politics. It is also the case that hybridity is occasionally constructed as simply another kind of authenticity, demonstrating the always-shifting nature of regimes of authenticity around what is commonly called "world music."

Chapter 6 addresses the music industry's policing of the "world music" category and explores why this label permits the inclusion of many different genres of music from elsewhere, rock in particular, but almost never country music. Central to this categorizing is the anthropological concept of culture, which became a well-known idea in America just before the Second World War. This chapter includes an extensive examination of what is to my knowledge the only album of country music that has been treated as world music, *Songs of the Hawaiian Cowboy*, a recording that was marketed and received (in reviews and in Internet newsgroup discussions) as world music through a complicated and overlapping set of discourses that construct this music as "cultural" (in the anthropological sense) and "historical" (rather than commercial, as country music is usually viewed). There is also an examination of the different class locations of the audiences of these musics, as country music is associated with working-class and lower-middle-class audiences, whereas world music is much more of a middle-class phenomenon.

The final chapter examines what is perhaps the most ubiquitous mode of representation in the United States—advertising—and the rise of what presents itself as world music in television commercials. These musics are increasingly used to try to sell something, whether a flight on an airplane, a cruise, or an automobile. More often than not, however, these musics are in no way related to any indigenous or traditional practices, but are instead entirely fabricated, either by performing musicians or by those who work in advertising. These musics often make use of what sound like choruses of children and of untexted vocal lines (usually sung by a solo woman vocalist); sometimes, as with the English group called Adiemus, the language heard is wholly invented. This chapter examines these musics and those who make them (composers, music production companies, and advertising agencies), and the uses to which these musics are put. The argument is that these musics tap into old western notions of escaping the ordinary, of using the voyage to signify "the world," but that they do this for new reasons. The myriad public discourses of globalization, transnationalism, the information age, and the information economy are reconfiguring conceptions of prestige and the kinds of capital that one needs to survive in the contemporary moment. As the concluding chapter also emphasizes, world music has been reduced to a single "style" that is used in these ads to signify "globalization," marking the most recent triumph of the capitalist market over this music.

PART I   COLONIALISM AND IMPERIALISM

CHAPTER 1

COLONIALISM, MODERNITY, AND MUSIC:
PRELIMINARY NOTES ON THE RISE OF
TONALITY AND OPERA

Hide your wives and daughters, hide the groceries too
The great nations of Europe comin' through.
—Randy Newman, "The Great Nations of Europe"

The emergence in the 1980s of scholarship on colonialism and postcolonialism has energized the study of history, allowing scholars to understand the extent to which some of the great metanarratives of modernity were caught up in Europe's colonial projects, so much so that earlier considerations of modernity have come to seem to be incomplete.[1] Scholars from historically marginalized groups have sought to dislodge the stories that western culture has told about itself, and histories and methods developed by students of western European colonial projects have destabilized western representations of its own history. "Modernity appears when Europe affirms itself as the 'center' of a *World* History that it inaugurates; the 'periphery' that surrounds this center is consequently part of its self-definition," writes Enrique Dussel.[2]

Music was not left unaffected by Europe's colonial endeavors and the course of modernity. This chapter will outline the impact of the "discovery" of the New World on European thought and culture, and how this discovery—and colonialism more generally—shaped western European musical practices. I will argue that colonialism's well-known effect of solidifying European conceptions of selfhood against nonwestern Others is registered in the establishment of tonality (the system of functional harmony that was dominant in art music in the west from around 1600 to 1900 and remains dominant in most western musics); and the rise of opera as a coherent genre. This is a big project for a single chapter, but I hope that it can play a role in stimulating more cultural and historical approaches to the study of musical systems and genres, adding to important work begun by Susan McClary and John Shepherd and others on tonality.[3]

Incorporating the histories of various western European colonial projects into our conceptions of European modernity allows—even forces—profound changes in our understanding of important events in early modern western European music history. The main axis along which European modernity was affected by its colonial projects was the conceptions of selfhood, which were caught up in a complex relationship to the Others at home and abroad.

Before embarking on the substance of this chapter I must make clear that the rise of tonality and the rise of opera were both multi-sited and messy; there is no singular narrative of origins that can adequately capture either. Yet it is nonetheless clear that both tonality as a musical system and opera as a genre coalesced into reasonably coherent and identifiable phenomena, though with local variations, especially with respect to opera. While the more localized stories of the rise of tonality and opera are extremely interesting and have been well documented by musicologists, my interest here is a broader set of issues: why local practices all over Europe eventually gave us tonality and opera as we have come to know them. In telling this story, some specifics will have to be omitted to keep in focus the larger question of the historical and cultural forces shaping the rise of tonality and opera.

COLONIALISM

The central argument of this chapter is simple: that tonality and opera gained a foothold, and then dominance, in western European culture when they did because of European conceptions of selfhood and otherness, particularly after the rise of European colonialism.[4] And so it is important here to outline the rise of European colonialism and the changes in ideology and culture that it wrought in western Europe, changes that were grappled with musically as in other arenas of the production of cultural forms. Much of this territory has been covered before, but it is necessary to rehearse it here to provide a context for the consideration of music to come.[5] The main thrust of the following history concerns new conceptions of self and Other, conceptions reconfigured in large part because of European colonial projects.

It is important to emphasize that while the New World was significant in European imaginations, Europe had long known of the existence of, and had traded on, both the Asian and African continents. Robert Brenner has written of the economic importance to England of both Asia and Africa, whereas America was not economically significant until well into the seventeenth century.[6]

Yet the discourses surrounding the discovery of the New World provide a number of writings that are very revealing of ideologies of self and Other. Some of the earliest European Renaissance humanist responses to the discovery of the New World reflected a belief that the indigenous Americans were living pure, free, ideal, even utopian lives, a well-known theme in this period.[7] Much of the New World and its inhabitants were greeted with a complex theory of wonder that has been widely written about.[8] I will not go over that material here, though I will treat the concept as an early modern phenomenon near the end of this chapter.

In the sixteenth and seventeenth centuries most Europeans believed all people to be God's children; conceptions of race as we would recognize them today didn't come into being until the nineteenth and twentieth centuries.[9] The problem for intellectuals in the sixteenth century was not one of "race" or "ethnicity" as we now think of them, but of what was called variety. If everyone was a child of God, how could there be variety, what we would now call cultural diversity? "How comes it to pass," wrote Robert Burton in *The Anatomy of Melancholy* in 1621, "that people separated only by a river or a mountain are dissimilar?"[10] Many an early modern scholar found himself advocating a position that would be called cultural relativism today.

Conceptions of variety produced studies, and much work in the sixteenth and seventeenth centuries was along the lines of finding correspondences between groups. Scholars were constantly seeking similarities between one group and another and writing about the similarities they thought they found. One result was the rise of an argument about the congruities between modern "savages" and the ancients. This ideological shift happened gradually, proceeding through a number of stages, but eventually it was held that contemporary savages had something in common with ancient savages, including those of European antiquity, and that contemporary savages could reveal something about ancient ones.[11] This conceptualization of the "savage" marks an important step toward distancing the "savage" from the rest of humanity, making it possible to judge him as inferior.

FUNGIBILITY

In large part, modern conceptions of self came to rest on binary conceptions of selfhood and otherness. Yet selves and Others can't be made out of thin air, or by just a few, no matter how culturally influential they might be. Cultural shifts require the efficient spread of information. In the case of Columbus and his "discovery," the news traveled fast. Columbus's first letter was printed and published nine times in 1493 and reached twenty editions by 1500; there were fifteen editions of Francanzano Montalboddo's collection of voyages, the *Paesi Novamente Retrovati*, first published at Venice in 1507, and more.[12]

Writers' comments on the New World have been thoroughly discussed by scholars but are worth reexamining here briefly. Descriptions of the New World and its inhabitants in writing were largely interchangeable; one traveler's reminiscences were replayed in Amerigo Vespucci's *Il Mondo Nuovo* (1504) and then again in Thomas More's *Utopia*.[13] This interchangeability was symptomatic of the dominant epistemology of the time, which was based on a system of resemblances, the search for similarities noted above; Michel Foucault writes that "resemblance played a constructive role in the knowledge of Western culture."[14] This changed by the beginning of the seventeenth century, giving way to a new configuration that Foucault calls "rationalism," for him a major epistemological shift.

But one cannot look for similarities or differences without data. To Europeans still in Europe, lack of concrete information was frustrating. Stephen Greenblatt notes that "the whole European project of writing about the New World rests upon the absence of the object—landscape, people, voice, culture—that has fascinated, repelled, or ravished the writer."[15] The lack of information resulted not in Europe's constructing the New World as *something*, but rather, as *anything*. Likewise, the inhabitants of the New World weren't conceived as Others, but as Not Selves: all that wasn't the modern northwestern European self, the New World Other could be, and was: wild, cannibalistic, irrational, sexually ravenous, monstrous.[16] Because of the lack of information on the New World, "the early modern discourse of discovery . . . is a superbly powerful register of the characteristic claims and limits of European representational practice."[17] Illustrations presented particular problems for Europeans fascinated by the New World. J. H. Elliott writes that "the European reader was hardly in a position to obtain a reliable picture of life among the Tupinambá savages of Brazil when the illustrations in his book included scenes of Turkish life, because the publisher happened to have them in stock."[18]

Musically, Europeans after the discovery of the New World represented these new others the same way as this publisher, whatever material was available for new representational purposes.[19] This wasn't sleight of hand; in early modern epistemology, these Others were interchangeable. And older forms of musical representation would get harnessed for new uses with the onset of colonialism. What may be the first recorded instance of a European treatment of another culture's forms in music dates from the late fourteenth century: "On the twenty-ninth of January, 1393, in Paris, the Duchesse de Berry gave a wedding party. One of the guests was King Charles VI of France, and during the evening he and five of his courtiers, disguised as savages, entertained the company with a 'furious Moresca.' . . . The Duc d'Orléans, accidentally or not, set the savages' headdresses afire with a torch and the flames spread, killing several guests and leaving the king (who was then recovering from a mental disturbance) permanently deranged."[20]

A *moresca* or *morisca* was a Moor's dance that reached its height of popularity in the fifteenth century.[21] Morescas parodied the music of slaves who were used as domestic servants in both Italy and Germany at this time. The dances usually involved performers putting on blackface, and probably gave rise to the English morris dance (a tradition still observable there, since a revival in the nineteenth century).[22] The moresca may also be related to the Spanish *matachín*, which goes back as far as the twelfth century in Spain. The conquistadores brought this dance to the New World, where they taught it to the indigenous peoples. This dance can now be found from Bolivia to New Mexico to the Philippines.[23]

Eventually, moresche predictably found their way into "higher" musical forms, adapted for broader representational purposes. Before opera, one of the most popular forms of entertainment among the nobility was drama, but plays usually appeared with music in some guise. The moresca was an important ingredient of the early *intermedio* in early modern Italy, a type of work performed beginning in the late fifteenth century. One author wrote in 1536 that intermedii were inserted between the acts of a play "so that the stage will not remain empty, music and songs, and *moresche* and buffoons are usually brought in mixed together."[24] In England the morris dance and its variants found their way into the masque, a precursor to opera in England, about which I will have more to say later.

GENDER

At this point I want to examine the extent to which modern attitudes toward difference are shaped by European colonial experiences, and the ways that existing attitudes of difference inflected the discourse of the discovery of the New World. Davies, Nandy, and Sardar argue that the discovery of the New World resulted in Europe's questioning itself, its identity, and thus forming the modern self: first, because moderns thought that "having" a self was possible at all; and second, that it could be made. The birth of the self could only come with the discovery of the Other.[25]

But who was this Other? Was it indigenous peoples only? I argue that modern, colonial attitudes toward racialized difference were shaped by existing attitudes toward difference; that new, racialized conceptions of difference drew upon older notions of gendered difference, and upon the racialized difference of Others closer to home—Turks, Arabs, Jews, Irish; and that these eventually informed one another.

As has been much discussed, colonized lands were feminized, and some have written of colonialism as a kind of rape. Early modern writings of the discovery put the question of gender on the surface. For example, Peter Martyr writes, "Smooth and pleasing words might be spoken of the sweet odors, and perfumes of these countries, which we purposely omit, because they make rather for the effeminating of men's minds, than for the maintenance of good behavior."[26] Much has been written about the feminization of the New World in particular. As many have noted, Europeans constructed the Americas as feminine, so that colonialism and rape were intertwining discourses, and by the end of the sixteenth century, America could be represented in paintings, engravings, maps, and title pages as a female nude with a feathered headdress. But the feminization of America presented problems for the English, particularly Sir Walter Raleigh, who served a woman monarch (Queen Elizabeth I). Europe's fascination for its newest Other was never stable, oscillating between "fascination and repulsion, likeness and strangeness, desires to destroy and to assimilate the Other; an oscillation between the confirmation and the subversion of familiar values, beliefs, and perceptual norms."[27]

Contemporary English texts amply illustrate this interpretation. Sir Walter Raleigh on the Spanish: "I made [Topiawari, a chieftain] knowe the cause of my comming thither, whose servant I was, and that the Queenes pleasure was, I should undertake the voyage for their defence, and to deliver them from the tyrannie of the Spaniards, dilating at large . . . her Majesties greatnesse, her justice, her charitie to all oppressed nations."[28] Queen Elizabeth herself participated in the construction of the New World as feminine: "I . . . think foul scorn that *Parma* or *Spain*, or any Prince of Europe should dare to invade the borders of my Realm, to which rather then any dishonour shall grow by me, I my self will take up arms, I my self will be your General, Judge, and Rewarder of everie one of your virtues in the field."[29]

What all this means is that questions of otherness, difference, gender, sexuality, ethnicity, nationality can't be easily separated, for constructions and representations of difference inform one another, a conclusion that the anthropologist Ann Laura Stoler also makes. Sex in the colonies could be about sexual access and reproduction, social class, race, nationalism, and conceptions of European identity.[30] For Stoler, racism, far from being a monolithic attitude, a byproduct (or product) of the colonial encounter, varies in quality and intensity from time to time and place to place, and generally the passage of time in colonial situations leads to intensified racial discrimination and rigidified boundaries.[31] In this and other writings, however, Stoler seems to want to prioritize gendered otherness over racial otherness: patriarchal ideas were brought to the colonies where they informed racist policies, which in turn were exported back to the metropoles as concepts of gendered and racial otherness. Women are the *ur*-Other in most cultures, and as such, attitudes toward women pervade all constructions of difference and otherness. That's true enough. Representations of other women as sexually licentious are well known and have been widely discussed.[32] But rather than say that one kind of construction of difference came first—which came first, difference or the Other?—it's more productive to try to explore how these constructions inform each other.

Clearly, various kinds of boundaries between self and Other were erected and exercised both in European colonies and in European metropoles: each fed off the other, and lessons learned in one place traveled to the other. So as we will see, cultural forms produced in European nations have as much to do with colonial attitudes as home attitudes do.

MODERN SELF-FASHIONING

This process of constructing difference, constructing selves and Others, particularly the far-off Others of the New World is, I am saying, a modern process. Look, for example, at the characterization of "self-fashioning" that Stephen Greenblatt offers in his introduction to *Renaissance Self-Fashioning*— in which he says, "there is in the early modern period a change in the intellectual, social, psychological, and aesthetic structures that govern the generation of identities."[33] Nearly all the criteria involve confrontations with Others, beginning with the third on his list. "Self-fashioning is achieved in relation to something perceived as alien, strange, or hostile."[34] This encounter with an alien or alien authority permeates just about all the rest of his ten criteria. The only substantial alteration I would make is to the ninth criterion: "Self-fashioning is always, though not exclusively, in language" should be "Self-fashioning is always in *representations*," a change that allows not only for language but for all sorts of cultural production, including music. Greenblatt's summary of his list hinges on the self-fashioner's confrontation with an "alien": "self-fashioning occurs at the point of encounter between an authority and an alien . . . and hence . . . any achieved identity always contains within itself the signs of its own subversion or loss."[35]

In short, western self-fashioning came to require an object, an Other. The power to fashion oneself was continuous with colonial power. "Colonialism is an abstract machine that produces alterity and identity," Hardt and Negri write.[36] Produces it, that is, as part of a dynamic in which European selfhood could define itself against those constructed as its Others.

TONALITY

The colossal fact of the "discovery" of the New World was registered in music, but at first without quotation of other peoples' music. Instead, European composers first grappled with the discovery of the New World and its subsequent colonialization in subtler and more fundamental ways. European composers, like writers and visual artists, struggled with new conceptions of difference by using representations of people nearby, and with materials to hand.

Simply put, the argument here is that the rise of tonality and opera facilitated representations and appropriations of Europe's cultural Others. The task is not to trace the musical and theoretical origins of tonality, which has been the primary mode of inquiry into this question.[37] Rather, I believe that it is crucial to examine the *cultural* and *historical* reasons for tonality's rise to dominance. Not that tonality "superseded" earlier, modal kinds of musical organization, but that tonality, as Carl Dahlhaus and others have pointed out, existed long before it became the primary musical language for roughly three hundred years in western European high culture.[38] Harold Powers has written cogently of modality and tonality as wholly different kinds of epistemologies, not merely as forms of the organization of pitches, a position with which it is easy to agree.[39] The question is then why one epistemology came to take over another in the particular historical moment when it did, and what the nature of this new epistemology was.

Admittedly, there were at first many tonalities, many local variants or dialects. But tonality as the now-familiar system did prevail in western Europe by the early eighteenth century among composers of art music, and it had many precursors, all of which, I maintain, registered to varying degrees changing western European ideologies of selfhood and otherness.

I argue that tonality arose to a long supremacy in western European music in part because it facilitated a concept of spatialization in music that provided for centers and margins, both geographically and psychologically. Largely because of the discovery of the New World, space in the sixteenth century was rethought, a rethinking that requires some discussion here.[40] Foucault writes that after Galileo, space began to be seen as infinite, and infinitely open; the sense of place in the Middle Ages became thrown into flux, so that, Foucault says, "with Galileo and the seventeenth century, extension was substituted for localization."[41]

Before Columbus, the world was conceptualized in an insular way, with oceans as the boundaries. But the discovery necessitated inventing the concept of the continent, and oceans as geographical entities. Before the "discovery" of the New World, maps were symbols to be read, deciphered, and meditated upon, but with the discovery, a map became something that could be practically used.[42] Exploration became possible in the sixteenth century.[43] The reconceptualization of Europe as a continent meant that there were thought to be other Europes—or non-Europes—out there, populated by people, or Others.

The discovery of a more radical otherness in the New World meant for Europeans that the Other had to be contained, the real space of the Other conquered by force, as it was by Christopher Marlowe's *Tamburlaine the Great* (1587), who made space the raw material of conquest:

Give me a Map, then let me see how much
Is left for me to conquer all the world,
That these my boys may finish all my wants.[44]

And later:

> I will confute those blind Geographers
> That make a triple region in the world,
> Excluding Regions which I mean to trace,
> And with this pen reduce them to a Map,
> Calling the Provinces, Cities and towns
> After my name and thine *Zenocrate* [daughter of the sultan of Egypt,
>   Tamburlaine's wife].[45]

Space was also conquered metaphorically with maps. It was not good enough that the Other was, for most Europeans, across the Atlantic; it had to be ideologically distanced, this distance represented cartographically. Cartography became an important tool in advancing the Enlightenment project, and the map became a totalizing device of European powers to control distant lands through their cartographic representation. For the first time after the discovery of the New World, the entire planet and its population could be graphically symbolized. The cartographic means of representation not only permitted new conceptions of otherness, but also allowed them to flourish.[46] Maps were thus a mode of containment as well as a mode of representation, a way of putting Others and their Elsewheres in view while keeping them safely at a distance.

Yet it was not just space that was at issue; it was Europe in this new conception of space, Europe at the center with the New World and other places at the margins, the European self at the center with Others at the margins. So while the concept of space took on great significance in this era in an abstract sense, space in terms of relationships, the relationships between centers and margins that maps represented, were no less important. "In the process of describing otherness," Walter Mignolo writes, Europeans "helped redfine the concept of the self-same."[47]

The epistemological changes wrought by the discovery of the New World and the Copernican revolution meant that for many scholars in the Renaissance, questions of space became paramount. Ernst Cassirer writes that one of the most important tasks of early modern philosophy was to construct a new concept of space; what he calls "aggregate space" had to be replaced by a "system space" which was homogenous, by which he refers to the project not of making all space homogeneous but of understanding the spatial world as a single system. This was the purpose to which maps were put in this period.[48]

Tonality as a type of musical organization achieves the same kind of spatal-ization that was being considered in cartography and in works such as *Tam-burlaine the Great*. Tonality works by establishing a main key, from which the composer can move to other, subordinate keys, and move back in a kind of exploratory, cartographic mode. Richard Norton, one of the few scholars of tonality to talk about it in more than strictly technical terms, shows how the tonic—the "home" or main key—came into being through its opposi-tion to the "nontonic," which eventually became known as the dominant (the tonal region most closely related to the tonic).[49] That is, early modern epistemology made a place for an idea and its negation; in music, this is the construction of a tonic key and its defining opposite nontonic, in technical terms the dominant.

Music theorists of the era tended to consider what they thought at the time were more pressing issues—the relationship of music to text, the role of counterpoint. The prevailing mode of inquiry was mechanistic, and me-chanical metaphors were typically used more frequently than those of move-ment through space, though metaphors about the heavens were also used.[50]

In the seventeenth century music theorists tended to be more concerned with making interventions in the large body of writings on the modal system, and only slowly grew to consider the changes in music happening around them. It took nearly the entire century for theorists to turn their attention to tonality.[51] And when they did, they frequently championed the new sys-tem at the expense of its predecessors. Johann David Heinichen (1683–1729) wrote in a letter in 1717, "I am no special friend either of the old imprison-ing musical modes . . . or of other dusty musical fads. I admit readily that many times I have pondered deeply over the fact that, for whatever reason, there are still people in our time who seek to bring up and defend the long since decayed musical rubbish of antiquity."[52] By the early eighteenth cen-tury theorists and composers began to rely on metaphors of movement and space to describe the workings of tonality. Heinichen, for example, offered a diagram of a "musical circle" in 1711, laying out the relationship of keys to one another.[53]

The first major theorist of tonality, the composer Jean-Philippe Rameau (1683–1764), employed Newtonian language for a time as a potent metaphor with which to describe aspects of tonality.[54] Thomas Christensen traces the influences of the Newtonian theory of gravity (first proposed in 1687) on Rameau and some of his acquaintances, noting that Rameau's language to describe tonal attraction (the feeling that one chord must move, or return, to another) is expressed in terms that Christensen identifies as distinctly Newtonian. Rameau writes that the tonic "must be seen as the center of the mode, towards which is drawn all our desires. It is effectively the middle term of the proportion to which the extremes are so tied that they cannot stray from it for a moment." If the chord progression "passes to one of them, it must return back right away."[55]

Implicit in Rameau's conception is the notion that tonal movement is more than a simple "from here to there" motivated by gravity. Rameau further theorizes the more peripatetic musical movement that tonal pieces take: "The mutual assistance lent by the dominant and subdominant [the tonal regions most closely related to the tonic] connect them to the principal sound such that they cannot stray from it. The harmonic sound of one, whose harmonic succession it has already determined, obliges the Other to submit to it, and consequently to return to the principal sound."[56] It is also significant that Rameau's metaphorization of tonality is naturalized: movement in tonality is the same as in nature.[57] Tonality and its ability to create centers and margins were construed as natural, inevitable, stable, just as Europeans naturalized their selfhood vis-à-vis non-European Others.

Metaphors of gravity have continued to the present, but some recent scholars have adopted different tacks that are still compatible with seeing tonality as a spatializing system. John Shepherd notes that tonality is "a center-oriented structure with margins," with a temporal dimension that articulates the social structure of industrialized societies.[58] Shepherd's main point, however, is not that tonality has a spatial aspect, though he acknowledges this, but rather that tonality is bound up with western European notions of progress toward a goal (a position that anticipates Susan McClary's numerous and convincing arguments about the teleological nature of tonality).[59] This is demonstrably true, but both Shepherd's and McClary's emphasis on the concepts of progress and teleology obscure the equally important spatial aspects of tonality. Indeed, it is possible to argue that tonality is *both* a spatializing system and a progressive, teleological system, with the spatializing aspect a way of grappling with and containing a distant Other, and the progressive aspect an articulation of a central ideology in western culture that can be used to assert western European superiority over "primitives" whose cultures do not seem to possess a similar concept of progress, or who are later thought to be far behind in a progressive march toward industrial and scientific modernity.

McClary in particular has explored the narrative schema of tonality and how tonality facilitates representations, arguing that the subordinate tonal regions and subordinate themes are virtually always perceived as feminine. Or "Other," one could say in a more general sense. Making this more general argument does not imply that all tonal works employ this schema; rather, tonality is as informed by modern western notions of center and margins, dominant and subordinate, as any other cultural form in western culture. McClary emphasizes the narrative aspects of tonality and the way that it encodes male heterosexual desire, a desire usually entangled with gendered, and sometimes racialized, otherness. But she also recognizes that the nature of tonality is caught up with representations of peoples from other cultures.[60] Endorsing this idea of tonality as desire is somewhat problematic, for "desire" is more of a psychological category than a cultural and historical one—though, of course, desire is imbricated in power relationships, all of which are caught up in social, cultural, and historical processes. It is these processes that are of interest, since I emphasize particular forms of desire in particular historical moments and geographical places. The desire that McClary writes of is not simply "desire" but in part a colonial artifact: the desire for the foreign, forbidden, female body, coupled with a trope of colonization as rape. The European notion of the licentious exotic woman is an old story, and a powerful one.[61] McClary's conception of heterosexual male desire, to the extent that we can situate it historically and culturally, could be put to other uses in the representation of ethnic and racial Others as well as women. And there is no more ingenious musical system to capture this ambivalence of western Europeans toward non-European Others—ambivalence composed of both desire and revulsion—than tonality.

McClary's characterization of tonality as a musical structuring of heterosexual male desire thus needs to be understood with the added valence of expanding European colonialism and all the ideologies of otherness that came with it. This further dimension helps us see desire not simply as an unwavering teleology but as a much more ambivalent and roundabout process that registers the many European ambivalences toward its cultural Others.

OPERA

As with tonality, the emergence of what we now call opera had deep roots in earlier musico-dramatic practices. The question is not when or how opera was "invented" but rather why what we now call opera arose when it did, and for what historical reasons. What we now call opera is delimited by certain newly conventionalized practices in this period, some of which were innovations. Opera, like tonality, did not arise out of nothing but represented a new dominance out of a coalescence of disparate tendencies, a coalescence marked in Italy (generally regarded as the birthplace of opera) by the melding of *stile rappresentativo* (a way of setting words to music that attempted to sound speechlike) with basso continuo (a kind of accompaniment consisting of a bass instrument playing the bassline and a keyboard instrument playing harmonies), as well as embracing a musico-dramatic unity achieved in part through a dramatic presentation coupled with continuous music.[62]

The following argument for a new history of the origins of opera is greatly indebted to the work of Lorenzo Bianconi, which has done much to call into question the standard history of opera as a genre that grew out of the revival by a few Florentine intellectuals of ancient Greek dramatic practices.[63] But opera's origins were more fraught. Ellen Rosand writes of how characters mixed together (resulting in the Jesuit Giovan Domenico Ottonelli condemning some Venetian operas in his *Della Cristiana moderatione del teatro* in 1652 as "mercenaria");[64] Richard Taruskin, drawing on Bianconi and Rosand, similarly writes of the less than lofty origins of this revered genre, noting that opera's "disruptive and destabilizing vectors" appear throughout its history.[65]

And with opera as with tonality, chronology cannot be ignored: the beginning of the seventeenth century witnesses not only the birth of modernity but the rise of tonality as the dominant musical system and the development of opera, as well as the growth of colonial territories and administration by what were to become the most powerful nations of modern Europe, England and France. Whaples tells us that the first French and English operas were based on "exotic" themes, an observation that points out the interrelationship of all these historical and musical events.[66]

In Italy, opera's subjects were frequently mythological, often drawn from Ovid. Bianconi notes the "flagrant contradiction" between the stated revival of the practices of Greek tragedy in Florence — the usual story of the rise of opera — and the dependence on plots from Ovid, observing that there are *no* heroic myths of ancient Greece represented in the earliest operas.[67]

At the same time as opera was developing, historical economic circumstances in Italy in the first decades of the seventeenth century resulted in the collapse of a humanistic principle in artistic production, according to Bianconi. Following the social and political events of the first part of the seventeenth century, musical representations matched the immediate and aggressive exercise of power, which was a far cry, Bianconi writes, from the "esoteric courteousness" of the madrigal.[68] The authority that the church invested in God resulted in a crackdown on science (and scientists — Galileo was disciplined by the church in 1616); the Reformation and Counter-Reformation pitted Protestants and Catholics against each other; and the new economic and political hegemony of Holland, England, and France reduced Italy to a second-rate power, as had happened so swiftly to Spain in the previous century.

All this, Bianconi says, makes for artworks that express authority at a new level. Music came to serve overtly ideological ends, purchased by church and state for representational and propagandistic purposes.[69] Music in the service of the powerful was an old story even by this period, but what was new was that tonality and opera provided potent new means of depiction and representation and thus, powerful new means of control and containment.

The ideological ends to which opera could be put contributed to its entry into the public sphere. The first public opera was performed in Venice in 1637, and it is the rise of Venetian opera that Bianconi focuses on in his history, not the earlier, more hermetic Florentine variety. Venetian opera was public, unlike the Florentine court operas, and it was the public nature of Venetian opera that ultimately led to the genre's institutionalization and longevity in Italy. Venice was also uniquely situated to grapple with ethnic and racial otherness in its works. Ellen Rosand and others have observed that the geographic position of Venice between East and West contributed to a cosmopolitan or even exotic atmosphere that could not have helped playing a role in the musical and dramatic treatment of racialized difference.[70]

Even before this period, however, operas meant to be performed at court — the earliest operas — were addressing the same issues. Claudio Monteverdi's *L'Orfeo* (1607), one of the earliest operas and usually hailed by musicologists as the first operatic masterwork, systematically explores different modal and tonal regions. The work is too early in the history of tonality to analyze exclusively in terms of tonality, yet it is clear that Monteverdi was thinking in spatial terms and was bending the modal system toward tonal ends, as Eric Chafe writes in a useful work on Monteverdi's musical language. Chafe's book is replete with metaphors of exploration and discovery in Monteverdi's employment of tonality, a use that Chafe characterizes as being ahead of its time, akin to the achievements of Galileo and Descartes.[71]

Monteverdi's music possesses qualities of "exploration and discovery," Chafe writes.[72]

For just one example, in act III of *L'Orfeo*, when Orpheus visits the underworld, the mode changes portentously to minor as a way of marking off that spatial region from the world of the sun. Perhaps even more significantly, the opera concludes with a moresca that invokes otherness and that systematically charts different tonal regions—cadencing on G major, then C Major, A major, and finally D major—as though revisiting them, claiming them, for a final time before drawing to a close.

Even though I am not arguing that the European "discovery" of non-European others "produced" or "determined" tonality and opera, some musicians and music theorists of opera bring difference into their discourse about opera and other musico-dramatic genres. Some early writings on opera include the representations of other peoples and practices within the arena of acceptable subjects. By the early eighteenth century exotic themes were commonplace; Barthold Feind (1678–1721) writes in *Gedanken von der Opera* (1708) that "the aim of the *entrées de ballet* [part of a French musico-dramatic work consisting of dances] is that of providing—by means of particular figures and bodily gestures—a theatrical simulation of those actions (good or evil) which form part of normal life: funeral lamentations, the sacrificial ceremonies of the Jews, Orientals or pagans, the behaviour of the master pedants, the guzzling of banquets, etc."[73] While nothing on Feind's list may sound like a part of "normal life" today, or in the seventeenth century for that matter, it is striking that Feind includes the "sacrificial ceremonies of the Jews, Orientals or pagans." Surely these were not "normal" in the early eighteenth century, but they were, however, already normally part of the legitimate concern of the opera composer. (Note also that Feind says "or," not "and," as though Jews, Orientals, and pagans were all interchangeable—they were to early moderns). That Feind lumps together all these peoples shows the kind of monolithic categorization of others that is a hallmark of the modern European worldview toward its Others.

OPERA, THE POLYGLOSSIC ART

Opera and its precursors facilitated a jumble of representations of different peoples, different social groups, frequently accomplished in a spirit of parody. Drama and thus languages could coexist, intermingle, creating the opera out of the same historical conditions that saw the rise of the novel, which makes similar use of the plethora of new kinds of voices, new races, new peoples, and new social classes, and which, not coincidentally, emerged around the same time as opera. "Thus," writes M. M. Bakhtin, "did the inter-animation of languages occur in the very epoch that saw the creation of the European novel. Laughter and polyglossia had paved the way for the novelistic discourse of modern times."[74] Not just novelistic discourse—operatic discourse.

Bakhtin's notion of the carnival has been widely employed in the last couple of decades or so outside of musicology and has some usefulness in understanding the workings of opera.[75] Let it be clear from the outset that Bakhtin's concern was with the bottom of the social ladder: carnival was a way for everyday people to articulate subversive acts, turn the everyday world upside down. This was clearly not the concern of those involved in producing the earliest operas.[76] So the usefulness of Bakhtin's carnival in understanding opera is not that it allows us to view opera as something subversive like the carnival, but rather that it provides a way for the powerful in western Europe to construct discursively and control the carnivalesque itself, the carnivalesque featuring Europe's internal others (women in particular, and ethnic minorities, and others), as well as the distant, racialized other on the far side of the Atlantic.

For Bakhtin, the carnival was a moment when the noisy juxtaposition of peoples from different social groups, its grotesque elements, the profane, could serve to create a kind of new evanescent moment, a kind of "grotesque realism" that "consecrates inventive freedom, to permit the combination of a variety of different elements and their rapprochement, to liberate from the prevailing point of view of the world, from conventions and established truths, from clichés, from all that is humdrum and universally accepted. This carnival spirit offers the chance to have a new outlook on the world, to realize the relative nature of all that exists, and to enter a completely new order of things."[77] If "grotesque realism" is the aesthetic and temporal dimension of the carnival, polyglossia is the discursive dimension. Indeed, Bakhtin used the idea of the carnival to argue for a conception of modernity much like the one being outlined here: modernity came in on the heels of new forms of social interactions and juxtapositions that destabilized the more rigid and hierarchical existing order of the Middle Ages.

Opera and its precursors, as entertainments of the powerful, were in a sense vehicles in which the carnivalesque as articulated by Bakhtin could be used against itself. The appropriations of forms from the arena of the everyday, the popular—Bakhtin's focus of interest—into opera's forerunners staged a kind of mock carnival in which otherness was ridiculed and controlled. Yet at the same time, the carnivalesque nature of the musico-dramatic works that led up to what became known as opera played a prominent role—perhaps the dominant one—in instantiating both tonality as a musical system and opera as a musico-dramatic system in western European high culture for centuries.

Bakhtin's concepts of polyglossia and carnival made it possible to interpret the novel itself as a kind of repository of different styles and discourses, and opera is no different. We shall see the extent to which one of opera's main precursors in England frequently had precisely these sociopolitical projects of hegemony.

Opera thus grew and was solidified out of this jumble of different musics and musical practices, representations and representational practices, that facilitated the representation of new peoples and new social roles and relationships in early modern Europe. It is no accident that one of the most important devices in opera, recitative (a mode of text declamation close to speech), was first called *stile rappresentativo* and appears in the earliest operas, including on the title page of what is usually regarded as one of the very first, Giulio Caccini's *Euridice* (1600). The questions then become, who is represented, how, and to what ends? Stile rappresentativo was called thus because it was supposed to represent people and the drama on stage in as lifelike a way as possible. Susan McClary has written that "music drama provides the incentive for the full-scale entry of gender construction into music";[78] replace "gender" with "difference" and one sees a different kind of power, although the two can resonate with one another strongly.

The development of opera provided a way of dealing with the powerful "discovery" of other peoples, from home and abroad; opera—especially once combined with a powerful new musical language, tonality—offered new and effective ways to (re)present and control difference.[79] Opera did not "cause" colonialism, and colonialism did not directly cause the rise of opera (or tonality), but as Edward Said writes of the rise of the novel, each is unthinkable without the other, and it is impossible to study one without grappling with the other.[80]

With the rise of opera we find a genre that in part grew out of existing forms, including those that played a role in the representations of Europe's

Others such as the moresca and intermedio, and in part coming to incorporate, contain, these other genres, eventually swallowing them up on its way to becoming its own genre. What Said calls the "consolidation of authority" of the novel is no less true for opera, in that the functioning of social power and governance in opera is normalized and presented as beyond questioning.[81] When the narrative of an opera plot is combined with the narrative implications of tonality, as McClary has examined, operatic narratives can seem even more normative and sovereign.

THE SEVENTEENTH-CENTURY ENGLISH MASQUE

Now let's turn to the question of how this new musical language and new dramatic genre work together by taking an example: the English masque, one of opera's many precursors.[82] The Jonsonian masques of the early seventeenth century tackled, in quite overt ways, problems of colonialism and difference. Masques functioned in part as rehearsals for managing space and the subordination of difference.[83]

The exigencies of empire as they were perceived in the early seventeenth century necessitated mastery of both space and peoples, a mastery that found analogues in music, dance, and theater. Perhaps the best examples of the masques for my purposes are those by William Lawes (baptized 1602, d. 1645), whose works register better than most the changing historical and cultural factors that led to the rise of tonality.[84] Additionally, since England was struggling to achieve dominance as a colonial power, colonial issues were often more frequently thematized in works produced there. My arguments here are bolstered by a number of studies by scholars of English literature of the same period and before who have explored some of the same issues.[85]

Scholars of Lawes's music agree that it displays an almost prescient use of tonality as a dramatic and unifying device (which has led Edward J. Dent and others to proclaim Lawes's music as an important precursor to opera). Dent singles out Lawes as an exceptional composer in his sense of tonality: in a historical moment when composers were only just learning how to write outside the modal system, Lawes's use of tonality is ahead of its time.[86]

For the purposes of this chapter, one of the most significant aspects of the masque was its employment of the antimasque. The masques themselves were usually on serious subjects, but for dramatic contrast Ben Jonson introduced the antimasque in 1609, at the request of Anne of Denmark, queen of James I, to serve as a foil to the main action. The characters of the anti-masque were similarly opposed: in *The Masque of Queens* (1609), twelve noble queens were contrasted with twelve hags. One of the antimasques in Lawes's *Britannia triumphans* (1638) contains the ubiquitous Turk.[87] The generic origins of the antimasque are unclear, though it may be derived from Tudor mummings, sometimes called "antics," that similarly featured grotesque dances and contrasts.[88]

The use of the antimasque to depict and ridicule the disreputable, the ugly, the low, the foreign—the Other—is significant, since the antimasque was the repository of all the music and dance most closely associated with the illicit, titillating Other (though masques could occasionally include "exotic" peoples). Peter Walls writes that Inigo Jones (1573–1652), a major English architect and designer of many of the court masques, usually depicted anti-masque characters in ungainly postures that were decried by dance manuals and courtesy books, whereas masquers were portrayed in elegant and dig-nified poses.[89] We are not far from the Bakhtinian carnivalesque here, and I should note that masques themselves also have some roots in the carnival, as it was the custom of the Caroline masque to begin with a procession in which all the masquers took part, a procession that would sometimes take to the streets of London.[90]

The importance of the antimasque is made clear in an exchange from *The Triumph of Peace* (1638), with text by John Shirley and music by Lawes. Char-acters in the masque are discussing the antimasque:

FANCY: How many antimasques have they? Of what nature?
For these are fancies that take most; your dull
And phlegmatic inventions are exploded.
Give me a nimble antiques.
OPINION: They have none, sir.
LAUGHTER: No antimasque! I'd laugh at that, i'faith.
JOLLITY: What make we here? No jollity!
FANCY: No antimasque!
Bid 'em down with the scene, and sell the timber,
Send Jupiter to grass, and bid Apollo
Keep cows again. . . .[91]

The salience here of play, parody, laughter, recalls the argument above with Bakhtin: it is laughter that makes possible the mixing of languages, sounds, representations—polyglossia—that paved the way for the novel, even opera.

Interestingly, it was the popularity of the antimasque that eventually brought an end to the masque itself.[92] Antimasques became progressively larger parts of masques, so that by 1640, Sir William Davenant's *Salmacida Spolia* included twenty antimasques.[93] Fascination with the Other in all its manifestations ultimately overwhelmed the part of the spectacle that was ostensibly a tale told by the tellers to themselves about themselves. But these selves were becoming increasingly dependent on these Others for their sense of selfhood.

These tales frequently had political and ideological meanings and designs. In this period of British history, the empire was fast growing. Queen Elizabeth had approved the charter of the British East India Company in 1600; the first fleet sailed in 1601.[94] Later incursions into North America are well known, brought about because of the conciliatory policies of James I toward England's colonial rival, Spain. In the treaty of London of 1604, James agreed to leave Spain largely alone, which meant that England was forced to shift its efforts to America if it were to continue its colonizing endeavors.[95]

England's rivalry with other colonial powers is faithfully reflected in many of the masques. Just some titles convey the masques' treatment of current issues, titles that appear, significantly, at the moment when the masques had become the earliest English operas: *The Siege of Rhodes* (1656), *The Cruelty of the Spaniards in Peru* (1658), and *The History of Sir Francis Drake* (1659).[96] The music is lost, but the texts, by Davenant, are extant and enunciate the kinds of propaganda that one might expect. The valiant Christian Rhodians stand up to the Turks in a setting of a historical event from 1522 with perhaps the first musical representation of a Noble Turk; the Peruvians experience mistreatment at the hands of the Spanish, in a masque written during Oliver Cromwell's war with Spain (1656–59); and in the last of these masques, Drake the heroic explorer works for queen, country, and God in a work that elaborates on the anti-Spanish propaganda of *The Cruelty of the Spaniards in Peru.*[97]

Earlier masques with music by Lawes were no less propagandistic but not quite as overt in their plotting. None of them tackle the subject of British colonialization as openly as the proto-operas just mentioned, but all in their antimasques make significant use of representations, in costume, music, and speech, of England's cultural Others, ranging from people from the North (presumably Scots) to hags, giants, dwarves, zanies, harlekins, Persians, and Turks.

William Lawes: *Britannia Triumphans*

I would like to spend some time discussing Lawes's *Britannia Triumphans* of 1638, the last court masque with extant music. *Britannia Triumphans* does not offer an explicitly colonialist plot, though the propaganda that it espouses meshes with the ambitions of a monarch bent on creating an empire. The prefatory remarks by Sir William Davenant (author of the entire text) refer to "Britanocles [played by Charles I], the glory of the western world hath by his wisdom, valour, and piety, not only vindicated his own, but far distant seas, infested with pirates, and reduc'd the land, by his example, to a real knowledge of all good acts and sciences,"[98] a "reduction" similar to the cartographic containment discussed earlier.[99] The absence of a blatantly colonialist plot, however, reinforces the more general point of this chapter—that the discovery of the New World had thoroughly infiltrated cultural production by the seventeenth century, and consequently even works seeming not to be dealing with colonialism on the surface were nonetheless wrestling with larger issues of racial, religious, ethnic, and gendered otherness.

This masque was essentially an advertisement for the wisdom of Charles I after he had made the far-fetched claim in the previous year of being "Sovereign of the Seas," and when he was in serious trouble with his own people.[100] Charles demanded that anyone fishing in the English Channel or the North Sea needed his consent. In this period, however, the English navy was not the power that it would become—the Dutch were strong, and the French were building. To raise funds to bolster the English navy, Charles imposed a "ship-money" tax without the consent of Parliament. This was a highly unpopular tax, and *Britannia Triumphans* was an attempt to justify it and restore some of Charles's prestige.[101]

The slight drama consists, as these masques did, of personifications of qualities intermingled with characters in an allegorical plot. Though not much happens, the plot is rather intricate in its depiction of an allegorical battle with the king's critics. Rather than summarize the entire plot, I will simply outline its bare bones. The opening allegory shows Action, representing the king's followers, and Imposture, representing the Puritans, in a verbal battle. Imposture eventually summons Merlin, who conjures the spirits of the multitude skeptical of learning. This invocation of the masses makes way for the six antimasques. After these are over, Bellerophon enters. Unimpressed by Imposture, Bellerophon orders him away, and calls for Fame to appear to help celebrate Britanocles's triumph. Britanocles appears. The scene shifts to the sea, where the sea-nymph, Galatea, appears riding a dolphin. She sings a song that extols the king's sovereignty over the seas.[102]

Britannia Triumphans trumpets the importance of extending British control over distant lands with peoples bereft of art and science: "So well Britanocles o'er seas doth reign, / Reducing what was wild before. . . ."[103] The civilizing influence of Britanocles is indicated with spatial metaphors:

> Move then in such a noble order here,
> As if you each his governed planet were,
> And he mov'd first to move you in each sphere. . . .[104]

There was probably a dance occurring while this was being sung, and the king's relation to the lords is compared to the movement of planets, further dramatizing the text through space and movement.[105] Lawes musically depicts the same idea: his music accompanying this text begins in A minor and ends in D major—a different sphere (example 1).

Most of Lawes's music to *Britannia Triumphans* is lost except a few arias and choruses from near the end, and it is thus difficult to get a sense of Lawes's long-range musical planning with respect to tonality; Murray Lefkowitz believes that Lawes's use of tonality is more interesting than what is found in the other masques and finds no reason to doubt that Lawes had a musical plan over the length of the work.[106] There was obviously at least some sort of local planning, as one aria or chorus ends in one key and the next begins in the same key; and there is an inexorable movement toward what Lefkowitz has referred to as the "royal" key of C major at the ending.[107]

It is also evident that Lawes uses keys to bring out meanings of texts, and not simply in an affective way. The chorus "On ever moving waves," for example, charts the swaying movement depicted in the text:

> On ever moving waves they us'd to dance
> Unto the whistling of the wind;
> Whose measures hit and meet by erring chance,
> Where music can no concord find.

The chorus starts in E-flat major and ends in C major. But Lawes ends each line of text on a different chord: "dance," E-flat major; "wind," G major; "chance," F minor; "find," C major. In other words, Lawes depicts with tonal means the lack of musical concord suggested by the text.

Lawes also employs a genre that was a rage at the time—the *ciaccona* (also spelled "*ciacona*," as it is by Lawes). This was a dance music genre that had its

Ex. 1 Lawes, *Britannia Triumphans*, "Move then in such a noble order here"

origins in the New World, though it is unclear whether it originated there or was brought there by African slaves.[108] According to Richard Hudson, the ciaccona was a Spanish genre employing a concept of mode that eventually led to tonality.[109] Susan McClary writes that the ciaccona to Europeans was associated with "forbidden bodily pleasures and potential social havoc."[110] Ciaconnas were not stylistically consistent, but Lawes's does make use of the main metrical and rhythmic features of the genre, including triple meter and the main syncopation associated with the ciaccona, the half note preceding the whole note, as in measures 4 and 12 (example 2).

The presence of the ciaccona in *Britannia Triumphans*—however remote from the stylistic conventions of the day—indicates how music associated with Others can be domesticated and smuggled in to more "respectable"

Ex. 2 Lawes, *Britannia Triumphans*, " 'Tis fit you mix that wonder with delight"

works. This ciaccona, after all, is part of the masque proper, not the antimasque. And the character responsible for presenting it is Fame, the aid to Britanocles himself. In *Britannia Triumphans*, however, those potential meanings are coupled with a more explicit reference to the New World, and Britannia's influence over it.

Reference to the New World is not simply musical, however: it is also important to note the text at this point, for wonder in the masque was frequently invoked to emphasize the power and magnificence of the king.[111] Wonder was also a term used to describe the frightening, the irrational, the unknown—concepts that were used to characterize the New World by the English in this era—so much so that wonder was one of the central concepts in the initial European response to the New World.[112] The masque's text reads:

'Tis fit you mix that wonder with delight,
As you were warm'd to motion with his sight,
To pay the expectation of the night.

Peter Platt writes that in the masque there is an interplay and dynamism between image and word, with image taking on the responsibility of offering the marvelous, the wonder-ful, while the word is responsible for the rational.[113] Music, it seems to me, is peculiarly placed to enter into this dynamic, because it offers neither spectacle akin to the stage-and-costume spectacles of the masque nor the measured rationality of texts; it can, instead, promiscuously side with either. Davenant's words served to remind the masque's audience of the wonder of the king — and empire — but Lawes's ciaccona was included to titillate it, and reminds it of the king's empire of racialized Others at the same time.

In all, Lawes's music, with its use of tonality, imposes a degree of unity on the rather disparate organization of the masque to the extent that the unruly masque with its antimasques — replete with laughter, polyglossia, and even the Bakhtinian carnivalesque — begins to emerge as something more than a propagandistic entertainment for social gatherings of nobility, and takes shape as a dramatically and musically unified whole: opera.

I have drawn extensively on musicological and other writings in this chapter to make an argument about the rise to dominance of a musical system and a musical representational system, a rise that could only have occurred for specific social, cultural, and historical reasons. This chapter exemplifies the need to go beyond consideration of European encounters with Others in stylistic terms — which is itself important — and to think about even more fundamental epistemological changes in this period, which were registered in many ways, including in music.

It is also clear from the foregoing that it is possible to make a more general claim about the importance of representations in advancing and solidifying music or other cultural forms. This is not the first time this point has needed to be made: that "newness enters the world" on the heels of the collision of cultures and representations of Others.[114] Yet perhaps it is an argument that cannot be enunciated frequently enough. Representations of Europe's cultural Others — women, as Susan McClary has written, and European colonialized subjects, as has been demonstrated here — helped make possible a genre that is still with us, and helped to establish a musical system that would last in the realm of western European art music for three hundred years. Until, that is, the age of empire around the beginning of the twentieth century. But that is the subject of another chapter.

PEOPLING THE STAGE: OPERA, OTHERNESS, AND NEW MUSICAL REPRESENTATIONS IN THE ENLIGHTENMENT

> ... power finds its place in lack of power. ...
> —George Eliot, *Middlemarch*

OTHERNESS IN THE ENLIGHTENMENT

In the eighteenth century issues of space that so occupied people in the seventeenth century do not disappear but become more prominent. The new literature of travelogues contributes to a new discourse of otherness.[1] Space as a continuing concept emerges from travel to, and descriptions of, European Elsewheres. If conceptions of otherness were complicated in the beginning of early modernity, things only become thornier in the eighteenth century. And of course, musical representations are part of the jumble of representational practices.

By the time of the Enlightenment, colonialism and science had compiled enough empirical data so that composers and other artists could begin to make use of the data in their work. While Europeans in the early modern era viewed Others as potential candidates for Christianity, by the onset of the Enlightenment the aims of rationality that drove the entire epoch sent scores of researchers into the wilds to study "primitives," to in effect write histories for them, since they were not thought to know them themselves.

These new primitives had to be subsumed into modern western ideology, not merely catalogued. One of the major projects of the early Enlightenment was to establish a world chronology, an attempt to establish one world, one temporally homogenous order, so that studies could be made.[2] This chronology was necessarily Christian, and was attempting to be a standard by which other chronologies could be judged, included, or excluded, a way of forcefully integrating nonwestern cultures into a Christian world.[3]

Writing the history of the world was a way of placing the world's peoples somewhere in that history.[4] Europeans came to think of themselves as civilized, peoples "with" civilization, while "primitives" did not "have" civilization, or at least, did not have it yet. Bernard McGrane writes of this radical transformation, in which "the European-Christians-and-Jews-as-opposed-to-the-savage-idolatrous-non-Christians became the civilized-Europeans-as-opposed-to-the-superstitious-ignorant-primitive."[5] McGrane identifies a crucial epistemological shift, one that would have decisive consequences for the continuing colonialization of much of the world, and for nineteenth- and early-twentieth-century constructions of other peoples.

The Other ceased being defined by his exclusion, his non-Christianity, and instead became contained by his designation as a member of a non-Christian religion.[6] In this way, McGrane argues, the early pagan and the contemporary Other came to be seen as essentially similar because neither was enlightened. "The self-identity of the Enlightenment is aligned with knowledge *as opposed to* the identity of the unenlightened, alien Other that is aligned with ignorance: Enlightenment knowledge consists in awareness of ignorance and ignorance consists of nonawareness of ignorance."[7]

Roxann Wheeler, in her meticulously researched study of changing conceptions of race in England in the eighteenth century, writes that when Christianity was the dominant lens through which other people were viewed, race was less of an issue than it later became in the eighteenth and nineteenth centuries. The eighteenth century witnessed the rise of a "four-stages theory" of society, she writes, in which commercial civilization, represented by modern Europe, was the final stage, preceded successively by the "primitive" stage, characterized by people who forage, the shepherd-based stage, characterized by the Scots Highlanders and the Arabs, and the agriculturally based stage of the ancient Greeks and Romans.[8] Wheeler writes that this model was not always conceived hierarchically; indeed, the many classifications and cataloguings of peoples in this era, which Wheeler covers with admirable thoroughness, were achieved with a fair amount of detachment (jettisoned in the next century).[9] Four-stages theory became orthodoxy in the last couple of decades of the eighteenth century.

The question of civilization was another concern. The word "civilization" in its modern sense was first used in France in 1766. Before that it was a legal term denoting the process of moving a case from the criminal to civil court. Then a M. Boulanger, perhaps a pseudonym for the Baron d'Holbach, wrote, "When the people of a savage race come to take on civilization, we must never set a term of the process by giving them fixed and irrevocable laws; they must be taught to regard the legislation imposed upon them as a stage in a continuous process."[10] From then on "civilization" took on the meaning still in use.[11] In the late eighteenth century "civilization" was at the top of a hierarchy of concepts, with the savage state at the bottom, followed in ascending order by barbarism, civility, politeness, "a wise control," and then civilization.[12]

At the same time, however, there were those writers who were bent on critiquing their society with reports of others, a common practice in the first half of the eighteenth century. An early and important Enlightenment text of this sort is the *Lettres Persanes* (1721) of Montesquieu (1689–1755), in which two Persian tourists travel to France and ridicule French society at every level: the church, war, politics, corruption, poverty. But it is Persian culture that is ultimately mocked, since one of the tourists, Usbek, learns of a crisis in the harem back home, nearly causing his wife to commit suicide. The message of the *Persian Letters* is that while things might not be ideal in France, it is better to live there than under the rule of an Oriental despot such as Usbek.[13]

The tactic of criticizing one's own culture by juxtaposing it with a "primitive" one received new life after the peoples of the Pacific were "discovered" in the latter half of the eighteenth century by Captain Cook. These peoples became emblematic of the unspoiled, happy native.[14] After the French explorer Louis-Antoine de Bougainville returned from the South Pacific after a voyage in 1766–69, Denis Diderot contributed a scathing portrayal of Europeans from the perspective of a wise old Tahitian man, written in 1772 but not published until 1796. " 'Weep, unfortunate Tahitians!,' " he wrote, "Weep! But over the arrival, not the departure, of these ambitious and wicked men. Some day you will come to know them better. Some day they will return. With the piece of wood, which you see attached to this man's girdle in one hand, and in the other the sword which hangs by that one's side, they will come to put you in chains, to slaughter you, to subject you to their wild fantasies and to their vices. Some day you will be made to serve under them, after you have become as corrupt, as vile, and as miserable as they are."[15]

Despite continued interest in this stratagem, Dorinda Outram writes that in the second half of the eighteenth century, intellectuals became increasingly occupied with the question of what constitutes civilization. By the end of the century it was common to conceptualize the Other as representing Europe's origins in classical civilization. Native peoples were depicted in paintings and statues in classical dress.

There were also the civilizing effects of trade, as English traders contrasted their civility with the barbarity of those who were traded as slaves. By the late eighteenth century it was consumption and the faculty of taste that were thought to make one civilized. Consumption of English goods could serve as an antidote to savagery.[16] Recall also that the pinnacle of humankind in the four-stages theory was commercial culture. The consumption of goods resulted in many public signs of England's civility and greatness. Many periodicals tackled this theme: "Every country must be luxurious before it can make any progress in human knowledge," one said in 1760.[17] Taste, that all-important ideology of the second half of the eighteenth century, became a major faculty found lacking in the African by English writers.

Probably most debates in this period, however, centered on the question of the savage, and the role of savages and other creatures in the overall scheme of things. By the eighteenth century, writings on the "savage" grew more virulent, even though the trope of the "noble savage" had been around for quite some time.[18] The cleric John Wesley (1703–91) wrote that the primitive peoples of the earth could not be compared to "horses or any of our domestic animals," which "would be doing them too much honour."[19] By the eighteenth century the concept of the "savage" had a long history of signifying European Christian superiority and encompassed many supposed qualities of nonwestern Others, such as cannibalism, paganism, social disorder, and nakedness.[20] Savages ultimately were placed in the existing chain of being—the hierarchy of God's creatures beloved by European scholars for centuries—which meant that the chain of being "had to be converted from a spatial arrangement of forms into an historical, developmental, or evolutionary series."[21]

But placing nonwestern Others into the chain of being proved difficult. Where would they go? Were they children of God? Lower than Europeans? Animals? This question was not resolved with any definitiveness until the publication in 1676–77 of Dr. Samuel Petty's *Scale of Creatures*, in which the Christian position was jettisoned: there were now thought to be many kinds of men, each of which occupied its own place in the chain of being, all in-

TABLE 1 Linnaeus's List of *Homo sapiens*, Varying by Education and Situation

1. Wild man	four-footed, mute, hairy.
2. American	copper-colored, choleric, erect. Paints self. Regulated by custom.
3. European	fair, sanguine, brawny. Covered with close vestments. Governed by laws.
4. Asiatic	sooty, melancholy, rigid. Covered with loose garments. Governed by opinions.
5. African	black, phlegmatic, relaxed. Anoints himself with grease. Governed by caprice.

Source: Sir Charles Linné, *A General System of Nature, through the Three Grand Kingdoms of Animals, Vegetables, Minerals, Systematically Divided into Their Several Classes, Orders, Genera, Species, and Variations* . . . (London: Lackington, Allen, 1806), I, 9, as quoted by Hodgen, *Early Anthropology*, 425.

ferior to European man.[22] Savages were thought to be unmanly, beastly, lacking in speech and reason—all "flat denials of the essential humanity of the savage."[23]

Petty's book, along with Sir William Tyson's *Orang-outang, sive homo silvestris; or the anatomy of a pygmie* (1708) and Carl Linnaeus's *System of Nature* (1735), represented a break in the thinking on nonwestern Others in the last quarter of the seventeenth century and the first quarter of the eighteenth. Humankind was no longer seen as a perfect whole, with all the children of God ranked above animals and below the angels. Naturalists had to somehow reconcile man and ape, and students of culture had to "compose an acceptable social or cultural hierarchy as an extension of the biological."[24] Margaret T. Hodgen writes that Linnaeus's inclusion of humans in his catalogue, dividing humankind into two major types, was an extremely important gesture.

Anne-Robert Jacques Turgot addressed a learned group at the Sorbonne on 11 December 1750, saying that the human race, unlike Nature, which is continually dying and coming to life, "is a vast whole which, like every individual being, has its time of childhood and of progress. . . . Manners become gentler; the mind becomes more enlightened; nations, hitherto living in isolation, draw nearer to one another; trade and political relations link up the various quarters of the globe; and the whole body of mankind, through vicissitudes of calm and tempest, of fair days and foul, continues its onward march, albeit with tardy steps, towards an ever nearing perfection."[25] This notion would gain greater traction in the nineteenth century, especially after Charles Darwin, and so I will leave a proper consideration of it until chapter 3.

TABLE 2 Linnaeus's List of *Homo monstrous*,
Varying by Climate and Art

1. Mountaineers	small, inactive, timid.
2. Patagonians	large, indolent.
3. Hottentots	less fertile.
4. American	beardless.
5. Chinese	head conic.
6. Canadian	head flattened.

Source: Linné, *A General System of Nature* I, 9, as quoted by
Hodgen, *Early Anthropology*, 425.

By the end of the eighteenth century and into the nineteenth, scholars and clerics classified non-Europeans, especially Africans and Native Americans, as species apart from Europeans. Failed colonial administrations and the absence of a perceptible influence of European civilization were arguments wielded to show that these peoples were inferior.[26]

Skin color and conceptions of race were also entering the debates, in ways that are somewhat familiar today. There was a problem with accepting the nonwestern Other as a Christian, however. Once these Others were Christianized, then what? And the term "Christian" changed over the course of the eighteenth century, no longer used to refer only to Europeans. The term thus declined over the eighteenth century in favor of terms such as "free" and "white."[27]

By the 1770s skin color became the dominant marker of difference, most prominently in Oliver Goldsmith's *History of the Earth and Animated Nature* (1774). Goldsmith made a connection between the appearance of Africans and Europeans and their mental capacities, attributing them, as was the norm in this period, to climate: "As their persons are thus naturally deformed, at least to our imaginations, their minds are equally incapable of strong exertions. The climate seems to relax their mental powers still more than those of the body."[28]

MUSICAL REPRESENTATIONS IN
THE EIGHTEENTH CENTURY

Students of music were as much interested in classification and compartmentalization as their counterparts in other intellectual endeavors. The influence of Père Lafitau's *Manners of the American Savages Compared to the Manners of Primi-*

tive Times (1724) found its way into studies of music, such as John Brown's *A Dissertation on the Rise, Union and Power, the Progressions, Separations, and Corruptions of Poetry and Music* (1763), which posited thirty-six stages in the development of music, with the ancient Greeks at the pinnacle moving downward to the inferior music of the present. Brown's work, its atomized bits of the development of music, represents a kind of chain of being, already discussed, in vogue in this period.[29]

Composition partook of the same ideologies, of course, and I want to consider how Enlightenment conceptions of otherness found their way into music. "Exoticism" in European music has long been a preoccupation of musicologists and historians, particularly with regard to Mozart's music, and to the eighteenth century in general.[30] What I hope to accomplish is to bring some of the insights of cultural and social history together with those offered by musicology, and attempt to examine them all with the benefit of current work in cultural theory.

I have already made clear that western European music for centuries has been concerned with representations and appropriations, as to some degree all musics are—no music is pure. As a scholar and musician I am interested in musical sounds themselves employed by musicians for representative purposes, not just representations in character, costume, or dance; to find these we must move through time to the early eighteenth century. Earlier western confrontations with peoples and musics from other cultures seldom resulted in anything but the grossest approximation of non-European music in western notation; western composers before the nineteenth century didn't yet possess concepts of authenticity, ethnography, even history that were constructed by late-eighteenth-century modernity, and so their transcriptions of the appropriated music look and sound rather like western European music of the time. By the early eighteenth century musical representation practices are set in place that remain for the better part of a century.

Even with the lack of musical sounds in dramatic works before the eighteenth century, musical dramatic works were frequently based on "exotic" themes. The rise of opera at the very end of the sixteenth century occurred in a historical moment that witnessed the increasing intercourse of peoples and travel of musical sounds and styles. Opera and tonality, as we have seen, grew out of this jumble of different musics and musical practices that facilitated as never before the representation of new peoples, new social roles, and new relationships in early modern Europe.

The question then becomes: Who is represented, how, to what ends, and to whose ends? New representational modalities entailed new musical devices, which themselves became aestheticized and used to enrich the musical vocabulary of all European musics, not just operas or other works with "exotic" themes.

The first nonwestern sounds to appear in western music were from the people geographically nearest to European metropoles. Mary Rowen Obelkevich makes a strong case for the appearance of Turkish musical elements in western European music by the end of the seventeenth century.[31] Interestingly, she writes that French composers' fascination with Turkey and its music stemmed first from the Renaissance desire to recapture the "lost" arts of ancient Greeks and not, as I will argue in a moment, the specter of the Ottoman Empire. For Obelkevich, the earliest use of Turkish music seemed to be more coloristic than anything else.[32]

We also have to note the way western Europeans would have come into contact with these other musics, which is of course mainly through political and military actions. The first borrowed sounds were Turkish primarily because the Ottoman Empire enjoyed such stunning success, so much so that for centuries, all foreign musics, if they were referred to at all in an idiom deviating from the norm, deviated in favor of Turkish sounds, particularly percussion: bass drum, tambourines, cymbals, triangle. Recall J. H. Elliott's account of a sixteenth-century publisher who, lacking any pictures of the Tupinambá people of Brazil, used pictures of Turks instead because he had those in stock.[33] Similarly, "Turkish" music was the all-purpose "exotic" music, and Turks the default foreign Others, in part because they commanded respect.[34]

The power and expanse of the Ottoman Empire cast its shadow over the European continent for centuries, even getting in the way of European expansion after the European discovery of the New World.[35] The Ottoman Empire was founded by Osman or Othman, a Turkish tribal chieftain early in the fourteenth century, and was ruled thereafter by several emperors who were portrayed in various works of European art: Selim I, whose name is among the most common in western representations of Turks as "noble savages"; and Süleyman I, the Magnificent. At the height of its power, the Ottoman Empire controlled all of Asia Minor, the Balkans, the islands of the eastern Mediterranean, parts of Hungary and Russia, Iraq, Syria, the Caucasus, Palestine, Egypt, parts of Arabia, and all of North Africa through Algeria. From a list of the names of the Sultans we can get an idea how many of them tend to be the most popular for names of Turkish characters in European treatments of Turkish topics for several centuries; Mozart, as we shall see, uses two in his *Die Entführung aus dem Serail*, Selim and Osmin (usually spelled Osman, the name of the founder of the Ottoman Empire in the fourteenth century); others include Bayezid (or Bajazet), Süleyman I the Magnificent, and Mohammed.

The longevity of the Ottoman Empire and, at its peak in the sixteenth century, its proximity to central Europe forced Europeans to deal, grudgingly or not, with its success. "By and large," Edward Said writes in *Orientalism*, "only the Arab and Islamic Orient presented Europe with an unresolved challenge on the political, intellectual, and for a time, economic levels."[36] According to Said, that the Orient presented a threat to Europe meant that Europeans treated other parts of the world that the term "Orient" could signify—such as India—with a degree of "proprietary hauteur." The Islamic world alone was treated with a "sense of danger."[37]

Said uses "orientalism" to denote not only a topic of study but also "that collection of dreams, images, and vocabularies available to anyone who has tried to talk about what lies east of the dividing line."[38] And there were plenty of dreams and images, as well as an interest in things Turkish. This fascination was part of a larger fascination for empire builders. I have counted nearly thirty operas on the life of Süleyman I the Magnificent from 1753 through 1799.[39] And there are over a dozen operas that follow roughly the same plot of a European damsel rescued from the clutches of the Turks.[40]

RAMEAU: *LES INDES GALANTES*

The important *opéra-ballet Les Indes galantes* (1735) by Jean-Philippe Rameau (baptized 1683, d. 1764) contains four "entrées" (acts): "Le Turc généreux" (which ends with "Tambourins I & II" featuring the tambourine, a musical instrument signifying "Turk" to contemporary ears), "Les Incas du Pérou," "Les Fleurs, fête persane," and "Les Sauvages."[41] The last entrée takes place in North America, where the "savages" are indigenous Americans.[42] The collection of entrées affords the composer the opportunity to represent different peoples, but the entrée that employs actual musical sounds to represent Others is "Le Turc généreux"; the other entrées make use of less unusual musical techniques within contemporary idioms to represent difference.

That Turks in this work are the subject of musical representations and other peoples are not is a result of the long history of Europe with the

Ottoman Empire, which had been represented in music before Rameau; one of the earliest treatments of Turkish music in a western European dramatic work appears in the *opéra-ballet L'Europe galante* (1697) by André Campra (1660–1744), which contains a prologue and four sections, moving from the French center to its peripheries: "La France," "L'Espagne," "L'Italie," "La Turqie."[43] The last section, subtitled "Le Théâtre des Jardins du Serail du Grand Seigneur, & dans le fond, l'Appartment des Sultanes," features a cast of sultans and others, as well as "La Discorde" and Venus.[44]

Most of the selections of Campra's "La Turqie" might not sound particularly "Turkish" to our ears, but they employ musical signs that Campra's audiences undoubtedly would have recognized as "Turkish." The text of the work concerns the triumph of love; Discord and Venus clash at the beginning, but after touring the world and viewing the power of love, Discord concedes. "La Turquie," the last aria, sung by Venus and Discord, ends with as good an example as any of what Stephen Greenblatt has called "Christian imperialism."[45]

> La Discorde à l'Amour, cède enfin la victoire.
> Vous, Jeux charmants, tendres Plaisirs,
> volez de toutes parts, pour servir ses désirs;
> allez accroître encor son Empire et sa gloire.

> Discord to Love at last cedes the victory.
> You, charming games, tender pleasures,
> fly to all parts of the world to serve his desires;
> go to increase his empire and his glory.[46]

Presumably the text refers to God's empire, but the slippage between spreading God's influence and the king's power isn't far away.

Rameau thus builds on a long tradition of European representations of Turkish otherness. What is comparatively new in *Les Indes galantes* is the dramatic, though not musical, representations of New World and peoples outside Europe and the Ottoman world. In a letter in 1727 Rameau refers to a performance by "savages" who appeared at the Théâtre-Italien "a year or so ago."[47] The musicologist Roger Savage tracked down an account of that event in the *Mercure de France* in September 1725, since Rameau himself did not provide one:

> Before leaving for Fontainebleau, the management of the Théâtre-Italien mounted a most unusual novelty. Two large and well-built sav-

ages, about 25 years old and only recently arrived from Louisiana, danced three kinds of dances (separately and together) in a style that left no room for doubt that the steps and leaps they executed were learnt a long way away from Paris. What the dances meant to signify by them would doubtless be perfectly easy to understand in their own country, but here nothing is harder to fathom. This is what we have been able to gather about them. The first dancer (dressed rather more modestly than would be the case in Louisiana but with a sufficiency of flesh visible nonetheless) represented a tribal chief. He wore a kind of crown on his head, not sumptuous but large and decorated with variegated plumes. There was nothing about the other dancer to distinguish him from a simple warrior. The one led the other to understand by the style and rhythm of his dance that he came to propose peace, and presented a calumet or banner to his enemy. Then they danced the dance of peace together. Next came a war-dance, depicting a gathering of savages resolved on waging war with such and such a tribe. One of their number acts out all the horror of so doing, while those in agreement with him signify their approval by joining in the dance. In the third dance the warrior, armed with a bow and quiverful of arrows, first tracks down an enemy while the other savage sits on the ground and beats a drum (a kind of kettledrum no bigger than a hatter's block). On discovering the enemy, the warrior goes back to inform his chief and then presents the combat during which he imagines himself defeating his foe. After this they dance the victory dance together.[48]

Around 1728 Rameau wrote *Nouvelles suites de pièces de clavecin* and included a movement entitled "Les Sauvages," a movement that he described as "characterizing the song and dance of the savages" he heard at the Théâtre-Italien.[49] Based on other historical reports, Savage surmises that Rameau probably heard members of the Natchez tribe, with whom the French had much contact in New Orleans after the city's founding in 1718. Savage believes that Rameau, subscribing to the current mimetic theory of art, attempted to imitate the song and dance of the Native Americans he had heard, modifying rhythms and melodies, and adding harmonies. Perhaps, though the music bears no resemblance to any Native American music, and Savage's arguments on this point aren't very convincing. It is far more likely that Rameau employed musical devices within existing norms, stretching them, so that the music sounded a bit strange, a bit odd to listeners of the day.

No matter how "authentic" the music of "Les Sauvages" is, for the composition of *Les Indes galantes* Rameau reused this music. And the press heard the music of *Les Indes galantes* as "authentic"; one critic wrote after the première, "I find the music truly Indian, allowing that this nation is capable of producing good music, for this extraordinary music is not without beauty."[50] Another reviewer wrote that "the music is a perpetual witchery; nature has no share in it. Nothing is more craggy and scabrous; it is a road of constant jolts. . . . What an excellent joggling chair [an armchair with springs for exercise] this opera is! Its airs are fit to stir up the benumbed nerves of a paralytic. How different are its violent shocks from the gentle stirring that Campra, [André Cardinal] Destouches [1672–1749], [Jean-Joseph] Mouret [1682–1738], [Michel Pignolet de] Montéclair [1667–1737], etc., know how to cause in us! I am racked, flayed, dislocated by this devilish *sonata* of *Les Indes galantes*; my head is all shaken up with it."[51] Note how the music is characterized — as witchery, as though somehow a "real" representation of Others, Others bereft of knowledge, ruled instead by superstition.

The work seems to have been particularly popular at the time of its composition; the philosopher and mathematician Jean le Rond d'Alembert (1717–83) singles out the "Ballet des fleurs" as the apex of instrumental composition — "where the dance airs, so well enacted as if in dialogue and so picturesque, form the most expressive mute scene"; and Diderot, writing in 1760, complains of the fleeting popularity and shallowness of contemporary operas compared to such long-lasting works as André Campra's *L'Europe galante* and *Les Indes galantes*.[52]

"Le Turc généreux" employs a plot that had gained currency long before Rameau and would be used throughout the eighteenth century. A Turkish nobleman captures a European woman and attempts to force her to have sex with him, but he relents in the face of the woman's affection for her European lover, who comes to her rescue. In Rameau's version of this old story (which Nicholas Till believes originated in the Renaissance, with a version in the *Decameron* and another in England, Thomas Heywood's romance-comedy *The Fair Maid of the West* of 1631),[53] the Turkish nobleman is Pasha Osman and the European characters Emilie and Valère are saved through Osman's recognition of Valère as his former master; Osman tells the two Europeans that he will "s'efforce aujourd'hui / D'imiter sa magnificence" ("attempt today / to imitate his magnanimity") by granting freedom.

This "generous Turk" is a type identified by Bernard McGrane as the

Ex. 3 Rameau, *Les Indes galantes*, "Le Turc généreux," "Air pour les esclaves africains"

"Other-as-saint," a type that emerged in the Renaissance.[54] Although the character is not particularly saintly in this old plot, the trope of the generous Other, as well as the Noble Savage, has a long history and survived into the Enlightenment even as other conceptions of difference were emerging.

Rameau's "Air pour les esclaves africains" occurs after this happy moment, as the assembled cast gathers onstage to sing Osman's praises (example 3). "Air pour les esclaves africains" stands out in *Les Indes galantes* as one of the most harmonically adventurous moments in the entire *opéra-ballet*, employing codes that signified otherness in extreme ways. First, it's in a minor

Ex. 4 Rameau, *Les Indes galantes*, "Le Turc généreux," "Premier Tambourin," opening

key, which would often be used in depicting racialized and gendered Others; second, there are surprising dissonances here and there, the most striking occurring as an appoggiatura—a note outside the prevailing harmony, but subsequently resolving on the harmony note—at measure 11, striking not only harmonically, where the A clashes with the B-flat in the bass, but in the sheer repetition of this A, the highest pitch in the movement.[55] The abrupt harmonic movement, deceptive cadences, great melodic leaps, and use of drum and tambourine (which I have combined into one staff, derived from the superb recording by William Christie and Les Arts Florissants) were all encodings of Turkish difference to Baroque ears. It is also interesting to note that in the second part, Rameau traverses several key areas as though exploring the real world.

Another "Turkish" example is "Premier Tambourin," which occurs after the previous "Air" and makes use of an upbeat-downbeat ambiguity as well as the familiar percussion instruments (example 4). This ambiguity is indeed great in that the passage would work perfectly well if the downbeat were heard on the first note. The only way one can know there is an ambiguity is by looking at the music (or perhaps a conductor at a live performance). While composers do occasionally play tricks in notation such as this, it is important to view Rameau's gesture not just as a trick, but as a device that also emphasizes the European perspective of the importance of literacy over orality: Rameau represents an uncoordinated Turk musically without the Turk's even hearing (or knowing).

These musical codes of difference were interchangeable, good for representing whatever Other the composer wanted. And they weren't just codes for women or racialized Others; as Susan McClary points out, extreme gestures within a tonal framework tended to occur when the composer was representing the feminine, the insane, racialized Others, and "natural" phenomena such as storms. In other words, all kinds of extremes of nature. Musical techniques such as chromaticism, dissonance, avoidance of a tonal center, and lack of goal orientation are some of the techniques that composers have used since the advent of tonality.[56] These are much the same as the procedures that Miriam K. Whaples identifies as those used to represent the "exotic" Other, whose difference could be musically signaled not by "authentic" borrowed materials but by the same eccentric musical techniques just noted, with some additions: chromaticism, metrical changes or ambiguity (including hemiola, a rhythmic device that resembles a temporary change in meter); minor keys in genres which didn't normally employ minor keys (such as marches); disjunct melodies; and disjunct ground basses. Operas for centuries made use of all these devices for representing Others, gendered or racialized.[57]

McClary has also argued that subordinate tonal regions and subordinate themes are virtually invariably perceived as feminine. Or "Other" in a more general sense.[58] Making this argument does not imply that all tonal works employ this schema; rather, tonality is as informed by modern western notions of center and margins, dominant and subordinate, as any other cultural form in western culture. I will draw on McClary's ideas in my discussion of Mozart's *Die Entführung aus dem Serail*.[59]

MOZART: DIE ENTFÜHRUNG AUS DEM SERAIL

Although Europeans during the Enlightenment were aware of a plurality of peoples on the earth, these Others rarely found their way into European music.[60] As we have seen in the discussion of Rameau's *Les Indes galantes*, few musical codes existed for portraying other peoples with any degree of accuracy. Perhaps as a result of this, musicologists have until recently been reluctant to explore modes of signification and representation, instead explaining the interest of Enlightenment Europe in *turquerie* as merely fashionable or faddish. Even when the composers involved are as well-known as Mozart (1756–91), this is the explanation usually advanced. But fashions and fads have historical, cultural, and social roots that are well worth examining. So it is interesting to note that Mozart was concerned with the political ramifications of *Die Entführung aus dem Serail*—the opera which, in the famous scene from the film *Amadeus*, the Habsburg emperor Joseph II (1741–90) describes as having "very many notes."[61]

During the composition of *Die Entführung*, and for nearly a decade thereafter, Joseph II was reforming the Habsburg Empire at every level. The power of the state was increased, mainly at the expense of the church; conscription, introduced in 1771, allowed Joseph in 1788 to mobilize 145,000 infantrymen, 37,000 cavalrymen, and 900 cannons for his war against Turkey, a war that proved to be his Vietnam.[62] The emperor was also attempting to expand his domain by trying to acquire Bavaria (twice) and the Balkans, where he tangled with the Ottoman Empire. Joseph was also conducting covert negotiations with Catherine the Great of Russia about quietly annexing parts of the Ottoman Empire. *Die Entführung* was scheduled to have its première while her emissary, the grand duke Paul Petrovich, was in Vienna.

The use of "Turkish" music was a way for Joseph II to remind the public of the treacherous Turks in the event that he and Catherine the Great managed to seize some of the territories of the Ottoman Empire.[63] Further, Volkmar Braunbehrens writes that by the time Mozart began work on *Die Entführung*, preparations had begun in Vienna to celebrate the one hundredth anniversary of the Austrian victory over the Turks in 1683, at the siege of Vienna.[64] The treaty that resulted between Catherine the Great and Joseph II dragged Joseph to war with the Ottoman Empire after it had been provoked by Catherine in 1787.

Moreover, the genre that Mozart employs is not, strictly speaking, an opera; it is rather a *Singspiel*, a German form of music drama that differs from opera in that spoken dialogue occurs (rather than dialogue set to music, like recitative in Italian operas). Joseph II in 1778 encouraged the composition of such works using the German language (which he had established as the administrative language of his empire) and founded a national theater to perform the "national singspiel." *Die Entführung* is one of the few memorable results, since the theater remained open only a decade. The success of *Die Entführung* encouraged Mozart to believe that he could produce an opera a year for the emperor's national theater, which he never got around to doing.[65]

In a letter to his father on 1 August 1781 Mozart writes, "the libretto is quite good. The subject is Turkish and the title is *Belmonte und Konstanze*, or *Die Verführung aus dem Serail*. I intend to write the overture, the chorus in Act I and the final chorus in the style of Turkish music."[66] Turkish Janissary music, that is, music played by the Janissary corps, which had been built up by Murad II in the first half of the fifteenth century. Edward J. Dent has written that "*Die Entführung* is a jumble of incompatible styles,"[67] but that of course is the point: characters from different cultures and social classes rub elbows throughout the opera, as does the music that represents them, all in polyglossic fashion.[68]

The plot revolves around the efforts of two Spanish men, Belmonte, a

Ex. 5 Mozart, *Die Entführung aus dem Serail*, act I, no. 5, "Chorus of Janissaries," opening

nobleman, and Pedrillo, his servant, to rescue two European women, Konstanze and Blonde, from the clutches of Pasha Selim, a Turkish nobleman, who has been described as representing the Voltairean ideal: a noble, pagan, philosophical, exotic, benevolent despot amenable to education—education, I should add, of the Enlightenment ideals.[69] Selim personifies McGrane's "Other-as-saint" or "noble savage," whereas Osmin is just a savage (in his letters Mozart refers to him as "a rude fellow," "stupid," "surly," and "malicious").[70] Selim has taken a particular fancy to Konstanze, the nobler of the two women. She has steadfastly refused his sexual advances throughout the early part of the opera (and, we assume, before the beginning of the opera), but he finally institutes a deadline. The European men must thus rescue the women before this rape.

Mozart's use of the "Turkish" music functions as parody, a sign of duplicity, and finally a sign of nobility. At the end of the opera it represents joy, celebration, and relief, and it's this particular meaning that lasts into the nineteenth century. What's interesting is that Mozart is in sole command of the material: he can manipulate it any way he pleases. And he uses it in different ways. The "Turkish" music represents Osmin, the "savage," and Pasha Selim, the "noble savage" or "Other-as-saint." It parodies Osmin's Muslim reluctance to drink wine; it concludes the entire opera, singing praise to Pasha Selim's generosity.

The music that represents the Turks in the opera is the familiar Janissary-derived sounds of eighteenth-century European music: percussion such as cymbals, triangles, and bass drums, as well as martial music (example 5). Note how Mozart, while offering Janissary music, at the same time emphasizes its difference by its very metrical duplicity: the opening of the chorus begins on an upbeat that sounds like a downbeat, then another upbeat-downbeat ambiguity. It doesn't take long to determine where the upbeat really is, but this requires listening backwards, in a sense, rehearing the opening music and construing it as an upbeat and not a downbeat, a demand on listeners that would have been more difficult before the modern hegemony of conceptions of linear time and history.[71] Such a gesture also has comic overtones, as though the chorus starts off on the wrong foot (which is probably why Giuseppe Verdi begins *Falstaff* with a similar, momentary upbeat-

Ex. 6 Mozart, *Die Entführung aus dem Serail*, act III, no. 18, Romanze, "In Mohrenland gefangen war," opening

downbeat ambiguity). This is the same technique, though more complex, used by Rameau (see example 4).

The phrase structures in example 5 tend to be asymmetrical, a characteristic which may well be derived from Janissary music. Also, the opening phrase is 9½ bars long, not an even number as was the norm. And the chorus phrasing is similarly asymmetrical; the first phrase consists of eleven bars, seven plus four, with the last four sounded almost like an afterthought, almost unheard of in Mozart's music. And it's unheard of here, since I would argue that it was purposeful, not inadvertent: Mozart represents the Turks through this asymmetry.

Although Whaples compared one example of "authentic" Turkish music to the "inauthentic" selections used by Jean-Baptiste Lully (1633–87), Rameau, Christoph Willibald von Gluck (1714–87), Mozart, and others, the example she chose doesn't bear much resemblance to the Janissary music referred to by Mozart. At this juncture it is probably impossible to know with any certainty just which sounds—apart from instrumentation—made their way from Janissary music into central European composers' works, though some recordings I have heard are suggestive.[72]

Mozart also takes pains to maintain other musical codes for the Orient, codes long established before this opera. In "In Mohrenland gefangen war" (example 6), the song that Pedrillo sings to cover up the European men's nocturnal effort to liberate the European women, he uses augmented seconds in measures 9 and 11, continuing a western construction of the sounds of the "Orient," a musical code that still signifies today:[73]

Pedrillo

In Mohrenland gefangen war
ein Mädel hübsch und fein;
sah rot und weiß, war schwarz von Haar,
seufzt Tag und Nacht und weinte gar,
wollt' gern erlöset sein.

Da kam aus fremdem Land daher
ein junger Rittersman;
den jammerte das Mädchen sehr.
"Jach," rief er, "wag' ich Kopf und Ehr,'
wenn ich sie retten kann."

Belmonte
Mach ein Ende, Pedrillo.

Pedrillo
An mir liegt es nicht, daß sie sich nicht
zeigen. Wir wollen's weiter versuchen. Bleiben Sie nur auf Ihren
     Posten.

"Ich komm zu dir in finstrer Nacht, laß, Liebchen, husch mich ein!
Ich fürchte weder Schloß noch Wacht,
holla, horch auf! Um Mitternacht
Sollst du erlöset sein."

Gesagt, getan; Glock' Zwölfe stand
der tapfre Ritter da;
sanft reicht' sie ihm die weiche Hand,
früh man die leere Zelle fand;
fort war sie, hopsasa!

Pedrillo
In a Moorish land was taken
a maid, pretty and fine;
pink and white was she, black her hair,
day and night she sighed and wept bitterly,
longing to be rescued.

From a foreign land
came a young knight
to whom the maid lamented loudly.
"Ah!" cried he, "I'll risk my head
and honor to rescue her."

Belmonte
Finish, Pedrillo.

Pedrillo

It's not my fault that they haven't appeared. Stay at your post.

"I'll come to you at dead of night;
let me in quickly, dearest!
I fear neither lock nor guard.
Holla there! Listen! At midnight
you shall be freed."

He kept his word: at the stroke of twelve
the bold knight was there;
she gently gave him her soft hand,
early her cell was found empty;
she was off and away!

I should note that Mozart has left the business of learning an Other's culture to Belmonte's servant, Pedrillo; Belmonte doesn't dirty his hands (or voice) singing a "Turkish" folk song.[74]

On the Significance of Keys

In a valuable article that draws on important work by Rita Steblin, Gretchen Wheelock argues that Mozart's use of minor keys provides examples of how he encoded gendered difference in his women characters, and in the case of *Die Entführung*, "exotic" Others. Wheelock notes that composers and theorists in the eighteenth century and into the nineteenth theorized associations between certain keys and affect, and that these associations were gendered. Minor keys, which tended to be considered weak and effeminate, would be used in important moments for female characters, and, Wheelock notes, "exotic" characters.[75]

Using Wheelock's work, it is possible to interpret Mozart's opera with respect to keys, though it should be understood that in order for these key associations to work as intelligible, socially understood codes, they need not be comprehensible in a technical sense to listeners, most of whom, after all, do not have perfect pitch. But if the composer chooses a key based on her perception of its affect, the other musical codes at work will fall in line.

The opera begins and ends in the same key—C major, the "Turkish" key—which, with Wheelock's research, one can hear with historicized ears as joyful.[76] So the "Turkish" music of the conclusion doesn't stand in relief after all, having signified exultation throughout. But this is the only time the plot and dialogue match the affect implied by the key; the plot and other musical characteristics intervened, prevented the key from signifying itself until the end. It is therefore significant that Mozart sets "In Mohrenland gefangen war" in the remotest key of the entire opera: B minor, a fairly unusual key; although the opera begins and ends in C major, the homiest of home keys, when it offers a "Turkish" folksong it moves almost as far from C major as possible.

The noble lovers long for each other and express anguish over their separation in B-flat major, Konstanze for Belmonte in act I, he for her in act II, the two for each other in act III, after Pasha Selim has sentenced them to death. But there's another aria in which Belmonte pines for Konstanze, no. 4, "Konstanze, dich wiederzusehen, dich!," in A major. How are we to account for this, given that the only other use of A major in the opera is in aria no. 8, Blonde's "Durch Zärtlichket und Schmeicheln," in which she instructs the brutish Osmin in the ways of love? Probably the closest explanation is that Blonde's aria explicates what Belmonte has already demonstrated: a declaration of love for Konstanze couched in the proper language of Enlightenment Europeans, a language of love and emotions, not lust.

> O wie ängstlich, o wie feurig
> klopft mein liebevolles Herz!
> Und des Wiedersehens Zähre
> lohnt der Trennung bange Schmerz.
> Schon zittr' ich und wanke,
> schon zag' ich und schwanke;
> es hebt sich die schwellende Brust!

> Oh how anxiously, how eagerly
> Beats my loving heart!
> And the tears on meeting again
> make amends for the pain of our separation.
> Already I am trembling and shaking,
> faltering and wavering,
> my heart is swelling.

Pasha Selim never sings (his parts are all spoken, as is acceptable in the singspiel genre), and is therefore something of a cardboard character, real in words but not quite three-dimensional, with the result that he stands apart from the other characters. When they sing his praise at the end of the opera he is silent, but not out of modesty, thus emphasizing the Pasha's outsiderness.

There is another twist, though. Near the opera's conclusion, when Selim discovers that Belmonte's father was his archenemy in Spain, he explains his hatred to Belmonte:

> Wisse, Elender! Dein Vater, dieser Barbar, ist schuld, daß ich mein Vaterland verlassen mußte. Sein unbiegsamer Geiz entriß mir eine Geliebte, die ich höher als mein Leben schätzte. Er brachte mich um Ehrenstellen, Vermögen, um alles. Kurz, er zernichtete mein ganzes Glück.

> You should know, wretch, that your barbarian father is the reason for my leaving my homeland. His unbending greed took my beloved from me, whom I treasured more than my own life. He destroyed my position and my fortune, and soon all my happiness.

Pasha Selim was a Muslim living in Turkey and banished from his "homeland"—Spain—from which he was likely expelled with the other Muslims and Jews in 1492, an interpretation possible not just because of this passage but because the libretto and score to the opera contain no mention of the time in which the drama takes place.[77] Pasha Selim is really a European, sort of, and the opera is thus partly about his rehabilitation to European Enlightenment ideals.

So Selim refrains from punishing the Europeans, and *Die Entführung* by its conclusion appears to be a meditation on power. It is no accident that in its overall trajectory, leaving the "Turkish" elements aside for a moment, the opera is quite similar to another popular opera of the day, *La Clemenza di Tito*, with a libretto later set by Mozart. Pietro Metastasio's libretto was set by at least forty composers, making it one of the most popular libretti of this well-known libretto writer. *La Clemenza di Tito* tells the story of the Roman emperor Titus who, as the title suggests, shows leniency in a moment when circumstances might suggest otherwise.

One of the accomplishments of *Die Entführung* is to recode the "Turkish" music—particularly the Janissary music—which by the conclusion of the opera has become music of celebration rather than of parody only (example 7). Instead of merely celebrating the Pasha himself, the music is recoded to signify celebration in general; this time the music celebrates the Pasha's generosity and more generally the triumph of the Enlightenment

Ex. 7 Mozart, *Die Entführung aus dem Serail*, act III, no. 21, "Chorus of Janissaries," opening

values of humanity and rationality, so profound—and "universal"—that they can influence non-Europeans (or, rather, former Europeans, as Pasha Selim is rehabilitated to his European self by the opera's conclusion).[78] This concluding musical code became so powerful that "Turkish" music and its devices—cymbals, bass drums, tambourines, and melodic procedures—became potent signs of celebration, so effective that they continue to be recognized as such today.

Thus musical codes could be presented as significant and not significant, presented as signifying one thing, then recoded. This is what happens in *Die Entführung*, in which music that Mozart identifies as "Turkish"—and which accompanies certain important scenes with the Turkish characters—ultimately becomes the celebratory music at the end of the opera, thus beginning what was to become a trend throughout the nineteenth century, and even into our own: the Others' music can become the music that celebrates its own defeat, or, in *Die Entführung*, reconciliation under the guise of Enlightenment universalism.

So I would argue that this concluding music signifies celebration more than anything else. Musical codes must have been well understood in Mozart's time, and for generations afterward. The most salient example of "Turkish" music recoded as celebratory is in the 9th symphony, op. 125 (1817–23), of Ludwig van Beethoven (1770–1827), which might receive most listeners' votes today as the deepest, most profound symphonic work ever written (example 8).

Beethoven perpetuates the more subtle signs of Turkish otherness in this excerpt, such as the upbeat-downbeat ambiguity that we saw in example 5, the first Janissary chorus in *Die Entführung*. The bigger question remains: What is this "Turkish" music doing here in what is probably the most fa-

Ex. 8 Beethoven, Symphony no. 9, IV, "Turkish March," opening

mous meditation on joy in all western European music? It *is* a meditation on joy, celebrating the decline of the Ottoman Empire and the triumph of European Enlightenment values. That is the most immediate meaning. But musical codes of joy came to rely on the devices learned from Janissary bands.

Other Forms of Otherness in *Die Entführung*

In *Die Entführung*, conceptions of cultural difference intersect with class and gender differences. And irrationality. In a letter to his father on 26 September 1781, Mozart wrote of the aria that was to become known as "Osmin's rage," no. 3, "Solche hergelauf'ne Laffen" (example 9):

> Osmin's rage is rendered comical by the use of the Turkish music. . . . The passage "Drum beim Barte des Propheten" is indeed in the same tempo, but with quick notes; and as Osmin's rage gradually increases, there comes (just when the aria seems to be at an end) the allegro assai, which is in a totally different metre and in a different key; this is bound to be very effective. For just as a man in such a towering rage oversteps all the bounds of order, moderation and propriety and completely forgets himself, so must the music too forget itself. But since passions, whether violent or not, must never be expressed to the point of exciting disgust, and as music, even in the most terrible situations, must

never offend the ear, but must please the listener, or in other words must never cease to be *music*, so I have not chosen a key foreign to F (in which the aria is written) but one related to it—not the nearest, D minor, but the more remote A minor.[79]

Mozart's representation of the "savage" Osmin in this extreme way was in keeping with the musical and dramatic ideas of representation of his time. The music theorist Johann Georg Sulzer wrote in *Allgemeine Theorie der schönen Künste* (1791), "In moral issues, nature can be either cruder, as is the case with relatively primitive peoples whose powers of reasoning are but little; or comparatively refined, according to the length of time over which the arts, sciences, ways of life and customs of a people have been developed. Crude moral nature is stronger: a Huron Indian's emotions are far more violent, his actions bolder, than would be those of a European in similar circumstances."[80] No doubt the emotions of a burly Turkish servant would fit well into this striking characterization, which speaks to the broader issues of European conceptions of otherness and representation of concern in this book.

Mozart's letter also provides an important caveat regarding the significance that can be read into keys, however, for it is clear that Mozart was not simply plugging in a key that signified this or that but rather was concerned with the relationship between keys. Not that Mozart disregarded conceptions of affect and key, but for him these associations were neither rigid nor formulaic. Modern aesthetics as "art for art's sake" may have gained hegemony in philosophical discourse, but in practice, connections between emotions and music persisted, and survive to this day.

In the same letter to his father, Mozart wrote: "I have sent you only fourteen bars of the overture, which is very short with alternate fortes and pianos, the Turkish music always coming in at the fortes. . . . The first act was finished more than three weeks ago, as was also one aria in Act II and the drunken duet [No. 14, Duet, "Vivat Bachus, Bachus lebe"] . . . which consists entirely of *my Turkish tattoo*."[81] Mozart refers here to the two moments in the opera when Enlightenment ideals of rationality lapse. But these lapses affect the Turkish and lower-class characters; Belmonte and Konstanze remain serenely rational throughout.

Then "Osmin's rage" moves to an "allegro assai," the section in A minor, changing meter from a more rational duple to a triple meter, in a kind of demented waltz (example 10).

Ex. 9 Mozart, *Die Entführung aus dem Serail*, act I, no. 3, "Solche hergelauf'ne Laffen," ("Osmin's Rage"), opening

Ex. 10 Mozart, *Die Entführung aus dem Serail*, act I, no. 3, "Solche hergelauf'ne Laffen," ("Osmin's Rage"), Allegro assai, opening

Osmin

Solche hergelauf'ne Laffen,
die nur nach den Weibern gaffen,
mag ich vor den Teufel nicht.
Denn ihr ganzes Tun und Lassen
ist, uns auf den Dienst zu passen,
doch mich trügt kein solch Gesicht.
Eure Tücken, eure Ränke,
eure Finten, eure Schwänke
sind mir ganz bekannt.
Mich zu hintergehen,
müßt ihr früh aufstehen;
ich hab' auch Verstand.
Drum, beim Barte des Propheten,
ich studiere Tag und Nacht,
dich so mit Manier zu töten,
nimm dich wie du willst in acht.

. . . .

Erst geköpft, dan gehangen,
dann gespieß auf heißen Stangen,
dan verbrannt, dann gebunden
und getaucht, zuletzt geschunden!

Osmin

These jumped-up dandies
who do nothing but gawp at women,
they're worse than the devil.
All they ever do
is watch us working,
but I'm not fooled by a face like that.
Your deceits, your schemes,
your ruses, your tricks,
I know them all.
You'd have to be up early
to put one over on me.
I'm not so stupid.
So, by the Prophet's beard,
day and night I'll search
without resting to have you put to death,
however careful you are.

. . . .

First beheaded, then hung,
then impaled on hot spikes,
burned, then bound,
and drowned, and finally flayed.

Osmin reasserts his rage in the "vaudeville" that precedes the final Chorus of Janissaries, and the reunited, reprieved Europeans scold him for his hatefulness, telling him, in effect, to be more like his master Pasha Selim:

Nichts ist so häßlich als die Rache.
Hingegn menschlich gütig sein
und ohne Eigennutz verzeihn,
ist nur der großen Seelen Sache!

Nothing is as unpleasant as revenge.
Instead to be human and kind
and to forgive without resentment
is the preserve of a great soul!

"Vivat Bachus, Bachus lebe" (example 11) begins with the now-familiar upbeat-downbeat ambiguity, making liberal use of "Turkish" instruments such as the triangle, cymbals, and bass drum.

Ex. 11 Mozart, *Die Entführung aus dem Serail*, act II, no. 14, "Vivat Bachus, Bachus lebe," opening

Apart from the European representations of Turks, an imperial attitude is also evident in the Europeans' superior view of themselves in their treatment of women. In act II there is a quarrel between Blonde and Osmin, in which he tries to persuade her to give up her body to him, much as his master is attempting to persuade Konstanze. There is much class symmetry across cultural borders, although Osmin still comes across as a boor. In this scene Blonde not only has to teach Osmin the arcane ways of polite seduction in the Enlightenment ("With tenderness and coaxing, / kindness and gaiety, / it's easy to win / a gentle maiden's heart"), but points out to him that she is from the freest and best of all races: an Englishwoman, and a blonde to boot. "I'm an Englishwoman, born to freedom!" Why English and not Austrian? England, as the center of capitalism and thus the bourgeois revolution, captured the fancy of many Enlightenment bourgeois. Mozart proclaimed that he was "an out and out Englishman."[82]

Although I have been detailing various kinds of difference evident in *Die Entführung*, it is crucial to point out how all the musical codes overlap. While Enlightenment Europeans might have thought that European women as Others were superior to racialized Others, the representational devices were the same and in a real sense, interchangeable: people without power are without power; a minor key could be a sign of a gendered Other or a racialized Other, or not represent anything at all. Sometimes a minor key is just a minor key. Stephen Greenblatt's argument concerning the flexibility of selfhood developed out of the colonial encounter works as well for European hegemonic *assignments* of selfhood, or otherness: the gendered Other could be particular, individuated, real, or lumped together with any Other marginalized group.

Having presented these musical works I now want to make explicit the central argument of this chapter: that political and geographical margins are peculiarly energetic sites where meanings are made, remade, altered, transformed, altered again. . . . It becomes clear that marginality—either as positionality or in representations—plays a pivotal role in forming and altering worldviews and thus, among other things, aesthetic processes. Musical treatments of difference also suggest that even though Rameau is considered a Baroque composer and Mozart a Classical one (in the musicological categorization of such things), there are nonetheless similarities across these stylistic divisions.

Mary Douglas discussed what she called the energy of the margins in *Purity and Danger*, a classic of anthropology, and writes of society as "potent in its own right to control or to stir men to action. This image [of society] has form; it has external boundaries, margins, internal structure. Its outlines contain power to reward conformity and repulse attack. There is energy in its margins and unstructured areas."[83] Douglas considers the strength and workings of these structures, paying particular attention to ideas of impurity and filth, and what she calls pollution behavior—reactions against anything that poses a threat to established orders. "All margins are dangerous," she says. "If they are pulled this way or that the shape of fundamental experience is altered. Any structure of ideas is vulnerable at its margins."[84]

Douglas's work strikes me as unusually insightful and useful. In Mozart's *Die Entführung*, a Turk, banished from the center, poses threats to it from his new marginal position. It takes the combined efforts of an aristocrat and a commoner to induce the powerful Turk to be generous. In the process, the symbolic power of Pasha Selim in the form of Mozart's "Turkish" music ultimately triumphs, only it is recoded by Mozart (as it would be by Beethoven and others) as "universal" celebratory music. Meanwhile, the immense, oafish Osmin, who might in other circumstances stand as a symbol of Pasha Selim's power, is rendered impotent.

Also drawing on Douglas, Peter Stallybrass and Allon White make a similar argument in their essential *The Politics and Poetics of Transgression* about how "art" or "high" culture thrives on representations and appropriations from the margins: "the *socially* peripheral is . . . frequently *symbolically* central."[85] Later they argue that two concepts of the "grotesque" inform western European practices, and that "when the bourgeoisie consolidated itself as a respectable and conventional body by withdrawing itself from the popular, it constructed the popular as grotesque otherness: but by this act of withdrawal and consolidation it produced *another grotesque*, an identity-in-difference which was nothing other than its fantasy relation, its negative symbols."[86]

We have observed this process in the preceding examples. What is interesting is that in Rameau's work, and more clearly in Mozart's, the noble Other is recuperated: Pasha Selim doesn't have his own music in *Die Entführung*, and thus isn't musically represented. Edward Said attributes the portrayal of the forgiving, noble Turk to Mozart's humanistic sympathy, but we have already seen the long currency and use of this plot.[87] The noble Turk is snipped cleanly out of the process of social purification theorized by Douglas, Stallybrass and White, and others, and it is Osmin alone who in the end serves as the Other of European aversion and fantasy, Pasha Selim rehabilitated but musically mute. Just as European colonialists generally made a practice of leaving the highest social groups partly intact in order to mediate between themselves and the masses, the noble Turk in these numerous libretti is allowed to retain his nobility in order to protect the Europeans.

These operatic representations freed later composers to use the musical results to advance music's technical vocabulary, which ultimately became harnessed to the goals of "absolute" music (instrumental music with no extramusical meanings intended by the composer—by the nineteenth century generally thought by aestheticians and most musicians to be the highest form of music).[88] In all the examples we have seen (and many more that we have not), technical musical means of representing Others—or technical musical means of representation *by* Others—ultimately increases the range of compositional options available to composers. Mozart may have modulated by a major third in "Osmin's rage" for dramatic reasons, but little more than a generation later, Franz Schubert (1797–1828) was routinely modulating by thirds, even in sonata-allegro forms which conventionally require that modulations work in other ways. Musical procedures that grew out of representational means ended up being laundered at the same time so that their appearance in later works made them seem abstract, pure, untainted.

Stuart Hall writes, in the passage quoted in the Introduction, that "The English are racist not because they hate the Blacks but because they don't know who they are without the Blacks. They have to know who they are *not* in order to know who they are."[89] Hall's potent observation describes not just the English but Europeans, not just Blacks but Others generally. This self-definition is negative, dependent not merely on an Other but on a negation of an Other, a process with deep roots, and one that continues to thrive. The Other, whether noble or common, is appropriated, represented, used, and then expunged, having served its purpose, but also having left its mark.

CHAPTER 3

THE RISE OF IMPERIALISM AND
NEW FORMS OF REPRESENTATION

When empire comes in at the door, logic goes out at
the window.
—Lord Peter Wimsey (Dorothy L. Sayers, *Have His Carcase*)

Chapter 1 concluded its discussion of the colonial rise of tonality by fore-casting that the decline of tonality would coincide with the rise of imperialism. This is accurate in terms of chronology but is a necessarily incomplete story, since a number of social, historical, and cultural factors contributed to the notion held by many musicians that tonality was a worn-out musical language. This chapter will not examine all of these developments, which are beyond the scope of this book. But some of the more prominent historical shifts—such as the rise of imperialism, urbanization and the changing nature of cities, and the rise of a new form of consumerism—and how these contributed to changes in conceptions of otherness are central to the work of this chapter.

Musical modes of representation changed slowly in the nineteenth century. Many composers, at least the self-identified Romantics who receive the most attention of musicologists, musicians, and audiences, were more interested in themselves than their Others. Yet musical treatments of otherness continued; the history of music since Beethoven in chapter 2 shows an increasing specificity of cross-cultural appropriations throughout the nineteenth century, made possible by publications of folksong collections beginning early in the nineteenth century, as well as the continuing European study of nonwestern peoples. Obsessions with Turkey continued, and explorations of other parts of the Orient and the Far East resulted in some works that are still active parts of the standard repertoire: Giuseppe Verdi's *Aida* (1871), Johannes Brahms's and Franz Liszt's many works based on Hungarian folk melodies, Antonín Dvořák's Symphony No. 9, "From the New World" (1893), and many others.

But it wasn't until the end of the nineteenth century and the early twentieth that an important break with the past was made. Composers in Europe and the United States dramatically altered their relationship to Other musics, or even other musics. Canonical twentieth-century moderns and modernists — such as Béla Bartók (1881–1945), Claude Debussy (1862–1918), Igor Stravinsky (1882–1971) — all took musical forms from outside their own cultures and manipulated them to such an extent that it usually requires a significant amount of exegesis to find the borrowed material. But representations of otherness are easier to elucidate, and I will start with some of these after examining the broad ways in which conceptions of otherness shifted.

Roxann Wheeler has examined the writings of John Prichard, who over the course of the first half of the nineteenth century tracked changes in attitudes towards race, shifting the emphasis from the resemblance between human groups to their differences, bolstered by scientific advances in this time.[1] Prichard's fellow Scot, Alexander Kinmont, inverted the prevailing conceptions of difference of the eighteenth century by arguing in a series of lectures in the late 1830s that human variety was not influenced by climate, trade, or more but rather by race, which had essential characteristics. "Thus," Wheeler writes, "national characteristics that had been considered *effects* of climate or of different stages of civilization during the eighteenth century became *causes* of European superiority and of other races' inferiority by the mid-nineteenth century."[2]

Other important works from the nineteenth century include Charles Lyell's *Principles of Geology* of 1830 (and *Elements of Geology* of 1838) and, most significantly, Charles Darwin's *The Origin of Species* of 1859, which had the result of contributing to a western European tendency to view Others as occupying a different, lower rung on the evolutionary ladder.[3] An ideology of superiority arose, as some Europeans came to think of themselves as masters of the universe, superior to peoples from other cultures. Conceptions of otherness and difference in the nineteenth century grew increasingly Manichean.[4] According to Bernard McGrane, it was time — geological, evolutionary time — that was the predominant mode of apprehending nonwestern Others.[5] So by the nineteenth century, McGrane writes, "the Other was no longer a representation of ignorance [as in the Enlightenment]; he was now a representation of historical evolution. *Beyond* Europe was henceforth *before* Europe."[6]

McGrane backs up this argument with a quotation from a passage by the anthropologist Charles Tylor, who wrote in an introductory anthropology book published in 1881 and reprinted in 1913, "No doubt the life of the less civilized peoples of the world, the savages and barbarians, is more wild, rough and cruel than ours is on the whole, but the difference between us and them does not lie altogether in this . . . savage and barbarous tribes often more or less fairly represent stages of culture through which our own ancestors passed long ago, and their customs and laws often explain to us in ways we should otherwise have hardly guessed, the sense and reason of our own."[7]

THE AGE OF EMPIRE

Such attitudes toward non-Europeans both shaped and were shaped by the rise of imperialism. The term first gained a foothold in the last quarter of the nineteenth century, and historians now seem generally agreed that the period of roughly 1875–1914 was the "age of imperialism," though of course its effects far exceed this narrow chronological boundary. And there is scant agreement on what the term means; as Raymond Williams notes, the term was used in a variety of ways, to refer to either a political system or an economic system.[8]

As always, it is important to think historically. What happened in the late nineteenth century and the early twentieth to make westerners believe that they had entered an "age of imperialism"? Colonialism had existed for centuries; what was new about this new phase, if indeed it was a phase at all?

Scale, for one thing. According to Eric Hobsbawm, "between 1876 and 1915 about one-quarter of the globe's land surface was distributed or redistributed as colonies among a half-dozen states."[9] Edward Said writes that "in 1800 Western powers claimed 55 percent but actually held approximately 35 percent of the earth's surface, and that by 1878 the proportion was 67 percent, a rate of increase of 83,000 square miles per year. By 1914, the annual rate had risen to an astonishing 240,000 square miles, and Europe held a grand total of roughly 85 percent of the earth as colonies, protectorates, dependencies, dominions, and commonwealths."[10] Imperialism thus had become the predominant unifying and integrating force in the world.

Ideological justifications for imperialism became even more necessary than they had been before. Representations of peoples from other cultures took a new turn, building on conceptions influenced by an interpretation of Darwin holding that peoples from nonwestern cultures were further down the evolutionary ladder, closer to apes or monkeys than the highly cultivated European or American.

Contemporary writings of all kinds, literary and other, are full of references to peoples of other cultures, especially Africans, as occupying a rung far down the evolutionary scale. Christine Haig has usefully gathered many materials on this subject, and I draw on her work for this discussion.[11] Jan Nederveen Pieterse writes of a drawing in the *Sunday Reading for the Young* (1877) that depicts Africans among vegetation, as though animals, who are described as "but one degree removed from the level of brute creation — the sole trace of civilization about them is that they cook their food, and that, it may be assumed, in the crudest manner."[12]

When not likened to an animal, the African Other was often assumed to be an infant. The famous doctor and musician Albert Schweitzer (1875–1965), who worked for many years in Gabon (then a province of French Equatorial Africa), wrote that "the Negro is a child, and with children nothing can be done without the use of authority. We must, therefore, so arrange the circumstances of daily life that my natural authority can find expression. With regard to the Negroes, then, I have coined the formula: 'I am your brother, it is true, but your elder brother.' "[13]

Europe's nearer Others hardly fared better, also frequently placed low on an evolutionary ladder. Chaim Weizmann wrote to the British statesman Arthur Balfour in 1918 that Arabs were "at least four centuries behind the times."[14] Karl Baedeker in 1914 advised travelers to Egypt: "While much caution and firmness are desirable in dealing with the people, it need hardly be added that the traveller should avoid being too exacting or suspicious. He should bear in mind that many of the natives with whom he comes in contact are mere children, whose demands should excite amusement rather than anger, and who often display a touching simplicity and kindliness of disposition."[15]

Characterizations of African and other nonwestern musics echoed the more general writings on peoples, with a whole school of evolutionism opening up after the publication in the mid-1880s of John Frederick Rowbotham's three-volume history of music until the Middle Ages, which included a discussion of the "law of development" in music. This "law" posited a kind of "progress" derived from Herbert Spencer, and ultimately Darwin, to explain the development of music, with Europeans of course assumed to be the most highly evolved:

> If these people (Samoans etc.) can be content nowadays with two notes in their songs, we may see that there is nothing improbable in the assumption that there was a period, probably a very long period, in the history of primitive music, when the whole resources of vocal music consisted of two notes. . . .
>
> There is one song of the Fuegians in which they get beyond their one note. By this it is clear that even the Fuegians are emerging from the one-note period in Music.[16]

Other musicians and musicologists after Rowbotham followed this same path. The English organist and composer Hubert Parry wrote that "At the very bottom of the process of development are those savage howls which have hardly any distinct notes in them at all," and that "the savage stage indicates a taste for design, but an incapacity for making the designs consistent and logical."[17] A music educator, also drawing on Rowbotham, wrote in 1928 of children:

> Being little savages, they can understand savage music. I shall find the child's own savage level, and lift him gradually up to higher forms. . . . The natural evolution of music shall be my guide in leading the child from the simple to the complex . . .
>
> Everything that a primitive savage can do in music, children can do. . . .
>
> Beginning at the drum stage, my children shall be little savages who know nothing of music, and then shall dance primitive dances and beat upon rude drums and shake rude rattles until they discover some way of making tone.[18]

As a last example, the great French composer Hector Berlioz wrote that "Chinese and Indian music would be similar to ours if it existed; but that, musically speaking, these nations are still plunged in a state of benighted barbarianism and childish ignorance where only a few vague and feeble instincts are dimly discernible; that, moreover, the Orientals call music what we should style cacophony, and that for them, as for Macbeth's witches, foul is fair."[19]

Europe increasingly needed the raw materials that the non-West had to offer, which may account in part for new otherizing discourses. Expanded transportation technologies meant that commodities could be more easily moved between European metropoles and their territories abroad. Hobsbawm writes that "the world's merchant shipping had only risen, between 1840 and 1870 from 10 to 16 million tons, whereas it doubled in the next forty years, as the world's railway network expanded from a little over 200,000 kilometres (1870) to over 1 million kilometres just before the First World War."[20] This transportation infrastructure was needed in part to transport new commodities made necessary by new technologies, commodities such as oil and rubber for the automobile; tin, which came from Asia and South America; gold; and more. And rising consumption at home required more foodstuffs, imported from several places.[21] Tea consumption was up in Britain; the average family in New York consumed one pound of coffee a week in the early years of the twentieth century.[22]

And as Hobsbawm notes, communications and transportation technologies meant that foreign lands, peoples, and their cultural forms were more accessible than ever before. The "exotic" increasingly became a part of everyday life, everyday culture, and everyday education, as in the writings of Kipling and Joseph Conrad, and the boys' novels of Karl May in Germany, whose hero traveled to foreign lands.

Imperialism was thus caught up in a complex dynamic in which it was both product and producer of new western attitudes toward otherness and difference abroad, which traveled and influenced broader notions of otherness and difference at home.

Changes at Home

Much of this book is about western conceptions of nonwestern difference, which over the course of modernity became increasingly intertwined with conceptions of selfhood. For a variety of reasons, these notions became increasingly problematized in the late nineteenth century and the early twentieth, but for social, cultural, and historical reasons that go beyond conceptions of difference. It is necessary to recount some of these latter shifts, even though they have been thoroughly discussed by historians. For one thing, these histories tend to leave out or marginalize music, and histories of music tend to leave out, well, history.

Even as the distant Other and thus the European metropolitan subject were being reconfigured, there were nonetheless threats to conceptions of selfhood. In Europe and the United States, major social, cultural, and historical changes were seen by many as threatening conceptions of selfhood that had been built up over centuries, conceptions that had been founded on ideas of otherness in the early modern era. I will examine some of these shifts, which along with imperialism shaped peoples' consciousness of themselves as selves.

Let's recall a vivid statement by Stuart Hall: "modernism is modernity experienced as trouble."[23] For Hall several intellectual shifts signaled the crisis. They originated with Karl Marx, whose understanding of history made the human subject more the object of history than an agential subject in it; Darwin, whose theory of natural selection tacitly held that humans were not the end result of a divine process but rather impersonal side effects; Freud, whose idea of the subconscious further challenged the agential subject; and Ferdinand de Saussure, whose theories of language allowed speech no life outside of language.[24]

I would argue that these intellectual shifts are more symptoms than causes, and that the causes are of more interest. So let me call the aforementioned shifts cultural, and turn now to substantial social and historical transformations that altered conceptions of the modern bourgeois subject: the rise of the modern city, the rise of mass culture, and changing gender roles.[25] These three social upheavals are connected to each other (and still more factors) in complicated ways, but I will treat them separately.

The many artistic movements that took root in European cities, particularly Vienna and Paris, in the late nineteenth century and the early twentieth probably could not have happened in any other historical moment or places.[26] Cities in this period were becoming more diverse and more dynamic than ever before. In Europe the percentage of people living in urban areas grew from 10 in 1800 to 16.7 in 1850 to 29 in 1890.[27] More specifically, during the second empire in France in the mid-nineteenth century, for example, the number of residents who moved from rural areas to Paris was huge, exceeding 500,000. By the end of the nineteenth century nearly two-thirds of the population of Paris had been born outside the city.[28] Most of the new residents were from rural parts of France, but there were also immigrants from Italy, and Jews from Eastern Europe. In Vienna, the other major capital of European modernism, the statistics are similar. In 1857 the population of the city was about 683,000; by 1910 it was nearly 2.1 million, though the profile of the population was less diverse than France, with most of the influx from other parts of the Austrian empire.[29]

Cities were not only growing in population but changing in nature. The

Parisian boulevards were built in the mid-nineteenth century, permitting people from different social groups to come into contact with one another in unprecedented ways.[30] In Vienna, after the Revolution of 1848, Emperor Franz Joseph took the throne of the Habsburg Empire; he was then seventeen years old and was to reign for sixty-eight years. Franz Joseph sought to rebuild the city, which he did from 1858 to 1888; one result of his efforts was the celebrated Ringstraße, a broad boulevard that still surrounds the city. Once this ring was completed it became the site of the coffeehouses for which Vienna is still famous.

The growing population of cities, and the changing composition of them, facilitated broader social contact as well as new forms of cosmopolitanism. I have discussed urbanization elsewhere at greater length.[31] In brief, these changes in population and in the experience of the city changed people's relationships to each other, affecting conceptions of selfhood. People increasingly began to feel lost in a crowd, in a welter of humanity. Nothing epitomizes this shift better than King Vidor's classic silent film *The Crowd* (1928), which opens in a small American town around the turn of the century, a town where everyone clearly knows everybody else. But when the hero matures and travels to New York City to work, he is at first shown at a sea of desks in a huge skyscraper. The film ends with the hero and his wife at a vaudeville show, the camera panning back and back until the couple dissolves in a sea of faces.

Even though cities could be the sites of impersonal crowds, at the same time they could afford their residents with opportunities to meet, to come into contact with people unlike themselves. Raymond Williams's insights on this point with respect to the arts are particularly useful. He notes that the rise of the avant-garde in the late nineteenth century and the early twentieth was mainly a metropolitan phenomenon, its manifestations largely autonomous and in part international, which he says is related to imperialism. Many contributors to avant-garde movements were immigrants to metropoles, either from other countries or from smaller national cultures closer by.[32]

Elsewhere, Williams writes that

the key cultural factor of the modernist shift is the character of the metropolis: in these general conditions, but then, even more decisively, in its direct effects on form. The most important general element of the innovations in form is the fact of immigration to the metropolis, and it cannot too often be emphasized how many of the major innovators were, in this precise sense, immigrants. At the level of theme, this underlies, in an obvious way, the elements of strangeness and distance, indeed of alienation, which so regularly form part of the repertory. But the decisive aesthetic effect is at a deeper level. Liberated or breaking from their national or provincial cultures, placed in quite new relations to those other native languages or native visual traditions, encountering meanwhile a novel and dynamic common environment from which many of the older forms were obviously distant, the artists and writers and thinkers of this phase found the only community available to them: a community of the medium; of their own practices.[33]

Generally, therefore, immigration to urban areas, themselves newly reconstructed, fostered a unique synergy that was utterly new, and in important ways constitutive of late-nineteenth-century and early-twentieth-century modernity, helping to give rise to modernism in the arts.

At the same time, the invention of the phonograph in the late nineteenth century, as well as the rise of radio and sound film in the 1920s, ushered in a new era of mass culture, which caused a great deal of consternation among some artists and intellectuals in the first half of the twentieth century. They saw this new popular or mass culture as a debased, mass-produced, un- or anti-intellectual heap of pap for the undiscriminating masses whose grasp on individuality and selfhood was threatened.[34] For these artists and intellectuals, the consumption of mass culture was another blow to the concept of self as an autonomous, rational being; mass culture was seen as cultivating legions of cultural dupes who were losing the ability to think for themselves and make judgments about art. This was to become a major theme of the writings of some intellectuals of the period, perhaps most prominently Theodor Adorno. This anxiety is also thematized in Vidor's *The Crowd*. When the hero tries to tell his estranged wife how he feels about her, he gives up in frustration and instead plays a recording of popular music—his subjectivity, his speech, seem to have been co-opted by mass-produced popular culture.

The rise of mass culture was perceived as such a threat that it was coupled to the gender conceptions of the time, a subject that has been written about extensively.[35] One ideological shift that is significant for my arguments has been written about by Andreas Huyssen, who has usefully described how writers in the early twentieth century demonized mass culture as effeminate; it is no accident that women were acquiring more power and freedom in this period, as has also been well documented: the growth of the middle class meant that more women were being educated; the invention of clothing such as the brassiere made for more freedom of movement; women agitated for the right to vote; early forms of birth control were becoming available — these changes and more further troubled male conceptions of individuality and selfhood.[36]

Just as intellectuals like Adorno decried mass culture, others effected a backlash against the aspirations to selfhood of women, which manifested itself in many ways: in Freud's extremely paternalistic treatment of his young patient, Dora, whose intelligence he recognized while at the same time refusing to take it seriously; in Otto Weininger's *Sex and Character* (1903), a bestseller that castigated women on every front; or in Richard Strauss's opera *Salome* (1906–7), based on Oscar Wilde's play of 1893, in which the title character, obsessed with John the Baptist, kisses him on the mouth after his head has been severed, in a grotesque depiction of women's sexuality and power from the vantage point of a representative of a threatened patriarchy.[37]

The city, mass culture, technology, gender — all become bound up in increasingly complicated ways, so that by the age of empire it had became difficult if not impossible to disarticulate "imperialism" from domestic cultural, historical, and social processes. Conceptions of selfhood became intricately connected to imperialism (and other developments that I have described above), to the extent that the self has had to be conceptualized as fluid and dynamic.

Such a flexible model is proposed by Ashis Nandy, who writes of "internal responses," that is, responses at home, to British colonialism in India. He disputes the conventional wisdom that the only subjects of colonialism are those in the occupied territories, claiming that this is a view produced by colonialism itself to make its purported problems and benefits seem clear and distinct. The ideology promulgated on British subjects in Britain was, simply, that away = bad, home = good. Attitudes of the colonializers — both home and in the colonies — is an avenue that has been underexplored by theorists of postcoloniality (who have tended to focus on the former colonialized, not the former colonialists).[38]

Nandy argues that colonialist attitudes resulted in a decline of tolerance for everything that western culture had coded as "feminine" — such as introspection, thoughtfulness, tenderness — and supported new kinds of violence inflicted on the social. This strategy, he writes, "was perfectly in tune with the needs of industrial capitalism and only a slightly modified version of the colonial concept of hierarchy was applied to the British society itself. The tragedy of colonialism was also the tragedy of the younger sons, the women, and all 'the etceteras and and-so-forths' of Britain."[39] Nandy's most fascinating example of a public figure disciplined by colonialist ideology proves to be the Anglo-Irish writer Oscar Wilde (1854–1900). Nandy argues that Wilde's public homosexuality was both a cultural phenomenon and a social protest, calling into question British ideas of well-defined sexual codes and ideas about orderly society based on the binary oppositions of (heterosexual) man and (heterosexual) woman. "What the élite culture of England could not tolerate was his blatant deviation from rigidly defined sexual roles in a society which, unknown to the hyper-aesthete Wilde, was working out the political meanings of these definitions in a colony thousands of miles away."[40]

MUSIC IN THE AGE OF EMPIRE

These are some of the troubles of modernity, tackled in various ways by the artists and intellectuals of the era. In music some composers sought to counter the erosion of subjectivity by embracing, or re-embracing, a revitalized nationalism along nineteenth-century lines, in their music (as Stravinsky did in his so-called Russian period) and in their discourses about their music (as in Schoenberg's repeated valorization of the Austro-German canon).[41] Another strategy was to forge aesthetic alliances with other artists and artistic movements, discussed above, which virtually all composers did—there was an efflorescence of various -isms in this period: expressionism, impressionism, primitivism, and more. Yet another response was the conscious cultivation of the primitive, pagan, and exotic, whose selves were perceived to be untroubled, not modern (Stravinsky again, Bartók, Debussy, and Ravel among the major composers of the period).

There were also some more idiosyncratic reactions, such as Stravinsky's attempts to deprive performers of their subjectivity by referring to them as "executants," decrying the idea of interpretation, while at the same time writing music that he described, with strikingly technocratic language, as "objective," seemingly without affect: "My *Octuor*," he wrote in 1924, the year after he composed it, "is a musical object," not an " 'emotive' work but a musical composition based on objective elements which are sufficient in themselves."[42] And one should not forget that Stravinsky, perhaps more than any other composer of the twentieth century, recorded exhaustively, attempting, I would argue, to make "definitive" recordings of his works.[43]

Or Erik Satie (1866–1925), who showed no interest in overcoming the problem of the subject in the age of empire, instead poking fun at it. While some commentators refer to Satie as an early postmodernist, I think it is more accurate to call him anti-modern, or anti-modernist: his solution to the troubles-of-modernity problem was to ridicule the idea of genius, mocking the monumentality of late-nineteenth-century and some early-twentieth-century works in both his musical works and his writings.[44]

Perhaps composers in Vienna felt the problem of waning selfhood most keenly. "Quite certainly the radio is a foe!," Schoenberg wrote in 1930, going on to say that radio, phonograph, and film had made available a "boundless surfeit of music. Here, perhaps the frightful expression 'consumption of music' really does apply after all. For perhaps this continuous tinkle, regardless of whether anyone wants to hear it or not, whether anyone can take it in, whether anyone can use it, will lead to a state where all music has been consumed, worn out."[45]

Theodor Adorno, the most thoughtful and insightful enunciator of the Schoenbergian perspective (I am reading him as a primary source rather than a secondary one with respect to this music), attacked composers such as Stravinsky for in effect selling out to mass culture and thereby surrendering subjectivity. Adorno noted that Stravinsky's ballet *Petrushka* (1910–11) grew out of the cabaret but that Stravinsky "rebelled against the elements of narcissistic elation and harlequin-like animation and he succeeded in asserting, against the Bohemian atmosphere, the destruction of everything intrinsically inaugurated by the cabaret number. This tendency leads from commercial art—which readied the soul for sale as a commercial good—to the negation of the soul in protest against the character of consumer goods: to music's declaration of loyalty to its physical basis, to its reduction to the phenomenon, which assumes objective meaning in that it renounces, of its own accord, any claim to meaning."[46]

Adorno compares *Petrushka* to Schoenberg's highly influential *Pierrot Lunaire* (1912), finding that Schoenberg's protagonist clown is "based upon that lonely subjectivity which withdraws into itself."[47] *Petrushka* "tends to take the part of those who ridicule the maltreated hero, rather than come to his defense."[48] In other words, *Petrushka* is on the side of the crowd, the undifferentiated mass, not the heroic, autonomous individual, who was becoming increasingly heroic in his stand against mass culture. Adorno further argues that *Petrushka* is like an intellectual's idea of the fairground: "This is analogous to the position of the intellectual who enjoys films and detective novels with well-mannered naiveté, thus preparing himself for his own function within mass culture."[49] The individual becomes lost in the crowd, partaking of mass culture, even making fun of the individual subject. "Wherever the subjective element is encountered, it is depraved: it is sickeningly over-sentimentalized or trodden to death."[50]

Schoenberg's musical solution to the problem of the crowd and mass culture—ardently supported, explained, and defended by Adorno—was to cultivate loneliness as a style. Schoenberg sought to make musical monuments to loneliness, to subjectivity, to the increasingly isolated, alienated subject. One of the ways he accomplished this musically was by eschewing virtually all quotation or reference to other works once he began writing atonal music, which in his aesthetic world would compromise the individuality of his music. It is interesting that in *Erwartung* (1909), the single quotation that anyone has been able to identify is from a song by Schoenberg himself entitled "Am Wegrand" from his op. 6 no. 6 (1905).[51] The quotation is quite buried and not indicated in the score. The song is based on poems from the Art Nouveau movement, with text by John Henry Mackay:

> Thousands of people march past,
> The one for whom I long,
> He is not among them!
> Restless glances fly past
> And ask the one in haste,
> Whether it is he. . . .
> But they ask and ask in vain.
> No one answers:
> "Here I am. Be still."
> Longing fills the realms of life,
> Left empty by fulfillment,
> And so I stand at the edge of the road,
> While the crowd flows past,
> Until—blinded by the burning sun—
> My tired eyes close.[52]

This loneliness is the loneliness of city dwellers who are totally unaware of each other.

By the time Schoenberg devised his method of composing with twelve tones in the early 1920s, he was firm in his insistence that any reference to tonality must be avoided, because tonal references would only encourage listeners to seek tonal harmony, tonics and dominants, thus preventing them from perceiving the new, nontonal method of organization.[53] This position was more than merely theoretical: it was also caught up in efforts by Schoenberg and other composers to distance themselves from the popular, from mass culture. For Schoenberg and his student Anton Webern (1883–1945), at least, the result was the composition of increasingly introspective and private works. They felt that the only way to preserve the future of music was to venture into new harmonic territory where most listeners feared to tread.

That was Schoenberg and his disciples' solution. Other composers and other artists were less doctrinaire about their interactions with cultural forms from other places. Hobsbawm notes that a number of Europeans took nonwestern cultures seriously — intellectuals, artists, even colonial administrators and soldiers. Hobsbawm singles out visual artists of the time, who he says "treated non-western cultures entirely as equals."[54] This may be going too far, but the impact that visual arts made on western artists in the late nineteenth century and the early twentieth is well known, and should not be underestimated. The impact of other cultures on music was scarcely less significant, though composers did not always view nonwestern music as favorably as visual artists appreciated nonwestern arts.

This was especially so in France, a country that possessed many foreign territories, unlike the Hapsburg Empire whose seat was Schoenberg's home; people in France had a greater awareness of other peoples and other cultures as a result of French colonialism. Additionally, mass culture was not so widely reviled; methods such as Schoenberg's were less influential; and there was a long history of incorporating sounds from other musics into art musics. This practice in the age of empire is best represented by many works of the most important French composers of the first half of the twentieth century, Debussy and Ravel.[55] Fascination for nonwestern cultures was so pronounced in this period that in the words of the composer Camille Saint-Saëns in 1879, "the ancient modes are making a comeback, to be hotly pursued by the scales of the East in all their tremendous variety."[56]

Some French composers such as Debussy freely admitted their debt to nonwestern musics. Debussy employed the sounds of the Javanese gamelan music in his own music, as in "Et la lune descend sur le temple qui fut" from *Images*, series II (1907), and the *Fantaisie* for piano and orchestra (1889–90). If the Dutch had not colonized Indonesia and sponsored the Javanese musicians' trip to the Paris Exposition of 1889, Debussy might not have heard this music and thus might have missed an encounter with another music that for him was particularly fruitful. And Debussy familiarly constructed Others as living in an idyllic, nonmodern world, writing in 1913: "There were, and still are, despite the evils of civilization, some delightful native peoples for whom music is as natural as breathing. Their conservatoire is the eternal rhythm of the sea, the wind among the leaves and the thousand sounds of nature which they understand without consulting an arbitrary treatise. Their traditions reside in old songs, combined with dances, built up throughout the centuries. Yet Javanese music is based on a type of counterpoint by comparison with which that of Palestrina is child's play. And if we listen without European prejudice to the charm of their percussion we must confess that our percussion is like primitive noises at a country fair."[57] For composers such as Debussy, these nonwestern musics provided a way to a new musical language that would reinvigorate a moribund tradition.

It is no accident, of course, that French composers were more interested in the non-West than their counterparts in the other capital of modernism, Vienna, for vast parts of the non-West were within the imperial reach of France. Edward Said writes that "between 1880 and 1895 French colonial possessions went from 1.0 to 9.5 million square kilometers, from five to fifty million inhabitants."[58] Academic disciplines increasingly turned their gazes toward imperial subjects and French colonies. Earlier modes of apprehending the Other were in part supplanted by theories of racial types that always saw Others as inferior. Said writes that "natives and their lands were not to be treated as entities that could be made French, but as possessions the immutable characteristics of which required separation and subservience, even though this did not rule out the *mission civilisatrice*."[59]

It is possible to talk about changes in the arts in more general terms. Said says that in the age of empire, a new encyclopedic form was necessary in literature that had three distinctive characteristics: "circularity of structure, inclusive and open at the same time"; "a novelty based almost entirely on the reformulation of old, even outdated fragments drawn self-consciously from disparate locations, sources, cultures"; and "the irony of a form that draws attention to itself as substituting art and its creations for the once-possible synthesis of world empires."[60]

I find this last point the most suggestive, since Said relates it to conceptions of selfhood: "When you can no longer assume that Britannia will rule the waves forever, you have to reconceive reality as something that can be held together by you the artist, in history rather than in geography. Spatiality becomes, ironically, the characteristic of an aesthetic rather than of political domination, as more and more regions—from India to Africa to the Caribbean—challenge the classical empires and their cultures."[61] Said's language makes me a little uncomfortable in that it sounds as though authors were languishing about, contemplating the demise of the empire and changing their forms. While of course author's intentions and style can tell us something, the purpose of this book has been to consider more than the surface manifestations of "exoticism" and to attempt to explicate the underlying cultural, social, and historical shifts that shaped cultural forms such as music. Nonetheless, I take seriously Said's point on form, because it is possible to discern how ideologies of form shifted during the age of empire, as well as forms themselves.

In another of the few writings on modernism and imperialism, Fredric Jameson has argued that the imperialist phase of capitalism moved much of the economic machine offshore, invisible to people back in the European metropoles, and that artistic content would therefore "always have something missing about it."[62] This explains, he says, the literary fascination with cartography and space in this period, and as illustrations he cites James Joyce's *Ulysses* and Joseph Conrad's *Heart of Darkness*. Space, in other words, becomes a major theme again, influenced powerfully by cinematic conceptions of space as well.

If, as I argued in chapter 1, tonality itself gained a foothold in western European musical practices because it was a spatializing system, how are we to account for its demise? The standard explanation is that for many composers in the early twentieth century, tonality as a musical language had outlived its usefulness. For example, George Lichtheim writes that "Schönberg, Bartók, Hindemith (1895–1963) and Debussy arrived at similar results by a more complex route, against the background of a tired romanticism which had ceased to convey hope to a sick civilization, and was duly replaced by a pessimism foreshadowing catastrophes yet to come."[63] This is not a social, cultural, or historical explanation, though it is one of several useful stories about the end of a powerful musical system.

What became evident with the rise of tonality was that it was more than a system of arranging pitches: it could also be used to create a sense of motion, form, and space. The language that musicians and musicologists still use to describe the workings of tonality is replete with metaphors of movement across space: the composer "explores" different tonal "regions," and uses this movement, this spatiality, as a way to create a sense of form by moving from one tonal region to another and back again (see chapter 1). What frequently happens with atonal musics is that this spatial movement is retained while the tonality is not. That is, composers frequently create a sense of movement through space, but without tonality as the organizing principle of this movement.

A favorite example is Arnold Schoenberg's Three Pieces for Piano, op. 11 (1909), an early atonal work (though not twelve-tone). The first piece is audibly tripartite, but what gives it a sense of form is not that the composer moves from one tonal region to another and back again, but that the sections of the work are wildly different stylistically: the first is in a kind of late romantic style taken to dissonant extremes; the middle ushers in an utterly new rhythmic and gestural rhetoric to contrast; and the end is an oblique recapitulation of the opening. Adorno writes that the piece is "traditionalist" in its "large-scale architectonics": a three-part song-form.[64]

Thus space as an outgrowth of tonality is gone, but the abstraction of form from pitch organization was continued by Schoenberg and his contemporaries. Space could still be signified, but the tonal voyages through it were jettisoned. Voyages instead became something for the imagination on the magic carpet of consumption, the subject to which I now turn.

FRANCE AND MAURICE RAVEL

I would like to expand here on the "French" version of modernism and changing conceptions of otherness, at least as refracted in the music of Maurice Ravel. Like Debussy he found much to admire in nonwestern musics, once writing that "I consider Javanese music the most sophisticated music of the Far East, and I frequently derive themes from it: 'Laideronnette' from *Ma mère l'oye* [1910], with the tolling of its temple bells, was derived from Java both harmonically and melodically."[65] To consider Ravel in light of earlier discussions, I need to outline another important cultural shift: the rise of a new form of consumption, also complicatedly intertwined with the other social, cultural, and historical changes already discussed.

Consumption is important because Europe's others were increasingly introduced to European through a new form of consumer culture. Generally, changes in manufacturing techniques in Europe meant that previously expensive goods could be made more cheaply and afforded by many more people, bringing about a democratization of luxury, with the result that consumer goods began to be valued more for their illusions than for their utility. Thanks in part to international expositions, the "exotic" was increasingly consumed, increasingly viewed as a stimulus of fantasy. Hobsbawm writes that the "colonial pavilions" at international expositions increased in number: there were eighteen at the Eiffel tower in 1889.[66]

Rosalind H. Williams, who has studied what she calls the "dream world of mass consumption" in France, writes vividly of the Trocadéro, the portion of the international expositions on the Right Bank of the Seine, directly across the river from the Eiffel Tower where the colonial exhibits were displayed. This was a jumble, containing, in the words of one contemporary observer in 1900, "Hindu temples, savage huts, pagodas, souks, Algerian alleys, Chinese, Japanese, Sudanese, Senegalese, Siamese, Cambodian quarters . . . a bazaar of climates, architectural styles, smells, colors, cuisine, music."[67]

All this was less "educational" than entertainment, fantastic, and a lot of it was for sale. The Trocadéro presented merchandising and dreaming, sales pitch and seduction, publicity and pleasure. Reveries were passed off as reality. This dream world escaped the Trocadéro and found its way into department stores, the major specimens of which arrived in this era in France.

At the same time, the idea of the "voyage" grew increasingly prominent in French culture. This theme was used at the 1900 exposition, where twenty-one of the thirty-three major attractions involved a dynamic illusion of voyage. In one exhibit at the Trocadéro, "The World Tour," the visitor walked along the length of an enormous circular canvas representing, in the words of a contemporary, "without solution of continuity, Spain, Athens, Constantinople, Suez, India, China, and Japan," as natives danced or charmed serpents or served tea before the painted picture of their homeland.[68] An "aesthetic" of exoticism emerged: seductive, not tasteful. It resembled art in that it had themes and styles, but its goals were different: it was not meant to create beauty, harmony, and spiritual significance. "In environments of mass consumption, the logic of an art gives way to the logic of fantasy," writes Williams, who calls the resulting new style "chaotic exotic."[69]

A series of poems written in the early part of the twentieth century by Tristan Klingsor (1874–1966, whose real name was Léon Leclère), called *Shéhérazade*, was influenced by the French publication of J. C. Mardrus's translation of *A Thousand and One Nights* (1899–1904) and celebrated this idea of the voyage, this iteration of the exotic, in the dreamlike way identified and discussed by Williams. The first poem, "Asie," employs lists of places and foreign words as if to impart a sense of authenticity. The poem is about collecting, or consuming, experiences in a detached way, so as to have a story to tell later.

Asie, Asie, Asie,
Vieux pays merveilleux des contes de nourrice
Où dort la fantaisie comme une impératrice
En sa forêt tout emplie de mystère.
Asie,
Je voudrais m'en aller avec la goëlette
Qui se berce ce soir dans le port
Mystérieuse et solitaire
Et qui déploie enfin ses voiles voilettes
Comme un immense oiseau de nuit dans le ciel d'or.
Je voudrais m'en aller vers les îles de fleurs
En écoutant chanter la mer perverse
Sur un vieux rythme ensorceleur.
Je voudrais voir Damas et les villes de Perse
Avec les minarets légers dans l'air.
Je voudrais voir de beaux turbans de soie
Sur des visages noirs aux dents claires;
Je voudrais voir des yeux sombres d'amour
Et des prunelles brillantes de joie
En des peaux jaunes comme des oranges;
Je voudrais voir des vêtements de velours
Et des habits à longues franges.
Je voudrais voir des calumets entre des bouches
Tout entourées de barbe blanche;
Je voudrais voir d'âpres marchands aux regards louches,
Et des cadis, et des vizirs
Qui du seul mouvement de leur doigt qui se penche
Accordent vie ou mort au gré de leur désir.
Je voudrais voir la Perse, et l'Inde et puis la Chine,
Les mandarins ventrus sous les ombrelles
Et les princesses aux mains fines,
Et les lettrés qui se querellent

Sur la poésie et sur la beauté;
Je voudrais m'attarder au palais enchanté
Et comme un voyageur étranger
Contempler à loisir des paysages peints
Sur des étoffes en des cadres de sapin
Avec un personnage au milieu d'un verger;
Je voudrais voir des assassins souriant
Du bourreau qui coupe un cou d'innocent
Avec son grand sabre courbé d'Orient.
Je voudrais voir des pauvres et des reines;
Je voudrais voir des roses et du sang;
Je voudrais voir mourir d'amour ou bien de haine.
Et puis m'en revenir plus tard
Narrer mon aventure aux curieux de rêves
En élevant comme Sinbad ma vielle tasse arabe
De temps en temps jusqu'à mes lèvres
Pour interrompre le conte avec art . . .

Asia, Asia, Asia
marvelous old land of nursery tales
where fantasy sleeps like an empress
in her forest so filled with mystery.
Asia,
I would like to go with the schooner
that rocks this evening in port
mysterious and solitary
and which will finally unfold its purple sails
like an immense bird of the night in the golden sky.
I would like to go to the islands of flowers
listening to the perverse sea sing
in an ancient enchanter's rhythm.
I would like to see Damascus and the cities of Persia
with their slender minarets in the air.
I would like to see the beautiful turbans of silk
on black faces with bright teeth;
I would like to see the dark eyes of love
and the pupils radiant with joy
in skin yellow as oranges;

I would like to see clothes of velvet

and apparel with long fringes.

I would like to see long pipes between lips

completely surrounded by a white beard;

I would like to see sharp merchants with suspicious eyes

and cadis and viziers

who with a single movement of their finger that they bend,

grant life or death in accord with their desires.

I would like to see Persia and India and then China

the mandarins paunchy beneath their umbrellas,

and the princesses with delicate hands,

and the learned ones who argue

about poetry and about beauty;

I would like to loiter in the enchanted palace

and like a foreign traveler

contemplate at leisure landscapes painted

on fabric in frames of fir

with a figure in the middle of an orchard;

I would like to see assassins smiling

as the executioner strikes an innocent neck

with his great, curved oriental saber.

I would like to see paupers and queens;

I would like to see roses and blood;

I would like to see those who die for love as well as those who die

    for hatred.

And then I would return later

to speak of my adventure to those curious about dreams,

raising, like Sinbad my old Arabian cup

from time to time to my lips

to interrupt the story artfully . . .[70]

The list of sights and sounds here is strikingly similar to the list of sights and sounds at the 1900 exposition as quoted by Williams above.

These poems were set to music by Ravel in 1903 and do not shy away from the exotic theme. Musically, this first song, set to Klingsor's "Asie," has been described by Derek B. Scott as containing a summary of turn-of-the-century musical Orientalism (example 12).[71] This may be an overstatement, but it is clear that Ravel is invoking known musical codes that signify the

Ex. 12 Ravel, *Shéhérazade*, "Asie," opening

Other. Near the beginning, for example, Ravel employs an augmented second, which Peter Kaminsky calls "ubiquitous" in this song and which had been used by composers for centuries to represent the Oriental Other; it is played by the oboe, an instrument that composers could use to approximate the sound of a surnāy (or zurna), a double-reed instrument of western and central Asia.[72] Kaminsky writes that the song uses a symmetrical hexatonic scale (D–C-sharp–B-flat–A–F-sharp [G-flat]–F), which with the augmented second and "octatonic flavouring" contributes to the Orientalist effect.

The song has a particularly dreamy quality, also evoking Williams's conception of the "dream world" of mass consumption. It is significant that this song, the first of three in the cycle, is by far the longest of the three, the "dream" getting as much play as "reality." It is perhaps also significant that a Klingsor poem not set by Ravel reads thus:

> For the dream is more beautiful than the reality,
> For the most beautiful countries are those one does not know,
> And the most beautiful voyage is that made in dream.[73]

Lawrence Kramer, writing about Ravel and the exotic, similarly addresses the changing consumption patterns of the era.[74] Yet it needs to be made clear that Klingsor, or Ravel, or whoever, was not simply "consuming" the exotic as Kramer writes. The Other first had to be made into an object of consumption—this was one of the results of this new phase of European imperialism. And more significantly, consumption is closer to being a relationship than an act. That is, consumption is a mode of interaction shot through with ideologies—historical, social, cultural, and more. The Other, through the international expositions, through the "chaotic exotic" style of display in department stores, then a novelty, was caught up in a complex relationship with its representers. It signified a premodern existence in which selfhood had not been as beleaguered; it signified simplicity, naturalness, and anti- or non-modernity. Short of going away, the best one could do was to construct a fantasy around this Other from home.

Kramer's article is useful in many respects but doesn't sufficiently historicize what were then new practices of consumption, instead focusing on what he calls the "fantasy of consumption"; it would be more accurate to describe fantasies *through* consumption.[75] New consumption practices allowed, even encouraged, many Europeans to construct fantasies, dreams, and daydreams out of the goods that they consumed generally, as Colin Campbell has written.[76] An under-historicized discussion of consumption, and of imperialism, leaves readers with the impression that Ravel and others were going to the Trocadéro and simply "consuming" others, or that Ravel's *Daphnis et Chloe* (1909–12), the central work of Kramer's discussion, exemplifies Ravel's use of "the symphonic ideal as a means of both containing and consuming the exotic." Rather, I would say, the advent of a new mode of consumption helped to shape a complex new relationship to France's Others, a relationship objectifying these Others in new ways that nonetheless preserved the European sense of superiority, simultaneously facilitating a new closeness to Otherness that had not been possible before.[77]

A later song cycle by Ravel, *Chansons madécasses* (1925–26), based on poems first published in 1878 by Evariste-Désiré de Parny, surrenders the dreamlike exotic for more realistic, even empathetic, depictions of nonwestern others. The second song, "Aoua!," is no longer the dreamlike exotic, but a harshly realistic warning written from the standpoint of a native Madagascan against the perils of slavery (Madagascar was a French colony from 1885 until it gained independence in 1960).

Aoua! Aoua! Méfiez-vous des Blancs,
habitants du rivage.
Du temps de nos pères,
des Blancs descendirent dans cette île.
On leur dit: Voilà des terres,
que vos femmes les cultivent;
soyez justes, soyez bons,
et devenez nos frères.
Les Blancs promirent, et cependant
ils faisaient des retranchements.
Un fort menaçant s'éleva;
le tonnerre fut renfermé

dans des bouches d'airain;
leurs prêtres voulurent nous donner
un Dieu que nous ne connaissons pas,
ils parlèrent enfin
d'obéissance et d'esclavage.
Plutôt la mort.
Le carnage fut long et terrible;
mais malgré la foudre qu'ils vormissaient,
et qui écrasait des armées entières,
ils furent tous exterminés.
Aoua! Aoua! Méfiez-vous des Blancs!
Nous avons vu de nouveaux tyrans,
plus forts et plus nombreaux,
planter leur pavillon sur le rivage:
le ciel a combattu pour nous;
il a fiat tomber sur eux les pluies,
les tempêtes et les vents empoisonnes.
Ils ne sont plus, et nous vivons,
et nous vivons libres.
Aoua! Méfiez-vous des Blancs,
habitants du rivage.

Aoua! Aoua! Do not trust the white men,
dwellers of the shore!
In time of our fathers,
white men came to this island.
They said: "Here is some land,"
your women may cultivate it;
be just, be good,
and become our brothers."
The whites promised, and yet
they were making entrenchments.
They built a menacing fort;
and they held thunder captive
in mouths of bronze [cannons];
their priests tried to give us
a God we did not know,
and later they spoke

of obedience and slavery.
Better death.
The carnage was long and terrible;
but despite the thunderbolts that they vomited,
and which crushed whole armies,
they were all wiped out.
Aoua! Aoua! Do not trust the white men!
We saw new tyrants,
stronger and more numerous,
planting their flag on the shore;
heaven fought for us;
it dropped rain on them,
tempests and poisoned winds.
They are dead, and we live,
and we live free.
Aoua! Do not trust the white men,
dwellers of the shore.[78]

Ravel's music similarly gives evidence of a different mode of representation, perhaps even signifying a change in thinking on the question of Europe's relationship to its Others. Kaminsky says that "Aoua!" makes use of bitonality after the dramatic opening (example 13)—F-sharp against G—and concludes that F-sharp represents blacks and G major whites (since F-sharp major uses all the black keys on the piano). "Aoua!" never resolves in one key or the other, suggesting that "white and native peoples cannot live in harmony but coexist only in a dissonant state."[79]

I think a more nuanced interpretation is possible. If one looks at what the instruments are actually playing in this bitonal passage apart from the keys they employ, it is clear that Ravel is pointing out commonalities: the piano, in F-sharp major, is sounding passages of fourths and fifths—the same as the cello in G major. I think it is probably better to conclude that even in different keys, there is no difference between peoples.

How are we to account for Ravel's seeming transition from the dream-world, the chaotic exotic, to this much more sympathetic, even realistic treatment? I would be reluctant simply to attribute it to second thoughts on Ravel's part, which is an interpretation too narrowly focused on the composer. Rather, it is important to remember just how volatile public sentiment in France was about colonialism, and the reasons why politicians sup-

Ex. 13 Ravel, *Chansons madécasses*, "Aoua!," opening

ported or opposed it. The dreamworld exotic was a rage for a time, but there was also opposition to French imperialism in the same period, which continued after the First World War. Proponents of France's colonial expansions rehearsed various justifications, but after France's humiliation in the Franco-Prussian war (1870–71), nationalism was rallied to the cause of promoting French colonialism; French prestige abroad could restore the prestige of France in Europe and the world. "If a nation wishes to remain or become great, it must undertake colonization," said the general secretary of the Valenciennes Society (of geography) in 1881.[80]

Positions on imperialism were complex and usually nuanced, with simple pro and con positions only at the extremes. It was possible, for example, to support the colonialization of one country while opposing it in another.[81] Jules Ferry, one of the main French politicians arguing for French colonial expansion, mustered justifications based on economics and the civilizing mission of Europeans: "the superior races have rights over the inferior races," and the so-called superior races "have a duty to civilize the inferior races." The opposition responded with cries such as "You dare to say this in the country where the rights of man were proclaimed?"[82] Yet even those who disliked rhetoric such as Ferry's nonetheless supported colonialism for reasons of trade.

Thus I would caution against making an interpretation that simply attributes a change in sentiment to Ravel himself. Rather, I would argue that his two works register complex and conflicting attitudes in France toward various French imperialist projects.

A SIDE TRIP INTO THE RISE OF AESTHETICS

Although this chapter is not about the eighteenth century, it is important to discuss the rise of aesthetics, an ideological complex that proved unusually effective in dealing with nonwestern Others in the age of empire. Let me be clear: by "aesthetic" I am referring to the notion of "art for art's sake," and the view of artworks as autonomous entities that emerged in the mid-eighteenth century, not the more localized use of the term to describe a particular composer's or particular group's style.

Aesthetics of course remained an important ideology throughout the nineteenth century, but for most composers it essentially provided a license to explore the limits of their art, the limits of their musicalized self-representations — at least it did so in romanticism, which musicologists take most seriously of all nineteenth-century artistic movements, and whose composers and works rank in the upper echelons of the canon. But aesthetics in the late nineteenth century and the early twentieth took on a new, previously undeveloped valance as a rubric for treating musics and peoples from other cultures, and so must be explored here.

The short version of the story of music turned into an autonomous entity for its own sake begins with the rise of rationality as the fundamental ideology of Enlightenment thought, which made way for the increasing commodification of knowledge, as well as culture.[83] With the growing commodification of music and other works of art into the commercial marketplace around the mid- to late eighteenth century, musical works were further reified in the Marxist sense, regarded as autonomous objects in "high" (that is, philosophical) discourses on music and the arts.[84] Musical meaning shifted from a vague connection with the emotions and an expression of a patron's relationship with his or her composer-employee to the composer's own expression; new meanings for artworks were sought, eventually resulting in the discourse of aesthetics. (The first use of the word "aesthetic" was by Alexander Baumgarten in his eight-volume *Aesthetica* of 1750–58.) This discourse gained hegemony fairly quickly, even though composers and listeners continued to seek and find earlier meanings, particularly those associated with emotions.[85] Aesthetics, which became the way of receiving artworks, is grounded on the idea of *art pour l'art*, a doctrine that tacitly acknowledges the lack of everyday use of art. John Ruskin, in *Modern Painters*, offered an ironic critique of this aesthetic, which he believed could lead to indifference: "Does a man die at your feet, your business is not to help him, but to note the colour of his lips."[86]

As the patronage system was declining and instrumental music was increasingly heard in public forums, musicians and listeners despaired about what this music might mean. Aesthetics grew out of a problem of instrumental music in the eighteenth century; vocal music, since it had words, could justify itself with meaning and plot. But instrumental music was another matter entirely. Jean-Jacques Rousseau wrote in his famous *Dictionnaire de Musique* (1767) in his entry on "sonata" that "in order to know what all these jumbles of *sonatas* mean, one would have to be like a crude painter who must write above his figures; *this is a tree, this is a man, this is a horse*. I shall never forget the flash of wit of the famous Fontenelle, who, finding himself overburdened with these interminable Symphonies, cried out in a fit of impatience: *sonata, what do you want of me?*"[87] The rise of aesthetics was thus a crisis in use-value. What could such works be for if not to glorify the Lord or the lord?

Given this change in the economic status of the composer and the products of his labor that I am claiming is responsible for the rise of aesthetics, it is significant that one of the early formulators of the concept was Adam Smith, whose essay "Of the Nature of That Imitation Which Takes Place in What Are Called the Imitative Arts" considers at length music's meanings and relationships to the other arts. Smith strides confidently into the arena of music at first, when he writes of meanings of music with words. With instrumental music, however, like many writers on the subject of musical meaning in the absence of text or action, Smith is less sure of himself, and far from presenting a unified argument about musical signification, he instead refines his argument throughout the essay: at first, instrumental music imitates discourse and passions; then it excites the passions; then (drawing here on Rousseau) he says that music disposes the mind toward the passions; then, he says, it does nothing of the sort.[88] Eventually Smith refines his "exciting the emotion" model to a "disposing the mind" model: listening to music is like walking through a beautiful garden, which disposes the mind, if it is in its "natural state," to the objects it perceives. "That music seldom means to tell any particular story, or to imitate any particular event, or in general to suggest any particular object, distinct from that combination of sounds of which itself is composed. Its meaning, therefore, may be said to be complete in itself, and to require no interpreters to explain it. What is called the subject of such Music is merely, as has already been said, a certain leading combination of notes, to which it frequently returns, and to which all its digressions and variations bear a certain affinity."[89]

For Smith, painting expresses something in the mind because it excites a sympathetic reaction in the beholder. "The melody and harmony of instrumental Music, on the contrary, do not distinctly and clearly suggest any thing that is different from that melody and harmony. Whatever effect it produces is the immediate effect of that melody and harmony, and not of something else which is signified and suggested by them: they in fact signify and suggest nothing."[90] In other words, aesthetics values the work of art for its own sake, but this very emptiness makes possible the work's entry into the marketplace as a commodity. Who better to argue for the exchange value of musical works than the first great economic theorist of capitalism?

Generally, I am arguing that the rise of modern aesthetic represents the radical beginning of a shift from use-value to exchange-value, as composers were learning how to profit from their works thanks to their release from the patronage system by the end of the eighteenth century and new copyright laws that arose in the same period. Additionally, this occurred in a period when, as Colin Campbell has written, there was a consumer revolution in which a growing middle-income market was increasingly the target of the goods produced by the industrial revolution, most of which were not essential but rather nonessential, including leisure goods.[91]

Throughout the nineteenth century, aesthetics was used primarily to justify composers' extravagances, experimentations with form and style, or what have you. But by the late nineteenth century and the early twentieth, when there was another consumer revolution, the concept of aesthetics was used by composers to recalibrate their relationships to music, theirs and others'. If a composer's music is increasingly a commodity, increasingly valued for its exchange-value because of the ideology of the aesthetic, then composers' relationships to other musics changes as well. This shift in western patterns of consumption is a main focus of this chapter. One could also argue that even though aesthetics was invented in the late eighteenth century, the age of empire offered it an opportunity to triumph: aesthetics as a form of modern exchange-value no longer justified only the composer's self-importance but justified everything, from the appropriation of music of other cultures to the leap into atonality.

Indeed, aesthetics, a system whereby use-values are replaced by exchange-values, was never needed as much as at the turn of the century. It was a way to deal with the new peoples, new artworks, and new sounds coming into European metropoles. Aesthetics is a kind of commodification machine: it strips everything of history, culture, and the social to render it fit for commodification, or for appropriation. Aesthetics is a major chapter in the history of the commodification of music, the masking of human relations by the reification of music and fetishization of works, recordings, and musicians.

It is this nexus of aesthetics, modernism, imperialism, and consumption that I pursue next. It is missing from the writings on modernism and imperialism cited earlier, which tend to focus on formal issues in works while sidestepping the ideological shift that was occurring around the texts with which the works were concerned.

FROM FRANCE TO AMERICA

I have spent some time outlining the major cultural, social, and historical upheavals in the early part of the twentieth century, though my primary focus was on Europe. In America, however, where Charles Ives (1874–1954) and Henry Cowell (1897–1965) were working, the situation was somewhat different. While population growth and the rise of mass culture were paralleling developments in Europe (along with other factors that are less central to the discussion), there was less of a sense of anomie and anti-modernity, though there were critics such as the film director King Vidor. But many Americans, at least in metropolitan areas, felt themselves to be living in a kind of modern, technological, paradise by the 1920s, their lives transformed by the phonograph, radio, the airplane, the automobile, electricity, and other inventions.

Charles Ives

The clearest example of the crucial shifts in aesthetics and consumption is in the work of Charles Ives, who provides some continuity with Ravel. A discussion of Ives will also help demonstrate what a radical break was made later by the younger Henry Cowell.

Ives, in the process of attempting to make an art music that was recogniz-

Ex. 14 Ives, "Concord" Sonata, "Hawthorne"

Ex. 15 Martyn ("Jesus, Lover of My Soul")

ably American and not European, borrowed sounds from both the European art music tradition and from various American vernacular musics. Ives took music indiscriminately, as though there were no difference between popular culture and high culture. I want to examine a particular work with this in mind, Ives's famous Piano Sonata No. 2, "Concord, Mass., 1840–1860" of 1910–15. In 1911 Ives wrote that the first movement he completed was "Hawthorne," followed by "Emerson," "The Alcotts," and finally "Thoreau" in May 1915.[92] "Hawthorne" contains a collision of two musics, the main motive from Beethoven's fifth symphony and a section of a gospel hymn, setting up the central dialectic of the work (example 14). The hymn tune that Ives uses here is "Martyn" ("Jesus, Lover of My Soul"; example 15).[93] All the other movements of the sonata contain the Beethoven motive, a hymn fragment, or a combination of the two.

Perhaps the most poignant moment in the entire sonata is this opening of "The Alcotts" (example 16), where the Beethoven 4-note motive meets Missionary Chant ("Ye Christian Heralds"). Since this is the most noticeable combination of Beethoven and the hymn, and since this appears to be a moment toward which Ives has been building throughout the sonata, it is important to note it here:

There are many more such instances of this kind of quotation and ma-

Ex. 16 Ives, "Concord" Sonata, "The Alcotts," opening

nipulation in the sonata and other works by Ives, so much so that the leading Ives scholar, J. Peter Burkholder, entitled his magnum opus on the composer *All Made of Tunes*.[94] Ives systematically quoted and manipulated musics by others to fashion an American art music, and an American art music composerly self. These other musics were simply "material" to him, exchangeable, aestheticized bits, available to be appropriated from other works into his own. Many other composers of roughly the same generation did the same, Stravinsky most prominently in works such as *Le sacre du printemps*, which makes extensive use of Russian folksongs, and *Pulcinella* (1920), which quotes liberally from various eighteenth-century works.

To be sure, these and other composers employ materials foreign to their musics for dramatic and significatory purposes. I am not concerned with these, however. Rather, I am interested in how these composers came to conceptualize the use of other musics, and I have linked their usages to the new aesthetics that was found in a particular historical moment in European and American history.

Usually I refrain from invoking composers' biographies, for I think it is more important to focus on their place and time, as I have been arguing throughout this book. But I cannot resist relating that Ives was not a professional composer. He was a successful insurance man in New York City. If it took Adam Smith to give us aesthetics, perhaps it took an American businessman, whose day job was essentially all about the principle of exchangeability in capitalist culture, to show how aesthetics can work in the early twentieth century in one of the world's great metropoles.

Thus in the early twentieth century, when conceptions of selfhood are in trouble, aesthetics is mobilized to play a role different from that in its period of origin, or even in the nineteenth century. The new form of consumption of the late nineteenth century and early twentieth, coupled with the rise of imperialism, gave composers and other artists a way to deal with non-European Others: aesthetics permitted these artists to keep Others at arm's length, while at the same time giving them an ideology that facilitated appropriation of these Others' cultural forms.

In this way, composers labeled "experimental" (as Ives usually is) or "avant-garde" are not apart from popular culture, or commercial culture, but in fact are part and parcel of it. "The new art and the new commerce were, and are, the same," John Xiros Cooper writes.[95] Modernism is not opposed to commercial or popular culture, but is a culture of capitalism. The "difficulty" of Ives's and other modernists' music (which has been described as one of the prime qualities of modernist music)[96] is not a critique of the modern world as much as a symptom of it. Thus, despite Adorno's championing of Schoenberg, it is impossible to see this composer as anything other than a product of his time, a product of a metropolitan capitalist culture in an age of empire.

Henry Cowell

Some musicologists lump Henry Cowell into the same category as Ives, as a pioneer of American experimental music. This is, as usual, a judgment based on style, not what actually might be going on in the music resulting from the underlying culture, history, and social relations that make a particular composer's practices possible.

Many of the recent writings on Cowell seek either to defend him from charges that he appropriated musics from other cultures (a charge made by Nancy Rao in a thorough article) or to represent him as a precursor figure to composers and musicians who frequently mingle different musics in their works (the view taken in the many writings by David Nicholls, who hails him as a "postmodern prophet").[97] Both strategies seem to me to be more about our time than Cowell's; "We live in multicultural times," Nicholls writes at the beginning of one article.[98] This itself is debatable, but the real question is: what about Cowell's times? Adherents of what I call the "classical music ideology" would hold that composers make works and imprint their individualities on them as "style," but as I have been arguing, it is crucial to remember that composers, and style, are profoundly shaped not just by their positionalities but by their times, and their places.

Cowell was a Californian who was influenced by nonwestern musics from an early age, and who studied with the pioneering ethnomusicologist Charles Seeger; Anthony Seeger tells me that the elder Seeger introduced Cowell to current anthropological ideas about culture, clearly evident in his writings.[99] Cowell's early influences and career have been well documented. John Varian (1863–1931), an Irish-American poet and influential friend of Cowell, wrote in 1930, "There is a new race birthing here in the West. In the ages coming, it will be a large factor in a new civilization now starting round the Pacific— of a quite different nature from that of the Atlantic. Oriental races will be in it. . . . We are germic embryonic seed of future majesties of growth."[100] Cowell was also influenced by the composer and philosopher Dane Rudhyar (1895–1985), who wrote in 1922 of "the possibility of *another* Truth" based on "Oriental civilization, art, science."[101]

Cowell's own writings and works show such ideas. In 1933 Cowell published an article entitled "Towards Neo-Primitivism," in which he calls for a new movement to counter neoclassicism (a style associated with Stravinsky most prominently and characterized by the use of Baroque and classical works as inspiration for modernist ones).[102] The new kind of music that Cowell envisioned was "not an attempt to imitate primitive music, but rather to draw on those materials common to the music of all the peoples of the world, to build a new music particularly related to our own century."[103] Cowell writes that "the music of various tribes is as different as the music of the various cultivated nations" and proceeds to give a long list of different cultures and their musical traditions, at the end of which he writes that "this list could of course be extended indefinitely; it is given here to dispel the idea of uniformity" among so-called primitive musics.[104]

While living in New York City, Cowell began teaching a course at the New School for Social Research in the late 1920s with the title "Music of the World's Peoples," a course taken by both John Cage and Lou Harrison in the mid-1930s.[105] Nancy Rao writes of Cowell's participation in the New York Musicological Society, which cultivated an interest in exoticism. She provides a list of meetings and speakers of the Society from early 1930 to mid-1934, with roughly one-sixth of the topics on exotic subjects. Rao quotes from an unpublished manuscript from just after this period entitled "Nature of Melody," in which Cowell writes of the importance of recognizing the conventions in music. "Conventions differ in different musical systems," he writes, and it is clear from similar statements that he possessed a kind of culturally relative notion of music.[106]

In a short essay from 1935 entitled "The Scientific Approach to Non-European Music," Cowell clearly shows his Seegerian background, arguing that nonwestern musics emanate from aesthetic perspectives so obviously different to the western ear that it is unacceptable to judge them as unmusical. He continues to say that an understanding of musics of other cultures "can be reached only upon the basis of a more extensive and profound knowledge firstly, of the technical processes and critical standards involved, and secondly, of the role of music in the social system from which it has sprung."[107] Cowell is mainly concerned with the first of the two approaches, yet the article makes clear his sympathies with the second. Indeed, after addressing itself to more technical concerns, the article concludes by reiterating the importance of studying musics as cultural forms, not simply forms (and includes a footnote to a publication by Charles Seeger). Cowell writes that musics should be studied not only from the standpoint of science "but from the point of view of the peoples themselves. An attempt should be made to discover which element of music most emphasized by the particular tribe in question, and what the native conventions are with regard to it."[108] It is important, he concludes, to work toward a study of music "that will give us not only a correct understanding of the musics of other peoples, but also a proper perspective in which to understand our own music, and its role in relation to the other musics of the world."[109]

In an article written late in life entitled "The Composer's World," Cowell speaks of being a young composer in the early part of the twentieth century and feeling dissatisfied with the harmonies available to him from the European tradition. "So I turned to explore rhythm and melody in actual musical traditions, and was surprised to discover that these aspects of music were not given the same orderly historical study in the West that polyphony and harmony were. Eventually I learned that to train myself in handling rhythmic and melodic possibilities systematically, I must go to Oriental teachers, and this I did."[110]

The question of course is: Where did such impulses come from? I have already mentioned Cowell's study with Charles Seeger, and it is now time to pick up that thread and discuss the kinds of ideas Cowell was drawing on that connect to my other themes.

Culture

Most significant among these was the culture concept usually attributed to the German-born anthropologist Franz Boas (1858–1942), who was important in overturning the old model of evolutionism discussed at the beginning of this chapter. Boas's critique of evolutionism, developed over many years of work, ultimately showed that "various elements of human culture did not march together in any sort of lock step or regular sequence. Once the 'one grand scheme' of evolutionism was rejected, the multiplicity of *cultures* which took the place of the cultural *stages* of savagery, barbarism, and civilization were no more easily brought within one standard of evaluation than they were within one system of explanation."[111] George Stocking points out that Boas's thinking on the culture concept can be seen as emerging from earlier ideas present in Boas's work, and that Boas's students were more responsible for fleshing out and disseminating the concept.[112]

Boas's writings contained the seeds of what his students would later cultivate. *The Mind of Primitive Man* (1911), for example, concludes: "I hope the discussions contained in these pages have shown that the data of anthropology teach us a greater tolerance of forms of civilization different from our own, and that we should learn to look upon foreign races with greater sympathy, and with the conviction, that, as all races have contributed in the past to cultural progress in one way or another, so they will be capable of advancing the interests of mankind, if we are only willing to give them a fair opportunity."[113] And, in a chapter entitled "Modern Life and Primitive Culture" in *Anthropology and Modern Life* (1928), Boas writes: "The social ideals of the Central African Negroes, of the Australians, Eskimo, and Chinese are so different from our own that the valuations given by them to human behavior are not comparable. What is considered good by one is considered bad by another."[114]

Stocking contends that Boas did not simply invent a new definition of culture, but made possible an intellectual space from which the concept could emerge. More than this, however; the last quotation from Boas was from a book written for the general public that is still in print. And of course, the concept found its way to Henry Cowell.

Thus Cowell did not simply have the experiences he had, but he learned to conceptualize them in a certain way, through the lens of a Boasian notion of culture and cultural relativism, and he attempted to relativize musics in his writings and compositions, many of which are musical workings-out of the culture concept that he first learned from Charles Seeger.

The *United Quartet* (1936)

A work considered by both David Nicholls and Nancy Rao is a string quartet from 1936 entitled the *United Quartet*. Rao writes that this work was composed shortly before Cowell began writing his treatise on melody, and therefore grew out of his intense interest in nonwestern methods of pitch organization. In language that is equally redolent of Boasian anthropology and Depression-era American populism, Cowell wrote that "the Quartet should not only be easy to understand, without following any known pathway, but it should be understood equally well by Americans, Europeans, Orientals, or higher primitives; or by anybody from a coal miner to a bank president. The main purpose of it, of course, is not in its technique, but in the message, which, of course, is not suitable for expression in words. It may be said that it concerns human and social relationships. The technique is for the purpose of conveying the message to the widely differentiated groups who need to be united in these relationships."[115]

He also wrote that

> the *United Quartet* is an attempt toward a more universal musical style. Although it is unique in form, style and content, it is easy to understand because of its use of fundamental elements as a basis, because of repetitions which enable the auditor to become accustomed to these elements, because the clarity and simplicity of its form, and because of the unity of form, rhythm and melody.
>
> There are in it elements suggested from many places and periods. For example, the classical feeling is represented not by the employment of a familiar classic form, but by building up a new form, carefully planned. . . . Primitive music is represented, not by imitating it, nor by taking a specific melody or rhythm from some tribe, but by using a three-tone scale, and exhausting all the different ways the three tones can appear, which is a procedure of some primitive music. . . . The Oriental is represented by modes which are constructed as Oriental modes are constructed, without being actual modes used in particular cultures. . . . The modern is represented by the use of unresolved discords, by free intervals in two-part counterpoint, and by the fact that the whole result is something new,—and all that is new is modern![116]

If we are to think beyond style and instead wonder where style comes from, where such utterances come from, it is important to take the *United Quartet* apart a bit, to see how Cowell puts the above ideas into practice. Nicholls offers an extensive analysis of the work, following on Cowell's discussion of it, to argue that the quartet is an example of "transethnicism" in music.

Cowell employs different pitch organization techniques, as he wrote in the above excerpts. Nicholls confirms this in his analysis, writing that the "Oriental" modes are akin to some ragas with similar scales, such as the scale C, D, E, F, G, A, B-flat, used in the fourth movement. Another scale used is C, D-flat, E-flat, F, G, A-flat, B-flat, C, which Nicholls claims is from the North Indian family of ragas called *Bhairavi*.[117]

Nicholls says that the fourth movement consists of three layers, each related to musics from other cultures. There is a melody, a countermelody plus a drone, and percussive accompaniment. The pitches used are derived from two-, three-, four-, five-, and six-note scales.[118]

What becomes clear from this work, and these useful analyses of it, is that far from simply viewing musics from other traditions aesthetically, as commodified bits, Cowell instead sought to imbue his music with ideas and techniques from other cultures in far deeper, more structural ways than Ives, or indeed anyone else of this period. One can raise the question of appropriation as some have done, but I think this is a less interesting subject of inquiry than attempting to understand what people are doing and why, given their social, cultural, and historical circumstances. Regardless of what one thinks of the results, Cowell, armed with Boasian notions of culture and cultural relativism, as well as Seegerian ideas of music, mounted a spirited critique in sounds and words of the marriage of aesthetics, modernism, and imperialism of his era.

Clearly, Ives and Cowell are worlds apart, although they usually rub elbows in standard histories of music. Ives did not see the need for, or lacked, a critique of the new consumer culture and the use of aesthetics that it facilitated. Cowell, on the other hand, enunciated a critique in work after work, writing after writing. Cowell's position was inclusive, anthropological, pluralist. Aesthetics cares little for any of this. It is alas no surprise that this latter attitude became dominant in the rest of the century, linked as it is to consumption and imperialism that continue in new guises.

PART II GLOBALIZATION

GLOBALIZATION AS A CULTURAL SYSTEM

G lobalization is the term most commonly used to refer to the recent regime under which nonwestern peoples are dominated and represented by the West. Most significantly for my purposes, globalization differs from earlier regimes in that in the so-called developed countries, the nation-state exerts less influence on the day-to-day lives of its citizens than multinational corporations do, as a spate of recent writings have suggested.[1] States still matter, for they continue to have the power to set the rules by which global commerce works. These rules, however, are increasingly written in favor of corporations, not citizens. Let me be clear: the question is not whether the nation-state no longer matters (as many argued in the early writings on globalization and postmodernism in the 1990s), but to what extent it has diminished power, diminished influence.

My emphasis is thus shifting from colonialism and imperialism, systems of domination grounded in the transition from late feudalism to capitalism and the practices of nascent and mature nation-states, and toward globalization, a cultural system in which the machinations of major companies can have tremendous impacts on peoples' lives, greater, in some respects, than that of states. The ideologies of colonialism and imperialism are still with us, but as systems of domination, these are largely though not wholly defunct. Now the state frequently follows the desires of corporations when it comes to dominating and oppressing, to enriching the wealthy at the expense of the poor (I write this on the day the U.S. Census Bureau released figures showing that the percentage of Americans living in poverty has risen for the fourth straight year).[2]

What this means is that western conceptions of otherness, no less significant than in the past, are less important in catalyzing conceptions of selfhood, and that consumption has become even more important in self-definition. In the last few decades, in an era that has witnessed the increased commodification and consumption of otherness, selfhood has come to be fashioned as much by the construction of identity through practices of consumption. Commodification has come to depend increasingly on the fabrication and valorization of sign-values—their value in a symbolic system of consumerism—which are largely made by media processes such as advertising and marketing.[3] In the realm of music, the role that the music industry can play in positioning musicians and musics is also extremely influential.

The following chapters, which are about the present and the recent past, pay more attention than the previous chapters to corporate structures (instead of court and state structures) and to sources that help us to understand musics and practices as deeply embedded in culture: music industry publications, web sites, internet newsgroups, the popular press.

GLOBALIZATION

Let me introduce and problematize the concept of globalization before proceeding further. Most people probably require no reminder of the success of the concept, for few terms have been employed as frequently in and out of academia as "globalization," so much so that in the view of Malcolm Waters "globalization may be *the* concept of the 1990s."[4] And in fact of the early twenty-first century as well.

Yet in some sense, globalization is not new. There has scarcely been a time when peoples and cultures didn't mix, didn't come up against each other.[5] Our much-vaunted "globalization" is just a recent, electronic, digitized incarnation of a process that has been around as long as there have been peoples and cultures. Most commentators have failed to think historically and wonder what might be unique to our globalization vis-à-vis earlier ones, allowing them to offer analyses of the present instead of triumphalist (or despairing) coverage of globalization in the present.

In *Global Pop* I wrote extensively about globalization as it was understood in the 1990s, when the term "flow" was frequently used to describe the movement of peoples, cultural forms, and more. Without recapitulating this discussion in full, I will give a short introduction to globalization, contrasting it with earlier regimes of economic exploitation.

The writings on globalization that have appeared since *Global Pop* pursue many of the ideas treated in that book: globalization, along with new technologies, has made the world smaller, producing what one recent publication calls the intensification of global interconnectedness (notwithstanding that some peoples lack access to the technologies of communication and transportation that make this interconnectedness possible).[6] Many authors emphasize deterritorialization, a time-space compression that has been widely discussed since the late 1980s.

It seems to me now that positions on globalization have hardened. While arguments concerning cultural imperialism, for example, have largely been dismissed by scholars for being too monolithic and rigid, there are many people around the world who complain that their cultures are being diluted by the importation of western, especially American, cultural forms.[7] But just as many scholars claim the opposite—that the forces of globalization are creating more diversity of cultural forms and practices, not less.

What is usually needed in such arguments is more ethnographic data to explain what happens in specific places and historical moments. Gathering more information with respect to globalization demonstrates both sides are right, sometimes, but that their views of globalization are incomplete and even misleading if no attention is paid to other practices such as consumption and the fashioning of identity. Jonathan Friedman, for example, writes interestingly of how people from different cultures have established relationships to the West and its modernities: "Congolese consume modernity to strengthen themselves. The Ainu [of Japan] produce traditional goods in order to create themselves. The former appropriate otherness while the latter produce selfhood for others. Hawaiians produce selfhood for themselves."[8] In other words, it is important to ask, what are people doing where, and why? Grand theorizing of globalization is possible, but not without attention to what people are actually doing.

CONSUMPTION

And what are they doing? Among other things: consuming. Taking the United States as an example, it is clear that consumption has been central to American life since at least the end of the nineteenth century, undergoing escalating regime shifts in the 1920s and 1950s but taking on a new importance, and a new urgency, in the 1980s, so much so that some argue for a rupture with the past modes of consumption.[9] Recent scholars have termed this more recent shift the "new consumerism" or "consumer culture reborn" or "postmodern markets" or "hyperconsumption" or "mallcondo" culture.[10] Whatever one calls it, a change in American consumption patterns has clearly occurred in the last couple of decades. As put succinctly by Sharon Zukin, "these days, workers are important because they consume, not because they produce anything the culture values."[11]

This cultural and ideological shift toward heightened consumption is marked generally by a much greater degree of acquisitiveness than in the past. For example, the average American today consumes twice as many goods and services as in 1950, and the average new home of today is twice as large as the average house constructed after the Second World War, partly to hold all of its owner's possessions.[12]

Americans are not just acquiring more, but are doing it in different places and in different ways than in the past. Gary Cross writes of the rise in the last couple of decades of warehouse superstores, and the conflation of shopping and entertainment into what he calls "shoppertainment." The Mall of America in Minnesota, for example, with 2.5 million square feet of retail space and over 520 shops, has become a tourist site, even a vacation site.[13] Additionally, the number of theme restaurants rose in this period, establishments that the industry categorizes as "eatertainment."[14] One such restaurant, Planet Hollywood, sells overpriced hamburgers and claims that 40 percent of its income is derived not from food but from T-shirts and other souvenir items.[15]

Two aspects of this new consumption are worth highlighting, though extensive treatment of them will be deferred until later. First, tourism in the United States rose in the period 1985–95, and some visited sites were dedicated to promoting consumption.[16] Several authors have written of the importance of television, Disneyland, and the rise of festival malls across the United States, malls that are symptoms of the new importance of consumption in American life in the 1980s and after. These festival malls usurp public space and are directed at tourists, turning, as George Lipsitz writes, "urban sites into urban sights."[17] The role of tourism is central to provoking interest in new sounds and other peoples' music, as will be discussed later.

Second, collecting has become more widespread and important with the advent of a new kind of superconsumer, a kind of a collector in the older sense, but not necessarily the type of collector who must have everything. As Russell W. Belk has noted, today's collectors are no longer members of élites who collect antiques or other valuables, but more frequently ordinary people who collect humble consumer goods.[18] Will Straw has written thoughtfully of male record collectors, and I have written elsewhere of the rise of collectors of "lounge" and "exotica" music.[19]

The causes of this new form of consumption have been theorized in different ways. The sociologist Juliet Schor has influentially written of an "aspirational gap," a term that describes the motivation for people to purchase the same expensive goods that celebrities own, even though these goods are usually not affordable to most purchasers. Schor locates this shift in the decline of neighborhoods, the resulting decline in the notion of "keeping up with the Joneses" (rather than with celebrities), and the growing income gap between rich and poor that began in the 1970s.[20]

One of the critics of Schor's argument makes a persuasive case for an alternative view of the new form of consumption, which he refers to as the "postmodern market." Douglas Holt notes the increasing marketization of areas of social life that were previously outside the market, such as health care and education. Holt also points to the ways that consumer identities have fragmented, proliferated, been recombined, and turned into commodities themselves.[21] Holt believes that Americans are overspending not because they are trying to keep up with celebrities, but because consumption has become what he calls an "open-ended project of self-creation." Today's consumers participate in a complex circulation of new experiences, commodities, and meanings, playing with different identities through their consumption habits and experiences.[22]

In one of the most thoroughgoing treatments of the new form of consumption, Martyn J. Lee chronicles the modes of consumption throughout the twentieth century. Contrasting contemporary consumption to earlier forms, Lee attributes the increased role of consumption in the contemporary West to a complex set of interrelated factors, including more sophisticated means of ascertaining demographic information, resulting in an increase of niche markets;[23] the spatial and temporal expansion of consumption, due in part to new technologies that make certain commodities more portable (such as personal stereos) and technologies that make consumption easier and more convenient than before, such as the internet (though this is not an example used by Lee); a transition from material to experiential forms of commodities such as tourism; deregulation;[24] a new form of advertising that eschews the traditional emphasis on utility and function and concentrates instead on style. The result, put simply, has been a transformation of both the modes of consumption and the role that consumption plays in peoples' lives. Consumption is now more flexible and fluid than ever before, and it occupies a more central role than ever before.[25]

Lee also discusses the rise of conservative movements in both the United Kingdom (Margaret Thatcher) and the United States (Ronald Reagan) that viewed consumption as a public good.[26] Several writers have commented on this overtly political and ideological shift; George Lipsitz, for example, says that Reagan skillfully sacralized consumption.[27] Don Slater writes that consumption in the Reagan and Thatcher years was projected as an "ideological miracle," and both political figures, he says, combined consumption with "the most profound, deep structural values and promises of modernity: personal freedom, economic progress, civic dynamism and political democracy."[28] American slogans from the 1980s, some of which were emblazoned on automobile bumper stickers, serve as powerful reminders of the growing importance of consumption: "Shop till you drop"; "A woman's place is in the mall"; "When the going gets tough, the tough go shopping."[29]

What has happened since the 1980s is a shift in American consumption toward an ever-increasing commodification and marketization of virtually everything, accompanied by ideologies that construct everything as either a commodity or commodifiable. Everything is for sale, everything is appropriable in the name of making one's identity—or music, as we shall see.[30]

FASHIONING SELVES, MAKING IDENTITIES

It is increasingly through practices of consumerism, many theorists of globalization have argued, that people in the so-called developed countries have come to make identities. This is quite a different project from self-fashioning, discussed earlier. Identity is a fairly recent concept that needs to be historicized. To do this I will pick up from chapter 3 and discuss further the culture concept and its success in American culture after its introduction to a broad public in the 1930s.

Outside the discipline of anthropology, it was intellectuals such as Henry Cowell who were at the vanguard of adopting and promoting the culture concept. The concept gained some foothold beginning in the 1930s. No longer was the term "culture" the province of anthropologists and intellectuals, or used to refer solely to high culture; the idea of culture as encompassing peoples' practices and symbols became widespread, in no small part because of what Warren Susman calls the "remarkable popularity" of the book *Patterns of Culture* (1934) by Ruth Benedict, one of Franz Boas's students.[31] It was in the 1930s, Susman suggests, that "the idea of culture was domesticated."[32]

Boas and Benedict rejected the earlier notion of racial and cultural difference as being evolutionary and instead argued for cultural relativism: cultures were merely different from one another, neither superior nor inferior, existing in a pluralist world. This concept took decades to catch on, not really becoming mainstream until the rise of multiculturalism.[33]

Simultaneously with the rise of a new postwar American culture, earlier conceptions of difference, and sameness, took new forms. The notion of "identity," influentially discussed by the psychologist Erik H. Erikson in *Childhood and Society* (1950), entered mainstream American discourse, where it remains to this day, though in different forms.[34] The identity concept later found a ready home in various social movements of the 1960s, as marginalized groups sought both to combat assimilationist ideologies and at the same time attempt to forge a common culture, a common identity (even though people in the same ethnic or racial group could be quite dissimilar in terms of social class, gender, age, sexual orientation, and other variables).[35]

Yet the rise of conceptions of identity based on race and ethnicity wasn't only the product of social movements but also a part of the crisis of the subject, first felt in the early decades of the twentieth century, and only intensifying after the Second World War. Immanuel Wallerstein writes that the end of the notion that the omnipotent individual is the subject of history has meant that people have begun to seek the protection of groups, largely organized around ethnic identities. The theme of identity, he writes, is "encrusted in a very elusive concept called 'culture,' or to be more exact in 'cultures.' But this new theme simply creates a new dilemma of the geocultural agenda. On the one hand, the call for multiple identities is a call for the equality of all 'cultures.' On the other hand, it is a call for the particularity, and therefore the tacit hierarchy, of all 'cultures.' As people move between the two contradictory thrusts, there will be the constant redefinition of the boundaries of the groups that have these 'cultures.' But the very concept of 'culture' is based on the assumed stability of these boundaries."[36]

Wallerstein goes on to examine different options that the concept provides to particular subjects who have been excluded from privilege, including what he calls "radical alterity."[37] Wallerstein's example is of Islamic fundamentalism, but taken more broadly (and moderately), it could just as well refer to the many forms of ethnic and racial difference or "differencing" that have taken hold in the United States in the last few decades.

It would be wrong to suggest, however, that earlier concerns for subjectivity, selfhood, or self-fashioning have merely been reorganized under the rubric of "identity," of membership in a (sub)culture. Identity making is an entirely different project, yet one that sometimes coexists with the older one of self-fashioning. So at this point, a definition of terms is necessary, and then a meditation on identity making as a project. I use "project" in the Sartrean sense: "The most rudimentary behavior must be determined both in relation to the real and present factors which condition it and in relation to a certain object, still to come, which it is trying to bring into being. This is what we call *the project*."[38] This is a simple, even obvious, formulation, yet it is quite useful in that it allows one to view something like self-fashioning not as some "natural" or "universal" characteristic of western modernity but an endeavor located in place, time, and social group. Self-fashioning can thus be seen as a modern project in which selves are made out of one's relationship to one's Others, from one's identification with one's profession, from one's relationship to production.

Identity making is quite a different project, one that gained momentum after the Second World War through changing consumption practices and the forging of new alliances based on ethnicity as a result of the diminishing ability of the nation-state to construct its subjects as citizens. And it is also a project associated with specific social groups.

Now, I realize that some of this may sound suspiciously like the claims about the death of the subject that have issued from many quarters, usually lumped under the umbrella of "postmodern" thought.[39] Such claims are almost never historical, or ethnographic, and are almost always painted in such broad strokes as to be useless, at least from the perspective of those who value attention to history, culture, and the multiplicity and uniqueness of social groups living in real places in the real world. But I am not asking whether the death of the subject has occurred—it is alive and well, at least in some social groups. Rather, I am asking which social groups have abandoned this project, and what they are doing instead. Additionally, I am not arguing that projects concerning identity have superseded selfhood projects; the two can coexist. It is not a question of periodizing, or of saying that one project existed in one historical moment and no longer exists in a later one.

Perhaps the most illuminating way to make this argument about these different projects would be by comparison, juxtaposing different generations, at least within the middle classes. To do this, I will draw on a fascinating study that Elizabeth Keenan has written concerning the conflicts that arose at a women's music festival over whether to permit transgendered people, both male-to-female and female-to-male, to participate.[40] One festival, long established, wanted to exclude transgendered people for not being born women; another, much more recent, accepted them. The first of these festivals espoused an older mode of feminism, an outgrowth of the women's and civil rights movements of the 1960s and 1970s, that understood womanhood as something given by nature; the other festival espoused a later version of feminism that respected transgendered peoples' choice of gender.

Choice appears to have been the key concept, indicating a shift in attitudes toward consumption. Earlier, "second wave" feminism shared many ideological characteristics with other countercultural thought at the time of its inception, in particular a deep distrust of postwar consumer culture. This consumer culture took women out of the workplace, where many had been during the war, placed them in the home, and attempted to placate them with shiny kitchens and a plethora of modern appliances. Later generations, though, as well as those positions loosely organized under the term "third wave" feminism, are much less opposed to consumption. As I have been arguing, it is a culture of consumption that helps, not hinders, the construction of identity, for example through what one purchases and how one dresses. These newer projects, among some younger generations, are concerned with the fashioning of identities more than selves. It's not that people think subjectivity, subjecthood, or selfhood has been achieved; rather, this modern project has been overshadowed, and in some social groups supplanted, by identity fashionings, largely through consumption practices and "style" in the Hebdigian sense.

The following chapters explore the workings of these concepts—globalization, consumption, identity—through examinations of the "culture industry" and its workers. First, I consider the rise of discourses of multiculturalism, how these discourses foster the concept of collaboration in popular music, and how they shape a particularly influential node in the music industry, that of the producer. Then I examine the music and advertising industries and their ideologies as they apply to world music, which they treat as a separate "style" or "genre" from others, policing its boundaries in an attempt to contain and congeal what is inside them.

CHAPTER 4

CONSUMPTION, GLOBALIZATION,
AND MUSIC IN THE 1980S AND AFTER

The culture concept was a powerful tool in understanding Others afar, and it became increasingly used in grappling with Others at home. The civil rights movements of the 1960s and 1970s lent a new urgency to the concept of culture and the rhetoric of cultural relativism established earlier in the twentieth century. What emerged were new discourses employing what were by then the familiar logics of cultural relativism, new discourses called multiculturalism to refer to Others at home, and globalization to refer to Others abroad or emigrating from their homes. Nonwestern cultures were celebrated as never before under the banners of globalization and multiculturalism, but Others were, at the same time, still kept at arm's length, and still used for profit and for individual artistic advancement by western musical stars. Aesthetics, revitalized at the beginning of the twentieth century as I have argued, are still at work.

My argument is that "globalization" and then multiculturalism, its domestic face in the (post)industrialized countries, are new incarnations of an older set of conceptions of difference, but that they entail a greater degree of the commodification of difference, as well as its consumption. This can be seen particularly in a recently influential position within the music industry, that of the producer.

GLOBALIZATION, MULTICULTURALISM, CONSUMPTION

Let me thus begin with a brief history of multiculturalism, with the proviso that it is important to view it not as a self-contained discourse but as one connected to larger ideas about selfhood, identity, and group belonging;

Arjun Appadurai prefers the single term "culturalism" to refer to a "movement of identities consciously in the making," itself part of larger global and historical processes, with multiculturalism thus one such manifestation.[1]

The multiculturalism concept first gained currency in Canada in the late 1960s and early 1970s, as Canadians wrestled with the question of Québec and the French language. Multiculturalism provided a way of moving beyond the old model of the melting pot and adopting a new image of the mosaic to describe not only Anglo- and Francophone Canadians but all the ethnic groups within the country.[2] The term quickly caught on outside Canada and inevitably took on a number of meanings, shadings, and usages, none of which, as Michel Wieviorka has pointed out, differ substantially from older conceptions of cultural pluralism.[3] Nonetheless, multiculturalism was the dominant discourse of ethnic and racial otherness of the last couple of decades, and it remains the human face of globalization in North America and beyond.[4]

The reinvigorated conception of culture discussed earlier, according to which "culture" has become attached to racial and ethnic otherness, has its downside, however, as many have observed. Étienne Balibar notes that racism today is based on culture, not biology, but that "culture" fills the slot once occupied by biology.[5] It is still used in essentialist ways, but in contrast to earlier conceptions of race, it is pluralist in that all cultures are assumed to be equal, at least in principle. This is also, some commentators say, a theory of segregation, not a theory of hierarchy. In this way nineteenth-century notions of different races and cultures have been left behind, though this may be only temporary.

The multivalent discourses of globalization and multiculturalism both contain notions of respect for other cultures and cultural forms. "Multiculturalism" should therefore not be seen as a newer, kinder, gentler set of conceptions of difference, but as a new term for old concepts that underwent a revival because of the civil rights and social movements of the 1960s and after in the United States and the cultural pluralism of Canada, and then took on a new importance with the rise of the discourses of globalization in the 1980s and 1990s.

Multiculturalism as a concept can mask some practices that would seem to contradict some of its tenets. David Rieff offered an early and trenchant critique, arguing that multiculturalism went hand in hand with global capitalism, perhaps its most salient ideological offshoot.[6] I would not take issue with this aspect of Rieff's argument; corporations have clearly perceived that they need to be more sensitive to different cultures at home and aboard, and have developed an approach called "multinational multiculturalism," which I will discuss in chapter 7.[7] Michael Lind makes much the same critique as Rieff, employing the term "divide-and-rule multiculturalism" to write of how multiculturalism serves the interests of what he calls the white overclass, resulting in a situation in which "the white elite is separated from the masses in taste and value, and the masses are divided among themselves along racial lines."[8]

Rieff's argument becomes more problematic, however, when he turns his analysis toward cultural production, saying that the multiculturalism conception of art as hierarchical, necessitating a change in the canon, plays into contemporary capitalistic ideas: "the multiculturalist mode is what any smart businessman would prefer. For if all art is deemed as good as all other art, and, for that matter, if the point of art is not greatness but the production of works of art that reflect the culture and aspirations of various ethnic, sexual, or racial subgroups within a society, then one is in a position to increase supply almost at will in order to meet increases in demand."[9] It has been my experience that the privileged position enjoyed by art is still intact, at least in the vast majority of university music departments, conservatories, and schools of music; other humanities departments have undergone more substantial, canon-displacing changes, it is true. Yet Rieff is correct, I think, in that almost all but the most extravagantly privileged forms of cultural production are more commodified, more conceptualized as "products" than ever.

And this leads to Rieff's next point, one that I would endorse, which is that multiculturalism "helps to legitimize whole new areas of consumerism."[10] Culture (he means high culture) was always a problem for the capitalist marketplace, because the world of high culture values artifacts and uniqueness, not reproducibility. But multiculturalism is helping to change all this, since it is incredulous toward the idea of the masterpiece; multiculturalism can democratize art, but this has the effect of turning art into a product, a commodity, even more than it had been in the past.[11] Not only that, but the tools for making cultural forms are increasingly commodified.

Most of the literature on consumption with respect to globalization is concerned with how American patterns of consumption are being exported in our so-called global era. What has been less studied is how ideologies of globalization and multiculturalism are helping to shape new patterns of consumption in European and American metropoles. I discussed this in *Global Pop* in a way, less framed by theories of consumption than by ideas of marketing: world music in the 1980s and 1990s was marketed as something fresh, new, exciting, and timeless, which helped anchor what was a fairly new "genre" in a rapidly changing landscape of music consumption.[12]

While "globalization" is a term used to cover all too many contemporary trends, it is important to note the ways that it is fostering a new way of taming difference in order to commodify it, thereby making an increasing number of goods and cultural forms available for consumption. And globalization, along with technological advances, is making these goods and cultural forms easier to consume than ever, by on-line purchasing, downloading, and file sharing.

The performance artist Guillermo Gómez-Peña argues that Americans now currently inhabit a world in which racism, sexism, civil rights, and other important issues no longer matter, an ideology complemented by a form of corporate multiculturalism. Our globalized world softens the edges of difference, making Others and their cultural forms desirable in new ways.[13] And this "transculture" is marked above all, Gómez-Peña says, by a "rabid consumerism," with everything available on-line and hundreds of channels on cable television. Later he writes that "the new global impresarios needn't be concerned with ethical boundaries. Ethics, ideology, border issues, and post-colonial dilemmas — they all belong to the immediate past, a past too painful to recall in any serious manner. The new praxis is to engage in a stylistically 'radical' but thoroughly apolitical type of transnational/multiculturalism that indulges a-critically in mild difference. The new praxis is to witness, document, 'sample,' and consume all thorny edges, 'alternative' expressions, antisocial behavior, and revolutionary kitsch."[14] Gómez-Peña calls the tendency for cultural producers to seek out the new and unusual — what he terms "lite difference" — the "Buena Vista Social Club syndrome."[15]

COLLABORATION

It is telling, and useful for my purposes, that Gómez-Peña names this condition by alluding to a hugely successful album of 1997 (in which the American guitarist Ry Cooder teamed with elderly and neglected Cuban musicians), and it provides an opportunity to discuss what I think has emerged as an important trope used to discuss musical production between westerners and their Others: collaboration. If in the last couple of decades the dominant discourses dealing with difference have been globalization and multiculturalism, collaboration has become the dominant trope in examining the interactions of western stars with nonwestern musicians. Some of the musicians of the 1980s and 1990s who gained fame (and sometimes notoriety) for their work with musicians from other cultures frequently employ the tropes of collaboration and respect.

In the early days of the "world music" boom of the late 1980s and early 1990s, the best way for nonwestern musicians to achieve an audience was to team up with a western star; this is still by and large true. This sort of collaboration helped the nonwestern musicians to gain international recognition, and western stars were frequently praised by fans and critics alike for their connoisseurship and knowledge of nonwestern musics. Many well-known musicians prolonged or resuscitated their careers by recording and sometimes performing with nonwestern musicians: most famously, Peter Gabriel, David Byrne, Paul Simon, and Cooder. "Collaboration" was the preferred trope to describe most of these interactions, for it smoothed over the often exploitative ways in which nonwestern musicians were used.

The first thoroughgoing scholarly treatment of this sort of collaboration with respect to world music, and western-nonwestern musical interactions, was an incisive article by Louise Meintjes in 1990 about Paul Simon's album *Graceland* (1986). In the article Meintjes convincingly argues that the album represented itself as a musical sign of collaboration, and was thus represented by critics. She examines Simon's and others' rhetoric about the album, the composition and production of the music itself, and the musicians' tours to show how the trope of "collaboration" was signified and promulgated.[16]

As Meintjes shows, Simon's discourse is replete with language of collaboration. For example, Simon said this in an interview in 1986:

> On a certain level this [*Graceland*] is really the evolution of an idea that began with "El Condor Pasa" [on *Bridge over Troubled Water*, 1970]. It was then that I thought there was no reason why music from another culture couldn't be popular music. "Condor" was Peruvian—I don't think there were any Peruvian hits before that—but I liked it.
>
> With "Mother and Child Reunion" [on *Paul Simon*, 1972], I went to Jamaica to record; I realized that if I want to write in that genre, for it to really work I had to go to the place and work with the musicians. That's what happened with the South African music.[17]

In a different interview, after the release of his *Rhythm of the Saints* (1990), Simon said that "the same thing happened with the music from South Africa. I heard that music and I liked it. The sound of Ladysmith Black Mambazo is the sound of a doo wop vocal group—except they take it to the pinnacle. Township jive? I didn't know what it was called and that it came from South Africa. It sounded to me like pop music from the '50s that I liked: three chords, simple, happy. So I asked 'Who is that band? I'd love to record with them.'"[18] Elsewhere in the same interview, Simon says that

> the idea that interacting with musicians from another culture could be viewed as cultural imperialism never occurred to me. I was reacting musically. I liked certain kind of music, I wanted to play with those musicians, I wanted to interact with those musicians and I treated them with my utmost musical respect. At the very minimum I was paying people very, very well.
>
> When it became an issue, I said, "Wait a minute, this has been going on forever. Musicians have always played with other musicians."[19]

Simon concludes:

> The big issue approaching another culture is respect. That's the key. If you come in with respect, as someone who doesn't know and doesn't pretend to know everything, I found that, overwhelmingly, people are friendly and open. But you must understand that you're a guest and you are privileged to be there.
>
> I am a white, Anglo, Jewish male, but I'm also more than that. We can transcend our little ghettos. People can communicate. It's hard, it takes work, it takes time, but it happens. And when you break through and make contact, the experience is exhilarating.[20]

These two interview excerpts encapsulate all of Simon's—and most others'—positions that are subsumed under a discourse of collaboration: they like music by a particular ethnicized, racialized Other and want to participate in making it. If someone is a major western star in a privileged position in the music industry, the likelihood that he will be able to act on the desire to make music with others is great (these collaborations are an overwhelmingly male phenomenon, for reasons that I will not investigate here). For these musicians, what is felt to be an authentic aesthetic connection is used to legitimate all kinds of collaborations across all kinds of borders—

geographic, ethnic, racial. And finally, the question of respect is explicitly raised.

Largely because of the success of *Graceland* in riding the wave of globalization triumphalism (it won a Grammy award for Record of the Year in 1987), I think it is now possible to argue that "collaboration" is not only significant in the production and reception of *Graceland* itself. The success and influence of the album have meant that the trope of collaboration has become a central aspect of how world music is heard and discussed, as most recently demonstrated by the success of *Buena Vista Social Club*. The term frequently appears in discourses about music as a sanitizing sign when western musicians work with nonwestern ones, making their music safe for mass consumption.

CONSUMPTION, PRODUCTION, AND CONTEMPORARY POPULAR MUSIC

"Collaboration" has become a trope used to describe a mode of production of music when musicians from other cultures appear together on the same stage or in the same recording, when a western star likes somebody else's music. But what about listeners' likes, their relationships to music, their consumption of music? Or the even more complicated situation that arises when a listener is in a position to make her own music? "Production" and "consumption" have become increasingly difficult to disentangle, but I will do so for analytical purposes, and will note that the main musical subject of this chapter, Bill Laswell (1950–), is a good example of how the boundaries between production and consumption are blurred for people who occupy a particular habitus, and a particular function in what Pierre Bourdieu has called the new bourgeoisie and the new petite bourgeoisie, groups that include many culture workers.[21]

At this point I want to pick up the thread concerning consumption in the current moment of globalization, with particular attention to how musicians situate themselves in this new era of consumption. That is, how have larger patterns of consumption in American culture changed how people produce music? Has the globalization of music, registered both in the rise of "world music" and in the increased use in music of samples (that is, exact digital copies of other musicians' recorded music), altered the consumption of music and its discursive constructions?

New consumption practices have played out in many ways with respect to music. I am especially interested in a relatively recent mode of record production that foregrounds the acquisition and deployment of samples and other sounds outside the sound world of the musicians being recorded—in effect a kind of collaboration without some of the musicians' being present.[22] This kind of record production has its roots in George Martin's work with the Beatles in the 1960s; Martin's immense influence on other producers has meant that his willingness to bring in stylistically different musics and sounds—including world music—has become an accepted mode of production. Two particularly well-known examples of this kind of producer are Brian Eno and the musical subject of this chapter, Bill Laswell.

However murky the term may be, "globalization" has made musics from many places much more easily available than ever, though not only as commercial recordings. Musical samples are increasingly available to musicians for use in making their own music. Even though sampling is thought of as a technological development made possible by the rise of machines made specifically for this purpose in the 1980s, the practice has been shaped by the changes in consumption outlined above. The sampler, as I have written elsewhere, was not a device to sample prerecorded music but a shortcut around the difficult problem of synthesizing the sound of an acoustic instrument, since it proved easier to just sample the actual sound.[23] The rise of the sampling of music has in a sense put all recorded sounds at the disposal of anyone, with musicians able to manipulate relatively inexpensive digital technologies for their own uses—music is now "consumable" in new ways. Additionally, however, the new digital technologies of the last couple of decades have made high-quality home recording possible, so that more and more musicians are producing their own music, as well as consuming others', providing a good example of how the boundaries between production and consumption have become increasingly porous.

Producers and Producing

The term "producer" describes the person who coordinates musicians and engineers, in some cases defining the overall sound of the album under construction. With the glut of musics currently available as recordings and samples, the role of the music producer has begun to shift in interesting ways. The music producer is undergoing the same sort of deification, or auteurization, that the film director experienced in the 1950s. Since George Martin worked with the Beatles, the producer has increasingly come to be a similar figure, at least among connoisseurs, achieving auteur status in the eyes—and ears—of some fans.

What is interesting is that producers, or at least some producers, are increasingly called upon for their knowledge of other musics—sometimes Other musics—and their collections of samples of these musics. As non-western musics enter North America with greater frequency and are heard in more and more places, it has become increasingly necessary for a mediator, a tour guide. Whereas a collaborator works with real musicians, onstage or in the studio, the producer is a mediator between sounds, some live and others not.

The discussions by Bill Laswell, the influential bassist and producer, of his role as a producer emphasize the collaborative discourses: "You get obsessed with the idea of being a catalyst, a person who can put things together. When a collaboration works between two people, that creates a kind of third power, a force or energy that becomes bigger than the two. That happens quite a bit in improvisation, where music can actually happen. It's not preconceived. It's not prerecorded. It's not predicted. It's not controlled. And it sometimes can produce a magical effect which is incredibly orchestrated and perhaps even handed down from somewhere else. But it can only happen if that door is open and you don't trap it with all the things we use to trap music—like chords and rhythms which come from a classical sense."[24] In a different interview, Laswell again stresses the collaborative mode of working: "On *Nagual Site* [1998], I had a lot of support track-by-track from different people. It's very much a collaboration and a collective effort. It included different people like Bill Buchen, who's a percussionist, and Gulam Mohamed Khan, who is a harmonium player. They constituted a great deal of the emotion and feeling of the music, and they contributed pieces too."[25]

In a recent interview while visiting his hometown of Albion, Michigan, Laswell compared his world music collaborations with other, more popular ones. Summarized by the interviewer:

> Laswell said his label promotes music from around the world, but is not the "world music" carefully selected for popular consumption, such as that of Peter Garbriel [*sic*].
>
> Laswell said his involvement with sounds from other nations is a collaboration, something that piqued his interest long before he left Michigan. His purpose, if it can be called that, is to interact with other musicians to create one sound, he said.[26]

The kind of role for the producer enunciated by Laswell has been called the "art mode" of production by Edward R. Kealy, who delineates three historical modes of music production. This is the most recent of his modes, which emerged around the same time as a new division between the functions of the producer and the engineer in the mid-1960s. In the old days, the producer's main job was to arrange music—that is, to manipulate the sound before it was recorded—and the engineer was responsible for sound recording.[27] Today the function of the producer is quite flexible. Some producers are more musicians than engineers, some are more engineers than musicians, others want to shape the sound of the band and play a creative role, while still others want to capture something unique that the band is doing.[28] The "art mode" embraces those producers such as George Martin who seek to play a creative role close to that of the musicians themselves.

Beginning in the 1980s with the introduction of digital technology such as the sampler and later MIDI (Musical Instrument Digital Interface, a standardized interface between computers and digital musical instruments), as well as the introduction of the compact disc format, the role of the record producer took on yet other dimensions. For some producers and musicians, the new digital technologies became, in the words of one historian of record production, "at least as important as the song."[29] These new technologies also blurred the line between musician and engineer, a line that in the past the producer was expected to mediate. But many musicians now know how to use these newer technologies themselves; they are probably already using computers and MIDI to make their music.[30] At the same time, however, there is also more complex and more expensive equipment than ever before.

I think that the shift in American consumption patterns discussed above has partly shaped this change in the "art" mode of record production. According to Brian Eno, perhaps the best-known of this new kind of record producer, the producer is no longer a mediator between the artistic and technical realms "but an interface between different areas of the existing culture."[31] This kind of producer, in addition to playing the roles typically assigned to him (and it is almost always a man), shapes already recorded sounds; yesterday's shaped the sounds before they were recorded. In a real sense, such a producer is in charge of the consumption project in recording: he acquires and brings in other and "Other" sounds to the recording studio. Because he is more of an "artist" or auteur, his job is not so much to be a collaborator but to realize his personal vision.

This version of the "art" mode of producing is concerned with bringing new sounds, new musics and new instruments into the studio, and has now become an accepted idiom of the art mode of production. Practitioners of this new kind of producing are more concerned with different kinds of musical styles and more likely to bring them into whatever project they are working on. Many of today's producers speak of the necessity of knowing other musical styles and sounds. George Martin says that "a good producer has got to really have an understanding of music, and a catholic love for it. Unless you're very specialized, I think that you have to have a very universal approach to music, to have the temperament to like a lot of music. Which, fortunately or unfortunately, I do! If you're very narrow in your outlook, you're not going to make a good record producer, because you have to be pretty tolerant, too."[32]

Because some producers are hired by bands to bring a certain sound to the studio, one should inquire about what sounds those might be. For Bill Laswell, those sounds often have nonwestern sources. Laswell participated in what is perhaps the seminal album that made use of sampled sounds, before digital sampling existed and engineers had to cut and splice tape, Brian Eno's and David Byrne's *My Life in the Bush of Ghosts* (1981), the album that more than any other demonstrated the usefulness of not just other sounds, but Others' sounds—sounds by peoples from nonwestern places.[33] All the sampled world music is from various Arab countries, Algeria, Lebanon, and Egypt.[34]

Joe Potoker, one of the engineers, provides a glimpse of the recording process of this album: "I remember a track . . . where we lifted a vocal track off another record. The interesting thing was that before [digital] sampling and all this controversy about lifting things from records, we were doing that [with tape]—I guess it was '79 or '80. We were lifting things off cassettes, off the radio, wherever we could get them. We would put them on ¼-inch tape and then fly them into different sections of the multitrack and actually make a tune out of them."[35] *My Life in the Bush of Ghosts*, perhaps more than any other album, marked the maturation of Martin's brand of producing and its acceptance in the United States and Europe. Now "collaboration," with the aid of technologies, could become simply "lifting," despite the best intentions of producer and musicians.

Since this album, the price of high-quality digital equipment has gone down, and sampling has become pervasive in popular music, including musics made at home. The ability of musicians at home to sample has enabled some professionals to turn themselves into connoisseurs of sampling other musics, to position themselves above the home studio owner. Thus Laswell doesn't sample in the strictest sense of the term—he doesn't employ previously recorded sounds—but travels all over the world to find new sounds, something he is able to do because of his success as a musician. One critic has observed that travel is central to Laswell's work, noting that he had visited Mongolia, China, and Japan, and that while "while some people go sightseeing, Laswell goes 'soundseeing.' "[36] Laswell himself says, "I've tried to branch out internationally, not just move out of the Village. I want to go everywhere and experience as much as possible, not as a tourist but as someone who's making real contact with people who are doing things musically. I want to document that music and present it more professionally and efficiently than it would be in a field recording."[37]

Laswell's travels, and his work with musicians in his studio in Brooklyn, allow him to make an argument about the importance of collaboration, a term that crops up in many of his interviews since the success of that discourse in *Graceland*. "Collaboration—that's the key," he says in one interview.[38] In another: "You have to look directly into the idea of collaboration with people. . . . It's not just a question of taking an instrument from a place, or a sound, or even a rhythm. It's not attaching or decorating something; it's really about interfacing with them and contributing back to them; not just taking from them."[39]

This sampling and collecting of "world music" is caught up in the complexly intertwined phenomena of travel, tourism, globalization, and new consumption patterns, covered and justified with the veneer of discourses of collaboration. Since Laswell has the means to travel and record in the field, he is able to amplify the collaboration trope in his discourse on his music. Laswell says: "a lot of the music I've released, which might be called ethnic, has been recorded in villages or in the music's place of origin. So, if I could call what we've been doing an achievement, it's because our field work involves capturing music for what it is and where it is, at the time it's happening."[40]

Collecting live samples also raises the question of whether the collector has greater discernment than those musicians who merely collect samples from previously recorded materials, the normal practice of musicians in home studios as well as many professionals. Inexpensive digital equipment has meant that more and more musicians can make their own music at home, can be producers in the broader sense, and one result of this ability has been to raise the stakes for professional musicians, who must position themselves above home musicians. Musicians such as Laswell who collect their own samples position themselves not just as collectors but as connoisseurs, superconsumers: they knew the music they sample before anybody else, they took the pains and trouble to find it, and they took the trouble to repackage it for listeners in what they claim is a serious and respectful way. Laswell's positioning of himself as a superconsumer is a familiar strategy in this era of hyperconsumption. Peter K. Lunt and Sonia M. Livingstone argue that because of the importance of consumption among all social groups, higher groups that wish to distinguish themselves must therefore seek out more exclusive goods and practices that mark them as different. "Intellectuals," they write, "oppose the spread of cultural capital by staying one step ahead of the supermarket shopper in their discovery of exotic products and practices."[41]

Laswell's travels and collecting facilitate his discourse of collaboration and allow him to place himself in a category above most musicians. He exploits this position, minimizing his role as a consumer by transforming it into that of a producer (in the nonmusical sense): Laswell has recently introduced some prerecorded loops of sampled music for users of the software application Acid Pro, which allows users to compose dance music on their computers.[42] Sony Pictures Digital, which recently purchased the company that manufactured Acid Pro, sells a four-volume set of royalty-free samples on CD-ROM for $199.95 (the original musicians are not paid anything other than a one-time fee, if that), attempting to capitalize on Laswell's reputation as an independent, noncommercial musician. The blurbs for the discs are so pregnant with material for analysis that it is difficult not to offer extensive quotations. The text for the set reads: "It's only natural that Laswell supply fuel for the enormous surge of ACID users who are redefining music just as Laswell himself does continuously—with total disregard for genre boundary restrictions and obsolete conventions in making, listening to, even conceptualizing, modern music and sound."[43] The texts for the individual discs, entitled "False Encryptions," "Undocument," "Letter of Law," and "Covert Diaspora," simultaneously hype the collection and exalt Laswell. "Bill Laswell reveals secret codes from the underground," reads the copy for the first volume. "The language of Bill Laswell is a musical Esperanto, an amalgam of cultures, subcultures, street cultures."[44]

What strikes me about these writings is how anticommercial they are: they reflect an underground or independent ("indie") attitude toward music. Sony knows who its target market is—young people, mostly men, making their own deliberately noncommercial dance music. But of course, instead of exhorting Acid Pro users to find their own prerecorded samples, Sony is trying to sell them these predigested ones, from which they can make their own sounds, find their own meanings, and even redefine music, at least for themselves. Buy these CD-ROMS and be anything you want, do anything you want, on the shoulders of Bill Laswell—traveler, sonic collector, musician, producer, visionary. Since his music is "fluid and derivative," according to Acid Pro's web site, since he pays no attention to boundaries or rules or conventions, using his loops means that your music will inevitably be equally rule-breaking and genre-defying.[45] In Acid's web pages hawking these loops, it's not just sound that is being turned into a consumable good but the concept of creativity itself.

In selling creativity, Acid Pro acknowledges the importance of the imagination in what Arjun Appadurai has called the "postelectronic" world (I would say the digital or digitized world).[46] The role that imagination plays in this increasingly globalized late capitalist world is central to Appadurai's project. For him, part of the new fuel of the imagination is the consumption of mass media, which can have the effect of engendering a sense of agency—viewers, listeners, are empowered by the mass media.[47] The descriptions provided by Acid Pro are clearly tapping into this: empower your musical imagination by purchasing our loops. I think that Appadurai could be right about the newly empowered imagination, but at the same time one has to note that the imagination and creativity are being commodified with sales talk such as this. Buy these (commodified) loops and combat the music industry . . . which sells commodified music.

Even while Acid Pro attempts to sell creativity and the power of the imagination, there is still the problem of the commodification of Laswell's creativity in all of this. Acid Pro's loops help transform Laswell into a brand, not just an individual. This process of branding is one of the ways that Laswell is transformed, and can transform himself, into a producer of samples, not just a collector of them; a maker of music, not just a consumer of sounds gathered around the world. Scott Lash and John Urry, in their indispensable *Economies of Signs and Space*, write of branding as one of the trends of production in the late capitalist economy, in which key players in the culture industry (major record labels, big publishers, major film studios) can consolidate their authority and maximize their profits by turning their most successful products into brands, beyond their origins as single individuals (one of their examples is Michael Jackson, whose brand life has probably expired).[48]

Acid Pro's web pages offer some examples of music made with their loops and shed light on their branding of Laswell. Acid Pro does not include any of Laswell's own music on the web site, but it includes some examples written by others that do sound much like Laswell's (except, of course, that Laswell's music has the bona fide Laswell brand name attached to it). The others are cheap imitations by contrast, but you can make music like this at home if you purchase the Laswell brand loops. Collaboration may be the key, as Laswell says, but the marketers for Laswell and other musicians seem more interested in selling individual "genius" and individual vision than collaborations which by definition are more modest enterprises. And it is easier to sell a recognizable brand name.

BILL LASWELL AS PRODUCER, SAMPLER, COLLABORATOR

This variation of Kealy's "art" mode of producing is predicated, as I have been arguing, on new relationships to music engendered by shifts in American consumption patterns and new digital technologies, presaged by George Martin's highly influential model of music production in the UK. But I have been talking about producers, not consumers. I would now like to flesh out the mediating role that a musician such as Laswell plays in this latest incarnation of the American consumer economy.

Laswell is one of these new producers who fulfill the traditional role(s) of the producer and augment it as a collector of samples while maintaining a discourse of collaboration all the while. It is perhaps no accident that Laswell was involved with *My Life in the Bush of Ghosts* (he is credited on the album as a bassist, but it is difficult to hear what his role was beyond that).[49] Whatever his function, he was clearly influenced by the result, given the trajectory of his subsequent work.

Yet it is generally not true collaborations, with musicians as equal partners, which make money. Discourses of collaboration are at odds with western — and especially American — ideologies of individualism, individual creation, and genius. It is easier to sell a recording with a branded star's name on the cover than an album that might more truthfully represent its contents. Laswell is not immune from market pressures, though they are incompatible with his stated desires for more truly collaborative modes of working with other musicians, western and nonwestern.

For example, Laswell has critiqued what he views as the underlying ideology of many "world music" recordings: "The one-big-happy-family-of-man thing has massive conceptual problems. It's fine that people around the world play drums or accordions, and we have that in common, but you put so much of that together, one little bit from here, another from there, it doesn't mean anything anymore. The other day I saw this world sampler CD *Planet Soup*. There's a lot of great music there, but the cover has these instruments floating into a soup pot, like the more the merrier. Geez. To me, the world's just a little more complicated than that."[50] In the same interview, invoking the collaboration discourse, Laswell said: "I'm not an ethnographer; I don't want to take this music, put a frame around it, and stick it in a museum. . . . I'm not saying indigenous music isn't important and, where it still exists, that it shouldn't be preserved as much as possible. It's just that I think of myself as a participant. To me, what people call world music right now, for better or worse, is a kind of global street sound. An ongoing thing. You can't stop that any place and make sense of it, because it doesn't stop."[51]

In statements such as these and in the marketing copy for the the Acid Pro loops, Laswell's rhetoric attempts to place him above the realm of the mere consumer and into the more prestigious category of producer (in the non-musical sense) or, as he says, "participant": he makes music in collaboration with others, but he doesn't buy it. And his collaborations are more equitable than those of some other musicians (he singles out Peter Gabriel and Paul Simon in his interviews as examples of more exploitative musicians). The discourses employed by Laswell make it appear that the level of distinction he possesses entitles him to be more than a consumer.

It is interesting to note that one of Laswell's most recent producing projects is a recording by the Beninoise musician Angélique Kidjo, which bears the credit "Reproduction and Mix Translation: Bill Laswell." I don't know what this means exactly—perhaps only Laswell himself does—but what comes through is his desire to label himself as something more than a producer. Perhaps the producer has become too authority-laden, too far from the more collaborative kind of work to which Laswell aspires.[52] When asked by an interviewer about how he manages to be so prolific (Laswell has been involved with hundreds of recordings), he replied, "It's responsibility really. A lot of it has to do with commitment. A lot of it has to do with the responsibility of helping people resolve or realize something. There's a part of it that's me just trying to get it done because I have that commitment."[53] Then he went on:

And certain times there's money involved. I have an overhead, so I have to create projects. The only way I make money is by making records. I'm not from a family of money. No-one's given me anything. I have to pay people, so I have to produce. I have to make records. That's combined with helping people who realize they're in trouble — you know, somebody from somewhere needs a record deal so they can have a family, so they can have a life. That's all part of it. So, we just keep pounding away to get everybody in place, including myself. It's not that I'm obsessed with an overabundance of activity. It's all just responsibility and commitment to staying alive — to keeping everything in place, not just for myself, but for a great deal of people. So, when people review things, they may not be talking about an artist who sat down and figured out something and said "This is my goal. This is what I want to do and I'm trying to impress somebody." It might be reviewing somebody who's trying to save somebody's life. So, good or bad, it means absolutely nothing compared to life. You're just trying to help.[54]

I have attempted to pull together different discourses usually seen as unrelated — multiculturalism, globalization, and collaboration, as well as music production and consumption — to show how they are complicatedly intertwined with each other, with new consumption patterns, and with new modes of making and consuming music. Michel de Certeau writes that "to a rationalized, expansionist and at the same time centralized, clamorous, and spectacular production corresponds *another* production, called 'consumption.' The latter is devious, it is dispersed, but it insinuates itself everywhere, silently and almost invisibly, because it does not manifest itself through its own products, but rather through its *ways of using* the products imposed by a dominant economic order."[55]

This statement effectively diagnoses the complex production-consumption dynamic as has been examined here with respect to music. What is less apparent, and what I have been attempting to draw out, is this: how "consumption," which in its current form has roots in the social, cultural, and historical shifts that are generally described by the terms "globalization" and "multiculturalism," can nonetheless leave room for collaboration, whereas "production" has increasingly become a vehicle for stardom, for creating an individual sound apart from that of anyone else.

CHAPTER 5

SOME VERSIONS OF DIFFERENCE:
DISCOURSES OF HYBRIDITY
IN TRANSNATIONAL MUSICS

I know from painful experience that when you upset
white people's categories, you'd better watch out.
—Mandawuy Yunupingu, bandleader, Yothu Yindi

Whereas interpersonal interactions in "world music" tend to be viewed as "collaborations," the resulting sound is often described as a "hybrid," when musics from different "cultures" mix. Few terms are bandied about more in discussions of contemporary musics than this one, a label believed to capture the mixtures of musics prevalent in this era of globalization and transnationalism. But the term "hybrid" has so many uses in and out of music that it has come to represent a variety of musics and other cultural forms, discourses, political strategies, and identity conceptions. These usages are frequently intertwined in complex ways that can complicate investigation into a particular facet of the term, and the musics and peoples that it is supposed to characterize.

In this chapter I continue my emphasis on the music industry and its practices, in particular its employment of a discourse to market musicians from other places. The popularity of the metaphor of hybridity has meant that older discourses of authenticity are no longer the only ways that the music industry labels musics from other places, and that western listeners apprehend musics from other places. Listeners to world music are now less likely to criticize music that doesn't seem authentic, and more likely to welcome it as a hybrid.[1] Hybridity at the same time, however, is also increasingly becoming construed as another kind of authenticity, demonstrating the constantly shifting nature of regimes of authenticity around world music.

My purpose is to confront the hybridity concept in discourses in and around what has come to be called world music. The hybridity concept exists in a number of discourses in academia, in the music industry, and among journalists, fans, and musicians, and these discourses of hybridity have become powerful means of shaping the perceptions and experiences of world music. While it is not my goal to explore hybridity as a "real," on-the-ground mode of cultural production, I am nonetheless interested in how the conceptions of hybridity, the discourses of hybridity, affect understandings of musicians and musics, and how identifiable musical hybrids are treated discursively.

HYBRIDITY DISCOURSES IN THE MUSIC INDUSTRY

Hybridity has become an important lens through which cross-cultural encounters are understood, sometimes displacing lenses of authenticity. But the widespread usage of the term as a descriptor has also meant that it is sometimes used as a prescriptor. Like the term "postmodern," the hybridity concept influences both the hearing and the production of popular musics.[2] There are now musicians who deliberately make hybrid musics and who use the term in describing their music. An early example is Michael Brook's album *Hybrid* from 1985; this album, realized with Brian Eno and Daniel Lanois, employed instruments and samples (that is, exact digital copies of previously recorded sounds) of musics from around the world.[3] Another example is offered by the band High Bird, led by one of my former students, who told me that the name was a deliberate play on the term "hybrid." The rap-rock fusion band Linkin Park released an album entitled *Hybrid Theory* in 2000. And there are many other examples.

Because of the increasing salience of the hybridity concept, it is now possible to argue that there has been a partial displacement of discourses: hybridity is now joining authenticity as a marketing handle for musics by Others, and as a criterion that shapes the ways musics by Others are heard by critics, fans, and listeners.[4] This means that listeners are now more likely to have multiple referents for their sense of the authentic when hearing world music.

As an example of the music industry's deliberate positioning of a particu-

lar music as hybrid, consider *Welenga*, a 1997 collaborative album between
the Cameroonian Wes Madiko (who goes by his first name only) and Michel
Sanchez, one of the two musicians behind the highly successful "band" Deep
Forest.[5] This album is accompanied by some of the most extravagant prose
to be found in the usually overheated rhetoric of the music industry marketing apparatus: "Having written his first traditional album (which only
appeared in the USA), Wes was wary of facile and over-artificial associations,
a form of white-gloved slavery that is at the heart of too many fashionable
cross-cultural projects. He was, however, reassured by the sincere passion
of Michel Sanchez, who for three years gave Wes his time and his know-
how. The combination of the two spirits, the irrational Wes and the virtuoso
Michel, was a fusion of fire and water, the meeting of a wild but fertile root
and the gifted loving caretaker of a musical garden where Wes could flourish."[6] A quite remarkable combination of the pseudo–politically correct with
the colonialist tropes of the African Other as "irrational," "wild," and un-
cultivated. These kinds of packagings simply reproduce old negative stereotypes dressed up in new language. Ashwani Sharma has commented on this
strategy, arguing that "the powerful redefinition of ethnicity evoked through
the concept of hybridity enters the dynamic of popular cultural politics to
be incorporated, reterritorialized and reworked by hegemonic structures to
produce new marginalized and essentialized identities."[7]

But it is not just identities that are marginalized and essentialized—the
same thing has happened to the world music category as a whole. While
major generic or stylistic categories such as "rock" can support a number of
independent record labels, the number of world music labels is decreasing,
and the remaining labels are increasingly hegemonic. One of this industry's
achievements with respect to world music has been to reduce this vast array
of musics to a recognizable "style" with only a few audible features that can
be easily managed (vocals in an unusual language, acoustic drums, and perhaps a wooden flute). This sort of reductionism makes it far easier for huge
companies to manage a potentially unruly category such as world music for
the purposes of sales calculation, marketing, and retailing.[8] Even so, an entire album of these sounds would still be too foreign for most of today's listeners, and thus the industry seems to prefer packaging them with a mediator
or broker such as Sanchez, who can introduce familiar western sounds and
techniques and add his star power to raise sales. This form of curatorship—
in which a known western musician (usually male) adds his name and sounds

to a nonwestern musician's work—has become an increasingly visible mode of world music marketing. Thus hybridity has become a marketing term, a way of identifying, commodifying, and selling what on the surface is a new form of difference, but one that reproduces old prejudices and hegemonies.[9]

World music journalists are no less enthusiastic than the music industry about hybridity in sound. In their coverage of the Beninoise musician Angé-lique Kidjo's album *Oremi* (1998), reviewers attempted to sound accepting of her not strictly authentic style, but used only updated terms from an older discourse that naturalized peoples from other, "Third World," cultures.[10] A reviewer in the *Boston Globe*, whose article is entitled "Listening to History," wrote that the album "balances the electronic and organic" with "electronic" presumably meaning "western" and "organic" presumably meaning "African."[11] Another reviewer wrote that "though Kidjo employs many elements familiar to techno fans, she makes that genre sound utterly sterile next to her funky, thoroughly organic hybrid."[12] The language of these reviewers is striking given that Kidjo's record company purposely marketed her not as a world but as an R&B musician, a strategy unusual enough to have achieved coverage on a front-page story in *Billboard*, the music industry's main trade magazine.[13] But she is still seen—heard—as an African musician, who by the western music industry's definition makes world music and only world music.

Hybridity in usages like this one, it seems, is simply a code for older forms of difference; nonwestern musicians who make world musics are still consigned to the Other, "savage slot."[14] Nonwestern musicians are still naturalized, still seen as nonmodern. Hybridity in this usage is not just a sign of Kidjo's and Wes's otherness but also a sign of their *authenticity* to western listeners as late-twentieth-century and early-twenty-first-century Africans. This is a far cry from the critical reception of just a few years ago, when Kidjo and some other Afropop musicians were excoriated by western world music journalists for sounding *too* western, or for selling out to commercial western pop styles, or for working with western producers.[15] For example, one critic wrote of Kidjo's album *Ayé* (1994) that it is "straight funk-rock, slickly packaged by a pop producer and, whichever way you look at it—not necessarily with any purist inflection—the songs on it are less engaging."[16] It was clearly the encroachment of western styles and production values that lessened the album for this writer.

Because of the shift of conceptions of authenticity-as-pure to authenticity-as-hybridity, the music industry's world music category appears to be bifurcated: it now includes "authentic" recordings (i.e., field recordings) of music, which don't sell well except to purists, aficionados, and musicians looking for music to sample in their own works; and music labeled as hybrid, such as that of Kidjo and Wes, even though their music is as slick and polished as any western pop music currently available. But because of its use of sounds that to the western music industry signify "world music," music that is in between these two poles gets little attention: too difficult to classify, it is altered so that it can be effectively marketed, or excluded from the category altogether.

The Australian aboriginal band Coloured Stone, for example, had trouble finding a white audience because of its members' "musical Aboriginality," according to Marcus Breen. They play musics associated with whites—rock and country rock—but their style frequently breaks accepted white expectations of square phrasing and constant rhythms, even when they perform cover versions of popular standards. White audiences tend to hear these alterations as mistakes.[17] Similarly, Jocelyne Guilbault writes of how zouk musicians in the West Indies have had to conform to an "international sound," which for them means adapting their music to European scales and tunings.[18] Conversely, however, it is possible for musicians to conceal sounds of their musical traditions that are nonetheless audible to members of their own community. Jill Stubington and Peter Dunbar-Hall, for example, write that in the music of Yothu Yindi, another Australian band composed of both white and aboriginal members, there is more going on than meets the average non-aboriginal pop or rock listener's ear.[19] But Yothu Yindi sounds enough like what the music industry desires in a "hybrid" that this band could succeed in terms that Coloured Stone could not.

Generally speaking, world music artists currently face growing expectations by western listeners that Others should produce hybrid musics.[20] It seems that a subaltern musician can only succeed in the world music market if her sound takes on a touch—but not too much—of the West; after all, the world music albums that sell the most are almost never recordings of traditional musics but rather of hybrids, whether Salif Keita's Afropop, Cesaria Evora's Portuguese *fado*-like *morna* from Cape Verde, or R. Carlos Nakai's Native American flute recordings. It appears, in other words, that world musicians may not be expected to be authentic anymore in the sense of being untouched by the sounds of the West; now it is their very hybridity that allows them to be constructed as authentic.

HYBRIDITY ON THE GROUND AND IN ACADEMIA

Yet musics do mix, as they have always done—hybridity isn't merely an industry or journalistic discourse, though it has become a powerful set of discourses around world music. Since I am interested in how the discourses of hybridity affect understandings of musics and musicians, it is necessary to examine academic conceptions of hybridity, as well as hybridity as an identifiable phenomenon on the ground. I am not claiming that academic considerations of hybridity are more accurate than nonacademic ones, but they do tend to be somewhat less influenced by the marketing hype surrounding hybridity, and thus academic usages of the hybridity concept exist somewhat apart from usages in industry and by critics.

One of the leading theorists of hybridity is the literary critic Homi K. Bhabha. Perhaps the most influential aspect of Bhabha's notion of hybridity is what he calls the "third space." He writes: "hybridity to me is the 'third space' that enables other positions to emerge. This third space displaces the histories that constitute it, and sets up new structures of authority, new political initiatives, which are inadequately understood through received wisdom. The process of cultural hybridity gives rise to something different, something new and unrecognisable, a new area of meaning and representation."[21]

But because of the prevalence of the marketing and journalistic hybridity discourses and the chauvinistic practices of the music industry, a hybrid cultural form of this third space frequently finds itself in an all-too-familiar opposition as the subordinate part of a dominant-subordinate binary, which is precisely what has happened to Angélique Kidjo and her music, despite her well-publicized efforts to achieve more mainstream success out of the narrow and marginal world music category. The "hybrid" can be recoded as "authentic," finding itself back in the "savage slot."

It has not been a major part of Bhabha's work to examine how the oppositional and destabilizing effects of hybridization might actually play out, for he has spent most of his attention on the activities of the oppressed, not the workings of the oppressors. By focusing on the counter-hegemonic practices of disempowered groups, Bhabha fails to consider that colonializing or other dominant powers might interpret the hybrid forms produced by subalterns as simply inaccurate, or mimetic, inferior versions of what the dominant culture has thrust upon them, or as new kinds of "authentic" cultural production.[22] Interpretations aren't made solely by those in power, of course, but hegemons have ways of ensuring that their interpretations prevail, at least in those institutions that they control, such as the major record labels, radio markets, and large retailers (and to some extent, the less responsible music journalists). The marketing of hybridity frequently triumphs over the third space.

Michael Hardt and Antonio Negri make a similar critique of Bhabha's work, noting his tendency to assume an older model of sovereignty that they believe no longer exists: states are less dependent on retaining power through hierarchies and binary oppositions than they once were.[23] And yet discourses that valorize hierarchies and binary oppositions remain, and peoples' practices are in part shaped by these discourses—the "real" and the discursive aren't easily disentangled. The world may "really" have changed, as Hardt and Negri argue, and it may have moved away from Bhabha's and others' interpretations of it, but older discourses of binary oppositions and hierarchies continue to operate.

DIASPORIC SOUTH ASIAN BHANGRA REMIX MUSIC

A case study will illustrate the complicated ways in which conceptions of hybridity are mixed up in what musicians, fans, record labels, critics, and scholars say and do in the name of "hybridity." The popular music made by diasporic South Asians known as bhangra remix music that relies on both traditional sounds and contemporary electronic dance sounds and techniques is far removed from the "world music" system constructed by the major labels: it is not a particularly popular music among world music aficionados, and there is usually little represented in the major retailers (although it received major coverage in both editions of *World Music: The Rough Guide*).[24] Yet the discourses of hybridity play an important role in this music, in part because of the hegemony of the major labels and retailers, and in part because musicians who create bhangra remix music and the listeners who listen to it use the term "hybridity" to describe both the music and their conceptions of their identity as diasporic South Asians.[25] And some of the South Asians who use the term have clearly learned it from academic treatments such as Bhabha's.

I should say at the outset that there was a time when bhangra and "Hindi remix"—music that sampled sounds primarily from Indian film music— were somewhat separate genres, but sampling has become so predominant that remix musicians sample bhangra sounds as well, clouding the difference between bhangra and remix music. So the music will be referred to here as "bhangra remix" unless it is necessary to make the distinction for historical reasons.[26]

When bhangra or bhangra remix music is discussed, the term "hybridity" is frequently invoked, often with its academic trappings. Sunita Sunder Mukhi, for example, quotes the academics Bhabha, Gayatri Gopinath (author of an early article on bhangra),[27] and Nabeel Zuberi (author of a book on transnational musics)[28] in her discussions of hybridity and Indian-American identities, demonstrating how the more popular discourses of hybridity are occasionally inflected by academic ones. "Being Indian American," she writes, "is being comfortable, smooth and cool amidst non Indians, in the playing fields of hybridity. It is being able to dance Bhangra unabashedly, wear contemporary Indian and western clothes smartly, enjoy the pleasures of an urban, cosmopolitan life in New York, as well as in Bombay, London, or Hongkong, and still care for mom and dad (at the very least), and go to the temple on occasion. . . . Indianizing fairy tales, American movies, and other such popular texts, dancing the Bhangra and the Hindi film dance, dressing in mixed styles, are hybrid forms which facilitate the expression of the hybrid self."[29] Elsewhere Mukhi writes:

> Though the Indian lyrics of Bhangra may be in Punjabi, now intermixed with pidgin English, Black English, Indian English, and Hindi film song lyrics, not necessarily understood by all of the diasporic Indians, the beat, some of the instruments, the melodies are identified as generally non-white, generically Indian, and specifically of Indian hybridity. . . .
>
> The energetic beat [of bhangra] allows for an exuberant, almost ecstatic, very physical and aerobic dancing. The dance is loud, expressive, rhythmic. The music hastens, and reaches a crescendo, making the body reach a peak of energy and awareness. When dancing the bhangra, one feels very alive, very present, absolutely not erased. Dancing the bhangra with others who are experiencing this self-same aliveness allows for the barriers of individuation to dissolve. We all dance together forming one pulsating body of "amorphous" South Asianness. It enlivens our hybridity kinesthetically.[30]

Writings such as this demonstrate the complex ways that the hybridity notion suffuses conceptions of self, musical style, and identity strategies in diasporic and cosmopolitan situations among South Asians in the United States, constituting a distinct, discursive usage of the term somewhat removed from the marketing usages.

The music industry's treatments of bhangra remix music have been no different; the hybridity descriptor crops up all the time without any academic trappings, usually in quite matter-of-fact ways. For example, the web site of CDNow describes *Rising from the East* by Bally Sagoo, a musician based in London, as follows: "Indian-born mixmaster Bally Sagoo helped to create the East-meets-West hybrid he calls 'bhangra beat,' and got American attention two years ago with *Bollywood Flash bash [Flashback]*, a collection of Indian film music made club-friendly by his remixes."[31] Journalistic representations tread much the same ground, often relying heavily on the press kits supplied by record labels. Ken Micallef, in a review of another British–South Asian album, Talvin Singh's *O.K.* (1997), writes that "his music blends state-of-the-art drum and bass with the surging rhythms of traditional Indian music to create one of the most exciting hybrids on the electronic dance scene."[32]

Simplistic treatments of bhangra remix music and other hybrid musics cause some of the more thoughtful academic commentators to react with some degree of exasperation.[33] Ashwani Sharma, for example, notes how the great Pakistani Qawwali singer Nusrat Fateh Ali Khan was marketed, especially once he started making recordings for Peter Gabriel's Real World label. His music is not bhangra remix, but a more iconoclastic blend of a South Asian music with western sounds. Real World represented Khan's music as an aesthetic object, not a critical part of a religious exercise, and the liner notes to one recording, Sharma writes, revealed how musics such as Khan's "can be celebrated and authenticated as hybrid within the logic of difference in global commodity capitalism."[34] Sharma tacitly assumes that Khan was a dupe in the process of making his own recordings, without agency. Frequently, however, nonwestern musicians in the shadow of major western stars relinquish control over representations of themselves and their music in exchange for the visibility they achieve from appearing with famous American and European musicians.[35] It is probably wrong to assume that the music industry's hybridity simply ran over Khan, but perhaps merged to some extent with his own notions of the hybrid, and his own reasons for achieving it.

The changes that bhangra and Hindi remix musics have undergone in the last few years, resulting in bhangra remix, point to the ways that these musics are caught up in complicated discourses and practices about diasporic South Asian youth identities, since bhangra remix has become a complex site of discursive contention around the issues of hybridity and authenticity. Much has been made of the supposed hybridity of bhangra remix, even though bhangra from the 1980s owed little to traditional bhangra; an occasional *dhol* drum and the language of the lyrics were often the only recognizable sonic signifiers from traditional bhangra, although some bands occasionally used synthesizers to simulate traditional instrumental sounds. This bhangra was more a kind of rock-pop played by South Asians in London than a music whose makers attempted to sound equally South Asian and western. But signaling the "traditional" was not of concern to the musicians who followed the first wave of popularized bhangra in the late 1970s and early 1980s. The first bhangra stars began to argue that what was called bhangra by the early 1990s wasn't really bhangra at all.[36]

About that time, however, bhangra musicians began to turn toward more traditional sounds, even as they introduced more and more techniques using digital technology to make bhangra remix. They increased the "South Asian" component of their hybrid sounds, for a number of reasons. First, this strategy of turning toward traditional sounds is fairly common among children and grandchildren of immigrant populations in the late twentieth century and the early twenty-first.[37] The new interest in musical and ancestral roots also highlights how bhangra is considered a hybrid, as are the people who make it, by themselves and others. The interest in the roots of bhangra was announced in 1996, when DJ Jiten, a DJ based in Toronto, said that "audiences are moving towards more traditional bhangra right now. The remix bhangra right now is nothing big. . . . The hardcore is coming straight out of Punjab. The real scene is so hardcore right now that you have to be a traditional Punjabi to be right in the scene."[38]

Also in 1996, Panjabi MC, a diasporic South Asian musician based in Britain, released a new recording called *Grass Roots*. According to an on-line report on this album, "1996 was the renaissance that traditional Bhangra had waited for. Panjabi MC headed back to his music heritage in India with his DAT [digital audio tape] machine in-hand and recorded the father-figures of Punjabi music in a way never before witnessed. Back home in England, he laced the vocals of Kuldip 'he is what James Brown is to soul—he's the Godfather of Bhangra. . . .' Manak and Surinder Shinda with street beats and melodies totally new to their style of vocals."[39] In other words, bhangra remix.

Bhangra, like any popular music, is constantly changing, as this quotation indicates; UK bhangra musicians' discussions of "getting back to their roots" are registered in the many bhangra recordings of the late 1990s with titles that refer to roots: *Bhangra Roots Do*, by the Sangeet group of California; Johnny Z's *Back to My Roots*; collections such as *Bhangra Roots* and *Bhangra Roots 2*; Shava Shava's *Diggin' the Roots*; *Roots of Bhangra*; and many others. But the way these roots were acquired was technological—sampling, or recording live vocals to manipulate later in the studio, bringing about bhangra remix.[40]

Like Punjabi MC, the UK superstar DJ Bally Sagoo also made a bhangra remix album that attempted to return to the roots of bhangra. Sagoo, who traveled to India to record musicians for his album *Aaja Nachle* (1998), said: "everybody around the world has been requesting that I make a bhangra album, and this one has taken me almost a year to put together." The CD was recorded mostly in India and features, among other musicians, what Sagoo called "new talent"[41]—that is, professional bhangra musicians. These musicians are less western-sounding than bhangra musicians outside India, but diasporic bhangra musicians audibly influence them.[42]

This shift from bhangra to bhangra remix illustrates the fluidity and changeability of conceptions of hybridity and the third space in Bhabha's formulation. Emphasizing fluidity, flux, and changeability helps us to understand the nature of cultural production, at least in the realm of popular musics. Popular musical styles change fast. So, however, can discourses, practices, and social formations. Hybridities are made in a series of open-ended social moments that move as people move and can overlap with each other, moments in which sounds or images or styles (or what have you) are thrown up against each other in ways that leave their different origins discernible. But most of the industry's discourses of hybridity are not about flux; they are rather concerned with fixing something for the purpose of easy categorization and marketing. The concept of hybridity has become a way for some diasporic South Asians to locate a sense of stability in a complex environment.

Let's examine this shift to bhangra remix in greater detail by comparing a track from a bhangra album before the turn toward roots and a track from Sagoo's *Aaja Nachle*. First, a song by Achanak, a UK bhangra band. "Lako Wadeya" was released on the collection *What Is Bhangra?* (1993). Achanak's song opens with an extended sample from James Brown's "Get Up (I Feel Like Being a) Sex Machine"; it's hard to tell for the first forty seconds or so what is South Asian about this song aside from a splash of tabla (a pair of tuned drums used in North Indian classical music, not bhangra): this song is clearly establishing links not with England—or India for that matter—but with African America. The connection to an African American musician is made overtly in both the liner notes and the back cover of the album with the following note: "Bhangra combines quintessential Asian music with a kaleidoscope of contemporary styles including reggae, pop, ska, hip-hop and house."[43] Except for one thing: "Lako Wadeya" employs a singsong percussion rhythm that is the signature bhangra dhol drum rhythm, a sound that creates a connection between James Brown's quite similar rhythm and bhangra that non-Punjabi listeners might not notice, in a kind of hidden link to tradition. After the extended sample from James Brown the bhangra sound begins, but the dhol drums and their swingy rhythm—one of the main sonic signifiers of bhangra—last only about fifteen seconds, long enough to tell us that this is bhangra music (though the drums do recur periodically throughout the song). The vocal style is less close to bhangra than to Indian film music, liquid and lilting.

Compare "Lako Wadeya" to Bally Sagoo's "Aaja Nachle" from the album of the same title. Sagoo's music, stemming from the dance-music wave of bhangra that led to bhangra remix, begins the track, but more traditional-sounding bhangra eventually appears, bhangra that we know Sagoo recorded in India. In fact the Punjabi musician on the track is credited in the liner notes: it's Hans Raj Hans, a well-known bhangra singer in India. Hans Raj Hans's vocal style is a little rougher than on the song by Achanak, and makes use of far more ornaments than in "Lako Wadeya." Sagoo is clearly participating in this roots movement, which for an international audience is a kind of authenticizing move. Links to African American musics are severed in favor of links to India, which Sagoo made himself in his travels and recording, not simply in the studio with pre-recorded bhangra albums.

Clearly I have chosen examples that are eons apart—five years—in the world of popular music. "Lako Wadeya" is still steeped in the African American phase of bhangra influence (which is still around but in a different guise). Bally Sagoo's music reflects the subsequent turn toward the traditional, as well as Sagoo's dance music background—bhangra remix. Styles in bhangra change as quickly as in mainstream popular musics, affording to musicians and listeners endless opportunities for affiliations, political commentary, and pleasure. Third spaces in this realm of the popular are moments of continual (re)invention.

Both Achanak's and Sagoo's musics are identifiably hybrids in the sense that more than one musical genre or style is audible. But what is interesting about these tracks is not so much their hybridity but the ways that their hybridity has been constructed and heard in particular historical and cultural and geographic instances, and the ways that the discourses of hybridity shape perceptions of the music by journalists and fans, and some academic commentators.

In keeping with my desire to get beyond questions of style to ask what style registers, it is important to pay attention to the social and historical situations that produced these recordings. In the early 1990s, when Achanak's album was released, bhangra was still a music particular to the UK, though it could become translocal through the Indian diaspora. Awareness of diasporic South Asians outside the UK was not high. But as it so often does, the West found a use for a South Asian Other in the upsurge of interest in yoga and various eastern spiritual practices in the 1990s. Children of those who had immigrated in the late 1960s and early 1970s came of age, and a new wave of immigration in the 1980s and 1990s brought an influx of highly educated South Asians.[44] Figures such as M. Night Shyamalan, director of the film *The Sixth Sense* (1999), helped to educate Americans about South Asians in their midst. Madonna prominently embraced some aspects of South Asian culture, reflected in her album *Ray of Light* (1998); in New York City, Somini Sengupta began covering the diasporic South Asian community in articles for the *New York Times*, including an important one that helped put the community's music on the map.[45] And Sony Music signed Bally Sagoo in 1994 to capitalize on the growing popularity of this music, and the growing knowledge of South Asians and world music in general.[46]

To complicate these issues further, it seems that many diasporic South Asian listeners may have only a theoretical notion of the Punjabi folk roots of bhangra and bhangra remixes. They know it's a hybrid, but aren't always clear on the underlying musical sounds and styles. On a visit to Jackson Heights, Queens, one of the most concentrated areas of South Asians in New York City, I stopped at three music stores on a single block and asked after traditional bhangra recordings—traditional, not the bhangra associated with diasporic South Asian youths, but the folk music of the Punjabis. I wanted to acquire the folk bhangra that gave rise to contemporary popular bhangra. Each person I spoke to had no idea what I was talking about. The store clerks brought out early bhangra recordings from the UK, which evidently are old enough now to be considered traditional, not hybrid. Bhangra (and it seems to me, any commodified music) ages in commercial time more, and faster, than in experiential distance from a musical source.[47] The clerks also showed me some recent recordings of musicians who were attempting to sound more traditional. "He's very traditional," said one clerk, handing me a brand-new album by a hot, young Punjabi musician.

Contemporary diasporic South Asian fans of South Asian popular musics, who seem largely unaware of traditional Punjabi bhangra, don't appear to be conceiving of their bhangra or bhangra remix as a hybrid of traditional bhangra and western pop music, but as a hybrid of East and West more generally, an unruly mixture that includes not only musical sounds and style but people and cultures as well. This binary of East and West can combine with others, such as old and new, traditional and modern, Punjabi and English, Punjabi and American, Indian and Anglo, acoustic and electronic, subordinate and superordinate, and doubtless still others. Further, bhangra remix, like most popular music genres, has become a diversifying category—there are many bhangras now, and there are many hybridities.

It also seems that early bhangra, hailed as a hybrid in its time, is now authentic, traditional bhangra to some of today's youth listeners. This points out another problem with the hybridity metaphor. Not only is it too focused on binary, asymmetrical social formations, it is too frequently ahistorical;[48] and while hybridity, particularly in Bhabha's writings, isn't a static formulation, most uses of the concept, such as those that we saw applied to Wes and Angélique Kidjo, too often ignore changing ideas of what is taken as the authentic, and thus constantly changing ideas of what constitutes the new or the traditional.

These hybridities are part of larger ones as well: there is the "East meets West" collision of sounds that is audible in both examples. But with respect to these recordings, one must ask: What counts as "East"? Traditional, Punjabi bhangra? Anything at all that sounds South Asian? Whatever alterations Sagoo brings to the music? And what counts as "West"? The electronics? Any western instrument? Further, the early collection *What Is Bhangra?* depicts on the cover a young South Asian male, or, rather half of a young South Asian male: the other half is a machinized skull, signifying the studio technology used in making bhangra today (figure 1). The hybrid on this cover is not necessarily of East and West, South Asian and African American, subordinate and superordinate, or even human and cyborg, but rather, I would

Fig. 1 *What is Bhangra?*, cover

argue, traditional and modern, a particularly complex binary under which other binaries are sometimes subsumed.

The changeability of discourses and perceptions makes it important to emphasize the fluidity of cultural production in Bhabha's third space. Even though the notion of the third space was formulated in a colonial and post-colonial framework, it is still useful even in the complicated world of mass-produced and mass-mediated cultural forms.

The anthropologist Sunaina Maira conducted an ethnography of South Asian youths in New York City and has examined the complex ways in which they conceive of themselves as ethnic and cultural hybrids. The discourses of hybridity figure prominently in their conceptions of themselves, revealing how the hybridity metaphor can frequently obscure more than it can clarify. Diasporic South Asians talk about themselves as hybrids culturally and generationally, and they use the term to describe everything from their music to clothing to food. Maira points out that simple assumptions about hybridity as being between "East" and "West," or "Asian music" and "African American music," can hide more complicated dynamics. For example, while some authors view diasporic South Asians' uses of African American musics as a way of sounding a political affiliation, Maira writes that hip-hop style was adopted among diasporic South Asian men more for reasons of fashion, since it "connotes a certain image of racialised, heterosexual masculinity that is the ultimate definition of 'cool.'"[49] Thus, to call bhangra remix a "hybrid" overlooks the ways its hybridity is produced for local reasons, forging stylistic alliances between two youth subcultural groups, while at the same time the simple label "hybrid" perpetuates old, gendered binary oppositions, as women are either made the repositories of South Asian "tradition," constructed as modern Americans, or, Maira writes, reconfigured as "virginally Indian or immodestly American."[50]

Maira is particularly insightful on the question of hybridity-as-identity, writing that the space of contradiction for her interlocutors in New York City was "between the discourse of ethnic authenticity among second-generation youth on the one hand, and the performance of hybridity in remix youth culture and in everyday life on the other, suggest[ing] that what is at stake in this youth subculture is not just a struggle over definitions of Indian music and dance; rather, this disjuncture also reveals conflicts over attempts by Indian American youth to be 'authentic' in both local and diasporic spaces, the belief of immigrant parents in the American Dream, and the complicity of Indian Americans with U.S. racial hierarchies."[51]

Diasporic South Asians' hybrid music negotiates the complex tensions between pressures to assimilate, to be authentic Indians, to be American and rebel against the older generation, and to use the older generation's knowledge of India to fashion what they believe to be authentic Indian selves.[52] It is only through studies such as Maira's that potent discourses such as those surrounding the concepts of hybridity and authenticity can be identified *as* discourses and real practices, and can be seen to work in particular practices, in particular social groups, in particular places and times.

BLACKNESS

The racial or ethnic category that is most problematized, or obscured, by the discourses of hybridity is blackness. Blackness represents a peculiar area in the hybridity discourses: sometimes it is so fetishized as a mode of affiliation and resistance that hybridity is constructed as the combination of blackness and something else; or blackness is subsumed into a larger category of "western" or "modern," thus obscuring the reasons for its presence in particular instances. There are plenty of discussions of how African American musics have influenced musicians around the world, but if the discussion in question is about "world music" and is framed by questions of authenticity or hybridity, blackness frequently falls by the wayside.

The problem of blackness in the hybridity discourses surfaces mainly as a result of the usual reductionist presumption that stylistic hybrids consist of two, and only two, "pures" that mix, even though more subtle theorists such as Bhabha and James Clifford contend that hybridity banishes concepts of the "pure" altogether.[53] It may already be evident that in most uses of the term "hybridity," the two "cultures" that hybridize are white and nonwhite Other, but the complex and multiple nature of the Other or Others is not always accounted for in the discourses of hybridity. And the nonwhite in popular musics can frequently be a third "culture" that interacts to form a more complex hybrid than is usually allowed for under most usages of the hybridity discourses. As with Achanak, African American musical sounds can be a crucial part of the music, resulting in a multifaceted hybrid sound that is South Asian, British, and African American, in various and shifting degrees, with audiences that find different things to value and different things with which to identify.

Take, for example, the Australian band Yothu Yindi (about which there is practically a scholarly cottage industry).[54] This is a band composed of aboriginal and white musicians, but as far as the music industry is concerned, it is an aboriginal band. And even though its music is rock, inflected by aboriginal musics—a rock–aboriginal traditional hybrid, if you will—the band's music is still classified as world music because of the presence of aboriginal members. These musicians foreground their aboriginality—in their album cover art, the costumes they wear, the instruments they use, and their lyrics—even as they make music that is, in generic and stylistic terms, rock.

Yothu Yindi and many aboriginal bands arrived at their musical style by heeding the belief of the reggae superstar Bob Marley that all black men are brothers. As Rosie Ryan, a music announcer in Adelaide, put it, "Bob Marley played Adelaide in early 1979. The dust raised by that tour never really settled."[55] While Yothu Yindi's music doesn't sound as though it has much to do with Marley's, or any reggae for that matter, Marley's influence does appear occasionally, as in the lyrics to "Tribal Voice" from the album of the same title (1992):

> All the people in the world are dreaming (get up stand up)
> Some of us cry cry cry for the rights of survival now (get up
>   stand up)
> Saying c'mon, c'mon! Stand up for your rights
> While other don't give a damn
> They're all waiting for a perfect day
> You better get up and fight for your rights

Don't be afraid of the move you make
You better listen to your tribal voice!

The "get up stand up" phrase comes from Marley's famous song of the same name, perhaps the most famous of all his songs that deliver a political message. Marley's chorus line, "Get up, Stand up, Stand up for your right" may well be the most potent injunction to black and brown people around the world, echoed and re-echoed in songs such as this one by Yothu Yindi.

In the scholarly literature on Yothu Yindi, ganma—an aboriginal philosophy of "both ways"—usually figures prominently, for this is essentially an indigenous theory of hybridity. According to the literature of the Both Ways school, with which the founder of Yothu Yindi, Mandawuy Yunupingu, is heavily involved: "Ganma is a metaphor describing the situation where a river of water from the sea (Western knowledge) and a river of water from the land (Yolngu [Yunupingu's tribe] knowledge) mutually engulf each other on flowing into a common lagoon and becoming one. In coming together the streams of water mix across the interface of the two currents and foam is created at the surface so that the process of ganma is marked by lines of foam along the interface of the two currents."[56]

Ganma specifically, and Yothu Yindi's aboriginal "culture" in general, are usually the focal point of scholarly analysis of the group.[57] But in discussions of Yothu Yindi and ganma, the band's attraction to Bob Marley and blackness is not always explicitly theorized (one important exception is George Lipsitz's *Dangerous Crossroads*); ganma is seen as occurring strictly between aboriginal people and whites, two groups constructed as occupying intractably opposite sides. In the same way that African American musics are not always mentioned in characterizations of bhangra music as hybrid, the power of reggae and other black musics to unite people of color around the world is frequently elided, or simply assumed to be part of the band's supposed hybridity. Usage of the hybridity metaphor tends to focus analysis on binary, asymmetrical power relations, not the myriad alliances that can be made by those on the subordinate side of those relations, or more specific local forms of alliances and critiques.[58]

In keeping with my argument that the discourses of hybridity shape the production and perception of world musics and can thus obscure as much as they clarify about a particular music, it is important to remember that musics labeled as hybrid are always more than mere mixtures of styles or genres. It is also important to remember the specific hybridities: Yothu Yindi's music, for example, isn't simply caught up in a global sense of a black brotherhood. Yothu Yindi's complex musical hybridity is further complicated by the band's relationships to white Australians, relationships that are imbricated in discourses of the politics of reconciliation and the land. Yothu Yindi makes connections to a global black brotherhood through music, but for specifically local reasons concerning land rights and land use, controlled by whites with whom ganma is being formed.

Some commentators call for, or champion, musicians who make radical critiques with African American musics, but again, hybridity emerges as something that occurs between whites and nonwhites; the cross-racial affiliative potential is overlooked or minimized. In a discussion of hybridity similar to this one in some respects, John Hutnyk asks *"What would a radical hybridity look like?"* [59] For him, the British band Asian Dub Foundation, another group of diasporic South Asians, exemplifies a radical hybridity, and seems radically hybrid not so much because of its music, its sounds, but because of its lyrics and political stances, which protest against anti–South Asian prejudice in the UK. Hutnyk also unquestioningly endorses Asian Dub Foundation's own characterization of its music in one song as not "ethnic, exotic or eclectic" but a vehicle for commentary. [60] But it is also music, and the genre—hip-hop—was not chosen accidentally.

Asian Dub Foundation's use of sounds associated with American blackness as a sign of solidarity with another oppressed people (in which it is emulating earlier diasporic South Asian bands in the UK such as Fun^Da^Mental) is, as in most discussions of hybridity, overlooked in favor of an opposition between white and something else not African American, in this case South Asian. Musically, Asian Dub Foundation's music is essentially hip-hop with a dash of South Asian sounds. One of the tracks that Hutnyk discusses is "Jericho," a song that aggressively proclaims the presence of these diasporic South Asians in the UK:

We ain't ethnic, exotic or eclectic
The only 'e' we use is electric
An Asian background
That's what's reflected
But this militant vibe
ain't what you expected.

"Jericho," which opens with a sample of a political speech, could have been by Public Enemy, except that the rapping voice of Master D (whose real name is Deeder Zaman) doesn't sound much like Chuck D's, though his name does. The dash of South Asian sounds here is not subtle; the sound of the tabla at the beginning serves, like Achanak's sample from James Brown, to situate the band in a history of a particular music and politics. The song also quotes the African American spiritual "Joshua Fit de Battle ob Jericho," which meshes with the band's own militancy. But while Joshua's Jericho was a place, the walls that come tumbling down in Asian Dub Foundation's song are the walls of racism. I would be remiss not to note that Asian Dub Foundation draws on more than African American culture: its very name of course refers to dub, the reggae studio remix technique; in the UK the members of a well-known movement called the Dub Poets are poets who deliver political messages over dub tracks.[61]

Yet Hutnyk sets aside Asian Dub Foundation's strong gestures of blackness, and affiliations with it; I suspect that he does so because of a common assumption of the hegemony of American popular musical sounds, which themselves are largely African American and African American–influenced —this is another instance of African American sounds being taken to signal "western" more generally. But the global dominance of African American popular musics does not mean that they have always been deracinated, or that their politics have always been aestheticized. Asian Dub Foundation is clearly making an affiliation with African Americans in its music, as do many youth music cultures, and as such it is making hybridities, a third space in Bhabha's sense of the term.

While I appreciate Hutnyk's interest in a radical hybridity as a potentially liberatory kind of cultural production, I am at the same time interested in showing how the discourses of hybridity fetishize hybridity, and indeed fetishize otherness, sometimes at the expense of another Other. Focusing on Asian Dub Foundation as "Asian" loses any diversity within that category, just as diversity within the category of "British" or "western" is lost as well.

In this chapter I have sought to demonstrate how the discourses of hybridity complicatedly influence each other, influence music-making, and influence listening, and how the marketing of hybridity shapes musical production and perception. Use of the term "hybridity" makes most of those who employ it occasionally complicit in perpetuating and intensifying historically unequal power relations, the entrenched conservatism of the cultural categories employed by the music industry, and the obstacles to changing those categories. In this era of unparalleled transnationalism and globalization, it is perhaps important to remember that it is not just commodities, money, sounds, images, and people that move but also, as Arjun Appadurai has famously written, ideologies.[62]

At one level, it is now demonstrably true that the hybridities perceived in popular cultural forms in this moment constitute merely another way that people in so-called developed countries perceive cultural forms from their Elsewheres, and construct them discursively. Hybridity has become, or perhaps always was, simply another form of difference, another subordinate category into which Others and their cultural forms can be put, another form of authenticity, another way that musics by people from western Elsewheres are relegated to the world music category and denied access to the more prestigious category of rock. If people with dark skin make a stylistically hybrid music, their music is world music; if white people, particularly superstars like Paul Simon or Peter Gabriel, make a stylistically hybrid music, their music is anything but world music—it is Simon's music, or Gabriel's music: rock.

At another level, perhaps Bhabha's concept of the "third space" as I have both critiqued and built upon it here can help obviate some of the problems of the hybridity metaphor and circumvent some of its ideological maneuverings. The term avoids the unfortunate organic roots, and racist history, of hybridity as a concept. And much as the music industry would like to reduce musics, styles, and genres to bland, knowable entities for easy categorization and marketing, the idea of third spaces is a corrective, implicitly referring to the momentary, evanescent nature of culture, social formations, and music.

This is an important point, and not just for the music industry and listeners. Theorization in the hands of Homi K. Bhabha resulted in an extraordinarily productive set of analytical tools. But like all terms and categories, you have to watch what happens to hybridity in practice. It becomes all too easy for those who follow—myself included—to find hybridities everywhere. Naming reifies, and reifications all too frequently prove surprisingly enduring.

Let's employ the notion of the "third space" to preempt reification. The third space recognizes the constant flux of cultural production and people and social formations, while at the same time retaining the potential for redressing imbalances of power relations, for forging distant and local affinities, for giving voice to political stances that oppose racism and other forms of discrimination. The third space concept recognizes the transitoriness of all these possibilities, but attempts never to lose sight of them.

CHAPTER 6

YOU CAN TAKE "COUNTRY" OUT OF THE
COUNTRY, BUT IT WILL NEVER BE "WORLD"

One of the powerful ways that the music industry shapes peoples' experiences of music, including the making of music, is by the categories that it erects and polices around musical styles and genres, categories that become associated with class, ethnic, and racial groups. This process has a long history but has accelerated in recent years as more musics, including world music, have become part of the purview of the music industry.

In this chapter I will juxtapose two musics to throw their generic constructedness into relief, showing just how much the music industry is invested in these categories, and how they perpetuate old notions of otherness. Despite the new and complicated kinds of mixtures of sounds being made today, the music industry works hard to place musics and their audiences into manageable boxes—of styles or genres, and of demographic groups. This is essentially a process of hardening style and genre categories, and of using techniques that effectively segment and target audiences, transforming "culture" into "demographics" and markets.

To understand how this works, it is useful to begin with a discussion of country music, which perhaps problematizes contemporary notions of culture, genre, politics, race, and class more than other musics do. This might not appear obvious on the surface, but if one places the category of country music up against world music, cracks and fissures begin to appear in the music industry's demarcations of these musics and their markets. The weakening of these demarcations in turn allows us to begin deconstructing the way the music industry uses categories, not just as a way of determining where to place a particular recording on a retailer's shelf or on what radio stations or programs to air it, but as a way of bundling all kinds of ideologies and stereotypes into a seemingly simple label that appears innocent, self-explanatory, even natural. As a result of the music industry's practices, country music seems less connected to "culture" than world music does; country music seems to be more of a category of styles—a genre—than world music is (although world music too is increasingly becoming a "genre," as I will discuss); country music's modes of being political are less well respected, and less expected, than those of world music; and country music is marketed to a working-class audience (despite the diversity of its audience), world music to a middle-class audience.

In this chapter I will attempt to dismantle some of the assumptions that the music industry has about these musics and their audiences, and to identify tensions between, on the one hand, the assumptions of the industry that certain musics belong or appeal to a broad social group such as the "working class" or "middle class" and, on the other hand, the industry's tendency to engage in niche marketing (and what Scott Lash and John Urry call "specialized consumption"), targeting ever-smaller subgroups for consumption with ever-greater accuracy.[1]

Lash and Urry have argued that the culture industries have become more like the advertising industry, intent on constructing and selling "brands" in the form of superstars such as Britney Spears. But if, by contrast, the music or musician being sold is not viewed as a brand, the music industry relies instead on what I would call brand-categories, categories that have taken on a kind of sign-value in and of themselves. Juxtaposing country music and world music brings this development into relief, which is the next order of business.

ON CATEGORIES AND AUTHENTICITY

If you ever looked up "country music" in the index to the original *World Music: The Rough Guide* you would have noticed that it refers you to a page in the chapter on Native Americans. Go to that page, and the only reference to country music is to *Ballads of the American Indian* (better known by its title, *Bitter Tears*, not the subtitle that *The Rough Guide* gives), a recording by Johnny Cash from 1964 that contains, we are told, "ballads on the plight of the Indian by several different composers."[2]

If you looked up "Rock"—which is the top-selling category in the United

States—you wouldn't have found anything, but musicians who make rock or rock-influenced musics are nonetheless all over the book. With the exception of Cash, however, country musicians are entirely omitted (though the *Guide* includes a section on Old-Time and Bluegrass).[3] The question is: Why is it that rock music can be considered world music, but country cannot? Why is music that sounds like American country music left out of the *Rough Guide*, the *Billboard* World Music Charts, the Grammy awards, and other official arbiters of music tastes and categorization, but musics that sound like rock are readily admitted? This is the question that guides this chapter, a question that cannot simply be answered by quick charges of chauvinism, classism, racism, or other -isms that might come to mind. Instead, I will argue that country music is left out because it doesn't seem to do what the (post)industrialized West wants "world music" to do: from a "world music" perspective, country music doesn't seem authentic in any way at all.[4]

This isn't to say that country musics are inauthentic in a larger sense, for there are many discourses of authenticity around country musics.[5] But these discourses are almost entirely distinct from those of world music. World musics are thought to be musics by premoderns who have been untouched by the West (which is usually conflated with modernity); in *Global Pop* I called this identification "authenticity as primality," and it is usually the most potent identification in any discussion of world music discourses.[6] Country musics, however, are viewed as musics by premoderns of the West who have been spoiled by modern, western commercial culture and, sadly, don't know it.[7]

There are many world musics that are also not authentic in the sense that they are thought to be related to some imagined original or pure music, but these, I would argue, are allowed into the world music category because they are assumed to be political. Or they are assumed to be black, and blackness is frequently conflated with the political in the music industry's view. It seems to me that the categorization of country music generally, and with respect to "world music" in particular, works through a series of binary exclusions: country isn't seen as authentic, it's commercial; it's not political, but commercial; it's not primal, authentic, or "cultural," it's commercial; it's not black, but white; it's not rebellious but complacent; it's not middle class but working class. These binary oppositions are cultural constructions and not necessarily realities, of course, but the way these constructions work to place country and world music as opposites means that they need to be addressed as ethnographic concerns in addition to being addressed as analytical ones.

"CULTURE"

The main reason why world musics are placed into a variety of categories of authenticity, and country musics are excluded, is that world musics are assumed to be—or constructed to be—"cultural," marking the success of that anthropological concept. In the last few years I have seen with increasing frequency the word "cultural" used as an adjective to describe music, as in "cultural music," "cultural instrument," and more. The western construction of some musics from outside the West as "cultural" is one way that country musics are excluded, since country musics are seen as not "cultural" but commercial.

First, a few examples of this new practice with respect to world music. An interviewer for *Mother Jones* paraphrased a comment by David Byrne by writing that "all popular U.S. music . . . is a synthesis of African, Latin, Celtic, and other *cultural music*."[8] According to the *Orlando Sentinel*, "the spiritual, one of the finest examples of *cultural music* in America, is more than just words sung to a tune."[9] The *Los Angeles Times*, in announcing a Vietnamese festival, wrote: "Celebrating the autumn full moon and farmers' hopes for a prosperous harvest, festivals will take place in churches, temples and parks throughout Orange County all weekend with parades of candle-lit lanterns, *cultural music and songs*, and the traditional lion dance."[10] Siouxsie Sioux, of Siouxie and the Banshees, told *Alternative Press* that she and the band traveled to Spain to work on their second album, *Boomerang* (1989), because "Spain was somewhere" that they had "touched upon in various forms, either through dance or through the Flamenco music. It could have been somewhere like Greece, as we touched upon their kind of *cultural music* as well."[11] And a reviewer of an album by Robert Palmer began his review thus: "British rocker Robert Palmer has always been intrigued by the different sounds of *cultural music*."[12] Finally, Shawn Bates of the Hearts of Space label says that "the didgeridoo [an Australian aboriginal instrument] has been around a lot longer than this kind of [contemporary electronic popular] music, and will be around long after we're gone. It's a perfect example of a *cultural instrument*."[13]

Anthropologists such as Richard G. Fox, Michel-Rolph Trouillot, and Akhil Gupta have discussed the operations of the term "culture," which, as Lila Abu-Lughod writes, "enforce[s] separations that inevitably carry a sense of hierarchy."[14] Anthropologists have also become concerned with how the very success of the term in something resembling its anthropological usage has meant that it has entered a more mainstream (nonacademic) lexicon, where it now does the same kind of segregating and marginalizing work that terms such as "blood" and "race" once did.[15] Inevitably, this "culture" is not what the West is thought to possess; in fact, the discourses around "world music" almost never refer to the West as the West, or as a "culture" (or complex of various "cultures"). Uses of the culture concept in world music talk operate under the assumption that whatever it is, the West isn't a culture in the anthropological sense; it is, rather, society or civilization. The term "culture" in the West, when used reflexively at all, usually refers to culture in the opera-house sense—high culture—or various ethnic (sub)cultures.

The construction of world musics as "cultural" distances them from the realm of the commodity; a music's relationship to perceptions of its commodification has much to do with its position in the music industry. Country music is manifestly not a "cultural" music from the rock and "world music" perspectives in that it employs no musical signifiers of the premodern, the nonwestern; there are no "exotic" instruments, no foreign languages, no unfamiliar vocal styles (though in the absence of the dichotomizing effect of world musics, country music has a long history of being culturalized in this sense, as Richard A. Peterson and others have written).[16] Because of the assumptions that the "cultural" is the uncommodified (but eminently commodifiable),[17] the inverse is also a common assumption in the discourse of popular musics: the Non-Cultural is the Commercial.

POLITICS

There are of course plenty of western popular musics that aren't viewed as authentically "cultural" and that are also not seen as having sold out to commercial interests. These musics, however, might be considered authentic in another sense if they critique their own status as a commodity, or take on overt political stances, or even covert ones. Again, however, country music is excluded from this group. If country music from the United States or elsewhere is viewed by the world music industry as Not Cultural, it is also viewed as Not Political. That is, it is seen as too obviously tainted by the West and commercial concerns to pass as the "real," authentic music of a people, and so whatever politics might be enunciated are so compromised as to be neutralized. Rock musics are no less commercial than country musics (and no more political), but the cultural assumption of rock as politically rebellious by definition means that politics can stand as an excuse for the absence of "culture."

Rock music's cultural history as rebellious is complex and for my purposes doesn't need to be recounted at length.[18] But Thomas Frank's book *The Conquest of Cool* has examined some of these same issues, although from an angle somewhat different from that of the usual rock history text. Frank tells of the complicity of the American advertising industry in promoting rebelliousness as hip, which is culturally viewed as diametrically opposed to "square." By the 1990s hip had become the "official capitalist style," as Frank's concluding chapter says in its title. The rebelliousness that is now generally associated with rock music was born out of reactions against perceptions in the 1950s of conformity, consumerism, and the banality of mass-produced culture.[19]

Frank writes that Norman Mailer's essay "The White Negro" (1957) both diagnosed the oppressiveness of middle-class white culture and helped to catalyze reactions against it; by embracing what was thought to be African American culture, dissatisfied white Americans could withdraw from mainstream American culture and be truly rebellious, a formula that has proven remarkably durable. By the 1960s, Frank writes, rebelliousness became "the motif of the age."[20] And music had a large role to play in this. Frank offers many anecdotes and primary source materials from people in the advertising industry that highlight the role of music; one of my favorites is a story about the chairman of an advertising agency who made a speech "encouraging his employees to broaden themselves creatively by attending the theater, going to movies, and listening to rock music like that of Bobby Dylan, mispronouncing the star's name ('Dile-in') egregiously."[21]

Other companies used rock music to promote their goods. As early as 1969 the clothing maker Jantzen hired a rock band to dress in its clothes; and, more relevantly to this discussion, Frank tells of a television ad for Jockey sportswear that "portrayed its consumers at a suburban living room 'recital of sitar music.'"[22] While rock was the music mainly associated with the counterculture, what we now call "world music" had its role to play too, and the sitar was perhaps the most salient example of it, both in this ad and in the well-publicized study by George Harrison of the Beatles with the Indian sitarist Ravi Shankar.[23]

For Frank, the cultural tensions that are registered and exploited by the advertising industry are at bottom located at two poles, the hip and the square. The concern in his book is more the construction of hip—or *The Conquest of Cool*—but he occasionally notes the other side of this gap, the square, the "central-casting prudes and squares": among these are, significantly for this argument, Southerners.[24] Although Frank doesn't say so, country music is assumed to be their music. Even with country's huge popularity today among a broad, diverse audience (it is one of the highest-selling categories), 45 percent of listeners to country music radio are in the South, and 26 percent are in the Midwest.[25]

Interestingly, Frank also writes that in the early 1990s, when discourses of globalization became rampant, business language of the 1960s returned.[26] In this same moment "world music" emerged as a category, one marketed as alternative, fresh, and occasionally rebellious music. It is also no accident that "Alternative" was the best selling subcategory in "Rock" in 1997.[27] So the question arises: If this is the biggest subcategory, what is it an alternative *to*? Nothing, really, but the idea of "alternative" fits well with the resurrection in the 1990s of the idea of rebellion, because "alternative" is viewed as alternative to the mainstream, alternative to the commercial. And country is just the same old, same old.

Some of the language currently used to describe world music recalls the slang of the 1960s, as if to reaffirm the perception of world musics as hip, and their potential transgressiveness. The writer j. poet's guide to "worldbeat" in the *All-Music Guide* uses old language as a way of positioning world music as something just as subversive as rock music: "Cats and chicks will always need to boogie," he tells us, and it is world music that will get the job done.[28] Or, in the words of Stanley Goman, head of retail operations for Tower Records, "Foreign Music is where all the hipsters are."[29]

Still, there are many "world musics" that are admitted into the world music category even though they sound like rock music; that is, like country music they aren't thought of as "pure" or "original" or "authentic" or "cultural." How can this be? Partly it can happen because the music or the musicians are nonetheless viewed as exotic enough — or they are exoticized — to still fit comfortably in the world music slot.

Perhaps the most startling example of the tendency to classify the music of a rock band as "world music" was the veritable whirlwind of scholarship surrounding the Australian band Yothu Yindi after the release of its "Treaty" in 1992, a song that lambastes the Australian government for never having made any formal agreement with aboriginal peoples about the disposition of land. None of this would be unusual, except that virtually all accounts of Yothu Yindi — all of which foreground their aboriginality — sidestep the seemingly hard fact that country music is the main music made and consumed by the native peoples of Australia: as one Australian observes, "to many Aboriginal people, country and western was traditional Aboriginal music."[30] Why is it that the "world music" industry excluded all that country music, but included rock music by Yothu Yindi, whose album *Tribal Voice* spent nineteen weeks on the *Billboard* World Music chart in 1992?[31]

It seems that if a nonwhite musician takes on an overt political position—though the politics must be national or global, not local—he or she might qualify for the "world music" bin. The construction seems to be something like oppressed people = authentic politics = authentic (or "cultural") music. As long as it doesn't sound like country music.[32]

Country Politics

One of the most useful and sophisticated analyses of country music vis-à-vis other kinds of popular musics appeared in Simon Frith's path-breaking book *Sound Effects*. Frith, though, is rather hard on the music. "There is no country equivalent of the aggressive political music developed by blacks in the 1960s. The message of country populism remains 'We're a loser!' "[33] Frith doesn't allow that many songs may be—and are—enunciating more localized critiques of bourgeois American culture. A song about losing a job is not voicing a national political position in the same way that Yothu Yindi did with "Treaty," but it's still a political position. Frith, despite his unparalleled deconstruction of rock ideologies, nonetheless falls prey to rock attitudes toward country music. For him, country music is populist and conservative, not radical (like rock); entertainment, not art (or politics); concerned with the past, not the present or future; rural, not urban; and oriented toward family and community (not group or nation).[34]

What gets rock-influenced world music recognized as political is rarely its local politics but rather its global politics. Albums that contain songs about European colonialism, westernization, and modernization often find an audience among world music fans (a predilection registered in *Global Pop*). Songs that tackle issues of local concern with which western listeners are unfamiliar are much less likely to be popular.

Mainstream and music industry perceptions of country music's seeming acceptance of itself as a hopelessly commodified genre, and perceptions that country musicians and fans accept themselves as hegemonized victims in American cultural (and other) politics, mean that the music will be heard as Not Political, even when it is. If the message of country music is, as Frith claims, "We're a loser," the message of rock is "The establishment is a loser," a position that country lyrics take less frequently.

Blackness

Let's pick up a thread here from Norman Mailer's "The White Negro" that Thomas Frank noted. The embrace of blackness was a way for whites to rebel in the 1950s and 1960s, and while the present moment is different in many ways, it is also similar. In the 1950s the hip was black; the square was white, and it was also southern (and Midwestern, and lower-middle- and working-class, and rural). The rise of the "world music" category corresponds with the West's "discovery" of African popular musics, exemplified by the success of Paul Simon's *Graceland* (1986), which won a Grammy award for Record of the Year in 1987. There were other signs that African popular musics were entering the music industry's—and thus the mainstream fan's—consciousnesses. Ronnie Graham's *The Da Capo Guide to Contemporary African Music* was published in 1988; the highly popular "Afropop Worldwide" program on public radio was first broadcast in the same year.[35] Musicians from Africa and the African diaspora dominated the *Billboard* World Music chart from its inception in 1990, usually accounting for 40 percent of the entries on the charts, more than for music from anywhere else until a "Celtic" explosion in the mid-1990s and after.[36]

A quotation from a relatively early writing on world music helps demonstrate the extent to which world music was constructed as a predominantly black category: "When you listen to the music of Latin America, Africa, Jamaica, Algeria, Java and other foreign climes you'll hear the kind of raw energy and hungry enthusiasm that's been missing from most pop music in this country for almost a decade. Most of the (white) world may suffer from an advanced case of xenophobic blindness (and deafness), but that's no reason to deprive yourself of some of the richest musical rewards our planet has to offer."[37] Because of the historical oppression of African Americans, most black musics are assumed to be transgressive, and so the aesthetic qualities of these musics—such as vocal quality, vocal style, and approaches to time—have taken on anti-hegemonic significations which were seized upon by rock musicians and are maintained in countless ways today.

Country music, on the other hand, is always seen as white, to the extent that African American country musicians like Charley Pride are usually discussed as though they are quite out of place. Richard A. Peterson writes that the music industry's creation of the category country was deliberate, noting that the early merchandisers of the music made "the strategic decision to market music by whites and African Americans separately," even though, I should note, early country musicians such as Jimmie Rodgers sang the blues, a genre mainly associated with African Americans as a result of the market in "race" records in the 1920s.[38] But this was the distinction: "race" music on the one hand, "hillbilly" on the other, no matter how much the musicians might have learned from each other and sounded like each other.[39] Peterson also writes of the separation that was made between "popular" music and "country," a separation that persists to some extent.

More recently, the African American country musician Trini Triggs discussed the treatment he gets from country fans, who tend to be incredulous at first but ultimately supportive of him and his music. An interviewer writes that Triggs "envisions a day when he'll no longer be referred to as a black country singer but as just a country singer."[40] A recorded collection, *From Where I Stand: The Black Experience in Country Music* (1998), attempted to dispel the myth of country music as white only. And yet this laudable release was discussed in the press as a kind of exotic oddity, with authors seemingly unable to understand how country music (and, it seems, the culture that surrounds it) refuses to be so neatly pigeonholed. Just some titles of reviews and commentaries on this album demonstrate the refusal of critics to admit African American music as country music, or rather country music as African American: " 'STAND' UP FOR COUNTRY SOUL!" (an editorial headline in *Billboard*);[41] "Blues Brothers under the Skin" (title of a review in the *Wall Street Journal*);[42] "The Neglected Soul of Country Music" (*Rolling Stone*).[43] As if country music by whites were soulless, or music by African Americans nothing other than an essential(ized) soulfulness.

CLASS

I need friends who don't pay their bills on home computers
and who buy their coffee beans already ground.
—Randy Travis, "Better Class of Losers"

In *Global Pop* I paid little attention to social class, which at the time was tangential to the constructions of western conceptions of otherness and music that I was considering. But in this dialectical juxtaposition of country music and world music, class comes to the surface. Compared to the class associations and assumptions of country music, the middle-classness of world music stands out in relief in ways that it did not before. And as we know from Pierre Bourdieu, nothing better indicates class position than taste in music.[44]

World Class

For example, Bob Haddad, president and producer for Music of the World, an independent record label based in Chapel Hill, North Carolina, that is now defunct, says that according to the cards that his label included in releases requesting information from buyers (called "bounce-back cards" in the trade), "the buyers of purer ethnic music tend to be well-educated, well-travelled, 25 and over—often between 35 and 60 years old—and might speak several languages."[45] This is a group, in other words, with high educational capital, and presumably high incomes as well. One record company executive, commenting on a radio station in Los Angeles that was in the process of changing from easy listening to what was described as "contemporary rock artists and singer-songwriters with a smattering of folk, soul, blues, reggae and world music" was a little more blunt: "The demographic it appeals to is one that advertisers find very appealing for their education and financial status. Even if the station only gets a certain level of success, those people are the ones that advertisers really want to get to."[46] Another record company representative said: "We discovered that the demographics of the people buying Irish albums were the same as for those buying reggae and world beat. Not the same individuals, necessarily, but the same demographic—mostly white, college-educated adults looking for something different."[47]

Some of the popular world music books that I interrogated in *Global Pop* for their assumptions of musical otherness and (post)colonialist racism are just as revealing in their assumption of a middle-class readership. I would like to reexamine two of those early guides to world music: *World Music: The Rough Guide* and Philip Spencer's *World Beat: A Listener's Guide to Contemporary World Music on CD*. They were published at a time when there was clearly a campaign on the part of the music industry, as well as some authors and critics (not wholly distinct from the industry), to establish world music as a legitimate category in the minds of consumers. Accordingly, the first guidebooks had a good deal of cultural work to do in creating and targeting a particular sector of the educated middle-class audience. More recent writings than those considered in *Global Pop* seem to take the world music audience for granted, since the groundwork had been laid by such important texts as the *Rough Guide* and *World Beat*.

Let's take a look at some of these writings. Philip Spencer writes in *World Beat*:

> Nowadays the music you play needs to be sophisticated but not obtrusive, easy to take but not at all bland, unfamiliar without being patronizing.
>
> World music gives the American listener a sense of freedom from the constraints of standardized Anglo-American pop, without the arid, over-intellectual pomposity of much "progressive" music. World music is both entertaining and different.[48]

Some of the world music guides are also rather cerebral. Philip Sweeney's *Virgin Directory of World Music* is, according to the readability statistics generator that came with my word processor, written in a far more difficult style than what you are reading now. Sweeney uses such terms as "*élan*" and "artistes" and scrupulously avoids contractions and slang. And the introduction to his book is one dense paragraph, nearly two pages long.

The audience for these books is a familiar educated middle class, but with a new global informational capital as I call it in chapter 7. The term reflects the increasing importance in developed countries of possessing a kind of capital that stands in for real knowledge of the world in this moment of globalization and transnationalism, a moment of triumph for the information age. This concept was developed in part out of Lash's and Urry's notion of "aesthetic reflexivity," brought about by the sheer availability of signs from all over. Contrary to the familiar postmodernist argument that the proliferation of signs is overwhelming, Lash and Urry argue instead that this phenomenon is instead producing a new aesthetic reflexivity, in which everyone is a kind of amateur hermeneutist.[49] It is clear from the rise of world music that "aesthetic reflexivity" evidences a receptivity toward an eclectic array of other kinds of musics, including even country, a taste and consumption pattern that one could call flexible consumption.

Country Class

In contrast to the world music audience, perceptions of country music's audience are mired in old-think about musics and social class. If world music belongs in some measure to new cosmopolitan classes, country music is still the province of premodern (or barely modern) rednecks. Or so many in the music industry would have one believe. Such a position is not new. From its outset, country music was consigned by the music industry as lowbrow and inferior. Richard A. Peterson and Paul DiMaggio write of the nascent American music industry's construction of country music, counterposing it with classical music. Classical music advocates—those possessing a view of civilization that they were attempting to promulgate nationally—effectively defined "folk country music as rustic, backward, old fashioned, and inferior to the musical products of the music industry which burgeoned after 1880. Thus, while the civilizers succeeded in denigrating indigenous musical forms and placing a piano in every proper middle-class home, the music that was played was more likely to be the latest product of the Tin Pan Alley music publisher than Chopin or Liszt. . . . The rustic, hayseed, country bumpkin character was added to the stock of ethnic-stereotype characters of the popular stage and vaudeville. Like his ethnic brethren, the rube was supposed to become "Americanized" into the urban bourgeois mold."[50] It is also true, however, that musics by rurals and rustics from elsewhere that are labeled "traditional" are perfectly admissible into the "world music" fold. It is acceptable for musicians to be rural and rustic elsewhere, as long as they don't make music associated with the rurals and rustics (and rubes) from here. Tolerance in the realm of world music of old time and bluegrass music usually employs a discourse that works hard to folklorize and authenticize these musics.[51]

This division between rural rube and hip sophisticate is still with us. According to one study, "among college graduates, the professional/managerial demographic, and those making $75,000-plus annually, Interep found that the most popular formats are news/talk, AC [Adult Contemporary], country, oldies, and top 40. For technical/clerical/sales listeners, the most-listened-to formats are country, AC, news/talk, top 40, and oldies."[52] Thus in the highest income group in this survey, country is quite popular (though not the most popular music listened to), but in the lower income group, it is the music most listened to. Around the same time, a survey revealed that among people who listened to country music radio, 72 percent owned a home (compared to 69 percent of the general population), 62 percent had a household income of $30,000 or more (compared to 61 percent of the general population), and 46 percent had one or more children (compared to 41 percent of the general population).[53] This information was trumpeted for a time on the

Country Music Association's web site. According to a more recent study, country music is the most popular music on the radio, and among typical country music radio listeners, 47 percent are married, 77 percent own their own home, and 49 percent have an annual house income of at least $50,000, yet the stigma of country's audience remains.[54]

The music industry also seems to view country music as a music for people without much educational capital. If you go to Tower Records, for example (at least, the one nearest me), you find that the world music section has books for sale on world music; the blues section has books on the blues; the jazz section, jazz books; the rock section, rock books. But the country music part of the store sells no books on country music, even though there is a significant number of books (popular and academic) that could appear there, certainly more than for world music.

By way of contrast, the venerable British classical recording review magazine *Gramophone* began a new spin-off magazine a few years ago called *The Songlines*. Its title recalls the practices of Australian aborigines made famous by Bruce Chatwin in a book of the same name. Before the first issue of the magazine was published, its editor, Simon Broughton (co-editor of *World Music: The Rough Guide*), told me that it would offer more serious and in-depth coverage of world music than its competitors.[55] This claim was borne out in the early issues of the magazine, though its more in-depth articles are fairly brief (sometimes only a page). Interestingly, the magazine was originally more journal-sized — less than 9½ inches high — which emphasized its status as a connoisseur's journal and not a slick magazine.[56] (More recently, however, the magazine has become a more glossy and commercial enterprise). BBC Radio 3, which until recently was solely a classical station, now airs world music as well. The record label Naxos, which occupied the low-budget classical niche, has now branched out into world music.

This growing relationship between a world music repositioned away from New Age music (where it was linked initially; see *Global Pop*) and toward classical music was also reflected in the practices of a major retailer of CDs in New York City. While most CD megastores block off the classical music section from the rest of the store (so that classical listeners don't have to endure the non-classical musics), this particular store downsized its classical section and moved it out altogether. World music now occupies the noise-proofed portion formerly dedicated to classical music.[57]

More than simply filling in the gap left by classical music, world music has begun to mix with classical music sounds. It is now possible to hear classi-calized world music performances such as Jonathan Elias's *The Prayer Cycle*, released in 1999, featuring singers ranging from Alanis Morissette to Nusrat Fateh Ali Khan.[58] The result is a mixture of world music, classical, and new age "styles," a sound that is increasingly common.[59] In the first movement of nine, the chorus sings in Swahili, Alanis Morrisette in Hungarian, and Salif Keïta in Malian. I should also note that this recording was released on the Sony Classical label, another sign of the classicalization of world music as the label seeks to broaden what may be included in the "classical" category. It is no coincidence that Jonathan Elias is the chief creative officer of one of the biggest music advertising companies, Elias Arts.

In one of the most trenchant of recent considerations of country music, Barbara Ching writes of the "sophisticates" who look down on country music; these sophisticates are pretty much the same as the hipsters that Thomas Frank writes about, and what we would call "cosmopolitans" in this era of globalization. Along the way, Ching introduces a provocative argument concerning "camp": country musicians do what they do with consciousness that they're doing it; and what they're doing is therefore camp. Now, there's nothing wrong with arguing that country musicians (and presumably fans) know what they're about. But country music, Ching says, is a performance "rather than a spontaneous expression of some pure emotion or state of being."[60] "In other words," she continues, "country music is capable of performing the rural role in such a way as to underline its construction and social purpose rather than its presumed natural essence, innocence, and/or bad taste."[61] Ching oversimplifies, I think—the "rather" hides the multiple interpretations that musicians and fans can make. Country music does tend to emphasize rurality (with class associations), but this rurality is reality for many of the musicians and fans; their consciousness of this, and knowledge of other kinds of lives in contemporary America, doesn't mean that their (self-) representations are performances only.

Still, Ching is on to something. The class and regional associations of country mark its discourses and practices as inferior, tainted. Rock musicians' performances are "honest" expressions of anger, lust, or what have you, and such performances are culturally acceptable. Country performances are culturally acceptable to its musicians and fans as well, but these performances are not those that the rock establishment—and much of the listening middle class—values. Ching is addressing the issue raised earlier: country musicians and fans are seen as premoderns who don't know that they've been spoiled, but she points out that they do know they've been spoiled by commercial culture as much (or as little) as anybody in America, and that the musicians address this consciousness in their self-presentations.

Last, it is important to point out that the "working class" of country music is as heterogeneous as the middle-class audience of world music; *pace* Lash and Urry, not everyone is a cosmopolitan. There are divisions within the working classes, different generations, different taste cultures, and different musics associated with them, associations both imposed by the music industry and made by listeners. New kinds of country music, whether under the rubric of "New Traditionalism," "New Country," or some other, could be viewed (though perhaps a little cynically) as sounds aimed at increasing a visibly middle-class audience for country music. It is interesting that these musics use sounds associated with folk music (that is, more "authentic" music, nearer "culture") more than much country music does, sounds such as acoustic instruments.[62] This country is thus nearer "world." At the same time, it's possible to identify another movement altogether: the entry of some country music superstars into mainstream (including middle-class) acceptance. The Garth Brooks phenomenon is probably the best example of this. But as Brooks is closer to rock than more mainstream country or "new traditional" or "new country," he can partake of rock's forms of, and claims to, authenticity.

SONGS OF THE HAWAIIAN COWBOY / NA MELE O PANIOLO

One of the few recordings of country music I have found that have entered the world music category, or perhaps the only recording, is a collection entitled *Songs of the Hawaiian Cowboy / Na mele O Paniolo* (1997), which features various performers who appeared in a documentary by Edgy Lee entitled *Paniolo O Hawai'i* (*paniolo* is the Hawai'ian term for cowboy). Paniolos are Hawai'ian cowboys who learned their trade from Mexican vaqueros; the term "paniolo" is thought to be a Hawai'ianized pronunciation of "español," and the music is the Hawai'ian version of cowboy songs. My discussion will concentrate on the representations and constructions of this recording that have permitted it to be considered world music: doing so will reveal the tensions that the music industry's categorizing practices creates, and the kinds of discourses and practices around world musics that such a recording triggers. Warner Western's marketing of the album, fans' responses, and reviewers have all labored to construe the music not as "country" but as "world" through a number of discursive means, many of which are intertwined, or occur in variations.

Let's begin by seeing how the album was pulled into the realm of world music. It was reviewed in at least two magazines that specialize in world music, *Rhythm Music* and *Dirty Linen*; and in Tower Records it is shelved in the "international" or "world music" category, as it is at various on-line venues. And the album has received airplay on National Public Radio and college radio, unlike country music, which is usually avoided by college stations and does not appeal to "your National Public Radio audience," according to a spot radio buyer in New York.[63] More interesting than the album's location in record stores (both physical and virtual) were the myriad discourses that cropped up in discussions of the music by Warner Western, reviewers, and fans. Some of these discourses were the same as those characteristic of world music, but others seemed more designed to cleanse the album of whatever country associations might have sprung from the title of the album (which refers to cowboys) and some of the sounds on it.

First, this album—and, more generally, this genre—are both always discussed as not commercial, which is what country music is usually taken to be. In a review in *USA Today*, Brian Mansfield wrote that "rather than beckoning to the tourist or would-be traveler, Na Mele o Paniolo is designed to tell the story of the island's cattlemen."[64] It's not tourist music—the music that most non-Hawai'ians know as "Hawai'ian music"—which is seen as commercial and thus inauthentic; paniolo music is usually immediately constructed by reviewers as "traditional," and thus "authentic" or "cultural."

Discussions of the album as traditional are a reminder that the "authenticity as primality" discourse takes various forms, the most common of which appeared at the end of the review in *Rhythm Music*: "More than a thoughtful collection of beautifully rendered tunes, *Songs of the Hawaiian Cowboy* is a discovery of little-known music that comes from a source as earthy, honest and unsullied as the weathered paniolo themselves."[65] And Warner Western's web site for the album opened by describing this idyllic scene: "They sang around the campfire, roped cattle and rode the range. But their history unfolded not on the vast expanses of the American Southwest, but beneath the cliffs of Kualoa on the windward coast of Oahu and on the rolling hills below Mauna Kea—they are paniolo O Hawaii, the Hawaiian cowboy."[66] Similarly, Warner Western's web pages emphasized the traditional, unsullied nature of the musicians and their music: "Throughout the album, paniolo artists perform songs . . . all of which tell about their way of life, their love for the land and their work."[67] This was expanded on elsewhere on the site, where Warner Western romanticizes the paniolos' relationship to the land: "Na Mele O Paniolo also shows the paniolos' love for the land. Being a cowboy meant learning from, and caring for, the land and passing along to future generations the hard-earned wisdom of a simple life."[68]

Songs of the Hawaiian Cowboy was released by Warner Western, a subdivision of Warner Bros.' country division (which has since been superseded by WBR Nashville). This compartmentalization by genre may appear to be logical from a bureaucratic standpoint, but as Maureen Mahon and others have written, divisions in the music industry have historically been quite racialized, as well as class-ized, as I am pointing out here.[69] Note also that the name of this division was Warner Western, not Warner Country. In a not entirely successful effort to make clear what this label is about, its web site opened with this mystifying, idealizing, and romanticizing statement:

> So what is Western music anyway?
>
> The answer is as broad and diverse as the people and places that it eloquently portrays. It speaks of a life and a land that is as mysterious as it is real. It is the sound of familiar melodies sung around a campfire. It is the rhyme and reason of a cowboy poet presenting his own brand of wit and wisdom. It is the driving rhythm and haunting melody of music inspired by the Native American experience.
>
> It is the modern day troubadour singing contemporary songs that speak passionately from a western perspective. Western music is all of this and more—it is a chance to explore a musical landscape where there are still no fences. Please take a look at what we have to offer.[70]

Warner Western seemed to be attempting to harness some of the varieties of world music authenticity for its western (Not Country) series, and we can see this effort operating in its presentation and marketing of their Hawai'ian CD. The mood that the web site sought to evoke is typical of representations of world music and musicians: natural, organic, and close to nature, thus emphasizing the supposed authenticity or quality of anthropological culture of the musicians.[71]

The producers of the album also helped position the music as folkloric and traditional by including a track of an ancient chant; this opening track, entitled "Li'uli'u Wale" and labeled "Traditional," is described in the notes thus:

"Chants have long been a way of expressing Hawaiian thought. It was this type of prose that was the forerunner of Hawaiian music. As time progressed, some were put to contemporary melody lines thus preserving many ancient compositions. We still honor the traditions of our ancestors and in doing this we perpetuate the music of the 'Paniolo,' Hawaiian cowboy. Li'uli'u Aloha in its humble intent is presented here as Hawaiian protocol. To ask in all modesty and to be kindly granted the liberty to proceed with aloha. In an effort to make clear and righteous 'pono' our path. Let us graciously ask and let the answer unfold."[72] This chant is used here as a marker of "authentic," indigenous Hawai'ian music, and sounds nothing like any of the other tracks on the album; the chant's function seems to vouch for the indigeneity of the paniolo music that follows it.

Many reports on the album emphasize that the paniolos were the first cowboys in America (even though Hawai'i wasn't "America" when the vaqueros were introduced in the 1830s; Hawai'i didn't become a U.S. possession until 1898). Warner Western's web site said that "Hawaiian cowboys preceded American cowboys by 40 years but were never included in America's frontier history."[73] This maneuver is rather interesting, for rather than assume that this world music is timeless and primordial (as do many accounts of more traditional-sounding musics)—that is, without history—Warner Western does permit these paniolos a history. But note that it is not their own history, but rather America's. Paniolos seem not to be important in and of themselves—only in their relationship to what is probably America's most important myth of itself, its frontier past. Paniolo history is only history when it is American history.

Even though the album is viewed as traditional, Hawai'ian music aficionados are careful to position it against an earlier, lesser-known release, a two-cassette set that was discussed by fans of Hawai'ian music on the Internet newsgroup alt.music.hawaiian. These fans were quick to point out the more commercial nature of the Warner Western recording; one wrote, "these are two different recordings. The one you have is brand new and very professionally recorded and produced. The older one, Na Mele Paniolo, was recorded in 1986 by Kindy Sproat going around to all the islands and recording the musicians in their living rooms (or whatever)."[74] Another fan wrote of this earlier recording: "Talk about grassroots music!! It doesn't get anymore grassroots then this with real paniolos singing paniolo songs . . . this is real grassroots music, just as you would hear if you were out on the 'range' with these folks."

Despite a little skepticism for Warner's release, however, the regulars at alt.music.hawaiian seemed to like *Songs of the Hawaiian Cowboy*, even though some made it clear that they didn't usually like country music. "Funny thing," one wrote, "I'm not a fan of country music, but give it a Hawai'ian style beat and it's just grand!" Another concurred: "Crank up Ernie Cruz's 'Molokai Cowboys' and I can't keep my feet or my hands still. But DONT make me listen to straight country!"[75] And so most posters argued on behalf of the authenticity of the album. "Good ol' traditional 'kanikapila sittin' on da lanai drinking a Primo' kine music," one wrote.

Constructing *Songs of the Hawaiian Cowboy* as not commercial but traditional and folkloric invited fans and reviewers to apprehend the album as an object of connoisseurship, a rare or unusual object, not as a commodity or even an object of fandom. The review in *USA Today* concludes: "Na Mele o Paniolo is a fascinating look at a little-known musical genre."[76] According to a review in *New Country* (one of the few reviews that I found in a country music publication), the album "captures an important piece of Americana that has been eclipsed by mainland frontier history and popular culture."[77] Other reviewers talk about the rarity and endangered nature of the music. Chiori Santiago writes that the arrangement of several songs "envelop[s] several compositions in a melancholy air entirely appropriate to this nostalgic look at a rapidly disappearing culture."[78] To one of the fans on alt.music.hawaiian, "Cowboy songs, from any frontier, are a lost art and probably destined to disappear completely unless people like those involved in the production of such projects as this are able to continue on, in some way, shape, or form."

In keeping with views of the album as traditional, authentic, and primal, discussions of the album almost always invoke historical or folkloric data, to reinforce the notion that the music is "cultural music." In some instances the references are reduced to factoids, as in *USA Today*, which notes that "Ke Anu e Ko Mai Nei, a love song in Hawai'ian and Spanish, was written by Queen Liliuokalani, the reigning monarch when the USA took over the island at the end of the 19th century."[79] (This is true, and most reviewers mention it, perhaps because it is in the liner notes.) The reviewer for *USA Today* began his article by saying, "Most Hawaiian music albums that hit the mainland emphasize its exotic qualities or the performers' abilities. But *Na Mele o Paniolo* (*Songs of the Hawaiian Cowboy*) . . . takes a more historical approach."[80] Many reviews echo or simply reproduce Warner Western's information about the

Fig. 2 *Songs of the Hawaiian Cowboy / Na Mele O Paniolo,* cover

introduction of cattle to Hawai'i in 1793, which precipitated the need for cowboys. This history is a sign of history as much as history itself; that is, it is not meant to explain or contextualize the music as much as authenticate it.

Songs of the Hawaiian Cowboy was positioned as folkloric by its association with Edgy Lee's documentary; as is well known, it is a companion CD to Lee's film, which had its première at the Smithsonian Institution. The review of the album by USA *Today* was accompanied by an article (much longer) about the documentary itself, another short article about Lee, and a still shorter article about traditional Hawai'ian music.[81] The album is further positioned as folkloric (that is, Not Country) by the absence of stars. Hawai'ian music connoisseurs will recognize some of the musicians, but the average world music fan will not. That the album is a collection gives it further credibility—it's not a star's vehicle—and makes the entire enterprise seem more folkloric. And the cover art is an artist's rendering of a generic Hawai'ian cowboy, not a real person.

All of the album's artwork also contributes to the notion that the album is folkloric and historical, not contemporary country music, which would make it an album compromised by the commerce of selling a star or brand. Not only is the cover a picture (credited to Herb Kawainui Kane; fig. 2), but all the photos on the CD liner and in the accompanying material are old black-and-whites from the Bishop Museum in Honolulu; the back cover of the liner notes is a photograph printed on warm-tone (that is, brown) paper, or made to appear so, and surrounded by a rough paper with all the imperfections visible, to emphasize or signify the age of the photograph. While the inclusion of these old photographs is welcome, we should also recall that this album was made to accompany a documentary film; surely there were recent photos available of real paniolos, including those who sang on the album. (News reports of the documentary and the album are accompanied by recent photographs of paniolos, some of whom are musicians.) Not including photographs of contemporary musicians anonymizes those musicians who appear on the album, which makes them seem more like the "authentic" folkloric musicians whose names are all too frequently omitted from recordings. In a familiar strategy, these musicians are placed in the past, as though further down the evolutionary ladder.

Now, some of the marketing strategies of this album are simply marketing strategies. But others are less strategies than the straightforward conveying of information that listeners are likely to find useful; the history of the paniolos will not be known to many fans, for example. And there are ways to view this album as a world music album, particularly since the songs are sung in Hawai'ian, not English, and language is the prime determinant of the category to which a music is assigned. But even such features as these that would make this album's inclusion in the "world music" category seem "natural" or inevitable do not mean that the recording needs to be so fully separated from its country music associations by its fans, its critics, and its labels. This is an album that falls between brand-category cracks: it could go into either the country or the world category, but people considering it from a "world music" standpoint seem determined to save it from the taint of "country."

What Warner Western practiced is no different from what the rest of the industry is doing these days; ever more like the advertising industry, as Lash and Urry have pointed out, Warner Western used whatever means were at its disposal to make its product appeal to the widest possible audience, while at the same time aiming its album at a thoroughly market-researched niche of "authentic" music aficionados. The resulting discursive, representational, and class confusions matter less than maximizing sales.

In the years that I spent writing *Global Pop* I became fascinated by categories, categories that ostensibly refer to musics, to peoples, to places; and I became interested in the ways that mixing up these categories was cause for much exploration in cultural theory, whether under the guise of "hybridity" or *mestizaje* or something else.[82] I am still fascinated by categories, and it still seems to me that even though cultural production increasingly emphasizes mixtures and juxtapositions, and even though contemporary American culture, and to some extent European cultures, are developing discourses of tolerating diversity—"multiculturalism" among them—these categories used by the music industry, and thus all of us, are more salient, more rigid, and more important than ever.

So the music industry and its consumers expect "aboriginals" or "Native Americans" to make what they take to be "aboriginal" or "Native American" music, which is to say anything with a didjeridu, or anything with a wooden flute that sounds meditative. Tolerance of difference ought to mean not only that we listen to didjeridu music as "aboriginal music," but that we pay attention to all the musics that people around the world make, including country.[83] Selling Australian aboriginal or Native American musics at Tower Records (or putting them in *World Music: The Rough Guide*) isn't as radical as clearing a space for all the musics that these and other peoples make. Until then, the West will remain "modern" (or "postmodern") and continue to force the non-West into positions that the West defines any way it wishes, but never as equal. And country music by those whom the West and its music industry have put in the "Other" pile will continue to be rendered invisible by their brand-categories, marginal and unheard.

CHAPTER 7

WORLD MUSIC IN TELEVISION ADS

This final chapter completes my analysis of the "culture industry" broadly understood, from the music industry into the world of advertising, which may be more responsible than any other single industry, or sector within the culture industry, for making—and selling—the meanings and values of music. Much of the chapter concerns the most recent triumph in the music industry's efforts to turn world music into a simple style or genre, a simple sign of itself, of globalization in sound. As we have seen, the West has a long history of grappling with its Others and attempting to manage them for its own purposes. This hasn't changed. What has changed, as I have attempted to show, is how the West has constructed its Others over time. The uses to which the West puts its Others are likewise never static, though there are some long continuities.

The musical subject of this chapter is television commercials, which in the 1980s became hipper and more aesthetically challenging, helping in part to drive a new phase of consumption.[1] Turn on the television these days and you are likely to hear what sounds like "world music" used to sell you something, whether a flight on an airplane, a cruise, or an automobile. More often than not, however, these musics are in no way related to any indigenous or traditional practices but are entirely fabricated, either by performing musicians or those who work in advertising. These musics often employ what sounds like choruses of children and untexted vocal lines (usually sung by a solo woman vocalist); sometimes, as with the English group Adiemus, the language sung is wholly invented.

This chapter examines these musics and those who make them (composers, music production companies, and advertising agencies), and the uses to which these musics are put. These musics tap into old western notions of escaping the ordinary, of the voyage, by signifying "the world," but they do this for new reasons. The myriad public discourses of globalization, transnationalism, the information age, and the information economy are reconfiguring conceptions of prestige and the kinds of capital that one needs to survive in the contemporary moment; today one needs a dictionary of global culture to succeed in business.

GENERIC "WORLD MUSIC"

The sounds used in these television ads are fairly standardized. There is almost always a soaring female vocalise employing nonsense syllables or more recognizable oohs and ahs; or, a children's or women's choir sings nonsense syllables or oohs and ahs; or, both a solo woman and a children's or women's chorus. Occasionally there is a male voice instead, but this is rare, and while a chorus might accompany a male voice, it is always a men's chorus, never a children's chorus. There are usually drums as well, and frequently the sound of a wooden flute. There are often many sequences (that is, repetitions of a rhythmic or melodic pattern starting on different pitches), which give the music a rather rudimentary or "primitive" sound; and the pitch organization is frequently modal rather than tonal, or sometimes a combination of both. The lyrics, when not simple nonsense syllables, are in an uncommon language or even a fake language, a technique that has been used for centuries in the West to depict Others.[2] The use of a woman's voice, child's voice, children's chorus, or some combination of the three is significant, since these sounds are the subjectivities most closely associated with otherness and thus most convertible to exotic otherness.[3] As Sherry B. Ortner has famously written, female is to male as nature is to culture.[4] That is, a musical representation of the primal, the elemental, and the natural may well be sounds made by or associated with women.

This lack of cultural and geographical specificity in these sounds is the point; as one composer, Danny Hulsizer of Elias Associates told me, clients don't want the music to refer to a particular culture or place. "World music" to them is music that makes use of sounds from all over the nonwestern world, not music from a particular nonwestern place that is lumped into the term concocted by the music industry, "world music."[5]

The way the ads are composed gives a clue to the genealogy of this sound.

According to Gabrielle Doré, a production manager at Michael Boyd Music in San Francisco, composition of the music for ads usually begins by choosing a tempo (probably for reasons of timing the entire ad). The next step is to listen to a lot of music commercially available to find a sound that seems to fit what the ad is about.[6] This description is seconded by Ann Haugen, an executive producer at Elias Associates, who says that her firm has a huge CD library with which staff members "needle-drop" to find the sounds they're looking for.[7] These sounds can be the rhythm of percussion, the timbre of a particular instrument, or anything that catches the ear of the musicians and producers. After finding sounds that the music people and advertising people can agree on, the music production companies' staff composers make their own music based on the sounds that they heard and selected from recordings. Many of the composers are performers (mostly guitarists, but they all learn how to operate synthesizers) and record the music themselves, sometimes hiring outside musicians. They only sample the sounds that they can't easily make themselves, which include orchestral music.

Given the industry practice of needle-dropping, it isn't difficult to speculate on the kinds of sounds that the advertising musicians are hearing. The rise in the popular realm of what has come to be known as "world music" since the late 1980s has made musics from all over much more widely available than ever before, and much more influential and audible in more mainstream musics. Ann Haugen told me that whatever music is "hot" clients want, and so she frequently receives requests to write music similar to something that is selling well.[8] One audible influence in many of these ads is the Irish singer known as Enya, whose solo voice and synthesized accompaniment have been popular with new age listeners. Enya sings in the Irish language, but to most listeners this is unfamiliar and might as well be nonsense syllables. Another audible influence is the Bulgarian State Radio and Television Female Choir, Le Mystère des Voix Bulgares, which was immensely popular (in world music terms) in the late 1980s and early 1990s and whose sound is still in the ears of many listeners. "Polegnala e Todora," a song from its first album, was recently used in a series of ads for the Audi A6 automobile and generated some interest on Internet newsgroups. Perhaps another sound source is Ennio Morricone's music for the film *The Mission* (1986), which included a chorus singing unintelligible words, a chorus widely heard outside the film on television and radio.

History

In the late 1980s Elias Associates—one of the giants of the industry—let it be known that it was beginning to listen to nonwestern musics, matching the rise of "world music" as a known category in the American and British music industry. According to a trade article that included an interview with Jonathan Elias, he "has begun . . . to focus on modern primitivism, among other things. 'Clients find it new and innovative,' he says."[9] A later feature on Elias Associates discusses the firm's composers as well as Elias himself, "whose major focus seems to be more compositional, orchestral and ethnic work."[10] A recent interviewer noted: "Apparently, [Jonathan Elias] also feels it's important to have an array of different sounds, since scattered throughout the company's spacious Santa Monica offices are a wide variety of international instruments. So, let's say, for example, a spot calls for some Third World drumming. 'What Third World?' he asks. 'I might do something African in one room, something Brazilian in another or something Native American in the third.'"[11]

One of the earliest noticeable uses of world music in an ad, a harbinger of the present trend, was Michael Boyd Music's accompaniment to an ad for Levi's Jeans for Women called "Woman Getting What She Wants" in 1994. This music, according to *Shoot* magazine, "is a mixture of sampling of recording artist Linda Tillery's voice—so-called body-generated percussion sounds—a Javanese gamelan and other percussion sounds."[12] (The gamelan sample, to my ears, consists of less than a dozen notes, however.) According to Boyd himself, "One of the things we were thinking about was how super-graphic and simple the computer animation was and that whatever style of music we used it would be something very arresting and stirring, but simple and stripped down as well. It's not a linear storytelling, western hemisphere-type of attitude. Therefore the music had to create a mood and also catch some of those things in a story, but not so literally."[13]

The ad depicts a wooden female doll figure attempting to find a ball that bounces in a large box of rubber balls. She is apparently having difficulty with this, and when she finally finds one that satisfies her, the Levi's logo flashes on the screen, along with the words "Levi's Jeans for Women." The appearance of this message is accompanied by a splash of a sitar that sounds a bit like Ravi Shankar's trademark opening gesture, a descending scalar passage.

This interest in world music seems to be part of a larger trend in the advertising music industry to bring more live music into the advertising recording studios. Instead of composing all the music with synthesizers, samplers, and drum machines, advertising clients, according to the composer Steve Shafer, "are interested in live organic sounds"; "They want it real," he says.[14] A recent guide to writing jingles by Jeffrey P. Fisher contains a list of studio equipment, all of which is electronic except, predictably, guitars, and almost as predictably these days, "lots of miscellaneous ethnic percussion (cabasa, bells, guiro, tabla, rain stick, tambourine, kalimba, etc.)"[15] Ann Haugen told me that her company is using far more vocals than it once did.[16]

Adiemus

Despite these pioneering efforts by Americans to use nonwestern sounds in their spots, the first ad with something resembling "world music" that received any real recognition outside the industry was a British commercial with music by the British band that later became known as Adiemus.[17] This group got its start with a commission from European Delta Airlines to score a commercial known as "Shadowlands" in 1994. This sixty-second spot features disjointed images: a boy and an old man, perhaps his grandfather, embracing; people hurrying on a city street; priests playing soccer outside a Greek (I think) church; four black men carrying fishing gear; jumping dolphins. A shadow of a fork, then a wine glass, and a ruler eventually come together to form an image of an airplane, just before a real Delta airplane appears. Many of the shots are from above, as though viewers are in a plane looking down. (Another spot with the same music produced by Saatchi and Saatchi in London, "Synchronised Flying," uses some of the same ethereal imagery, though without the travelogue flavor).

The juxtaposition of different images, although seemingly haphazard, nonetheless captures the availability of the many experiences that today's consumers believe they have at their disposal. The premodern world is idealized, with the joyful priests, the African fishermen close to nature. Meanwhile, since many of the shots are from the air, and since this is after all an ad for Delta Airlines, the overall message conveyed is that if you get in a plane, you can have all these things, see all these sights. The only voiceover in the entire ad is at the conclusion: "At Delta, we believe that the best service on earth . . . shouldn't be on earth."

It would be hard to predict what might be the most effective music for such an ad. While music is capable of pulling together the many juxtaposed scenes of the spot, this ability does not of course suggest a particular style for this ad. The Welsh composer, arranger, and conductor Karl Jenkins (who has a background in both rock and classical music) fashioned a sound that seemed to unite in the song "Adiemus" the modern and premodern signi-fieds of these images in its combination of "classical" music and world music, with an overall sound that is neither one nor the other, though clearly highly arranged.

The resulting music was so popular in the Delta ads that it was eventually released as a single, and precipitated the formation of a "band" as something more than an ad hoc assemblage of musicians gathered to record one com-mercial. Based on the success of the single, Adiemus the band ultimately released an album, *Songs of Sanctuary*, in 1995. This quickly sold 100,000 copies in Germany, rising to number 13 on the pop charts there.[18] Interestingly, there was some question about where to position this recording on charts in the UK. The Classical Chart Eligibility Panel met to discuss the album and decided that it wasn't classical and therefore couldn't be listed on the British classical charts. This ruling was appealed by Adiemus's label Venture, part of Virgin, with the support of the London Philharmonic, which appears on the album. The British Phonographic Industry finally changed its mind, and the album entered the chart in the number 3 position, eventually making number 1, where it remained for seven straight weeks.[19] *Songs of Sanctuary* sold roughly 1.5 million copies worldwide, a significant number for almost any kind of music.

Arguments over whether this music is classical point less to the much-discussed blurring of genres in the contemporary moment than increasingly flexible ideas of what can be considered classical music in the music indus-try.[20] Partly as a result of this new openness, world music is becoming in-creasingly classicalized. I discussed this tendency in chapter 6, and will here simply note the ways world music is being repositioned as a connoisseur's music, a music that requires knowledge to understand. It is important to note that the score of *Adiemus I: Songs of Sanctuary* is published by a presti-gious British classical music publisher, Boosey and Hawkes (publishers of Igor Stravinsky and Béla Bartók, among others),[21] and that Karl Jenkins's albums after *Songs of Sanctuary*, *Diamond Music* (1996), *Adiemus 2: Cantata Mundi* (1997), and *Imagined Oceans* (1998), were released by Sony Classical.

Songs of Sanctuary is an amalgam of classical and world music that clearly

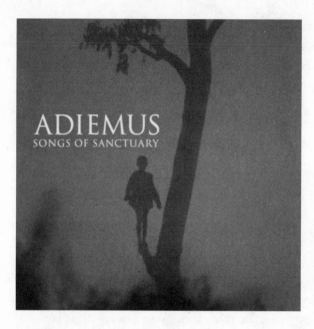

Fig. 3 Adiemus, *Songs of Sanctuary*, cover

represents an extension and elaboration of the "Adiemus" song, and the cover art of the album is in keeping with the sound. The artwork includes photographs that represent the timeless Other and Elsewhere, still down the evolutionary ladder. The album's cover depicts a child standing on a limb in a tree; it is impossible to discern this person's race, age, or gender (figure 3). This photograph is also emblazoned on the CD itself. The photographs inside show a person in a long boat with a pole, and a person wearing a baseball hat and holding on to a bicycle, the only gesture toward modernity in any of the album's photographs (figure 4). Another interior shot shows a similar boat, but this time with a group of people holding their bicycles (figure 5). These photographs seemingly bear no relationship to the music other than their similar lack of specificity to any place, culture, historical moment, or people: They are all timeless Others.

Despite the placeless ambiguity of both the music and the album's imagery, the band's principals nonetheless attempt to ground the music in a tradition, and in particular in ethnicized, racialized subject positions. The lead vocalist, Miriam Stockley, says: "I'm a native of South Africa whose grandparents were Russian Jews, and I combine sounds not really words from Zulu, Xhosa and Yiddish."[22] Karl Jenkins capitalizes even more on this perception of Stockley's authenticity as a South African, even though she is white. In arguing for the "ethnic" or "world" music sounds he wanted, he

Fig. 4 Adiemus, *Songs of Sanctuary*, liner notes photograph

first described them, then said that "Miriam grew up in South Africa and was exposed to these kinds of sound."[23]

Even with this claim to ethnic and racial credibility, the main strategy of Jenkins and the other musicians is to make a kind of timeless, placeless, unidentifiable sound that can stand as the music of the world, or better perhaps, *any* music of the world. This quality is enhanced by the songs' language, which is wholly invented. Jenkins says: "The text in *Adiemus* is written phonetically, with the words viewed as instrumental sound. The human voice is the oldest instrument and by removing the distraction of lyrics, we hope to create a sound that is universal and timeless. The knowledge that Adiemus [the word] has a meaning—'We will draw near'—invokes what I feel to be an appropriate concept of bringing people together." Thus the texts of the selections "actually do not have any meaning," Jenkins says. "They were just strings of sounds to give the album an ethnic feel, but [Stockley] is a professional and she understands how and what to do with the words to put across the feel and the emotions we needed. It turned out beautifully. The string and percussion sections of the orchestra were augmented with the horn section to provide a fuller sound necessary for the cantatas. The ethnic percussion sounds were initially sampled and then performed alongside the orchestra performances by my son Jody."[24] Also, the name of the band was invented, though Jenkins said he found out later there is a similar-sounding

Fig. 5 Adiemus, *Songs of Sanctuary*, liner notes photograph

Latin word that means, as he says above, "we will draw near."[25] The name works the same way: it invokes Latin, the premodern, without actually being Latin, though it turned out to be almost-Latin after all.

Jenkins's approach, like that of many in the world of advertising music, is to construe many kinds of musics in the broadest possible terms, such as "classical" or "world" or "new age," in order to emulate, manipulate, and master them. A feature in the magazine *Keyboard* contained interviews with several leading composers of advertising music in Chicago and included an observation by the interviewer that advertising composers seem to need to be "fluent in almost all musical styles." The composer Larry Peccorella responded by saying, "Definitely. And not just modern styles. One thing we have to be aware of is history. We're called on all the time to recreate things from the past. We often wonder if the new kids coming up are going to be able to do that. When I came up . . . the world wasn't as diverse. We all watched Ed Sullivan with our parents. So I learned who Vic Damone was, or who the Rolling Stones were. But today's kids have grown up with MTV, and they don't seem to know much of what happened before 1980. The point is, we're called upon every day to know these diverse musical styles, and we *really* have to know them."[26]

Sony Music recently introduced a web site that makes it possible for advertising agencies, broadcasters, and others to search its music catalogue by genre, style, and mood. World music is listed as a "genre," of course; the list of "styles" that appears in the pull-down menu contains geographical regions (excluding North America) and "styles" themselves:

Afro-Cuban
Andean Folk
Avant-Garde
Bachata
Big Band
Bolero
CCM [Contemporary Christian Music]
Central Asia
Cha-Cha
Charanga
Christmas
Classical
Country-Pop
Country-Rock
Dance-Pop
Eastern Europe
Ethnic Fusion
Euro-pop
Far East
Flamenco
Folk Songs
Foreign Language Rock
French Pop
Hip-Hop
Indian Pop
Italian Folk
Klezmer
Latin Folk
Latin Jazz
Latin Pop
Mariachi
Mediterranean
Merengue
Norteño

Opera
Orchestral Pop
Progressive Bluegrass
Qawwali
Rock & Roll
Rock en Español
Salsa
Samba
South Asia
Tango
Tejano
Tex-Mex
Third Wave Ska Revival
Traditional Chinese
Tropical
Vocal Pop
Western Europe
World Fusion
Worldbeat
Zouk[27]

Many of the more obscure (or unexpected) "styles" have few recordings associated with them. For example, searching for "Avant-Garde" without inputting a mood results in only Tan Dun's homage to Peking opera, *Bitter Love* (1998). Searching similarly for the style "Classical" results only in *A Nordic Festival* (1991), with Esa-Pekka Salonen conducting the Swedish Radio Symphony Orchestra in compositions by well-known and lesser-known Scandinavian composers.[28] A search for "Country Pop" results in a handful of songs, sung by singers such as Willie Nelson and George Jones, making one wonder what this particular "style" is for; "Country Rock" has a single album, *Poco* (1970), by Poco.

Reducing vast amounts of music to manageably knowable "genres" and "styles" enables musicians in the advertising business to attempt to bring together these different "styles," which for Karl Jenkins was the point of "Adiemus" and then of *Songs of Sanctuary* (example 17). This is how Jenkins describes *Songs of Sanctuary* in the album's liner notes: "Songs of Sanctuary is an extended choral-type work based on the European classical tradition, but where the vocal sound is more akin to 'Ethnic' or 'World' music. . . . We

Ex. 17 Adiemus, "Adiemus," opening

wanted the choruses to sound 'Tribal,' therefore Miriam [Stockley] and Mary
Carewe, who also sang on those sections, were required to sing fortissimo
and without vibrato. If you listen to most ethnic music (African, Maori, etc)
this is a feature of the genre."[29]

Clients think in the same terms. Adiemus's lead vocalist, Stockley, re-
counts the sound of the song "Adiemus," using language that would strike
most in academia as fairly shocking: "The advertising agency liked the lead
vocal but wanted much more of an 'African/child like' approach. So I suggested bringing in Mary Carewe, who has a much brighter younger sound
to sing with me in the choruses."[30]

The music of the song "Adiemus" used in the Delta Airlines spots, part
of which appears in the excerpt that I have reproduced, is quintessential advertising "world music": it employs many sequences (as in measures 5–6),
women's and children's voices only, and modal melodies. Since the lyrics consist solely of nonsense syllables I have not included them with the musical
notation (though it is interesting to note that the Boosey and Hawkes published version, from which my example is adapted, includes the syllables;
and several enterprising fans have posted their phonetic transcriptions of the
lyrics on the Internet as well).

Unusually in the world of advertising music, this piece continued to be
used in Delta spots even after Delta moved its account from Abbott Mead
Vickers/BBDO to Saatchi and Saatchi in New York City in 1997. A new series
employing this music called "Individuals," released in 1997 and produced by

Saatchi and Saatchi, was voted number 1 in *Shoot* magazine's Summer Top 10 Spots.[31] "Individuals" depicts different scenes of passengers alone in a huge airplane cabin, being served in various ways by an army of impeccable flight attendants. For a time this music was practically Delta's theme song; it became so closely associated with Delta that I heard the music played on a Delta flight as we were boarding (as we "deplaned" we heard a Mozart piano concerto). The letter from Saatchi and Saatchi accompanying the videotape of their ads says that "the Adiemus music is now considered a strong brand equity of Delta's."[32]

Adiemus and its music raise most of the theoretical issues that I hope to address in this chapter, though I will note only one here, which concerns the sound of spirituality in its music. This music's signification of a vague kind of spirituality or mysticism is in keeping with the clear mission of most of the ads of taking viewers away from the here and now and toward an exoticized elsewhere. In this the ads echo centuries of western notions of other places as spiritual, in contrast to the modern West. Little of this advertising music has been discussed in any great detail on the Internet, beyond questions of authorship and identification, and so it is difficult to get a sense of how listeners are hearing it. Adiemus, however, unlike most advertising musicians, has a dedicated following outside the realm of advertising, and so some fan reactions are known. One woman fan wrote in to another band's mailing list in January 1999, saying, "i only have 'songs of sanctuary' so far . . . its like someone took out my soul and made a cd out of it."

Fans weren't the only ones to receive a message of spirituality. An article in *Shoot* magazine discussing "Individuals," the spot produced by Saatchi and Saatchi that reused the music of Adiemus, also mentioned the spiritual quality of the imagery and music:

> If cleanliness is next to Godliness, then good service is downright divine. . . .
>
> The spots, with an ethereal soft-focus touch, evoke a mythic space where service on Delta's business class is seemingly provided by the Gods themselves, and passengers are treated like kings. . . .
>
> How better to score such a scene than by providing a backdrop of angels.[33]

Adiemus's composer Karl Jenkins has himself acknowledged that fans find spirituality in his music: "I write music that connects with a lot of people and gives them, they say, some spiritual solace."[34] This is the level of affect. But what about audiences? To whom are these sounds directed? With the next examples, I will begin to pursue this question.

Michael Boyd Music

Michael Boyd Music, based in San Francisco, provided music for the "Wings" ad for Chrysler automobiles in 1999 that "has an Indian feel to it," according to Andrea Marcaccio of Bozell Worldwide in Southfield, Michigan, the agency that produced the ad.[35] She is referring, I think, to both the opening drone on an octave with a perfect fifth up from the bottom, a sound that for at least a couple of centuries has signified "rustic" or "primitive" to western listeners.[36] This drone is followed by a woman's voice singing nonsense syllables to a modal melody. Drums then enter, followed, unusually in this genre, by a rock rhythm section. Also unusual is the entry of a male voice near the end, singing more nonsense syllables in duet with the woman singer. While the music is credited to Michael Boyd Music, Gabrielle Doré of the firm told me that it was the firm's house band, Mox, that performed it. Mox includes Michael Boyd himself and released three albums, the last of which, *Mox*, includes a good deal of music that sounds as though "Wings" would be right at home among it. The CD cellophane bears a sticker on the front: "Instrumental Pop for a shrinking world. A wicked stylish mix of classic electric guitars, ambient electronics, world beats and tasty samples."[37]

The "Wings" ad shows the cars being driven, with no sign of any drivers, a common tactic in automobile ads. These images convey a sense of freedom from the vicissitudes of everyday life: Bozell's title "Wings" probably refers to the opening shots of a kite that looks like a butterfly; real monarch butterflies then appear, flying in the sun. Chrysler's press release says that "the three new Concorde ads further develop the concept of 'ideas in flight' from the Chrysler brand spot, 'Wings,' and captures the youthful elegance of the Chrysler Concorde by highlighting the vehicle's distinctive design, performance, roominess and value."[38] Scenes of Daimler-Chrysler's finest are interspersed with flying birds and airplanes. As in the Delta "Shadowlands" spot, many shots are taken from the air, which imparts a feeling of freedom, buoyancy, and loftiness. One shot shows a car parked in front of a large, grand house; two other scenes show what could be buildings on an Italian estate. Shots of statues flit through; a man paints on a large canvas. And lest the European flavor offend customers who might need to be reassured to buy American after the merger of Daimler-Benz and Chrysler, one of the statues looks a good deal like the Statue of Liberty. Taken as a whole, the images clearly convey the idea of high culture. Not coincidentally, these Chryslers were expensive: the manufacturer's suggested retail prices on the seven models depicted in "Wings" ranged from $20,290 to $34,815: this was Chrysler's high end at the time the ad appeared.

The ad's visuals would not seem to require an accompaniment of Mox's brand of world music. If anything, given the high-culture, European imagery of the ads, classical music would seem to convey best the idea of class, old money, and haut bourgeois superiority. Two points are important. One is the classicalization of world music, with advertisers attempting to reach the desirable high-end market for world music; the other is the explicit linkage, both in the ads for Delta and in these for Chrysler automobiles, of world music with high culture. The increasing classicalization of world music has meant that it is more and more closely associated with high culture, a kind of classical music of the globe, of the global, informational, transnational moment. The ads are saying not only that knowledge about the world is important, but that this kind of knowledge is what matters most—it's the way to get ahead in today's global economy.

Despite the elevation of world music into a kind of high culture, a connoisseur's music, its mode of signification is somewhat different from classical music's. In the context of advertising, marketing, and consumption, classical music signifies old money, Old World, heritage, and prestige.

Danny Hulsizer and Elias Associates

Danny Hulsizer, a composer at Elias Associates in Santa Monica, provided music for three ads for Royal Caribbean Cruise Lines produced by McKinney and Silver, an advertising agency based in Raleigh. The spot entitled "Fling" features images from an ideal tropical cruise and depicts an authentic tourist experience. The tourists in question are a beautiful young African American couple—yuppies, judging by their hairstyles and clothes. The first scene shows them riding bicycles on a deserted, unpaved road lined with palm trees. In the next they are riding horses on the beach, again without any other tourists (or locals for that matter). Then they are swimming in a lovely natural pool into which a high waterfall cascades; later they are snorkeling with beautiful tropical fishes. The final shot is of the couple knee-deep in the sea, with a Royal Caribbean ship in the background. They are the only people in the entire ad, as if they have the cruise ship and its ports of call to themselves. This idea of the personal, private cruise in which authentic places are seen and authentic experiences had is emphasized in another Royal Caribbean spot, this one suggestively entitled "Spices," in which another beautiful young couple (white this time) finds its way through the woods and "happens" upon a native (i.e., black) ritual with drumming men wearing shorts and T-shirts.

Both these ads for Royal Caribbean (and a third called "First Date") feature music composed by Hulsizer. Ann Haugen of Elias Associates told me that the music for "Fling" was supposed to sound "native" and "tribal," and make use of "drum stuff."[39] Hulsizer's music for "Fling" starts with a drone on a perfect fifth (as did Michael Boyd Music's music for "Wings" for Chrysler), followed by the usual woman's voice with no or unintelligible words, and finally some "miscellaneous ethnic percussion," as Jeffrey P. Fisher would have it.[40] Added to this are synthesized sounds that contribute to the affect of the spot.

Earlier, in 1996, the San Francisco firm of Publicis and Hal Riney produced several ads for Sprint PCS, the long-distance telephone company. These all had a similar theme: that in the premodern era, communication over long distances was difficult, cumbersome, inefficient, requiring a lot of people and effort. So the spot called "Romans" shows many Roman soldiers lighting bonfires to communicate by smoke; "Incas" shows Incas running up and down the Andes; and "Egyptians" shows people on the Nile using birds to relay messages. It is "Egyptians" that I want to examine, because its music comes closest to this genre that I am focusing on, the untexted-female-voice-and-assorted-"world"-instruments genre, once again composed by Danny Hulsizer.

The music starts with something that sounds like an Armenian duduk, best known to western listeners through Peter Gabriel's music for Martin Scorsese's film *The Last Temptation of Christ*, released as *Passion: Music for "The Last Temptation of Christ"*; the original source material, that Gabriel sampled for his music, was released as *Passion: Sources*. There is also a Native American flute, an Indian tabla (along with other drums), and the ubiquitous woman's voice singing nonsense syllables. "Egyptians" features the imagery just described, with a voiceover by a suave, deep, British male voice:

In 2,700 BC, along the fertile valley of the River Nile, nobility of the fourth Egyptian dynasty domesticated birds . . . and used them to dispatch information swiftly across the far reaches of their advanced civilization. It's information that has carried nearly 5,000 years: a simple truth that bridges our past and our future: that a culture is defined by how well its people connect.

Introducing the connection for our time: Sprint PCS. The replacement for cellular is here.

This copy, combining history (or "history") and serious-sounding music, effectively emphasizes the distance that civilization is thought to have covered with communication technology, and the importance of worldwide communication today.

THE INFORMATION AGE, GLOBALIZATION, AND POST-TOURISM

Faux world music as a symptom of the importance of global informational capital needs to be understood in part by examining the recent emphasis in the business world on globalization, and more generally on discourses of globalization in the public domain. While the idea of the voyage, of escaping the ordinary, is not new in the realm of mass consumption in western European history, today's discourses of globalization, transnationalism, multiculturalism, and diversity are comparatively recent developments. One would have to be far out of the loop of contemporary American culture not to have been told that everyone now lives in an information economy or an information age or a global economy. And so consumers are constantly bombarded with ads in all media for a faster computer that can "multitask"; a pager that takes messages; a cellular phone whose signal travels further; a PDA (personal digital assistant) that can connect to the computer and the Internet—anything to be in control of the information that threatens to become overwhelming as people travel further, faster, and more frequently.

Globalization and Business

Even though most people know that the business world has been talking about globalization for some time, business discourse on the subject has scarcely been examined by scholars of globalization.

In this Global Information Age, the problem for business has been to find ways of selling their products further and further afield; the problem for businesspeople is to learn more and more about these places. Many businesses today cultivate an approach labeled "multinational multiculturalism," popularized by Percy Barnevik, the Swedish founder of ASEA Brown Boveri

(ABB, a manufacturer of heavy-industrial products), that advocated adaptation to whatever markets the company cultivated; Barnevik himself calls his company "multidomestic." As one ABB executive stated, "We are not a global business. We are a collection of local businesses with intense global coordination."[41] Barnevik is lionized in an influential, award-winning book that purports to cut through management gurus' smoke and mirrors — *The Witch Doctors* by John Micklethwait and Adrian Wooldridge — that includes an entire chapter on globalization. "Of all the words in the management gurus' lexicon, none is used with quite so much relish as 'globalization.' Go into the business section of any bookstore and you will see the word emblazoned on almost every other book; talk to the chairman of any big company and before long, you will find that it starts dominating the conversation. Globalization — and how to deal with it — is now the leading concern (some would say the raison d'être) of nearly every big multinational company."[42] The authors of *The New Portable MBA* write in its concluding chapter, "Leadership for the Year 2000," that "future leaders will have to be well schooled in foreign markets, geopolitical forces, global economics, and local cultures to manage overseas operations and to negotiate deals and joint ventures with foreigners"; they continue by admonishing readers that "we have to develop a transnational vision for our organization while at the same time appreciating the many and critical nuances of each geographic market even though we may only partially understand them."[43]

Tom Peters, another popular and influential writer on management, includes an anecdote in his *Liberation Management* that emphasizes how regional differences can affect business transactions in the United States, and he uses this anecdote to instruct the reader that "Appreciation of the fact that regional differences in the U.S. are as important as income or age variations has *begun* to affect everything from product design to advertising strategy among leading companies. . . . Such concerns explode, of course, when national borders are crossed, whether Canada's or Japan's."[44]

In these and other writings, Percy Barnevik is either mentioned specifically or, as in Peters's book, discussed extensively (and in fact Barnevik is one of the book's dedicatees). The idea of "multinational multiculturalism," whether or not it can be neatly traced to Barnevik, is clearly becoming an important, perhaps even defining, strategy of European and American businesses.[45] More generally, somehow grappling with the new informational and global economy has become a crucial task for business.[46]

Global Informational Capital and Social Élites

Business is changing, businesspeople are changing, marketers are changing, and so of course are consumers. But even though businesses are increasingly cultivating a "multinational multicultural" approach, this does not mean that all consumers are interpellated in the same ways. The term "interpellation," as is well known, is from Louis Althusser's influential work on ideology and refers to the ways that ideology constitutes subjects by interpellating, or hailing, them.[47] Indeed, marketers know how to reach consumers. As Roy Gattinella, vice president of sales and marketing for EMI Entertainment Properties in Los Angeles, says in a recent interview about marketers releasing promotional compact discs, "More than anything else, music allows marketers to target demographics with absolutely bulls-eye precision, because there are just so many forms of it and so many artists,"[48] a comment echoing Pierre Bourdieu's observation that music is the best classifier of taste.[49]

These fabricated world musics are part of a newer kind of cultural and educational capital that I will call, drawing on Bourdieu's influential work, global informational capital: distinction, knowledge, and the ability to travel, learn, and discriminate.[50] This in itself isn't a new development: the European upper classes have for quite some time acquired objects from other cultures to display their wealth and worldliness. More recently, the advent of mass consumption as we now know it was accompanied by a hodgepodge of exotic artifacts—the "chaotic-exotic style" discussed in chapter 3—intended to entice people into department stores and make purchases.[51]

Today's emphasis on representations and icons of otherness has come about for different reasons. Familiarity with world music isn't needed only for reasons of prestige, but rather signifies the kind of capital that one needs to get ahead in today's world; the concocted world music that one hears in today's ads is the soundtrack for the global information age. To get ahead today, one needs to know something about the world. This position is signified in the ads by the use of music that isn't really "world music" in the music-industry sense—that is, music made by people from outside the West—but is nonetheless music that signifies world music and thus the global, which is what matters in the context of the ads. An example of this is that during a recent layover at Heathrow Airport, I spotted the *Dictionary of Global Culture* by Kwame Anthony Appiah, Michael Colin Vazquez, and Henry Louis Gates Jr. for sale in a bookstore, in the business section.

Information is an important part of the equation, as shown in the Sprint ads, which are symptoms of the increasingly intertwined nature of this global era and information age. Manuel Castells says of this complex intertwining that today's economy can be called informational "because the productivity and competitiveness of units or agents in this economy . . . fundamentally depend upon their capacity to generate, process, and apply efficiently knowledge-based information." It is global, he says, "because the core activities of production, consumption, and circulation, as well as their components . . . are organized on a global scale. . . . It is informational *and* global because, under the new historical conditions, productivity is generated through and competition is played out in a global network of interaction."[52] Hence I use the term global informational capital to describe the kinds of ideologies in which these ads and their music are caught up.

It is important to point out here the distinction I am making between "real" knowledges, knowledges of specific places and peoples, and what I am calling global informational capital, which symbolizes a broad knowledge of and experience of the world without actually being knowledge itself. It is a form of capital in the sense that it is associated with, and convertible into, prestige. Just as the advertising world musics that I have been studying aren't traceable to any particular nonwestern place or places but nonetheless symbolize "world music," global informational capital isn't knowledge of a real place or places but stands in for that knowledge.

The global informational capital I am theorizing is associated with certain highly placed social groups, even though it is theoretically available to anyone. Manuel Castells writes of changes in social class wrought by the Information Age, arguing that there has been a split between information producers and replaceable generic labor.[53] Castells resists naming the élite group that he mentions, though it has been called "information users" by some researchers[54] and a new "transnational corporate class" by another;[55] politicians and popular press accounts make more simplified arguments about the growing gap between the "information rich" and the "information poor," and some scholars prefer the term "cosmopolitan."[56] Whatever one labels this group, I would argue that it is less a new social class than a familiar élite class advocating and acquiring a new kind of capital, which is why I have chosen to discuss global informational capital here rather than theorizing a new social group or class.

Yet it is still possible to talk about new modes of subjectivity in this context. The pressures for keeping on top of information flows, of being in near constant communication with colleagues, friends, and family, has become seen by many as a necessity. This progression from luxury to necessity is seen frequently with successful technologies, whether radio, automobile, cellular phone, or personal computer: at first they are expensive and difficult to use, but as prices come down and as technologies develop social lives, they become increasingly seen not as fads or gimmicks but as necessities of life.[57] More than necessities, however, these and other technologies shape everyday life, shape consciousness, shape experience, shape even subjectivity.

And new technologies can change what is thought to be important to know. Knowledge of the world is fast becoming the most important prerequisite for success in business, an idea that is registered and refracted in many domains of contemporary life. But this success in business is aimed at, and achieved by, a particular high social group, not everyone. According to Juliana Koranteng in *Advertising Age*, Delta Airlines aimed its "Shadowlands" ad campaign at business flyers: "the idea was to communicate to rational, but cynical, business fliers Delta's vast size as an enterprise, the human side to its high-quality services, plus the never-ending excitement of flying." The campaign worked: it boosted business and first-class cabin sales; Delta's European revenues rose $600 million less than two years after the campaign's launch.[58]

Saatchi and Saatchi has continued this business-class focus in its "Individuals" spot and in others for Delta that use Adiemus's music. The message of "Individuals" seems to be that while everyone lives in a global economy, only a few have the necessary global informational capital—and economic capital—to cope with it. And coping means being able to retain historical haut bourgeois ideals such as that of the the autonomous individual. Saatchi and Saatchi, with the music of Adiemus, is saying that business passengers don't need to be bothered with the outside world except to the extent that they require global informational capital for business—they're busy wrapped up in their own minds and worlds as "Individuals." The lack of social interaction, except by those serving the passenger, conflates the conception of the modern bourgeois subject with privacy, also noticeable in the rise in recent years of gated communities and other retreats from public spaces.

Post-Tourism and the Post-Tourist

I have been talking about social élites, but it is clear that this new cultural dominant, suffused with icons and representations of otherness, is not simply inhabited and navigated by élite groups, though as I have been saying, they are able to make the most of it and place the most emphasis on what I have termed global informational capital. Building on the discussion of tourism in chapter 4, I want to talk in more general terms about this cultural dominant by employing the notions of post-tourism and the post-tourist, an idea that originated with Maxine Feifer and is fruitfully explored by Scott Lash and John Urry. They write that the current moment can be thought of (among other things) as the era of "the end of tourism," or even "post-tourism."[59]

While images and sounds of the "exotic" have long fascinated people in western culture, whether "Turkish" music in Vienna in the eighteenth century, the "chaotic exotic" in France in the late nineteenth century and the early twentieth, the "exotica" music of Les Baxter and Martin Denny in America after the Second World War, or today's world music, what is different today is that in some sense, according to Feifer and to Lash and Urry is that everyone is in some sense a (post)tourist: there is very little in the world that is not accessible, whether in person or in commodity form. A touch of the exotic as local çolor, as decoration, or as chaotic-exotic is giving way to a more pervasive series of representations and icons of otherness as a cultural dominant, not simply as an occasional style. This accessibility is one way of grasping one of the concrete effects of the global informational economy.

Employing the literature of post-tourism isn't just an abstract theoretical application, for it is striking how many ads that employ similar kinds of "world music" evoke the idea of travel, of seeing other peoples and escaping the ordinary. (One of the ads I have not examined here, which features the same kind of music, is for the Arts and Entertainment network (A&E), whose motto is "A&E: Escape the Ordinary.") This pervasive world music is not simply a feature of these ads, but an older phenomenon newly configured in this historical moment.

For Lash and Urry, tourism does not simply register changes in socio-politico-economic realities but is a useful lens through which to understand these changes. For them, the contemporary moment is one in which tourism has lost specificity, and thus structures and even dominates contemporary social and cultural experience. "People are tourists most of the time," they write, "whether they are literally mobile or only experience simulated mobility through the incredible fluidity of multiple signs and electronic images."[60]

This does not mean that people are no longer tourists as they were in earlier eras; I would be reluctant to adopt the periodizing aspect of a "post-tourism" formulation that does not allow for tourism in older senses. Post-tourism is one available mode of tourism, not a successor to earlier ones. There are, after all, still old-fashioned guidebooks, both for places and for musics. For example, *World Music: The Rough Guide* was the first of the Rough Guide series to cover music; previously, it had only included travel guides. Currently in its second edition, the world music guide is the longest of all the guides except the one on rock. That this book was first published by a company specializing in guides for tourists says much about the present: the interest in world music arose at roughly the same time as discourses of globalization and transnationalism, when everyone (at least in the West) is in some sense a "post-tourist." But some post-tourists are more fortunate than others, have a greater quantity of old-fashioned capital than others, and are thus in a position to accumulate more global informational capital than others.

Ours is an era, Lash and Urry write, in which practically anything can be manufactured—including, as is evident here, world music. And "these processes appear homogenizing, reducing differences between places through the proliferation of essentially the same signs and images," as we have seen with respect to this advertising music.[61]

These arguments help clarify the use of culturally nonspecific musics and nonlanguage syllables. They are a kind of a metonym for "the world," with listeners understanding that they are exchanging this for a more particular experience of real music from a certain people, place, and culture, which would require a good deal of time, energy, and work. Also, while some theorists of cosmopolitanism such as Urry have argued that tourism includes a certain risk—to try the unfamiliar, to go someplace new—these sounds obviate those risks for those who don't want to, or don't have the opportunity, to take them.

Celia Lury has written of how various kinds of tourist objects are packaged as "friendly" or "fun"—that is, nonthreatening.[62] But another strategy is the one used in the ads. Fans who like this music do not risk being accused of neocolonialism, neoimperialism, racism, or other -isms, because the music doesn't come from hegemonized places, even as it seems to refer to such places. This music is safe to like, because if you're afraid of visiting the peoples and places with which this music is associated, you are far from them, whether riding in business class or in an expensive automobile, or simply sitting in front of the television set. And it requires no specialized, "real" knowledge on the part of the listener, since the music does not come from a particular place or people.

Even though much of the foregoing developments are new, and provide the most useful lens through which to view the ads and their music, it is necessary to reiterate how they still engage with older western narratives of travel and escaping the ordinary. The desire for the journey, the voyage, the encounter with the Other, has not dissipated in the era of post-tourism; in fact it may seem heightened, even as tourists of all kinds understand that it is increasingly difficult to accomplish as the "Other" seems to become more and more like "us."

I acknowledge that I seem to be sidestepping what some would argue is the most salient theoretical framework for the ads: consumption. There is no straight line, however, between advertising and consumption. Recent theorists of contemporary culture such as Jean Baudrillard are right, I think, in arguing that lifestyle choices are playing a more important role than ever before, and that's what these advertisements are selling as much as a particular commodity.[63]

But signs and lifestyle choices depicted in an ad do not mean that everyone has equal access to them. I am mainly interested in for whom these advertisements were produced, and what this targeting tells us about this historical moment. In other words, what are these lifestyles, who has access to them, and what can we learn from them? As we have seen, the ads were clearly aimed at those who could afford the commodities being sold. Familiar, historical social groupings such as social class may be less stable with the proliferation of signs and the rise of sign-value that Baudrillard writes of, but they are not gone.

Although many have argued that the contemporary moment is now global, or "post-Fordist" or "post-tourist" or "postmodern" or "postindustrial" or post-whatever, it is nonetheless true that those flows that everyone has been theorizing for over a decade now are themselves caught up in flows: there are different kinds of tourists, different modes of travel and tourism, and different kinds of touristed sites. To argue, as Lash and Urry do, that the contemporary moment is marked by the "end of tourism" ignores the simultaneity of different modes of travel, tourism, and consumption in operation today.

The commercials that I have been discussing are no different. They betray a number of diverse, and sometimes conflicting and contradictory, attitudes about the contemporary world. Authenticity, far from being a quality no longer sought or discussed in disparaging or ironic terms, is still significant, as Miriam Stockley and Karl Jenkins of Adiemus demonstrate. Royal Caribbean Cruise Lines is still trying to sell voyages that take those fortunate enough to be able to afford them into remote places where "natives" behave as they always have, even though their "ritual" looks staged. Delta Airlines still proffers the modern bourgeois individual subject to élites.

And yet, the kinds of skills and knowledge available today do seem to have changed. Lash and Urry argue for a form of aesthetic cosmopolitanism, in which everyone has some interaction with cultural forms from elsewhere, but I am arguing that aesthetic cosmopolitanism exists as a crucial new kind of global informational capital associated with élite social groups, a kind of comfortable experience of the world. As such, it isn't available to everyone, who must instead settle for Dick Hebdige's "mundane cosmopolitanism,"[64] or—perhaps a better term in this context—what one could call "armchair cosmopolitanism"—much cheaper and thus more pervasive. The sounds—musical and syllabic—in these ads signal to viewers that even though the world seems smaller, it is still as unknowable in any real or total way as it has always been, and therefore those who have the opportunity to participate in it can have a leg up on the rest. "World music" as a kind of empty sonic signifier is thus linked with business-class travel, expensive automobiles, and cruises on which there are no other tourists.

SELVES/OTHERS, HISTORY, AND CULTURE

Much of this book has been about the changing conceptions of otherness held by Europeans and Americans, how these have been implicated in western notions of selfhood, and how these conceptions have left traces in music, sometimes overt, sometimes less so. "Exoticism," as I wrote in the Introduction, was too messy and vague a term to cover the extremely complex and numerous ways that these (not to mention many other) ideologies shape the production and consumption of music.

Much of the problem is that "exoticism" is a stylistic label; it does not explain anything in and of itself. Instead, it obscures. Calling a work, or a trend, or an oeuvre "exotic" can impede the deeper historical, cultural, and social analysis that I have been calling for in the preceding pages. Style labels such as "exoticism" stand in for more complex, and accurate, answers to the questions posed by the major theorists—Weber, Foucault, Williams—in the Introduction, which can be simply summed up: Why is this piece the way it is? Relying on the exoticism label also creates music(ologic)al commonalities where none may exist by putting composers whose works are quite distinct from a social, cultural, and historical perspective into the same narrow stylistic box. Style can tell us much of value, but it is time, at the very least, to question our obeisance to it. It has become a fetish, as works themselves have become, standing in for approaches to music that can help us understand it as part of the workings of culture and history.

And relying on style labels such as "exoticism" masks just how quickly things can change. If modernity, as Anthony Giddens has vividly written, is a juggernaut, it shows no sign of slowing down.[1] All that is solid is melting into air at an ever-increasing pace: representations that might once have seemed stable are destabilized, reused, recombined. Ideologies questioned can nonetheless resurface in another guise, endlessly recycled in the proliferation of cultural commodities.

It is one thing to know all this intellectually, but quite another when a phenomenon such as music and globalization that one has been studying for many years turns out to have been less stable than any of us thought. After the publication of my *Global Pop: World Music, World Markets* in 1997, I realized with some alarm just how quickly the musical landscape could change, as we saw with the example of the authenticizing of hybridity in chapter 5.

The fact that things change is, one would think, elementary, yet it is striking just how little historicizing work gets done, as though "exoticism" or "globalization" or "identity" or what have you is a fixed entity without a history. One of the points I would like to reiterate isn't so much about the content of the foregoing, but this book's underlying arguments concerning contemporary academic work. Although this book is organized as a loosely chronologized series of case studies, I hope that readers find in these cases a deep engagement with historical views of culture and society, and the social and cultural views of history, as a way of facilitating further conversations on the issues contained here.

Admittedly, the culture concept has become embattled lately, having escaped its anthropological usages to find footing in everyday discourse. But this doesn't mean that the anthropological concept is no longer useful, that peoples are no longer organized into groups with systems of symbols and communication. "For it is still the case," Clifford Geertz writes, "that no one lives in the world in general."[2] People live in cultures as the products—and makers—of history.

The engagement with social and cultural views of history and historical views of society and culture drives every chapter of this book. Chapter 1, for example, while participating in an old discussion about the rise of tonality (and secondarily, opera) nonetheless attempted to ask historical and cultural questions about the rise of tonality, not only technical ones. What were the cultural and historical and social circumstances of the rise of this particular musical system, instead of another one? My answer was to situate tonality in discourses and ideologies of the "discovery" of the New World, which for many Europeans necessitated representational systems that allowed them to manage a world in which they placed themselves at the center, and others at various peripheries.

Chapter 2 continued this interest in selfhood and otherness, two notions which found their way into musical sound, conventionalized in ways that audiences could understand. These kinds of representations, which might have had a surface value of titillating audiences with a soupçon of the illicit Other, also served practical purposes for composers by facilitating melodic, harmonic, and rhythmic innovations. Representations of otherness in music in this period were in effect akin to the colonial exploitation of natural resources, advancing musical innovation and what was increasingly becoming the composer's stock-in-trade, his originality.

This was no less true for the musicians discussed in chapter 3, though the rise of the culture concept gave musicians such as Henry Cowell a way to conceive a world in which the modern western subject was no longer at the center of the universe but on an equal footing with peoples from other cultures. In the hands of musicians such as Cowell, modern western selfhood might have been compromised, but it also permitted one to view Others as selves at the same time.

The rate of change accelerated rapidly with the rise of mass media technologies: radio and later sound film in the 1920s, followed by television in the late 1940s. Old modes of apprehending Others and representing them weren't jettisoned but found themselves reused, recycled, and updated. The Boasian culture concept got a facelift with multiculturalism. Now the Other could be considered less of a threat but just as profitable as ever, perhaps more so under rubrics of, for example, "collaboration" that permit nonwestern musicians to be on the same stage as western stars, though not nearly as well paid. Style and genre boundaries such as "country" and "world music," the subject of chapter 6, became increasingly fixed by the music industry in an attempt to maintain control over the proliferation of new sounds and new musics, which themselves continue to change as musicians fulfill their obligation in a consumer culture of producing something newer, faster, sooner, and as fans construct meanings through membership in little cultures that value one increasingly narrowly defined subgenre over others.[3]

And then there is advertising. My recent work on music and advertising has colored my take on chapter 7: I now find it difficult not to view contemporary American culture as consumerized through and through, making the advertising industry perhaps the most important and influential of all the sectors of the culture industry, helping to promulgate and solidify yet another form of selfhood as the consumer.

This gives me pause, as it has many others. I am not ready to follow the Adornian route and assume that everyone is an automaton fulfilling a role scripted by the culture industry—I am still an avowed Birmingham Schooler, though in the dynamic way I discussed in *Strange Sounds*.[4] Yet it is clear that ever-greater attention is required of those who study the workings of culture and history and how they leave traces in forms such as music.

So let me conclude with a plea, for the stakes have never been higher if we are going to understand our world and attempt to leave it for the better. History and culture must be put into dialogue with one another. Past and present must be put into dialogue with one another. As the slide toward theo-fascism in America continues, it is ever more important to go beyond the text and reclaim the social, the cultural, and the historical. Why were things the way they were? Why are things the way they are?

Notes

INTRODUCTION: BEYOND EXOTICISM

1. Some of these recent works include Jonathan Bellman, ed., *The Exotic in Western Music* (Boston: Northeastern University Press, 1998); Georgina Born and David Hesmondhalgh, eds., *Western Music and Its Others: Difference, Representation, and Appropriation in Music* (Berkeley: University of California Press, 2000); Yayoi Uno Everett and Frederick Lau, eds., *Locating East Asia in Western Art Music* (Middletown, Conn.: Wesleyan University Press, 2004); and Glenn Watkins, *Pyramids at the Louvre: Music, Culture, and Collage from Stravinsky to the Postmodernists* (Cambridge: Belknap Press of Harvard University Press, 1994). And many recent articles, including Philip Brett, "Eros and Orientalism in Britten's Operas," *Queering the Pitch: The New Gay and Lesbian Musicology*, ed. Philip Brett, Elizabeth Wood, and Gary C. Thomas (New York: Routledge, 1994); Victor Anand Coelho, "Kapsberger's *Apotheosis* . . . of Francis Xavier (1622) and the Conquering of India," *The Work of Opera: Genre, Nationhood, and Sexual Difference*, ed. Richard Dellamora and Daniel Fischlin (New York: Columbia University Press, 1997); Ralph Locke, "Constructing the Oriental 'Other': Saint-Saëns's *Samson et Dalila*," *The Work of Opera*; Locke, "Exoticism and Orientalism in Music: Problems for the Worldly Critic," *Edward Said and the Work of the Critic: Speaking Truth to Power*, ed. Paul Bové (Durham: Duke University Press, 2000); and Paul Robinson, "Is *Aida* an Orientalist Opera?," *Cambridge Opera Journal* 5 (July 1993): 133–40.
2. Ralph P. Locke, "Exoticism," *Grove Music Online*, ed. L. Macy (visited 22 August 2005), http://www.grovemusic.com.
3. On genius, a favorite source is Christine Battersby, *Gender and Genius: Towards a Feminist Aesthetics* (Bloomington: Indiana University Press, 1989). For a musicological account see Edward Lowinsky, "Musical Genius: Evolution and Origins of a Concept," *Musical Quarterly* 50 (July 1964): 321–40, and "Musical Genius: Evolution and Origins of a Concept, II," *Musical Quarterly* 50 (October 1964): 476–95.

4. Raymond Williams, "Base and Superstructure in Marxist Cultural Theory," *Problems in Materialism and Culture* (London: Verso, 1980), 47.

5. Much of Greenblatt's work makes his debt to Geertz explicit. For a recent homage see Greenblatt's "The Touch of the Real," *The Fate of Culture: Geertz and Beyond*, ed. Sherry B. Ortner (Berkeley: University of California Press, 1999).

6. Max Weber, *The Methodology of the Social Sciences*, 72, as quoted by Anthony Giddens, *Capitalism and Modern Social Theory: An Analysis of the Writings of Marx, Durkheim and Max Weber* (Cambridge: Cambridge University Press, 1971), 138.

7. Michel Foucault, *The Archaeology of Knowledge*, trans. A. M. Sheridan Smith (New York: Pantheon, 1972), 27.

8. Richard Leppert and Susan McClary, eds., *Music and Society: The Politics of Composition, Performance, and Reception* (Cambridge: Cambridge University Press, 1987); Jacques Attali, *Noise: The Political Economy of Music*, trans. Brian Massumi (Minneapolis: University of Minnesota Press, 1985); Rose Rosengard Subotnik, *Developing Variations: Style and Ideology in Western Music* (Minneapolis: University of Minnesota Press, 1991); Susan McClary, *Feminine Endings: Music, Gender, and Sexuality* (Minneapolis: University of Minnesota Press, 1991); Simon Frith, *Sound Effects: Youth, Leisure, Politics and Rock 'n' Roll* (London: Constable, 1983); and Robert Walser, *Running with the Devil: Power, Gender, and Madness in Heavy Metal Music* (Middletown, Conn.: Wesleyan University Press, 1993).

9. See Lawrence Grossberg, "Toward a Genealogy of the State of Cultural Studies: The Discipline of Communication and the Reception of Cultural Studies in the United States," *Disciplinarity and Dissent in Cultural Studies*, ed. Cary Nelson and Dilip P. Gaonkar (New York: Routledge, 1996), for a similar point about cultural studies.

10. Born and Hesmondhalgh, "Introduction: On Difference, Representation, and Appropriation in Music," *Western Music and Its Others*, ed. Born and Hesmondhalgh, 39.

11. Born and Hesmondhalgh, Introduction, *Western Music and Its Others*, ed. Born and Hesmondhalgh, 16.

12. See Veit Erlmann, *Music, Modernity, and the Global Imagination: South Africa and the West* (New York: Oxford University Press, 1999); and Ronald Radano, *Lying Up a Nation: Race and Black Music* (Chicago: University of Chicago Press, 2003).

13. Steven Feld, "Notes on 'World Beat,'" *Music Grooves: Essays and Dialogues*, by Charles Keil and Steven Feld (Chicago: University of Chicago Press, 1994). Feld has continued work in this area in many subsequent writings that I will draw upon in what follows.

14. Louise Meintjes, *Sound of Africa! Making Music Zulu in a South African Studio* (Durham: Duke University Press, 2003).

15. Sunaina Marr Maira, *Desis in the House: Indian American Youth Culture in New York City* (Philadelphia: Temple University Press, 2002).

16. On this point see Fredric Jameson, "Modernism and Imperialism," *Nationalism, Colonialism, and Literature*, by Terry Eagleton, Fredric Jameson, and Edward W. Said (Minneapolis: University of Minnesota Press, 1990).

17. Marshall Berman, *All That Is Solid Melts into Air: The Experience of Modernity* (New York: Penguin, 1988), 5.

18. Race and skin color, though they may seem "natural" determinants of otherness today (particularly in America), were inconsequential to the premoderns, as Nancy Stepan submits, arguing that racism didn't arise until the slave trade. Nancy Stepan, *The Idea of Race in Science: Great Britain, 1800–1960* (London: Macmillan, 1982); see also Frank M. Snowden, *Before Color Prejudice: The Ancient View of the Blacks* (Cambridge: Harvard University Press, 1983).

19. Stuart Hall, "Ethnicity: Identity and Difference," *Radical America* 23 (October–December 1989), 16.

20. Timothy D. Taylor, *Global Pop: World Music, World Markets* (New York: Routledge, 1997).

CHAPTER 1: COLONIALISM, MODERNITY, AND MUSIC

1. See Dipesh Chakrabarty, "Postcoloniality and the Artifice of History: Who Speaks for 'Indian' Pasts?," *Representations* 32 (winter 1992): 1–26; and Homi K. Bhabha, *The Location of Culture*, especially "Conclusion: 'Race,' Time and the Revision of Modernity" (New York: Routledge, 1994).

2. Enrique Dussel, "Eurocentrism and Modernity (Introduction to the Frankfurt Lectures)," *boundary 2* 20 (autumn 1993): 65; emphasis in original.

3. Susan McClary, *Conventional Wisdom: The Content of Musical Form* (Berkeley: University of California Press, 2000), and *Feminine Endings: Music, Gender, and Sexuality* (Minneapolis: University of Minnesota Press, 1991); and John Shepherd, *Music as Social Text* (Cambridge, England: Polity, 1991).

4. For an important treatment of subjectivity in music just before the rise of tonality, see Susan McClary, *Modal Subjectivities: Self-Fashioning in the Italian Madrigal* (Berkeley: University of California Press, 2004).

5. For a particularly useful discussion of European history in this period, see Immanuel Wallerstein, *The Modern World-System: Capitalist Agriculture and the Origins of the European World-Economy in the Sixteenth Century* (New York: Academic, 1974).

6. In contrast to the East India Company, the early activities of the Virginia Company never showed a profit, and in fact the company was dissolved in 1624, only fifteen years after it was founded. The Massachusetts Bay Company, founded in 1627, was scarcely more profitable. See Robert Brenner, *Merchants and Revolution: Commercial Change, Political Conflict, and London's Overseas Traders, 1550–1653* (Princeton: Princeton University Press, 1993), especially chapters 3 and 4. I am grateful to Jean Howard for her insight on this point.

   For more sources on the rise of British colonialism see David Armitage, *The Ideological Origins of the British Empire* (Cambridge: Cambridge University Press, 2000); and Nicholas Canny, ed., *The Origins of Empire*, vol. 1 of *The Oxford History of the British Empire*, ed. Wm. Roger Louis (New York: Oxford University Press, 1998–99).

7. See for example J. Martin Evans, *America: The View from Europe* (San Francisco: San Francisco Book Company, 1976).

8. See, most importantly, Stephen Greenblatt, *Marvelous Possessions: The Wonder of the New World* (Chicago: University of Chicago Press, 1991).

9. Margaret T. Hodgen, *Early Anthropology in the Sixteenth and Seventeenth Centuries* (Philadelphia: University of Pennsylvania Press, 1964), 213.

10. Robert Burton, *The Anatomy of Melancholy*, as quoted by Hodgen, *Early Anthropology*, 222.

11. Hodgen, *Early Anthropology*, 332–33.

12. J. H. Elliott, *The Old World and the New* (Cambridge: Cambridge University Press, 1970), 9.

13. Peter Mason, *Deconstructing America: Representations of the Other* (New York: Routledge, 1990), 32.

14. Michel Foucault, *The Order of Things: An Archaeology of the Human Sciences* (London: Tavistock, 1970), 17.

15. Stephen Greenblatt, "Introduction: New World Encounters," *New World Encounters*, ed. Greenblatt (Berkeley: University of California Press, 1993), xvii.

16. See Mason, *Deconstructing America*, for a discussion of the European demonization of New World peoples.

17. Greenblatt, *Marvelous Possessions*, 23. Other works on early modern encounters between Europeans and non-Europeans include Urs Bitterli, *Cultures in Conflict: Encounters between European and Non-European Cultures, 1492–1800*, trans. Ritchie Robinson (Stanford: Stanford University Press, 1989); Brian Fagan, *Clash of Cultures* (New York: W. H. Freeman, 1984); Anthony Pagden, *European Encounters with the New World: From Renaissance to Romanticism* (New Haven: Yale University Press, 1993), and *Peoples and Empires: A Short History of European Migration, Exploration, and Conquest, from Greece to the Present* (New York: Modern Library, 2001); and Kirkpatrick Sale, *The Conquest of Paradise: The Columbian Legacy* (New York: Alfred A. Knopf, 1990).

18. Elliott, *The Old World and the New*, 23. Merryl Wyn Davies, Ashis Nandy, and Ziauddin Sardar believe that such substitutions were really a widespread practice: "The same woodcuts kept being re-used: many of the illustrations used for early accounts of the Americas were swiftly amended versions of woodcuts that had previously been used for texts that had nothing to do with the Americas." *Barbaric Others: A Manifesto on Western Racism* (Boulder: Pluto, 1993), 46.

19. See Olivia A. Bloechl, "The Pedagogy of Polyphony in Gabriel Sagard's *Histoire du Canada*," *Journal of Musicology* 22 (summer 2005): 365–411, for a discussion of the life of transcriptions of indigenous music from Brazil.

20. Miriam K. Whaples, "Exoticism in Dramatic Music, 1600–1800," Ph.D. diss., Indiana University, 1958, 13.

21. See Paul Nettl, "Die Moresca," *Archiv für Musikwissenchaft* 14 (1957): 165–74.

22. See Cecil Sharp and Herbert C. MacIlwaine, *The Morris Book: A History of Morris Dancing, with a Description of Eleven Dances as Performed by the Morrismen of England*, rev. ed.

(London: Novello, 1912–24); and Curt Sachs, *World History of the Dance*, trans. Bessie Schönberg (New York: W. W. Norton, 1963). The choreographer Thoinot Arbeau wrote of the morris dance in his *Orchesography* of 1589 (the editors of the edition I consulted note that Arbeau probably witnessed a French version of an English morris dance, which may have been imported into England from Spain by John of Gaunt): "In fashionable society when I was young, a small boy, his face daubed with black and his forehead swathed in a white or yellow kerchief, would make an appearance after supper. He wore leggings covered with little bells and performed a morris, wherein he advanced the length of the room, made a kind of passage and then moving backwards retraced his steps to the place from whence he started. Then he executed a new passage and he continued thus making various passages, which delighted the spectators." Thoinot Arbeau, *Orchesography*, trans. Mary Stewart Evans (New York: Dover, 1967), 177.

23. See Carol Robertson, "Introduction: The Dance of Conquest," *Musical Repercussions of 1492: Encounters in Text and Performance*, ed. Robertson (Washington: Smithsonian Institution Press, 1992); and Flavia Waters Chapme, *The Matachines Dance of the Upper Rio Grande: History, Music, and Choreography* (Lincoln: University of Nebraska Press, 1983).

24. Bernardino Daniello, as quoted by Tim Carter in "The Seventeenth Century," *The Oxford Illustrated History of Opera*, ed. Roger Parker (Oxford: Oxford University Press, 1994), 3. See Howard Mayer Brown, *Sixteenth-Century Instrumentation: The Music for the Florentine Intermedii*, Musicological Studies and Documents 30 (1973). A contemporary report of a Medici wedding in 1565 includes a description of a *moresca*: "All of them together sang and played a madrigal of arms and war, while executing, in the excitement of combatants, a new and extravagant *Moresca* at the end of which, rushing hither and thither across the stage as if in confusion, they fled in simulated terror from the gaze of the spectators." O. G. Sonneck, *Miscellaneous Studies in the History of Music* (New York: Macmillan, 1921), 281.

25. Davies, Nandy, and Sardar write that the "Reformation is dated from Martin Luther pinning his 95 theses to the cathedral door of Wittenburg in 1517. It did not develop into a full rupture until the Diet of Worms in that fateful year of 1521. No sooner had Magellan brought a whole globe into European orbit that the world of Europe was split apart and vital questions concerning Europe's understanding of itself had to be answered afresh. Newness, change and the invention of progress as historical process in the present impressed themselves on European consciousness under the impact of the Reformation. However, these ideas were legitimated by the worldview of early Christianity, and the development of this worldview into a reformulated conception of human nature and civil society would have been impossible without the medieval gaze that *oculus mundi* turned on the New World."

"Thus," they argue, "there was no rupture in the application of medieval iconography and ideas to the peoples of the New World. The invention of the Other was a vital tool for European self-consciousness, whether influenced by Protestantism or the Counter-Reformation." Davies, Nandy, and Sardar, *Barbaric Others*, 57.

26. Peter Martyr, *The Decades of the New World*, trans. Michael Lok, in *A Selection of Curious, Rare, and Early Voyages and Histories of Interesting Discoveries chiefly published by Hakluyt* . . . (London: R. H. Evans and R. Priestly, 1812), 539, as quoted by Stephen Greenblatt, *Renaissance Self-Fashioning: From More to Shakespeare* (Chicago: University of Chicago Press, 1980), 181.

27. Louis Montrose, "The Work of Gender in the Discourse of Discovery," *New World Encounters*, ed. Greenblatt, 182.

28. As quoted by Montrose, "The Work of Gender," 193.

29. Undated letter, "Dr. [Leonel] Sharp to the Duke of Buckingham," printed in *Cabala, Mysteries of State, in Letters of the great Ministers of K. James and K. Charles* (London, 1654), 259, as quoted by Montrose, "The Work of Gender," 204.

30. Ann Laura Stoler, "Carnal Knowledge and Imperial Power: Gender, Race, and Morality in Colonial Asia," *Gender at the Crossroads of Knowledge: Feminist Anthropology in the Postmodern Era*, ed. Micaela di Leonardo (Berkeley: University of California Press, 1991), 87. See also Mason's *Deconstructing America*, in which he notes the ways the Irish were otherized and re-otherized based on England's colonial experiences in the New World.

31. Ann Laura Stoler, "Rethinking Colonial Categories: European Communities and the Boundaries of Rule," *Comparative Studies in Society and History* 31 (January 1989): 137.

32. Perhaps most famously in Edward W. Said's *Orientalism* (New York: Vintage 1979).

33. Greenblatt, *Renaissance Self-Fashioning*, 1. Greenblatt notes that this characterization of defining individual identities goes far back in academic writing, as far as Jacob Burckhardt's classic *The Civilization of the Renaissance in Italy*, trans. S. G. C. Middlemore (Harmondsworth: Penguin, 1990), first published in 1860.

34. Greenblatt, *Renaissance Self-Fashioning*, 9.

35. Greenblatt, *Renaissance Self-Fashioning*, 9.

36. Michael Hardt and Antonio Negri, *Empire* (Cambridge: Harvard University Press, 2000), 129.

37. See, for just a few of the classic and recent examples, Heinrich Besseler, *Bourdon und Fauxbourdon: Studien zur Ursprung der niederländischen Musik*, ed. and rev. Peter Gulke (Leipzig: Breitkopf and Härtel, 1974); Richard Crocker, "Discant, Counterpoint, and Harmony," *Journal of the American Musicological Society* 15 (spring 1962): 1–21; Carl Dahlhaus, *Studies on the Origin of Harmonic Tonality*, trans. Robert O. Gjerdingen (Princeton: Princeton University Press, 1990); Cristle Collins Judd, ed., *Tonal Structures in Early Music* (New York: Garland, 1998); Edward E. Lowinsky, *Tonality and Atonality in Sixteenth-Century Music* (Berkeley: University of California Press, 1961); Bernhard Meier, *The Modes of Classical Vocal Polyphony, Described According to the Sources*, trans. Ellen S. Beebe (New York: Broude Brothers, 1988); Don Randel, "Emerging Triadic Tonality in the Fifteenth Century," *Musical Quarterly* 57 (1971): 73–86; and Benito Rivera, "Harmonic Theory in Musical Treatises of the Late Fifteenth and Early Sixteenth Centuries," *Music Theory Spectrum* 1 (1979): 80–95.

38. Dahlhaus, *Studies on the Origin of Harmonic Tonality*.

39. Harold Powers, "Is Mode Real? Pietro Aron, the Octenary System, and Polyphony," *Basler Jahrbuch für historische Musikpraxis* 16 (1992): 12. Carl E. Schorske, the great student of fin-de-siècle Vienna, writing on the demise of tonality, says that it "belonged to the same socio-cultural system as the science of perspective in art, with its centralized focus; the Baroque status system in society, and legal absolutism in politics. It was part of the same culture that favored the geometric garden—the garden as the extension of rational architecture over nature. Not for nothing was Rameau, the court musician of Louis XV, the clearest and most uncompromising theorist of the laws of harmony. The tonal system was a musical frame in which tones had *un*equal power to express, to validate, and to make bearable the life of man under a rationally organized, hierarchical culture." Carl E. Schorske, *Fin-de-siècle Vienna: Politics and Culture* (New York: Vintage, 1981), 346; emphasis in original.

40. The idea of space itself was also addressed by composers of this era. One of the earliest ways in which European colonialism and new conceptions of selves and others found its way into music was through the rise of the antiphonal choir, or, in Italy, the *cori spezzati* ("broken choirs"), which became popular around 1550 particularly, and not coincidentally, in Venice. The rise in popularity of this spatial division of two choirs at this historical moment is another of the many ways that composers attempted to come to grips with the changes in the spatial configuration of the world itself.

41. Michel Foucault, "Of Other Spaces," *Diacritics* 16 (1986): 23.

42. Bernard McGrane, *Beyond Anthropology: Society and the Other* (New York: Columbia University Press, 1989), 30.

43. McGrane, *Beyond Anthropology*, 36.

44. As quoted by Greenblatt, *Renaissance Self-Fashioning*, 195.

45. Greenblatt, *Renaissance Self-Fashioning*, 198. For a further discussion of Marlowe's *Tamburlaine* with respect to changing conceptions of space, see John Gillies, "Marlowe, the Timur Myth, and the Motives of Geography," *Playing the Globe: Genre and Geography in English Renaissance Drama*, ed. Gillies and Virginia Mason Vaughan (Madison, N.J.: Fairleigh Dickinson University Press, 1998), 8.

   The fascination for Timor or Tamerlane, the Turkic empire builder (and for his nemesis Bajazet, about whom Jean Racine wrote a play in 1672), was picked up by composers and librettists by the end of the seventeenth century and over forty operas were written about him from 1689 to 1840, including some by major composers such as Alessandro Scarlatti (*Il gran Tamerlano*, first performed in 1706), George Frideric Handel (*Tamerlano*, 1724), and Antonio Vivaldi (*Tamerlano*, 1735).

46. David Harvey, *The Condition of Postmodernity: An Enquiry into the Origins of Cultural Change* (Cambridge, Mass.: Basil Blackwell, 1989), 250. For more on maps and geography in this era see C. Raymond Beazley, *The Dawn of Modern Geography* (New York: P. Smith, 1949); J. R. Hale, *Renaissance Exploration* (New York: W. W. Norton, 1968); J. H. Parry, *The Age of Reconnaissance* (Berkeley: University of California Press, 1981); and R. V. Tooley, *Maps and Map-Makers*, 7th ed. (London: B. T. Batsford, 1987).

47. Walter D. Mignolo, *The Darker Side of the Renaissance: Literacy, Territoriality, and Coloni-zation*, 2d ed. (Ann Arbor: University of Michigan Press, 2003), 264. I would like to thank Olivia Bloechl for recommending this book.

48. Ernst Cassirer, *The Individual and the Cosmos in Renaissance Philosophy*, trans. Mario Domandi (New York: Barnes and Noble, 1963), 182.

49. Richard Norton, *Tonality in Western Culture: A Critical and Historical Perspective* (University Park: Pennsylvania State University Press, 1984), 140.

50. Thomas Christensen, *Rameau and Musical Thought in the Enlightenment* (Cambridge: Cambridge University Press, 1993). See Penelope Gouk, "The Role of Harmonics in the Scientific Revolution," *The Cambridge History of Western Music Theory*, ed. Thomas Christensen (New York: Cambridge University Press, 2002).

51. Gregory Barnett, "Tonal Organization in Seventeenth-Century Music Theory," *The Cambridge History of Western Music Theory*, ed. Christensen, 408.

52. Johann David Heinichen, *Criticae musicae*, II (1725; facsimile Amsterdam: Knuf, 1964), 212–13, as quoted by Joel Lester, *Between Modes and Keys: German Theory, 1592–1802* (Stuyvesant, N.Y.: Pendragon, 1989), 112. Lester's work provides similar examples by other theorists.

53. Barnett, "Tonal Organization," 444; Lester, *Between Modes and Keys*, 108–9. An early spatial representation of the movement of keys is discussed in Thomas Christensen, "The Spanish Baroque Guitar and Seventeenth-Century Triadic Theory," *Journal of Music Theory* 36 (spring 1992): 1–42.

54. Rameau was also one of the major composers of his time to have tackled issues of otherness in his work; see the next chapter.

55. Jean-Philippe Rameau, *Génération harmonique* (1737), 109, as quoted by Christensen, *Rameau and Musical Thought*, 189.

56. Rameau, *Génération harmonique*, 112, as quoted by Christensen, *Rameau and Musical Thought*, 189.

57. See also John Zerzan, "Tonality and the Totality," *Future Primitive and Other Essays* (Brooklyn, N.Y.: Autonomedia, 1994).

58. Shepherd, *Music as Social Text*, 122.

59. McClary has written widely and influentially on this subject. See "Constructions of Subjectivity in Schubert's Music," *Queering the Pitch: The New Gay and Lesbian Musicology*, ed. Philip Brett, Elizabeth Wood, and Gary C. Thomas (New York: Routledge, 1994); "Narrative Agendas in 'Absolute' Music: Identity and Difference in Brahms's Third Symphony," *Musicology and Difference: Gender and Sexuality in Music Scholarship*, ed. Ruth A. Solie (Berkeley: University of California Press, 1994); and "What Was Tonality?," *Conventional Wisdom*.

60. Susan McClary, "Music, the Pythagoreans, and the Body," *Choreographing History*, ed. Susan Leigh Foster (Bloomington: Indiana University Press, 1995), 88.

61. Jack P. Greene includes a reproduction of a fascinating engraving from a book published in 1600 that depicts the Italian explorer Amerigo Vespucci awakening a slumbering America, represented by a woman in a hammock clothed only in cap and

belt. Greene, *The Intellectual Construction of America: Exceptionalism and Identity from 1492 to 1800* (Chapel Hill: University of North Carolina Press, 1993), 9.

62. See Barnett, "Tonal Organization," 441.

63. Lorenzo Bianconi, *Music in the Seventeenth Century*, trans. David Bryant (New York: Cambridge University Press, 1987).

64. Ellen Rosand, *Opera in Seventeenth-Century Venice: The Creation of a Genre* (Berkeley: University of California Press, 1991), 11.

65. Richard Taruskin, "Of Kings and Divas," *New Republic*, 13 December 1993, 35.

66. Whaples, "Exoticism in Dramatic Music," 21.

67. Bianconi, *Music in the Seventeenth Century*, 174. Rosand makes much the same argument in *Opera in Seventeenth-Century Venice*, 59–65. For histories of opera that tell the standard story of opera's origins, see Robert Donington, *The Rise of Opera* (New York: Charles Scribner's Sons, 1981); Donald Jay Grout and Hermine Weigel Williams, *A Short History of Opera*, 3d ed. (New York: Columbia University Press, 1988); Ruth Katz, *The Powers of Music: Aesthetic Theory and the Invention of Opera* (New Brunswick, N.J.: Transaction, 1994); Michael F. Robinson, *Opera before Mozart* (New York: William Morrow, 1966); and F. W. Sternfeld, *The Birth of Opera* (Oxford: Clarendon, 1993).

68. Bianconi, *Music in the Seventeenth Century*, 29.

69. Bianconi, *Music in the Seventeenth Century*, 33.

70. Rosand, *Opera in Seventeenth-Century Venice*, 13. See also Irene Alm, "Dances from the 'Four Corners of the Earth': Exoticism in Seventeenth-Century Venetian Opera," *Musica Franca: Essays in Honor of Frank A. D'Accone*, ed. Irene Alm, Alyson McLamore, and Colleen Reardon (Stuyvesant, N.Y.: Pendragon, 1996).

71. Eric Chafe, *Monteverdi's Tonal Language* (New York: Schirmer, 1992), 1. I am grateful to Susan Boynton for telling me of this book.

72. Chafe, *Monteverdi's Tonal Language*, 2; emphasis in original.

73. Barthold Feind, *Dramaturgy of Opera* (1708), repr. in Bianconi, *Music in the Seventeenth Century*, 322.

74. M. M. Bakhtin, *The Dialogic Imagination*, ed. Michael Holquist, trans. Caryl Emerson and Michael Holquist (Austin: University of Texas Press, 1981), 82.

75. Bakhtin used the concept in *Rabelais and His World*, trans. Helene Iswolsky (Bloomington: Indiana University Press, 1981). For a comment on the overuse of the term see Caryl Emerson, "Problems with Baxtin's Poetics," *Slavic and East European Journal* 32 (1988): 503–25.

   It is interesting to note, as Rosand writes, that the earliest audiences for opera in Venice were drawn from the annual carnival crowds. Rosand, *Opera in Seventeenth-Century Venice*, 1–2.

76. For a particularly lucid discussion of Bakhtin and the carnival as a transgressive mode, see Peter Stallybrass and Allon White, *The Politics and Poetics of Transgression* (Ithaca: Cornell University Press, 1986).

77. Bakhtin, *Rabelais and His World*, 34.

78. McClary, *Feminine Endings*, 36.

79. For an examination of how music was used in gendered representations in this era, see Susan McClary, "Representations of Gender in Monteverdi's Dramatic Music," *Feminine Endings*.

80. Edward W. Said, *Culture and Imperialism* (New York: Alfred A. Knopf, 1993), 70–71.

81. Said, *Culture and Imperialism*, 77.

82. Jean Howard cautions me that the dramatic practices of the court were quite different from those of the public theater. For a consideration of the latter see John Gillies, *Shakespeare and the Geography of Difference* (Cambridge: Cambridge University Press, 1994); Gillies and Vaughan, eds., *Playing the Globe*; Jean Howard, *Theater of a City: Social Change and Generic Innovation on the Early Modern Stage*, forthcoming; and Jeffrey Masten and Wendy Wall, eds., "The Space of the Stage," *Renaissance Drama* 28 (Evanston: Northwestern University Press, 1999).

83. Skiles Howard, *The Politics of Courtly Dancing in Early Modern England* (Amherst: University of Massachusetts Press, 1998), 111. I would like to thank Jean Howard for recommending this book.

   For more on the Jonsonian masque see Jonathan Goldberg, *James I and the Politics of Literature: Jonson, Shakespeare, Donne, and Their Contemporaries* (Baltimore: Johns Hopkins University Press, 1983); D. J. Gordon, *The Renaissance Imagination: Essays and Lectures*, ed. Stephen Orgel (Berkeley: University of California Press, 1975); Susan Gossett, "Recent Studies in the English Masque," *English Renaissance* 26 (1996): 587–627; David Lindley, ed., *The Court Masque* (Manchester: Manchester University Press, 1984); Stephen Orgel, *The Jonsonian Masque*, 2d ed. (New York: Columbia University Press, 1981), and *The Illusion of Power: Political Theater in the English Renaissance* (Berkeley: University of California Press, 1975); Roy Strong, *Art and Power: Renaissance Festivals, 1450–1650* (Berkeley: University of California Press, 1984). For a study of the music that accompanies Jonson's masques see Mary Chan, *Music in the Theatre of Ben Jonson* (New York: Oxford University Press, 1980). For a study of Jonson's and other early masques see Kristin Rygg, *Masqued Mysteries Unmasked: Early Modern Music Theater and Its Pythagorean Subtext* (Hillsdale, N.Y.: Pendragon, 2000).

84. An established genre of English adventure plays tackled the same issues of otherness earlier than the masques but in similar ways. See Jean Howard "Gender on the Periphery," Feminist Interventions Series, Institute for Research on Women and Gender, Columbia University, 12 February 2001.

85. Such as Gillies, *Shakespeare and the Geography of Difference*; Gillies and Vaughan, eds., *Playing the Globe*; Howard, *Theater of a City*; and Masten and Wall, eds., *The Space of the Stage*.

86. Edward J. Dent, *Foundations of English Opera* (Cambridge: Cambridge University Press, 1928), 39. See also Peter Walls, *Music in the English Courtly Masque, 1604–1640* (Oxford: Clarendon, 1996), 177–78.

87. A reproduction of Inigo Jones's drawing of this character is included in Murray Lefkowitz, ed., *Trois Masques à la cour de Charles Ier d'Angleterre* (Paris: Centre National de la Recherche Scientifique, 1970), plate XIV.

88. Enid Welsford, *The Court Masque: A Study in the Relationship between Poetry and the Revels* (Cambridge: Cambridge University Press, 1927), 184.

89. Walls, *Music in the English Courtly Masque*, 115.

90. Murray Lefkowitz, *William Lawes* (London: Routledge and Kegan Paul, 1960), 206.

91. Lefkowitz, *William Lawes*, 214.

92. Similarly, in Italy, the *intermedii* threatened to overtake the dramas into which they were inserted. A Florentine playwright, Antonfrancesco Grazzini, wrote in the late sixteenth century that "Once intermedi were made to serve the comedy, but now comedies are made to serve the intermedi" (as quoted by Carter, "The Seventeenth Century," 3). And like masques and antimasques, *intermedii* were used for political and ideological purposes.

93. Lefkowitz, *William Lawes*, 207.

94. J. H. Parry, *The Establishment of the European Hegemony, 1415–1715: Trade and Exploration in the Age of the Renaissance* (New York: Harper and Row, 1966), 89.

95. Parry, *Establishment of the European Hegemony*, 93.

96. A. M. Gibbs writes that the source material for *The Cruelty of the Spaniards in Peru* was probably a book entitled *The Royal Commentaries of Peru* published in Lisbon by the Inca Garcilas de la Vega; a French version was published in Paris in 1633. Other contemporary sources to which Gibbs believes Davenant might have had access are Thomas Nicholas's *The Discoverie and Conquest of the Provinces of Peru* from 1581, a translation of a book by Augustin de Zarate; and the folios of de Bry's *Grandes Voyages*. Sir William Davenant, *The Shorter Poems, and Songs from the Plays and Masques*, ed. A. M. Gibbs (Oxford: Clarendon, 1972), 458.

  For a discussion of the ideological battle over the right to colonialize based on religious differences, see Olivia A. Bloechl, "Protestant Imperialism and the Representation of Native American Song," *Musical Quarterly* 87 (2004): 44–86.

97. Gibbs writes that *The History of Sir Francis Drake* is probably based on Philip Nichols's *Sir Francis Drake Reviv'd*, first published in 1626; Davenant, *The Shorter Poems*, 460. *The History of Sir Francis Drake* includes a "morisco," that is, a moresca or morris dance, which the native Cimaroons dance "for joy of the arrival of Sir Francis Drake"; Gibbs, *The History of Sir Francis Drake*, 461.

98. Lefkowitz, *Trois Masques*, 188.

99. The preface also admits the Italian influence mentioned earlier by admitting the influence of *intermedii* in *Britannia Triumphans*.

100. I am indebted to Olivia Bloechl for this last point.

101. This history is from Lefkowitz, *William Lawes*, 225–26.

102. For a detailed summary of the plot see Lefkowitz, *William Lawes*, 226–28.

103. Lefkowitz, *Trois Masques*, 207.

104. Lefkowitz, *Trois Masques*, 206.

105. Davenant, *The Shorter Poems*, 447.

106. Lefkowitz, *Trois Masques*, 183.

107. Murray Lefkowitz, "Lawes, William," *The New Grove Dictionary of Music and Musicians*, ed. Stanley Sadie (London: Macmillan, 1980).

108. See McClary, "Music, the Pythagoreans, and the Body," for a particularly useful discussion of this genre.

109. Richard Hudson, "The Concept of Mode in Italian Guitar Music during the First Half of the 17th Century," *Acta Musicologica* 42 (1970): 163–83.

110. McClary, "Music, the Pythagoreans, and the Body," 87.

111. Peter Platt, *Reason Diminished: Shakespeare and the Marvelous* (Omaha: University of Nebraska Press, 1997), 99.

112. Greenblatt, *Marvelous Possessions*, 14.

113. Platt, *Reason Diminished*, 103.

114. Salman Rushdie, *Imaginary Homelands* (London: Granta, 1991), 394. See also the next chapter.

CHAPTER 2: PEOPLING THE STAGE

1. Johannes Fabian, *Time and the Other: How Anthropology Makes Its Object* (New York: Columbia University Press, 1983), 7. For discussions of some of these travel accounts see Mary B. Campbell, *The Witness and the Other World: Exotic European Travel Writing, 400–1600* (Ithaca: Cornell University Press, 1988); Mary Louise Pratt, *Imperial Eyes: Travel Writing and Transculturation* (New York: Routledge, 1992); and David Spurr, *The Rhetoric of Empire: Colonial Discourse in Journalism, Travel Writing, and Imperial Administration* (Durham: Duke University Press, 1993).

2. Bernard McGrane, *Beyond Anthropology: Society and the Other* (New York: Columbia University Press, 1989), 59.

3. McGrane, *Beyond Anthropology*, 60.

4. For example, Jacques-Benigne Bossuet's *Discours sur l'histoire universelle* (1681), Antoine-Nicholas de Condorcet's *Sketch for a Historical Picture of the Progress of the Human Mind* (1795), Bernard le Bovier de Fontenelle's *Conversation on the Plurality of Worlds* (1724), Johann Gottfried Herder's *Ideas on a Philosophy of History of Mankind* (1784), Isaac Newton's *The Chronology of the Ancient Kingdoms Amended* (1728), and many others.

5. McGrane, *Beyond Anthropology*, 56.

6. McGrane, *Beyond Anthropology*, 57.

7. McGrane, *Beyond Anthropology*, 71.

8. Roxann Wheeler, *The Complexion of Race: Categories of Difference in Eighteenth-Century British Culture* (Philadelphia: University of Pennsylvania Press, 2000), 35. Thanks to Roe-Min Kok for suggesting this book.

9. See Nancy Stepan, *The Idea of Race in Science: Great Britain, 1800–1960* (London: Macmillan, 1982).

10. M. Boulanger, *L'antiquité dévoilée par ses usages*, as quoted by Paul Hazard, *European Thought in the Eighteenth Century: From Montesquieu to Lessing* (Cleveland: World, 1969), 371.

11. Hazard, *European Thought*, 372.

12. Hazard, *European Thought*, 372, citing Lucien Febvre, *Civilisation: Évolution d'un mot et d'un groupe d'idées*, 1930. He provides no citation information, but this seems to be

from Lucien Febvre, "*Civilisation*: Evolution of a Word and a Group of Ideas," *A New Kind of History and Other Essays*, ed. Peter Burke, trans. K. Folca (New York: Harper and Row, 1973).

13. See Hazard, *European Thought*, for a discussion of Montesquieu and intellectual history.

14. Dorinda Outram, *The Enlightenment* (Cambridge: Cambridge University Press, 1995), 68–70.

15. Denis Diderot, "Supplement to Bougainville's 'Voyage,'" *The Enlightenment*, ed. Frank E. Manuel (Englewood Cliffs, N.J.: Prentice-Hall, 1965), 99.

16. Wheeler, *The Complexion of Race*, 178.

17. *Royal Magazine; or, Gentleman's Monthly Companion* 2 (June 1760): 341, as quoted by Wheeler, *The Complexion of Race*, 191.

18. This is not the place to discourse on the phrase "noble savage," though a little history is in order. Dorinda Outram writes that the term was first used by Dryden in *The Conquest of Grenada* of 1670, in which a character says:

> "I am as free as Nature first made man,
> Ere the base laws of servitude began,
> When wild in woods the noble savage ran" (Outram, *Enlightenment*, 66)

Some commentators, such as Bence Szabolcsi, "Exoticisms in Mozart," *Music and Letters* 37 (October 1956): 323–32, have attributed the rehabilitation of the Turks into the noble savage type to the influence of Rousseau's writings, but Tzvetan Todorov writes that this type had been prevalent in travel narratives throughout the sixteenth to the eighteenth centuries; see *On Human Diversity: Nationalism, Racism, and Exoticism in French Thought*, trans. Catherine Porter (Cambridge: Harvard University Press, 1995). Last, for an admirable study, see Ter Ellingson, *The Myth of the Noble Savage* (Berkeley: University of California Press, 2001).

19. John Wesley, as quoted by Margaret T. Hodgen, *Early Anthropology in the Sixteenth and Seventeenth Centuries* (Philadelphia: University of Pennsylvania Press, 1964), 367.

20. Wheeler, *The Complexion of Race*, 67.

21. Hodgen, *Early Anthropology*, 390.

22. Hodgen, *Early Anthropology*, 408.

23. Hodgen, *Early Anthropology*, 413.

24. Hodgen, *Early Anthropology*, 418.

25. As quoted by Hazard, *European Thought in the Eighteenth Century*, 369.

26. Hodgen, *Early Anthropology*, 380–82.

27. Wheeler, *The Complexion of Race*, 74.

28. Oliver Goldsmith, *History of the Earth and Animated Nature in Four Volumes* (1774; repr. Philadelphia: Carey, 1795), 373, as quoted by Wheeler, *The Complexion of Race*, 180.

29. Warren Dwight Allen, *Philosophies of Music History: A Study of General Histories of Music, 1600–1900* (New York: Dover, 1962), 82.

30. Beginning with Walter Preibisch, "Quellenstudien zu Mozart's 'Entführung aus

dem Serail': Ein Beitrag zu der Geschichte der Türkenoper," *Sammelbände der Internationalen Musik-Gesellschaft* 10 (1908–9): 430–76; followed by Szabolcsi, "Exoticisms in Mozart"; Eve R. Meyer, "Turquerie and Eighteenth-Century Music," *Eighteenth-Century Studies* 7 (1973/4): 474–88; and others.

31. Mary Rowan Obelkevich, "Turkish Affect in the Land of the Sun King," *Musical Quarterly* 63 (July 1977): 367–89, includes many contemporary European reports on Turkish music that are well worth reading.

32. For an analysis of how Turks could have been constructed by Europeans as somehow equivalent to the ancients, see McGrane's chapter "The Other in the Enlightenment" in *Beyond Anthropology*.

33. J. H. Elliott, *The Old World and the New, 1492–1650* (New York: Cambridge University Press, 1970), 23.

34. The Islamic Middle East, of course, became the principal Other of Europeans, as Edward W. Said wrote so cogently in *Orientalism* (New York: Vintage, 1979). Jews, as has been widely discussed, were long the default domestic Others, as they were in music.

35. Henry Magdoff, *Imperialism in the Modern Phase*, vol. 1, Papers of the International Seminar on Imperialism, Independence and Social Transformation in the Contemporary World [Delhi, 1972], ed. Baudhayan Chattopadhyay (New Delhi: People's Publishing House, 1974), 7.

36. Said, *Orientalism*, 74–75.

37. Said, *Orientalism*, 75.

38. Said, *Orientalism*, 74.

39. See also Stephen Greenblatt for an important chapter on Christopher Marlowe's *Tamburlane the Great* (1587) in *Marvelous Possessions: The Wonder of the New World* (Chicago: University of Chicago Press, 1991).

40. From W. Daniel Wilson, "Turks on the Eighteenth-Century Operatic Stage and European Political, Military, and Cultural History," *Eighteenth-Century Life* 2 (1985): 79–92, who provides an excellent history of Europe in this moment which convincingly links political developments to Europeans' fascination with Turkey in this period.

41. Such organization is typical of this Baroque genre, which normally has different sets of characters for each act; musicologists believe Rameau to be the greatest composer in this genre.

42. For a discussion of the longevity of "Les Sauvages," see Howard Brofsky, "Rameau and the Indians: The Popularity of *Les Sauvages*," *Music in the Classic Period: Essays in Honor of Barry S. Brook*, ed. Allan W. Atlas (New York: Pendragon, 1985). See also Olivia A. Bloechl, *Native American Song at the Frontiers of Early Modern Music* (Cambridge: Cambridge University Press, forthcoming), for another treatment of this work, as well as a particularly thoughtful consideration of music and colonialism in the seventeenth century more generally.

43. I am not forgetting about *Le Bourgeois gentilhomme* (1670) by Jean-Baptiste Lully (1632–

87), but this work, as far as I can tell, employs no Turkish sounds. Its "La Cérémonie Turque" includes a "Marche pour la Cérémonie des Turcs," with these stage directions:

> La cérémonie turque pour ennoblir le bourgeois se fait en danse et en musique et compose le quatrième intermède.
>
> Le Mufti, quatre Dervis, six Turcs dansants, six Turcs musiciens, et autres joueurs d'instruments à la turque, sont les acteurs de cette cérémonie.

> The Turkish ceremony for ennobling the bourgeois is performed with dance and music and constitutes the fourth interlude.
>
> The Mufti, four Dervishes, six dancing Turks, six Turkish musicians, and other players of Turkish instruments, are the actors of this ceremony. (Author's translation)

Le Bourgeois gentilhomme does employ musical procedures within contemporary practices that its listeners would have heard as "exotic." Miriam K. Whaples includes a long analysis of this work in "Exoticism in Dramatic Music, 1600–1800," Ph.D. diss., Indiana University, 1958, and in her more recent "Early Exoticism Revisited," *The Exotic in Western Music*, ed. Jonathan Bellman (Boston: Northeastern University Press, 1998).

There were earlier works that tackled the subject of the Turks, but none of these make use of "Turkish" sounds, or representations of those sounds that contemporary listeners would have recognized. Earlier treatments of the Turks in texts of musical works go far back. Guillaume Dufay, for example, wrote a motet entitled *Ecclesie militantis/Sanctorum arbitrio* for the inauguration of Pope Eugenius IV in 1431. The text celebrates the church, but the contratenor's text contains overtly political and military sentiments:

> Bella canunt gentes: querimur, pater optime, tempus;
> Expediet multos, si cupis, una dies.
> Nummus et hora fluunt, magnumque iter orbis agendum,
> Nec suus in toto noscitur orbe deus.

> The gentiles are calling for war: we lament the times, best of fathers;
> a single day, if you so wish, will send out many men.
> Money and time are flowing away, and a great march through the world has
>   to be complete;
> and yet, God is not known to the whole world.

Reinhard Strohm (to whom I owe this passage and translation) writes that "this can only be a call upon the Holy Father to expedite troops against the Ottoman Empire, which was threatening Constantinople and the Venetian possessions in the eastern Mediterranean." Strohm, *The Rise of European Music, 1380–1500* (Cambridge: Cambridge University Press, 1993), 164.

The composer Robert Morton provides a particularly interesting case, in which the famous popular tune "L'homme armé"—used by many composers of liturgical music—appears in a work celebrating a defeat of the Ottoman Empire. *Il sera pour vous / L'homme armé* (probably by Morton) uses the famous tune in combination with a new written text praising Symon le Breton, a Burgundian chaplain and a conqueror of the Turks. Strohm, *The Rise of European Music*, 456.

44. It is important to note here that the *opéra-ballet* itself was an invention of Houdar de Lamotte and Campra, defined in 1754 by Louis de Cahusac as "a spectacle of singing and dancing made up of several different actions, each one complete and with no link one with the other except a vague and indeterminate relation." Louis de Cahusac, *La Danse ancienne et modern* (1754), 108, as quoted by Cuthbert Girdlestone, *Jean-Philippe Rameau: His Life and Work* (1957; repr. New York: Dover, 1969), 322.

45. Greenblatt, *Marvelous Possessions*. See especially chapter 3, "Marvelous Possessions."

46. André Campra, *L'Europe galante* (Farnborough, Hants., England: Gregg, 1967).

47. Letter to Houdar de la Motte, quoted by Girdlestone, *Jean-Philippe Rameau*, 10, as translated and quoted by Roger Savage in "Rameau's American Dancers," *Early Music* 11 (October 1983): 444.

48. *Mercure de France*, September 1725, 2274–76, as quoted by Savage, "Rameau's American Dancers," 444.

49. Letter to Houdar de la Motte, as quoted by Savage, "Rameau's American Dancers," 444.

50. Rameau, *Œuvres Complètes* VII, as quoted by Girdlestone, *Jean-Philippe Rameau*, 349.

51. As quoted by Girdlestone, *Jean-Philippe Rameau*, 349.

52. Enrico Fubini, *Music and Culture in Eighteenth-Century Europe: A Source Book* (Chicago: University of Chicago Press, 1994), 90, 106.

53. Nicholas Till, *Mozart and the Enlightenment: Truth, Virtue and Beauty in Mozart's Operas* (New York: W. W. Norton, 1992), 111. See also Wilson, "Turks on the Eighteenth-Century Operatic Stage."

54. McGrane, *Beyond Anthropology*, 26.

55. Whaples points out in "Exoticism in Dramatic Music" the thematic relationship between this and the "Ritournelle" of the same entrée, which makes use of the same devices that encode otherness, particularly wide leaps, although Whaples notes that this melody can be heard as a four-voice fugue and the leaps are thus not integral to the melody. I don't think this matters, though, for the audience would more than likely have heard the leaps as a musical sign of otherness, not as a hidden fugue.

56. See especially the introduction, "A Material Girl in Bluebeard's Castle," in *Feminine Endings* (Minneapolis: University of Minnesota Press, 1991); and the essays "Constructions of Gender in Monteverdi's Dramatic Music" and "Excess and Frame: The Musical Representation of Madwomen." See also McClary's *Georges Bizet: "Carmen"* (Cambridge: Cambridge University Press, 1992).

57. Other musical representations of otherness that I won't be discussing can be found in Thomas Bauman, *W. A. Mozart: "Die Entführung aus dem Serail"* (New York: Cam-

bridge University Press, 1987); and Jonathan Bellman, *The "Style Hongrois" in the Music of Western Europe* (Boston: Northeastern University Press, 1993). Both authors rely heavily on Whaples's pioneering work.

58. In addition to McClary's works already cited, see her "Narrative Agendas in 'Absolute' Music: Identity and Difference in Brahms's Third Symphony," *Musicology and Difference: Gender and Sexuality in Music Scholarship*, ed. Ruth A. Solie (Berkeley: University of California Press, 1993); and "Constructions of Subjectivity in Schubert's Music," *Queering the Pitch: The New Gay and Lesbian Musicology*, ed. Philip Brett, Elizabeth Wood, and Gary C. Thomas (New York: Routledge, 1994).

59. Mary Hunter's "The *Alla Turca* Style in the Late Eighteenth Century: Race and Gender in the Symphony and the Seraglio," *The Exotic in Western Music*, ed. Jonathan Bellman (Boston: Northeastern University Press, 1998), which appeared after the publication of the article on which this chapter is based, makes some of the same points as this discussion of Mozart.

60. Space doesn't permit discussing the changes in European perspective on peoples of other cultures. Writings that I have found useful include Fabian, *Time and the Other*; Line Grenier, "From 'Diversity' to 'Difference,'" *New Formations* 9 (1989): 125–42; McGrane, *Beyond Anthropology*; and Nicholas Thomas, *Colonialism's Culture: Anthropology, Travel, and Government* (Princeton: Princeton University Press, 1994).

61. To which Mozart is said to have replied, "Exactly the necessary number, your majesty." This comes from the biography of Mozart by F. X. Niemetschek's *Leben des k. k. Kapellmeisters Wolfgang Gottlieb Mozart nach Originalquellen beschrieben* (Prague, 1798), as quoted by Stanley Sadie, *The New Grove Mozart* (New York: W. W. Norton, 1983), 82.

62. Emily Anderson, ed. and trans., *The Letters of Mozart and His Family* (London: Macmillan, 1985), 319; William J. Baumol and Hilda Baumol, "On the Economics of Musical Composition in Mozart's Vienna," *On Mozart*, ed. James M. Morris (Washington: Woodrow Wilson Center Press), 96. For more on the economic impact on Austria of Joseph II in this period see David P. Good, *The Economic Rise of the Habsburg Empire, 1750–1914* (Berkeley: University of California Press, 1984).

63. Till, *Mozart and the Enlightenment*, 104.

64. Volkmar Braunbehrens, *Mozart in Vienna, 1781–1791*, trans. Timothy Bell (New York: Grove Weidenfeld, 1990), 74.

65. See Giorgio Pestelli, *The Age of Mozart and Beethoven*, trans. Eric Cross (New York: Cambridge University Press, 1984).

66. Anderson, *The Letters of Mozart and His Family*, 755.

67. Edward J. Dent, *Mozart's Operas: A Critical Study*, 2d ed. (Oxford: Clarendon, 1947), 82.

68. Wye J. Allanbrook also notes the wide range of musical signs employed by Mozart and other classical composers in instrumental music. Allanbrook accounts for this practice by describing the loosening of musical signs from *opera buffa* conventions. "The Secular Commedia: Comic Mimesis in Late Eighteenth-Century Music," Ernest Bloch Lectures, University of California, Berkeley, fall 1994.

69. Brigid Brophy, *Mozart the Dramatist: The Value of His Operas to Him, to His Age and to Us*, rev. ed. (New York: Da Capo, 1988), 223.

70. Anderson, *The Letters of Mozart and His Family*, 768, 772.

71. See also Jonathan Bellman's discussion of this passage in *The "Style Hongrois,"* 41, in which, drawing on Bauman, *W. A. Mozart: "Die Entführung,"* and Whaples, "Exoticism in Dramatic Music," he points out the use of upper neighbor notes to descending scale passages.

72. For example on *Turkish Military Band Music of the Ottoman Empire*, King Record Co., KICC 5101, 1987.

73. All translations are adapted from the translation by Kenneth Chalmers accompanying the recording of *Die Entführung aus dem Serail* on L'Oiseau-Lyre 430 339-2, 1991.

74. Szabolcsi notes that this song by Pedrillo may be more closely related to Italian folk music than anything else, basing this supposition on Mozart's having visited Italy in 1782; Szabolcsi, "Exoticisms in Mozart," 330–31. This could be, but the sound of the augmented second signifies the "Orient," if it is employed in other musics. Besides, it seems a little far-fetched for a Spaniard to be singing an Italian love song in Turkey to an audience of Spaniards (Belmonte and Konstanze), an Englishwoman (Blonde), and eavesdropping Turks.

75. Gretchen Wheelock, "Schwarze Gredel and the Engendered Minor Mode in Mozart's Operas," *Musicology and Difference*, ed. Solie.

76. See Bauman, *W. A. Mozart: "Die Entführung,"* 73.

77. Some scores state that the action takes place in the "mid 16th century," though this assumption seems to be based on some performances that adopted this time setting, not the wishes of Mozart or his librettist, Gottlieb Stephanie.

78. I am not saying that the older meanings of this music were "lost"; on the contrary, they are all alive and well, and employed by Mozart himself in later works (such as the piano sonatas K. 331 and K. 332, and many other works). But I am suggesting that Mozart successfully added another layer of signification to those "Turkish sounds," one that reappeared occasionally afterward.

79. Anderson, *The Letters of Mozart and His Family*, 769; emphasis in original.

80. Johann Georg Sulzer, "Allgemeine Theorie der schönen Künste, in einzelnen, nach alphabetischer Ordnung der Künstwörter aufeinanderfolgenden Artikeln abgehandelt," *Music and Aesthetics in the Eighteenth and Early-Nineteenth Centuries*, abridged and ed. Peter le Huray and James Day (Cambridge University Press, 1988), 112.

81. Anderson, *The Letters of Mozart and His Family*, 770; emphasis in original.

82. Anderson, *The Letters of Mozart and His Family*, 828.

83. Mary Douglas, *Purity and Danger: An Analysis of Concepts of Pollution and Taboo* (Harmondsworth: Penguin, 1970), 137.

84. Douglas, *Purity and Danger*, 145.

85. Peter Stallybrass and Allon White, *The Politics and Poetics of Transgression* (Ithaca: Cornell University Press, 1986), 5; emphasis in original.

86. Stallybrass and White, *The Politics and Poetics of Transgression*, 193; emphasis in original.

87. Said, *Orientalism*, 118.

88. For a discussion of absolute music see Carl Dahlhaus, *The Idea of Absolute Music*, trans. Roger Lustig (Chicago: University of Chicago Press, 1989).

89. Stuart Hall, "Ethnicity: Identity and Difference," *Radical America* 23 (October–December 1989), 16; emphasis in original.

CHAPTER 3: THE RISE OF IMPERIALISM

1. Roxann Wheeler, *The Complexion of Race: Categories of Difference in Eighteenth-Century British Culture* (Philadelphia: University of Pennsylvania Press, 2000), 291–97.

2. Wheeler, *The Complexion of Race*, 299; emphasis in original.

3. For this argument I am indebted primarily to Bernard McGrane's *Beyond Anthropology: Society and the Other* (New York: Columbia University Press, 1989); and Nicholas Thomas, *Colonialism's Culture: Anthropology, Travel, and Government* (Princeton: Princeton University Press, 1994).

4. "The Negro is a being, whose nature and dispositions are not merely different from those of the Europeans, they are the *reverse* of them," *An Inquiry into the Causes of the Insurrection of Negroes in the Island of St. Domingo* (London: Crukshank, 1792), 5, as quoted by Michael Hardt and Antonio Negri, *Empire* (Cambridge: Harvard University Press, 2000), 127.

5. McGrane, *Beyond Anthropology*, 77.

6. McGrane, *Beyond Anthropology*, 94.

7. E. B. Tylor, *Anthropology, an Introduction to the Study of Man and Civilization* (1881; repr. New York: D. Appleton, 1913), 388, as quoted by McGrane, *Beyond Anthropology*, 93.

8. Raymond Williams, *Keywords: A Vocabulary of Culture and Society* (London: Fontana, 1976), 159–60.

9. Eric Hobsbawm, *The Age of Empire, 1874–1915* (New York: Pantheon, 1987), 59.

10. Edward W. Said, *Culture and Imperialism* (New York: Alfred A. Knopf, 1993), 8.

11. Christine Haig, "Our Music, Their Music: Identifying Meaning in Musical Experiences," Ph.D. diss., University of Otago, New Zealand, 2004.

12. Jan Nederveen Pieterse, *White on Black: Images of Africa and Blacks in Western Popular Culture* (New Haven: Yale University Press, 1992), 35.

13. Albert Schweitzer, *The Primeval Forest* (New York: Pyramid, 1964), 99, as quoted by Felix N. Okoye, *The American Image of Africa: Myth and Reality* (Buffalo: Black Academy, 1971), 114.

14. Chaim Weizmann, in Doreen Ingrams, *Palestine Papers, 1917–1922: Seeds of Conflict* (London: John Murray, 1972), 32, as quoted by Edward W. Said, *Orientalism* (New York: Vintage, 1979), 318.

15. Karl Baedeker, *Egypt and the Suday: Handbook for Travelers* (London: T. Fisher Unwin, 1914), xxv, as quoted by Michael Gilsenan, "Imagined Cities of the East," an inaugural lecture delivered before the University of Oxford, 27 May 1985 (Oxford: Clarendon, 1986), 7.

16. John Frederick Rowbotham, *A History of Music to the Time of the Troubadours* (London:

Trübner, 1885–87), as quoted by Warren Dwight Allen, *Philosophies of Music History: A Study of General Histories of Music, 1600–1900* (New York: Dover, 1962), 111–12.

17. Sir Charles Hubert Hastings Parry, *Evolution of the Art of Music* (London: Kegan Paul, 1893), 53, as quoted by Allen, *Philosophies of Music History*, 228; Parry, *Evolution of the Art of Music*, 82, as quoted by Allen, *Philosophies of Music History*, 113.

18. Satis N. Coleman, *Creative Music for Children: A Plan of Training Based on the Natural Evolution of Music, Including the Making and Playing of Instruments* (New York: G. P. Putnam's Sons, 1922, 1928), 29–30, as quoted by Allen, *Philosophies of Music History*, 158–59.

19. Hector Berlioz, "Twenty-First Evening," *Evenings in the Orchestra*, trans. C. R. Fortescue (Harmondsworth: Penguin, 1963), 218–19, as quoted by Robert Orledge, "Evocations of Exoticism," *The Cambridge Companion to Ravel*, ed. Deborah Mawer (New York: Cambridge University Press, 2000), 28.

20. Hobsbawm, *The Age of Empire*, 62.

21. Hobsbawm, *The Age of Empire*, 63.

22. Hobsbawm, *The Age of Empire*, 64.

23. Stuart Hall, "Ethnicity: Identity and Difference," *Radical America* 23 (October–December 1989), 12.

24. Hall, "Ethnicity," 11.

25. There are other shifts that one could discuss, but I am concentrating on only the most salient factors here.

26. For a classic discussion of the Viennese case see Carl E. Schorske, *Fin-de-siècle Vienna: Politics and Culture* (New York: Vintage, 1981); for a discussion of Paris see David Harvey, *Paris, Capital of Modernity* (New York: Routledge, 2003). For a broader discussion of France see Paul Rabinow, *French Modern: Norms and Forms of the Social Environment* (Chicago: University of Chicago Press, 1995).

27. Hobsbawm, *The Age of Empire*, table 2, 343.

28. Nancy L. Green, Laura Levine Frader, and Pierre Milza, "Paris: City of Light and Shadow," *Distant Magnets: Expectations and Realities in the Immigrant Experience, 1840–1930*, ed. Dirk Hoerder and Horst Rössler (New York: Holmes and Meier, 1992), 47.

29. Michael John and Albert Lichtblau, "Vienna around 1900: Images, Expectations, and Experiences of Labor Migrants," *Distant Magnets*, ed. Hoerder and Rössler, 53.

30. See the chapter "Baudelaire: Modernism in the Streets" in Marshall Berman, *All That Is Solid Melts into Air: The Experience of Modernity* (New York: Penguin, 1988).

31. See my "Bad World Music" in *Bad Music: The Music We Love to Hate*, ed. Chris Washburne and Maiken Derno (New York: Routledge, 2004).

32. Raymond Williams, *Culture* (Glasgow: William Collins Sons, 1981), 83–85.

33. Raymond Williams, "Metropolitan Perceptions and the Emergence of Modernism," *The Politics of Modernism: Against the New Conformists* (New York: Verso, 1989), 45.

34. For writings on these new technologies see Mark Katz, *Capturing Sound: How Technology Has Changed Music* (Berkeley: University of California Press, 2004); Jonathan Sterne, *The Audible Past: Cultural Origins of Sound Reproduction* (Durham: Duke University Press, 2003); my "Music and the Rise of Radio in Twenties America: Techno-

logical Imperialism, Socialization, and the Transformation of Intimacy," *Wired for Sound: Engineering and Technology in Sonic Cultures*, ed. Thomas Porcello and Paul Greene (Middletown, Conn.: Wesleyan University Press, 2004); and Emily Thompson, *The Soundscape of Modernity: Architectural Acoustics and the Culture of Listening in America, 1900–1933* (Cambridge: MIT Press, 2002).

35. For a good overview of the changing status of women in this era see Hobsbawm's chapter "The New Woman" in *The Age of Empire*.

36. Andreas Huyssen, "Mass Culture as Woman: Modernism's Other," *After the Great Divide: Modernism, Mass Culture, Postmodernism* (Bloomington: Indiana University Press, 1986).

37. Sigmund Freud, *Dora: An Analysis of a Case of Hysteria* (New York: Touchstone, 1997); Otto Weininger, *Sex and Character: An Investigation of Fundamental Principles*, ed. Daniel Steuer and Laura Marcus, trans. Ladislaus Löb (Bloomington: Indiana University Press, 2005). Tamara Levitz informs me that the history of *Salome* is complicated by the rise of a Salome dancing craze, a liberatory interpretation of the opera.

38. For more on the academy's lack of attention to the colonializers see "Tensions of Empire: Colonial Control and Visions of Rule" by Frederick Cooper and Ann L. Stoler, an introductory essay to a volume on colonialism, *American Ethnologist* 16 (November 1989): 609–21. See also Thomas, *Colonialism's Culture*.

39. Ashis Nandy, *The Intimate Enemy: Loss and Recovery of Self under Colonialism* (Delhi: Oxford University Press, 1983), 32.

40. Nandy, *The Intimate Enemy*, 44–45.

41. See the essays in Arnold Schoenberg, *Style and Idea: Selected Writings of Arnold Schoenberg*, ed. Leonard Stein, trans. Leo Black (Berkeley: University of California Press, 1985).

42. Igor Stravinsky, "Some Ideas about My Octuor," *Stravinsky: The Composer and His Works*, by Eric Walter White, 2d ed. (Berkeley: University of California Press, 1979), 574, 575.

43. See Igor Stravinsky, *An Autobiography* (1936; repr. New York: W. W. Norton, 1962).

44. Satie's "autobiography" provides many examples of his satirical writings: *A Mammal's Notebook: Collected Writings of Erik Satie*, ed. Ornella Volta, trans. Antony Melville (London: Atlas, 2002).

45. Arnold Schoenberg, "Reply to a Questionnaire," *Style and Idea*, 147.

46. Theodor Adorno, *Philosophy of Modern Music*, trans. Anne G. Mitchell and Wesley V. Blomster (London: Sheed and Ward, 1973), 142.

47. Adorno, *Philosophy of Modern Music*, 142.

48. Adorno, *Philosophy of Modern Music*, 143.

49. Adorno, *Philosophy of Modern Music*, 143.

50. Adorno, *Philosophy of Modern Music*, 144.

51. For more on this work and the importance of the quotation see Adorno's discussion entitled "Loneliness as Style" in *Philosophy of Modern Music*.

52. John Henry Mackay, as quoted by Adorno, *Philosophy of Modern Music*, 47.

53. See Schoenberg's "Composition with Twelve Tones" in *Style and Idea*.

54. Hobsbawm, *The Age of Empire*, 81.

55. For more on these composers' relationships to musics from other cultures see Jürgen Arndt, *Der Einfluß der javanischen Gamelan-Musik auf Kompositionen von Claude Debussy* (Frankfurt: Peter Lang, 1993); Jonathan Bellman, ed., *The Exotic in Western Music* (Boston: Northeastern University Press, 1998); Roy Howat, "Debussy and the Orient," *Recovering the Orient: Artists, Scholars, Appropriations*, ed. Andrew Gerstle and Anthony Milner (London: Harwood, 1995); Richard James, "Ravel's *Chansons madécasses*: Ethnic Fantasy or Ethnic Borrowing?," *Musical Quarterly* 74 (1990): 360–85; Richard Mueller, "Javanese Influence on Debussy's *Fantaisie* and Beyond," *Nineteenth-Century Music* 10 (autumn 1986–87): 157–86; and Glenn Watkins, *Pyramids at the Louvre: Music, Culture, and Collage from Stravinsky to the Postmodernists* (Cambridge: Harvard University Press, 1994).

56. As quoted by Roger Nichols, *Debussy* (London: Oxford University Press, 1973), 7.

57. Debussy, *Revue S.I.M.*, 1913, as quoted by Edward Lockspeiser, *Debussy: His Life and Mind* (New York: Cambridge University Press, 1978), 2:115.

58. Said, *Culture and Imperialism*, 169.

59. Said, *Culture and Imperialism*, 170.

60. Said, *Culture and Imperialism*, 189.

61. Said, *Culture and Imperialism*, 189–90.

62. Fredric Jameson, "Modernism and Imperialism," *Nationalism, Colonialism, and Literature*, by Terry Eagleton, Fredric Jameson, and Edward W. Said (Minneapolis: University of Minnesota Press, 1990), 51.

63. George Lichtheim, *Europe in the 20th Century* (London: Phoenix, 1972), 88.

64. Theodor Adorno, *Quasi una Fantasia: Essays on Modern Music*, trans. Rodney Livingstone (New York: Verso, 1992), 278.

65. "A Visit with Maurice Ravel," *De Telegraaf*, 31 March 1931, 473, as quoted by Orledge, "Evocations of Exoticism," 29.

66. Hobsbawm, *The Age of Empire*, 70.

67. Maurice Talmeyr, "L'École du Trocadéro," *Revue des deux mondes*, 1 November 1900, as quoted by Rosalind H. Williams, *Dream Worlds: Mass Consumption in Late Nineteenth-Century France* (Berkeley: University of California Press, 1982), 61. For a musicological study of the exposition of 1889 see Annegret Fauser, *Musical Encounters at the 1889 Paris World's Fair* (Rochester, N.Y.: University of Rochester Press, 2005). I am indebted to Tamara Levitz for telling me of this book.

68. Michel Corday, "À l'Exposition: Visions lointaines," *Revue de Paris*, 15 March 1900, as quoted by Williams, *Dream Worlds*, 74.

69. Williams, *Dream Worlds*.

70. Translation adapted from Glenn Watkins, *Soundings: Music in the Twentieth Century* (New York: Schirmer, 1995), 124–25.

71. Derek B. Scott, "Orientalism and Musical Style," *Critical Musicology Journal*, http://www.leeds.ac.uk/music/info/critmus/articles/1997/02/01.html, last visited 24 July 2004.

72. Peter Kaminsky, "Vocal Music and the Lures of Exoticism and Irony," *The Cambridge Companion to Ravel*, ed. Mawer, 165.

73. As quoted by Orledge, "Evocations of Exoticism," 32.

74. Lawrence Kramer, "Consuming the Exotic: Ravel's *Daphnis and Chloe*," *Classical Music and Postmodern Knowledge* (Berkeley: University of California Press, 1995), 201–25.

75. Kramer, "Consuming the Exotic," 219.

76. Colin Campbell, *The Romantic Ethic and the Spirit of Modern Consumerism* (Cambridge, Mass.: Basil Blackwell, 1989).

77. Kramer, "Consuming the Exotic," 220.

78. Translation by author.

79. Kaminsky, "Vocal Music," 184.

80. As quoted by Henri Brunschwig, *French Colonialism, 1871–1914: Myths and Realities*, trans. William Glanville Brown (New York: Frederick A. Praeger, 1966), 25. Thanks are due to Daniel Sherman for suggesting this book.

81. I am indebted to Daniel Sherman for making this point clear to me.

82. As quoted by Brunschwig, *French Colonialism*, 78.

83. On the question of the commodification of music see Max Horkheimer and Theodor Adorno, *Dialectic of Enlightenment*, trans. John Cumming (New York Continuum, 1990); and my "The Commodification of Music at the Dawn of the Era of 'Mechanical Music,'" in preparation.

84. This is a complex concept, relevant to all cultural products. One way of verifying and illuminating it is to trace the development of copyright laws—first used around this same period, the mid- to late eighteenth century—for as the work of art entered the commercial marketplace, questions of ownership and use became extremely important. See Richard Petzoldt, "The Economic Conditions of the 18th-Century Musician," *The Social Status of the Professional Musician from the Middle Ages to the 19th Century*, ed. Walter Salmen, trans. Herbert Kaufman and Barbara Reisner (New York: Pendragon, 1983); and my "Aesthetic and Cultural Issues in Schumann's *Kinderszenen*," *International Review of the Aesthetics and Sociology of Music* 21 (December 1990): 161–78.

85. A good overview of the rise of modern aesthetics appears in Neil Nehring, *Flowers in the Dustbin: Culture, Anarchy, and Postwar England* (Ann Arbor: University of Michigan Press, 1993), 46–52. See also Janet Wolff, "The Ideology of Autonomous Art," *Music and Society: The Politics of Composition, Performance, and Reception*, ed. Richard Leppert and Susan McClary (Cambridge: Cambridge University Press, 1987).

86. John Ruskin, appendix, *Modern Painters* (London: Library Edition, 1903–12), 2:388–89, as quoted by Raymond Williams, *Marxism and Literature* (New York: Oxford University Press, 1977), 156–57.

87. "Pour savoir ce que veulent tire tous ces fatras de *sonates* dont on est accablé, il faudroit faire comme ce peintre grossier qui étoit obligé d'écrire au-dessous de ses figures; *c'est un arbre, c'est un homme, c'est un cheval*. Je n'oublierai jamais la saillie du célèbre Fontenelle, qui se trouvant excédé de ces éternelles Symphonies, s'écria tout haut dans un transport d'impatience : *sonate, que me veux-tu ?*" Jean Jacques Rousseau, "Sonate,"

Dictionnaire de Musique (Hildesheim: Georg Olms Verlagsbuchhandlung; New York: Johnson Reprint, 1969), 452; emphases in original, translation by author. Fontenelle is Bernard le Bovier de Fontenelle (1657–1757), scientist and man of letters highly regarded by Voltaire.

88. Adam Smith, *Essays on Philosophical Subjects*, ed. W. P. D. Wightman and J. C. Bryce (Oxford: Clarendon, 1980), 207.

89. Smith, *Essays on Philosophical Subjects*, 205.

90. Smith, *Essays on Philosophical Subjects*, 205–6.

91. Campbell, *The Romantic Ethic*. For more on this period with respect to the consumption of music see Richard Leppert, "Social Order and the Domestic Consumption of Music: The Politics of Sound in the Policing of Gender Construction in Eighteenth-Century England," *The Consumption of Culture, 1600–1800: Image, Object, Text*, ed. Ann Bermingham and John Brewer (New York: Routledge, 1995).

92. Chronology in Ives is notoriously difficult, and I am indebted to John Kirkpatrick's thoughts on the chronology of the sonata. His order of movements corresponds to Ives's own: "The Alcotts," 1902–4; "Emerson," 1907 (?1905); "Hawthorne," 1910; and "Thoreau," 1915. See Vivian Perlis, *Charles Ives Remembered: An Oral History* (New York: W. W. Norton, 1974), 215.

93. From W. Howard Doane and E. H. Johnson, eds., *The Baptist Hymnal* (Philadelphia: American Baptist Publication Society, 1883).

94. J. Peter Burkholder, *All Made of Tunes: Charles Ives and the Uses of Musical Borrowing* (New Haven: Yale University Press, 1995).

95. John Xiros Cooper, *Modernism and the Culture of Market Society* (New York: Cambridge University Press, 2004), 22.

96. Daniel Albright, Introduction, *Modernism and Music: An Anthology of Sources* (Chicago: University of Chicago Press, 2004).

97. David Nicholls, "Cowell, Henry," *Grove Music Online*, ed. L. Macy, http://www.grovemusic.com, last visited 28 June 2005. Nancy Rao clearly seeks to defend Cowell from charges of appropriating nonwestern musics, and draws on his writings and biography to do so. Cowell writes: "As a child I grew up in San Francisco, living near the Chinese and Japanese districts. Among other music which I heard and sang was included many Chinese and Japanese tunes from my playmates, and I was taken to hear a Chinese opera before I heard a European one, although I went at this time to hear concerts of string quartets, etc. As a result, Oriental music has never seemed strange to me, and I have often in composing thought quite naturally of themes in Oriental modes, or in which Oriental and Occidental elements are integrated. Later I studied the music of North India with a Bengali musician, and the music of Java with a Javanese." Henry Cowell, "Influence of Oriental Music on American Composers," unpublished manuscript, New York Public Library, as quoted by Nancy Rao, "American Compositional Theory: American Compositional Theory in the 1930s: Scale and Exoticism in 'The Nature of Melody' by Henry Cowell," *Musical Quarterly* 85 (2001): 625. Rao takes this to mean that nonwestern musics were

"native to Cowell's musical imagination." Rao, "American Compositional Theory," 626. Cowell's strategy, however, is a familiar one. People who have appropriated, quoted, borrowed music from other cultures frequently employ discourses of long-time knowledge of that music as a way of inoculating themselves against charges of appropriation.

Rao uses her interpretation to argue with John Corbett's charges of appropriation of nonwestern musics as a way to dislocate conventional European practices, saying that Cowell could not be interpreted as having appropriated nonwestern music since this music is an "almost instinctive procedure" in Cowell's music, inseparable from "his musical being." Rao, "American Compositional Theory," 626. The article by Corbett that Rao is arguing with is "Experimental Oriental: New Music and Other Others," *Western Music and Its Others: Difference, Representation, and Appropriation in Music*, ed. Georgina Born and David Hesmondhalgh (Berkeley: University of California Press, 2000).

But it seems to me that this argument is beside the point. Corbett, Rao, and Nicholls root their positions far too much in composers' psyches, biographies, and musical works, failing to consider the broader historical and cultural reasons underlying Cowell's discourses and musical practices. This is not to avoid the question of whether Cowell appropriated musics and musical practices from other cultures—arguments can be made for both sides. But the question is not particularly interesting. What is interesting is why Cowell and others were doing what they were doing, how their practices and discourses emanated from ideologies in play at any given moment.

98. David Nicholls, "Transethnicism and the American Experimental Tradition," *Musical Quarterly* 80 (winter 1996): 659–94.

99. Anthony Seeger, personal communication, 7 June 2005.

100. John Varian, foreword to *Tirawa* (San Diego: Troubadour Press, 1930), as quoted by Steven Johnson, "Henry Cowell, John Varian, and Halcyon," *American Music* 11 (spring 1993): 16.

101. Dane Rudhyar, "The Relativity of Our Musical Conceptions," *Musical Quarterly* 8 (January 1922): 108, as quoted by Carol Oja, *Making Music Modern: New York in the 1920s* (New York: Oxford University Press, 2000), 131.

102. See Scott Messing, *Neoclassicism in Music: From the Genesis of the Concept through the Schoenberg/Stravinsky Polemic* (Ann Arbor: UMI Research Press, 1988).

103. Henry Cowell, "Towards Neo-Primitivism," *Modern Music* 10 (March–April 1933): 151.

104. Cowell, "Towards Neo-Primitivism," 151.

105. David Nicholls, "Henry Cowell's *United Quartet*," *American Music* 13 (summer 1995): 199.

106. Henry Cowell, "The Nature of Melody," sec. III, 1–2, as quoted by Nancy Rao, "American Compositional Theory," 608.

107. Henry Cowell, "The Scientific Approach to Non-European Music," *Music Vanguard* 1 (summer 1935): 62.

108. Cowell, "The Scientific Approach," 66.

109. Cowell, "The Scientific Approach," 67.

110. Henry Cowell, "The Composer's World," *The Preservation of Traditional Forms of the Learned and Popular Music of the Orient and the Occident*, ed. William Kay Archer (Urbana: Center for Comparative Psycholinguistics, Institute of Communications Research, University of Illinois [1964]), 101–2.

111. George W. Stocking Jr., *Race, Culture, and Evolution: Essays in the History of Anthropology* (New York: Free Press, 1968), 228–29; emphases in original.

112. Stocking, *Race, Culture, and Evolution*, 230–31.

113. Franz Boas, *The Mind of Primitive Man* (New York: Macmillan, 1911), 278.

114. Franz Boas, *Anthropology and Modern Life* (New York: Dover, 1986), 204.

115. Henry Cowell, note to String Quartet no. 4, *United Quartet* (San Francisco: New Music Edition, 1936), as quoted by Nicholls, "Henry Cowell's *United Quartet*," 199.

116. Henry Cowell, note to String Quartet no. 4, *United Quartet* (New York: C. F. Peters, 1966).

117. Nicholls, "Henry Cowell's *United Quartet*," 200, 202.

118. Nicholls, "Transethnicism," 573.

INTRODUCTION TO PART II:
GLOBALIZATION AS A CULTURAL SYSTEM

1. See, for just a few examples, Jean Comaroff and John L. Comaroff, "Millennial Capitalism: First Thoughts on a Second Coming," *Millennial Capitalism and the Culture of Neoliberalism* (Durham: Duke University Press, 2001); Naomi Klein, *No Logo: Taking Aim at the Brand Bullies* (New York: Picador, 2000); David C. Korten, *When Corporations Rule the World* (West Hartford, Conn.: Kumarian, 1995); and Daniel Yergin and Joseph Stanislaw, *The Commanding Heights: The Battle for the World Economy* (New York: Simon and Schuster, 1998).

2. While income in North America, western Europe, and some other countries has generally risen, there has nonetheless been a polarizing tendency, with "decline and stagnation at the bottom, moderate growth and relative loss in the middle, and big growth at the top." Michael Storper, "Lived Effects of the Contemporary Economy: Globalization, Inequality, and Consumer Society," *Millennial Capitalism and the Culture of Neoliberalism*, ed. Jean Comaroff and John L. Comaroff (Durham: Duke University Press, 2001), 91.

3. William Mazzarella, "Culture, Globalization, Mediation," *Annual Review of Anthropology* (2004), 352.

4. Malcolm Waters, *Globalization* (New York: Routledge, 1995), 1; emphasis in original. For another useful treatment of the concept see John Tomlinson, *Globalization and Culture* (Chicago: University of Chicago Press, 1999).

5. See also Immanuel Wallerstein's *The Modern World-System: Capitalist Agriculture and the Origins of the European World-Economy in the Sixteenth Century* (New York: Academic,

1974); and Jerry H. Bentley, *Old World Encounters: Cross-Cultural Contacts and Exchanges in Pre-modern Times* (New York: Oxford University Press, 1993).

6. Jonathan Xavier Inda and Renato Rosaldo, "Introduction: A World in Motion," *The Anthropology of Globalization: A Reader*, ed. Inda and Rosaldo (Malden, Mass.: Blackwell, 2002).

7. For a discussion of cultural imperialism from this perspective see my "World Music Revisited," 13th Internationaler Kongress der Gesellschaft für Musikforschung, Weimar, 20 September 2004. See also Martin Stokes, "Music and the Global Order," *Annual Review of Anthropology* (2004): 47–72.

8. Jonathan Friedman, "Being in the World: Globalization and Localization," *Global Culture: Nationalism, Globalization and Modernity*, ed. Mike Featherstone (Newbury Park, Calif.: Sage, 1990).

9. I am referring here to Arjun Appadurai's chapter "Consumption, Duration, and History" in his *Modernity at Large: Cultural Dimensions of Globalization* (Minneapolis: University of Minnesota Press, 1996).

10. "New consumerism" is used by Juliet Schor in *Do Americans Shop too Much?* (Boston: Beacon, 2000); "consumer culture reborn" by Martyn J. Lee in *Consumer Culture Reborn: The Cultural Politics of Consumption* (New York: Routledge, 1993); "postmodern markets" by Douglas Holt in his chapter of the same name in *Do Americans Shop too Much?*; "hyperconsumption" by George Ritzer in *Enchanting a Disenchanted World: Revolutionizing the Means of Consumption* (Thousand Oaks, Calif.: Pine Forge, 1999); and "mallcondo" by James B. Twitchell in *Lead Us into Temptation: The Triumph of American Materialism* (New York: Columbia University Press, 1999).

11. Sharon Zukin, *Landscapes of Power: From Detroit to Disney World* (Berkeley: University of California Press, 1991), 4.

12. Twitchell, *Lead Us into Temptation*, 18.

13. See Gary Cross, *An All-Consuming Century: Why Commercialism Won in Modern America* (New York: Columbia University Press, 2000), 215. For information on the Mall of America, see http://www.mallofamerica.com; last visited 9 February 2004.

14. See Mark Gottdiener, "The Consumption of Space and the Spaces of Consumption," *New Forms of Consumption: Consumers, Culture, and Commodification*, ed. Gottdiener (Lanham, Md.: Rowan and Littlefield, 2000), and Ritzer, *Enchanting a Disenchanted World*.

15. Ritzer, *Enchanting a Disenchanted World*, 22.

16. Cross, *An All-Consuming Century*, 214–15.

17. George Lipsitz, "Consumer Spending as State Project: Yesterday's Solutions and Today's Problems," *Getting and Spending: European and American Consumer Societies in the Twentieth Century*, ed. Susan Strasser, Charles McGovern, and Matthias Judt (Cambridge: Cambridge University Press, 1998), 141.

18. Russell W. Belk, *Collecting in a Consumer Society* (New York: Routledge, 1995), 139.

19. Will Straw, "Sizing Up Record Collections: Gender and Connoisseurship in Rock Music Culture," *Sexing the Groove: Popular Music and Gender*, ed. Sheila Whiteley (New

York: Routledge, 1997); and my *Strange Sounds: Music, Technology and Culture* (New York: Routledge, 2001). See also Evan Eisenberg, *The Recording Angel: The Experience of Music from Aristotle to Zappa* (New York: Penguin, 1988); and Grant McCracken, *Culture and Consumption: New Approaches to the Symbolic Character of Consumer Goods and Activities* (Bloomington: Indiana University Press, 1990).

20. Schor, *Do Americans Shop too Much?*, 7–11.

21. Holt, "Postmodern Markets," 64–65; see also Grant McCracken, *Plenitude* (Toronto: Periph.: Fluide, 1997).

22. Holt, "Postmodern Markets," 65. Craig J. Thompson, in another response to Schor, echoes Holt's emphasis on the social construction of identities and the complex role that consumption plays in this construction. Craig J. Thompson, "A New Puritanism?," *Do Americans Shop too Much?*, 69–70.

23. See Scott Lash and John Urry, *The End of Organized Capitalism* (Madison: University of Wisconsin Press, 1987).

24. On this point see also Lizabeth Cohen, *A Consumer's Republic: The Politics of Mass Consumption in Postwar America* (New York: Alfred A. Knopf, 2003).

25. Lee, *Consumer Culture Reborn*. This is only a brief summary of many points from Lee's useful book.

26. Thatcher and Reagan were not enunciating new positions, however, but amplifying an existing ideological relationship between consumption and citizenship that dates back to the beginning of the twentieth century. See Charles McGovern, "Consumption and Citizenship in the United States, 1900–1940," *Getting and Spending*, ed. Strasser, McGovern, and Judt.

27. Lipsitz, "Consumer Spending as State Project," 142.

28. Don Slater, *Consumer Culture and Modernity* (Malden, Mass.: Blackwell, 1997), 11.

29. I would like to thank John Smalley for reminding me of this last bumper sticker.

30. The new aesthetic resulting from this shift has been called "postmodern" (a term that Lee uses), though nowadays that label has become overused to the point of banalization. But the "postmodern" aesthetic itself, whatever one calls it, is a recognizable one, characterized by Lee as an attitude that "transforms all cultural content into objects for immediate consumption rather than texts of contemplative reception or detached and intellectual interpretation." Lee, *Consumer Culture Reborn*, 143.

31. Warren Susman, *Culture as History: The Transformation of American Society in the Twentieth Century* (New York: Pantheon, 1984), 153.

32. Susman, *Culture as History*, 154.

33. Also in the 1950s, "culture" came to be used most prominently to describe mass culture, as in essays by Adorno and Horkheimer, Dwight Macdonald, and others. Michael Denning, *Culture in the Age of Three Worlds* (New York: Verso, 2004), 79–81.

34. Christopher Shannon, *A World Made Safe for Differences: Cold War Intellectuals and the Politics of Identity* (Lanham, Md.: Rowan and Littlefield, 2001).

35. Frederick Buell, "National Postnationalism: Globalist Discourse in Contemporary American Culture," *American Quarterly* 50 (September 1998): 548–91.

36. Immanuel Wallerstein, *Historical Capitalism*, pubd. with *Capitalist Civilization* (New York: Verso 1983), 159.

37. On this point see also Arjun Appadurai's chapter "Life after Primordialism" in *Modernity at Large*.

38. Jean-Paul Sartre, *Search for a Method*, trans. Hazel E. Barnes (New York: Alfred A. Knopf, 1967), 91; emphasis in original.

39. See James Heartfield, *The "Death of the Subject" Explained* (Sheffield: Sheffield Hallam University Press, 2002).

40. Elizabeth Keenan, "Ladies, Womyn, and Grrls: Policing the Borders of Gender and Generations at Women's Rock Music Festivals," paper delivered at the annual meeting of the Society for Ethnomusicology, Atlanta, 19 November 2005.

CHAPTER 4: CONSUMPTION, GLOBALIZATION, AND MUSIC

1. Arjun Appadurai, *Modernity at Large: Cultural Dimensions of Globalization* (Minneapolis: University of Minnesota Press, 1996), 15.

2. Michel Wieviorka, "Is Multiculturalism the Solution?," *Ethnic and Racial Studies* 21 (September 1998): 884.

3. Wieviorka, "Is Multiculturalism the Solution?," 882.

4. For a useful overview see C. W. Watson, *Multiculturalism* (Philadelphia: Open University Press, 2000); for dissents and critiques see Nathan Glazer, *We Are All Multiculturalists Now* (Cambridge: Harvard University Press, 1997), David A. Hollinger, *Postethnic America: Beyond Multiculturalism* (New York: Basic, 1995), and Charles Taylor, *Multiculturalism: Examining the Politics of Recognition*, ed. Amy Gutmann (Princeton: Princeton University Press, 1994). For a thoughtful critique see Frederick Buell, "National Postnationalism: Globalist Discourse in Contemporary American Culture," *American Quarterly* 50 (September 1998): 548–91.

5. Étienne Balibar, "Is There a 'Neo-Racism'?," *Race, Nation, Class: Ambiguous Identities*, by Étienne Balibar and Immanuel Wallerstein (New York: Verso, 1991).

6. David Rieff, "Multiculturalism's Silent Partner," *Harper's*, August 1993, 62, 63.

7. For more on this perspective see Roger Rouse, "Thinking through Transnationalism: Notes on the Cultural Politics of Class Relations in the Contemporary United States," *Public Culture* 7 (spring 1995): 353–402.

8. Michael Lind, *The Next American Nation: The New Nationalism and the Fourth American Revolution* (New York: Free Press, 1995).

9. Rieff, "Multiculturalism's Silent Partner," 64.

10. Rieff, "Multiculturalism's Silent Partner," 64.

11. Rieff, "Multiculturalism's Silent Partner," 64.

12. Timothy D. Taylor, "Popular Musics and Globalization," *Global Pop: World Music, World Markets* (New York: Routledge, 1997).

13. Guillermo Gómez-Peña, "The New Global Culture: Somewhere between Corporate Multiculturalism and the Mainstream Bizarre (a Border Perspective)," *TDR* 45 (spring 2001): 12.

14. Gómez-Peña, "The New Global Culture," 16.

15. Gómez-Peña, "The New Global Culture," 16.

16. Louise Meintjes, "Paul Simon's *Graceland*, South Africa, and the Mediation of Musical Meaning," *Ethnomusicology* 34 (winter 1990): 37–73. See also Steven Feld, "From Schizophonia to Schismogenesis: On the Discourses and Commodification Practices of 'World Music' and 'World Beat,'" *Music Grooves: Essays and Dialogues*, by Charles Keil and Steven Feld (Chicago: University of Chicago Press, 1994).

17. Steven Williams, "State of 'Graceland,'" *Los Angeles Times*, 24 August 1986, 92.

18. Fernando Gonzalez, "Paul Simon's World Beat," *Boston Globe*, 14 October 1990, § B, 25.

19. Gonzalez, "Paul Simon's World Beat."

20. Gonzalez, "Paul Simon's World Beat."

21. Pierre Bourdieu, *Distinction: A Social Critique of the Judgement of Taste*, trans. Richard Nice (Cambridge: Harvard University Press, 1984). For a longer discussion of these bourgeois groups with respect to the production of music, see my "The Changing Shape of the Culture Industry; or, How Did Electronica Music Get into Television Commercials?," *Journal of Television and New Media*, forthcoming.

22. For useful discussions of sampling see Hugh Davies, "A History of Sampling," *Organised Sound* 1 (April 1996): 3–11; Andrew Goodwin, "Sample and Hold: Pop Music in the Digital Age of Reproduction," *On Record: Rock, Pop, and the Written World*, ed. Simon Frith and Andrew Goodwin (New York: Pantheon, 1990); Martin Russ, *Sound Synthesis and Sampling* (Oxford: Focal Press, 1996); and my "Sampling and Consumption," *Sound Unbound: Music, Multimedia, and Contemporary Sound Art: An Anthology of Writings on Contemporary Culture*, ed. Paul D. Miller (Cambridge: MIT Press, forthcoming).

23. Taylor, "Sampling and Consumption."

24. Matt Golosinski, "Outer Bass: Bill Laswell Is a Deep-Groove Guerrilla Who's Not Afraid to Lay Down the Bottom Line," *Phoenix New Times*, 26 March 1998.

25. Anil Prasad, "Extending Energy and Experimentation" [interview with Bill Laswell, 27 April 1999], http://www.innerviews.org/inner/laswell.html, last visited 17 August 2004.

26. Christine Iwan, "Albion's Own Ace of Bass; Grammy-Winning Bill Laswell Returns to His Hometown," *Enquirer* (Battle Creek), 16 June 2003.

27. Edward R. Kealy, "From Craft to Art: The Case of Sound Mixers and Popular Music," *Sociology of Work and Occupations* 6 (February 1979): 3–29. See also Edward R. Kealy, "The Real Rock Revolution: Sound Mixers, Social Inequality, and the Aesthetics of Popular Music Production," Ph.D. diss., Northwestern University, 1974.

28. Producers speak of this in interviews. George Martin, for example, says that "the role of the producer has already changed. There are more engineer/producers now. I'm the old-fashioned type, a producer who is a musician and likes to work with an engineer who's an engineer. I think that the two roles are very difficult to combine. I feel that the guy who concentrates on the art, the production and the music,

shouldn't really be bothered with whether the microphone is on the blink or not, or whether the EQ switch is dirty or not." "High Tea" [interview with George Martin and John Burgess by Mr. Bonzai], *Music Producers: Conversations with Today's Top Record Makers*, ed. Terri Stone (Emeryville, Calif.: Mix, 1992), 75.

29. Mark Cunningham, *Good Vibrations: A History of Record Production* (Chessington, England: Castle, 1996), 251. See also Jari Muikku, who writes that the role of the producer became more important in the 1980s. Muikku, "On the Role of the Tasks of a Record Producer," *Popular Music and Society* 14 (spring 1990): 25–34.

30. The producer Steve Albini speaks of the technical knowledge once required by producers, knowledge that is less necessary now since equipment has got easier to use since the 1970s. For that reason, he says, few self-respecting engineers would call themselves producers. Steve Albini, "The Problem with Music," http://www.musicianassist.com/archive/article/ART/a-1098-1.htm, last visited 18 August 2004; Steve Albini, "Nemesis of Corporate Rock" [interview by Camran Afsari], *Music Producers: Conversations with Today's Hottest Hitmakers*, ed. Barbara Schultz (Emeryville, Calif.: Mix, 2000). I would like to thank Louise Meintjes for recommending the first of these.

31. Cunningham, *Good Vibrations*, 313.

32. George Martin, "Yesterday & Today" [interview by Mel Lambert], *Music Producers*, ed. Schultz, 228.

33. The sampled sounds on this album weren't just from other places, however; they included excerpts from a radio talk show host, a caller, a politician's reply, the Reverend Paul Morton, an exorcist, African American singers from the Georgia Sea Islands, and a radio evangelist.

34. Eric Tamm, in *Brian Eno: His Music and the Vertical Color of Sound* (Boston: Faber and Faber, 1989), writes that Eno and Byrne had been interested in Arab music for some time before making *My Life in the Bush of Ghosts* in 1979. For Tamm, the artistic value of the album, and its accurate depiction of an enactment of a McLuhanesque "global village," lent the project an aura of intellectual legitimacy, which he defends by invoking earlier western artists who appropriated forms from other parts of the world: Picasso, Stravinsky, and the Beatles.

35. "Doing What Feels Right" [interview with John Potoker by Nick Vallelonga], *Music Producers*, ed. Stone, 89.

36. Mark Jacobson, "Playing the Synthesizer," *Natural History*, March 1996, 25.

37. "International Enigma" [interview with Bill Laswell by Bill Milkowski], *Music Producers: Conversations with Today's Top Record Makers*, ed. Terri Stone (Emeryville, Calif.: Mix, 1992), 51.

38. David Toop, *Exotica* (New York: Serpent's Tail, 1999), 177.

39. Geoffrey Sherrard, "The Illustrious Industrious Bill Laswell," http://www.glowmag.com/laswell/laswell.html [URL no longer active].

40. Leslie Sly, "Bill Laswell: World Music Mixes from a Material Guy," *Keyboard*, June 1994, 10.

41. Peter K. Lunt and Sonia M. Livingstone, *Mass Consumption and Personal Identity: Everyday Economic Experience* (Philadelphia: Open University Press, 1992), 171.

42. I would like to thank Morgan Lang for telling me of these loops.

43. http://mediasoftware.sonypictures.com/loop_libraries/showloop.asp?PID=636 &ms=1, last visited 22 August 2004.

44. http://mediasoftware.sonypictures.com/loop_libraries/showloop.asp?PID=628 &ms=1, last visited 22 August 2004.

45. http://mediasoftware.sonypictures.com/loop_libraries/ShowLoop.asp?PID=634 &ms=1, last visited 22 August 2004.

46. Appadurai, *Modernity at Large*, 4. For an ethnomusicological treatment of this idea see Veit Erlmann, *Music, Modernity, and the Global Imagination: South Africa and the West* (New York: Oxford University Press, 1999).

47. Appadurai, *Modernity at Large*, 7.

48. Scott Lash and John Urry, *Economies of Signs and Space* (Newbury Park, Calif.: Sage Publications, 1994), 137–38. Their argument could be extended to include not just individuals but also books (e.g. the Harry Potter stories) or films (e.g. the *Star Wars* films), and more.

49. Laswell discusses his experience on this recording in Prasad, "Extending Energy and Experimentation."

50. Jacobson, "Playing the Synthesizer," 27.

51. Jacboson, "Playing the Synthesizer," 24; ellipsis in original.

52. See Morgan Luker, " 'Deconstructing Havana': Bill Laswell's *Imaginary Cuba* and the Critical Revision of Authenticity," paper presented at the Society for Ethnomusicology, Estes Park, Colo., 27 October 2002.

53. Prasad, "Extending Energy and Experimentation."

54. Prasad, "Extending Energy and Experimentation."

55. Michel de Certeau, *The Practice of Everyday Life*, trans. Steven Rendall (Berkeley: University of California Press, 1984), xii–xiii; emphasis in original.

CHAPTER 5: SOME VERSIONS OF DIFFERENCE

1. There are other kinds of mixes that have been theorized — *mestizaje*, *métissage*, creolization — and that I could discuss, but they are not nearly as visible in considerations of music as hybridity. On *mestizaje* see Gloria Anzaldúa, *Borderlands: The New Mestiza* (San Francisco: Aunt Lute, 1991); and J. Jorge Klor de Alva, "The Postcolonization of the (Latin) American Experience: A Reconsideration of 'Colonialism,' 'Postcolonialism,' and 'Mestizaje,' " *After Colonialism: Imperial Histories and Postcolonial Displacements*, ed. Gyan Prakash (Princeton: Princeton University Press, 1995). On *métissage* see Ann Laura Stoler, "Sexual Affronts and Racial Frontiers: European Identities and the Cultural Politics of Exclusion in Colonial Southeast Asia," *Tensions of Empire: Colonial Cultures in a Bourgeois World*, ed. Frederick Cooper and Ann Laura Stoler (Berkeley: University of California Press, 1997). On creolization see Line Grenier and Jocelyne Guilbault, "Créolité and Francophonie in Music: Socio-Musical Re-

positioning Where It Matters," *Cultural Studies* 11 (May 1997): 207–34; Ulf Hannerz, *Transnational Connections: Culture, People, Places* (New York: Routledge, 1996); and David Parkin, "Nemi in the Modern World: Return of the Exotic?," *Man* 28 (March 1993): 79–99. For another useful article that touches on the concept of hybridity see Lisa Lowe, *Immigrant Acts: On Asian American Cultural Politics* (Durham: Duke University Press, 1996).

2. See Andrew Goodwin, "Popular Music and Postmodern Theory," *Cultural Studies* 5 (May 1991): 174–90.

3. Brook has achieved more recent fame as the collaborator with the late Nusrat Fateh Ali Khan on *Night Song*, Real World 2354, 1996.

4. See also Simon Frith, "The Discourse of World Music," *Western Music and Its Others: Difference, Representation, and Appropriation in Music*, ed. Georgina Born and David Hesmondhalgh (Berkeley: University of California Press, 2000).

5. The CD *Deep Forest* by the group of the same name was released in 1992 and sold over 1.5 million copies. For more on Deep Forest see Carrie Borzillo, "Deep Forest Growing in Popularity; 550's World Music-Dance Hybrid Climbs Charts," *Billboard*, 19 February 1994, 8, and "U.S. Ad Use Adds to Commercial Success of Deep Forest," *Billboard*, 11 June 1994, 44; Andrew Ross, review of *Deep Forest*, *Artforum*, December 1993, 11; Al Weisel, "Deep Forest's Lush Lullaby," *Rolling Stone*, 21 April 1994, 26; Hugo Zemp, "The/An Ethnomusicologist and the Record Business," *Yearbook for Traditional Music* 28 (1996): 36–56; and most importantly Steven Feld, "pygmy POP: A Genealogy of Schizophonic Mimesis," *Yearbook for Traditional Music* 28 (1996): 1–35.

6. Liner notes to Wes, *Welenga*, Sony Music 48146-2, 1997. I would like to thank Harriet Whitehead for introducing me to this album.

7. Ashwani Sharma, "Sounds Oriental: The (Im)Possibility of Theorizing Asian Musical Cultures," *Dis-Orienting Rhythms: The Politics of the New Asian Dance Music*, ed. Sanjay Sharma, John Hutnyk, and Ashwani Sharma (Atlantic Highlands, N.J.: Zed, 1996), 20.

8. For more on "world music" as style see chapter 7.

9. For a similar point see John Hutnyk, "Adorno at Womad: South Asian Crossovers and the Limits of Hybridity-Talk," *Debating Cultural Hybridity: Multi-Cultural Identities and the Politics of Anti-Racism*, ed. Pnina Werbner and Tariq Modood (Atlantic Highlands, N.J.: Zed, 1997).

10. This process of naturalization is discussed at length in my *Global Pop: World Music, World Markets* (New York: Routledge, 1997).

11. Paul Robicheau, "Listening to History," *Boston Globe*, 25 September 1998, § D, 15.

12. "Kidjo's 'Oremi' Is Heavenly," *Boston Herald*, 25 September 1998, S25. Robert Young argues in *Colonial Desire: Hybridity in Theory, Culture and Race* (New York: Routledge, 1995) that the concept of hybridity recapitulates nineteenth-century discourses on race and racism in that it naturalizes peoples from other cultures by employing a term from agriculture, and indeed the term is usually applied to musics by peoples from other cultures. Paul Simon's *Graceland* (1986), for example, was widely hailed as an

important rock album, not as a hybrid of South African (and other African) popular musics and American popular musics. Paul Simon's prominence as an international star, American and white, ensured that *Graceland* would be interpreted as the product of his individual artistic genius, not as a hybrid of styles. See Louise Meintjes, "Paul Simon's *Graceland*, South Africa, and the Mediation of Musical Meaning," *Ethnomusicology* 34 (winter 1990): 37–73, for a consideration of Simon's *Graceland*.

13. Elena Oumano, "Island Targets R&B Market with New Album from Kidjo," *Billboard*, 23 May 1998, 1.

14. The term "savage slot" was introduced by Michel-Rolph Trouillot, "Anthropology and the Savage Slot: The Poetics and Politics of Otherness," *Recapturing Anthropology: Working in the Present*, ed. Richard G. Fox (Santa Fe: School of American Research Press, 1991).

15. This is discussed in *Global Pop*, chapter 5. For some of the criticisms of Kidjo see especially Philip Sweeney, *The Virgin Directory of World Music* (London: Virgin, 1991); Brooke Wentz, "No Kid Stuff," *Beat*, 1993, 42–45; and Wentz, "Youssou N'Dour: Is He Shaking the Tree or Cutting It Down?," *Rhythm Music*, May–June 1994, 38.

16. Simon Broughton, Mark Ellingham, David Muddyman, and Richard Trillo, eds., *World Music: The Rough Guide* (London: Rough Guides, 1994), 298. The newer edition of the *Rough Guide* is more circumspect, reporting that Kidjo "goes from strength to strength" and that her albums "vary widely in style." Simon Broughton, Mark Ellingham, and Richard Trillo, eds., *World Music: The Rough Guide*, vol. 1, *Africa, Europe and the Middle East* (London: Rough Guides, 1999), 433, 434.

17. Marcus Breen, ed., *Our Place, Our Music*, Australian Popular Music in Perspective, vol. 2 (Canberra: Aboriginal Studies Press, 1989), 65.

18. Jocelyne Guilbault, *Zouk: World Music in the West Indies* (Chicago: University of Chicago Press, 1993), 150.

19. Jill Stubington and Peter Dunbar-Hall, "Yothu Yindi's 'Treaty': Ganma in Music," *Popular Music* 13 (October 1994): 250.

20. See Leela Gandhi, *Postcolonial Theory: An Introduction* (New York: Columbia University Press, 1998), for a similar point about literature.

21. Homi K. Bhabha, "The Third Space: Interview with Homi Bhabha," *Identity: Community, Culture, Difference*, ed. Jonathan Rutherford (London: Lawrence and Wishart, 1990), 211. For more of Bhabha's influential writings on these and other issues see his *The Location of Culture* (New York: Routledge, 1994).

22. See James Clifford, *Routes: Travel and Translation in the Late Twentieth Century* (Cambridge: Harvard University Press, 1997), especially chapter 6.

23. Michael Hardt and Antonio Negri, *Empire* (Cambridge: Harvard University Press, 2000), 144–46.

24. *World Music: The Rough Guide*, Broughton, Ellingham, and Trillio, eds.; *World Music: The Rough Guide*, Broughton, Ellingham, Muddyman, and Trillio, eds., vol. 1.

25. There are many examples of uses of the hybridity concept by South Asians in discussions of bhangra remix. A few: Lavina Melwani, "It's a Party," *Welcome to Little*

India, January 1997, 21; Sunita Sunder Mukhi, "Forging an Indian American Identity: Guess Who's Coming to Dinner?," *Little India*, May 1996, 49, Mukhi, "Forging an Indian American Identity: Something to Dance About," *Little India*, April 1996, 53, and Mukhi, *Doing the Desi Thing: Performing Indianness in New York City* (New York: Garland, 2000).

26. Bhangra is a folk music of the Punjabis of Northern India and Pakistan, a lively music celebrating the end of the harvest that eventually became popular all over the Punjab. Punjabis migrating to England and Canada in the 1960s and 1970s brought bhangra with them. These Punjabis mixed bhangra with the instruments and sounds they found in their new homes, at first using mainly acoustic instruments (such as accordion, violin, and acoustic guitar) before moving to a fairly standard rock band instrumentation (drum kits, synthesizers, guitars). In the 1980s bhangra musicians incorporated elements from electronic dance music such as drum machines to match the singsong beat of the *dhol* drums, thus creating the signature sound of bhangra. Later, Caribbean and African American musical influences dominated. While these changes in sound were occurring, in the UK and other parts of the South Asian diaspora, bhangra evolved into a pan–South Asian music that became extremely popular among diasporic South Asian youths, not just those of Punjabi heritage but Hindus, Muslims, Sikhs, and Jains alike. For more on bhangra see, in addition to the articles cited in the discussion, Sabita Banerji, "Ghazals of Bhangra in Great Britain," *Popular Music* 7 (May 1988): 207–13; and Sabita Banerji and Gerd Baumann, "Bhangra 1984–8: Fusion and Professionalization in a Genre of South Asian Dance Music," *Black Music in Britain: Essays on the Afro-Asian Contribution to Popular Music*, ed. Paul Oliver (Buckingham: Open University Press, 1990).

27. Gayatri Gopinath, " 'Bombay, U.K., Yuba City': Bhangra Music and the Engendering of Diaspora," *Diaspora* 4 (winter 1995): 303–21.

28. Nabeel Zuberi, *Sounds English: Transnational Popular Music* (Urbana: University of Illinois Press, 2001).

29. Mukhi, "Guess Who's Coming to Dinner?," 49.

30. Mukhi, "Forging an Indian American Identity," 53.

31. http://www.cdnow.com/cgi-bin/mserver/SID=1261988902/pagename=/RP/CDN/FIND/album.html/ArtistID=SAGOO*BALLY/ITEMID=630225 [URL no longer active].

32. Ken Micallef, "Talvin Singh," *Rolling Stone*, 21 August 1997, 36.

33. For some examples of music journalists' use of the term with respect to bhangra remix music, see Neil McCormack, "At the Speed of Sound on Pop," *Daily Telegraph*, 15 February 2001, 26; David Lister, "Mercury Prize," *Independent* (London), 26 July 2000, 7; Marty Lipp, "On the Record," *Newsday*, 11 June 2000, § D, 26; D. James Romero, "His Drum-and-Bass Is Served with Some Spice," *Los Angeles Times*, 20 July 1997, 56; Paul H. B. Shin, "Hot New Music Has Some Very Old Roots," *Daily News* (New York), 18 February 1998, 3; and Neil Spencer, "Kaftans Are Back but Singh Wants No Part of Any Indian Summer," *Observer* (London), 16 February 1997, 10.

34. Sharma, "Sounds Oriental," 25.

35. The best known of these "collaborations" is probably Paul Simon's recording with the South African chorus Ladysmith Black Mambazo on the album *Graceland*, discussed in chapter 4.

36. Channi, from Alaap, the first major bhangra band in the UK, says, "I would not class the music in the bhangra charts as proper bhangra because they have lost the [South] Asian touch. Bhangra is when you have more authentic sounds like the dhol and the alghoza [flute]" (quoted by Broughton, Ellingham, and Trillo, eds., *World Music*, 231).

37. See Sunaina Marr Maira, *Desis in the House: Indian American Youth Culture in New York City* (Philadelphia: Temple University Press, 2002), and Maira, "Identity Dub: Second-Generation Indian Americans and Youth Culture," *Cultural Anthropology* 14 (February 1999): 29–60, for extensive treatments of the question of generation among diasporic South Asians.

38. DJ Jiten, interview, http://www.streetsound.com/bhangra/intjiten83.html [URL no longer active]. All quotations from the Internet appear with their original spelling and punctuation unless otherwise noted.

39. Jatender S. Heer, "Revolutionizing Bhangra: Punjabi MC Gives Bhangra a Much Needed Jolt," *Welcome to Little India*, July 1998, 56.

40. It may be that these musicians are getting back to their roots to combat the appropriation of South Asian sounds and symbols by westerners. Madonna's album *Ray of Light* (1998) was one culprit here; see Lavina Melwani, "Indian Chic: OM to the Music," *Little India*, April 1998, 20; and Sunaina Maria, "Henna and Hip Hop: The Politics of Cultural Production and the Work of Cultural Studies," *Journal of Asian American Studies* 3 (October 2000): 239–69. Another case concerned Aerosmith's album cover for *Nine Lives* (1997), which was changed after protests from Hindus; see "Hindu Protest Forces Sony to Remake CD," *Hinduism Today*, July 1997, 47. Thanks are due to Irene Nexica for suggesting this line of inquiry.

41. Lisa Tsering, "Bally Gets Busy with Bhangra, Film Projects," *India West*, August 1998, http://members.tripod.com/~LisaTsering/index-8.html [URL no longer active].

42. For more on Sagoo and other South Asian musicians based in the UK see Zuberi, *Sounds English*, chapter 5.

43. Liner notes to *What Is Bhangra?*, IRS Records 7243 8 29242 27, 1994.

44. Maira, "Henna and Hip Hop," 335.

45. Somini Sengupta, "To Be Young, Indian and Hip," *New York Times*, 30 July 1996, § 13, 11.

46. Sagoo has since left to found his own label, ISHQ records, which has a web site at http:///www.ishqrecords.com.

47. I would like to thank Steven Feld for his insights on this point.

48. This point is also raised by Aijaz Ahmad, "The Politics of Literary Postcoloniality," *Race and Class* 36 (January–March 1995): 1–20.

49. Sunaina Maira, "Desis Reprazent: Bhangra Remix and Hip Hop in New York City," *Postcolonial Studies* 1 (November 1998): 361.

50. Maira, "Desis Reprazent," 361.

51. Maira, *Desis in the House*, 56–57.

52. See Sengupta, "To Be Young, Indian and Hip," for a fascinating example of a second-generation South Asian seeking advice from his mother about which Indian film music to sample in his remix.

53. See Clifford, *Routes*.

54. John Castles, "Tjungaringanyi: Aboriginal Rock," *From Pop to Punk to Postmodernism: Popular Music and Australian Culture from the 1960s to the 1990s*, ed. Philip Hayward (North Sydney: Allen and Unwin, 1992); Philip Hayward, "Music Video, the Bicentenary (and After)," *From Pop to Punk to Postmodernism*, and "Safe, Exotic and Somewhere Else: Yothu Yindi, Treaty, and the Mediation of Aboriginality," *Perfect Beat* 1 (January 1993): 33–42; Philip Hayward and Karl Neuenfeldt, "Yothu Yindi: Context and Significance," *Sound Alliances: Indigenous Peoples, Cultural Politics and Popular Music in the Pacific*, ed. Philip Hayward (London: Cassell, 1998); George Lipsitz, *Dangerous Crossroads: Popular Music, Postmodernism and the Poetics of Place* (New York: Verso, 1994); Fiona Magowan, " 'The Land Is Our Mäar (Essence), It Stays Forever': The Yothu-Yindi Relationship in Australian Aboriginal Traditional and Popular Musics," *Ethnicity, Identity and Music: The Musical Construction of Place*, ed. Martin Stokes (Providence, R.I.: Berg, 1994), and "Traditions of the Mind or the Music Video: Imagining the Imagination in Yothu Yindi's Tribal Voice," *Arena* 7 (1996): 99–111; Tony Mitchell, *Popular Music and Local Identity: Rock, Pop and Rap in Europe and Oceania* (New York: Leicester University Press, 1997); Stephen Muecke, *Textual Spaces: Aboriginality and Cultural Studies* (Kensington: New South Wales University Press, 1992); Karl Neuenfeldt, "Yothu Yindi and Ganma: The Cultural Transposition of Aboriginal Agenda through Metaphor and Music," *Journal of Australian Studies* 38 (September 1993): 1–11, and "Yothu Yindi: Agendas and Aspirations," *Sound Alliances*, ed. Hayward; Lisa Nicol, "Culture, Custom and Collaboration: The Production of Yothu Yindi's Treaty Videos," *Perfect Beat* 1 (January 1993): 23–32; Adam Shoemaker, "The Politics of Yothu Yindi," *Working Papers in Australian Studies*, ed. Kate Darian-Smith (London: Institute of Commonwealth Studies, 1994), 88–96, and "Selling Yothu Yindi," *Republica: All Same as Family in a Big 'Ouse*, ed. George Papaellinas (Sydney: Angus and Robertson, 1994); Stubington and Dunbar-Hall, "Yothu Yindi's 'Treaty' "; Graeme Turner, *Making It National: Nationalism and Australian Popular Culture* (St. Leonards, N.S.W., Australia: Allen and Unwin, 1994); and Mandawuy Yunupingu, "Yothu Yindi: Finding Balance," *Race and Class* 35 (April–June 1994): 113–20.

55. Breen, ed., *Our Place. Our Music*, 121. For more on the importance of Bob Marley and reggae music for Australian and New Zealand Aboriginal popular musics see also John Dix, *Stranded in Paradise: New Zealand Rock and Roll, 1955–1985* (Wellington: Paradise, 1988); and Lipsitz, *Dangerous Crossroads*. For more on cross-racial and cross-ethnic affiliations see Juan Flores, " 'Que Assimilated, Brother, Yo Soy Asimilao': The Structuring of Puerto Rican Identity in the U.S.," *Journal of Ethnic Studies* 13 (fall 1984): 1–16.

56. Helen Watson, "The Ganma Project: Research in Mathematics Education by the Yolngu Community in the Schools of the Laynhapuy (N.E. Arnhemland)," *Yirrkala Community School Action Group*, 1988, 2, as quoted by Neuenfeldt, "Yothu Yindi and Ganma," 1.

57. Thanks to Irene Nexica for pointing this out. For a similar critique see Turner, *Making It National*.

58. This last point is the main thrust of Sherry B. Ortner, "Resistance and the Problem of Ethnographic Refusal," *Comparative Studies in Society and History* 37 (January 1995): 173–93.

59. Hutnyk, "Adorno at Womad," 128; emphasis in original.

60. Hutnyk, "Adorno at Womad," 129.

61. The best-known of the dub poets are probably Linton Kwesi Johnson and Benjamin Zephaniah.

62. Appadurai coined the term "ideoscapes," among others, to describe the kinds of global flows. Arjun Appadurai, *Modernity at Large: Cultural Dimensions of Globalization* (Minneapolis: University of Minnesota Press, 1996).

CHAPTER 6: YOU CAN TAKE "COUNTRY" OUT OF THE COUNTRY

1. Scott Lash and John Urry, *Economies of Signs and Space* (Thousand Oaks, Calif.: Sage, 1994).

2. Simon Broughton, Mark Ellingham, David Muddyman, and Richard Trillo, eds., *World Music: The Rough Guide* (London: Rough Guides, 1994), 602. This album is actually entitled *Bitter Tears: Ballads of the American Indian*. A little research outside of the *Rough Guide* reveals that at least one of these composers is a Native American, and that Cash once thought himself one-quarter Cherokee, so perhaps the editors of the *Rough Guide* thought this was an "authentic" Native American album.

3. The newer *World Music: The Rough Guide*, vol. 2, omits country music (and rock) from the index entirely, though there are sections on bluegrass and gospel. Simon Broughton and Mark Ellingham, *World Music: The Rough Guide*, vol. 2, *Latin and North America, Caribbean, India, Asia and Pacific* (London: Rough Guides, 2000).

4. Aaron Fox reminds me, however, that the earlier edition of *World Music: The Rough Guide* includes country gospel.

5. See Richard A. Peterson, *Creating Country Music: Fabricating Authenticity* (Chicago: University of Chicago Press, 1997), for a history of the music industry's creation of some of these discourses of authenticity.

6. *Global Pop: World Music, World Markets* (New York: Routledge, 1997), chapter 1.

7. See Barbara Ching, "Acting Naturally: Cultural Distinction and Critiques of Pure Country," *White Trash: Race and Class in America*, ed. Matt Wray and Annalee Newitz (New York: Routledge, 1997), for a discussion of this issue of consciousness of subject position and country music.

8. Rebecca Carroll, "Rodriguez Meets Byrne," *Mother Jones*, July–August 1991, 9; emphasis added.

9. "Black History Month: Spirituals," *Orlando Sentinel*, 6 February 1998, § X, 1; emphasis added.

10. Cathy Werblin, "Vietnamese Full Moon Celebration Planned," *Los Angeles Times* (Orange County Edition), 28 September 1996, § B, 2; emphasis added.

11. "The Creatures," *Alternative Press*, November 1990, http://www.vamp.org/Siouxsie/Text/ap2.html, last visited 9 February 2004; emphasis added.

12. Peter Ramjug, "Robert Palmer Has a Little Bit of Everything in His Music," Reuters, 22 December 1998; emphasis added.

13. Quoted by Colin Berry, "The Sound of Silence: San Francisco's Ambient Music Labels Find Their Groove," *SF Weekly*, 17–23 May 1995, 17; emphasis added.

14. Lila Abu-Lughod, "Writing against Culture," *Recapturing Anthropology: Working in the Present*, ed. Richard G. Fox (Santa Fe: School of American Research Press, 1991), 138.

15. See, perhaps most importantly, several essays collected in *Recapturing Anthropology*: Abu-Lughod, "Writing against Culture"; and Michel-Rolph Trouillot, "Anthropology and the Savage Slot: The Poetics and Politics of Otherness." See also Akhil Gupta and James Ferguson, "Beyond 'Culture': Space, Identity, and the Politics of Difference," *Cultural Anthropology* 7 (February 1992): 7–23; and Ulf Hannerz, *Transnational Connections: Culture, People, Places* (New York: Routledge, 1996).

16. Peterson, *Creating Country Music*.

17. See *Global Pop* and my *Strange Sounds: Music, Technology and Culture* (New York: Routledge, 2001) for a discussion of the presumptively commodifiable nature of world musics.

18. See Simon Frith, *Sound Effects: Youth, Leisure, Politics and Rock n' Roll* (London: Constable, 1983), for this, especially the chapter "Rock, the Liberal Consensus and Everyday Life."

19. Thomas Frank, *The Conquest of Cool: Business Culture, Counterculture, and the Rise of Hip Consumerism* (Chicago: University of Chicago Press, 1997), 11.

20. Frank, *The Conquest of Cool*, 15.

21. Frank, *The Conquest of Cool*, 113.

22. Frank, *The Conquest of Cool*, 216.

23. See Gerry Farrell, *Indian Music and the West* (Oxford: Clarendon, 1997), for a discussion of the West's fascination with Indian music, and India in music; Farrell devotes one chapter to the 1960s. See also David Reck, "The Neon Electric Sarswati," *Contributions to Asian Studies* 12 (1978): 3–19.

24. Frank, *The Conquest of Cool*, 228.

25. John Merli, "Country Riding High," *Broadcasting and Cable*, 2 March 1998, 30.

26. Frank, *The Conquest of Cool*, 28.

27. For insights into the "alternative" category in music see Thomas Frank, "Alternative to What?," *Sounding Off! Music as Subversion/Resistance/Revolution*, ed. Ron Sakolsky and Fred Wei-Han Ho (Brooklyn, N.Y.: Autonomedia, 1995).

28. j. poet, "Worldbeat," *All-Music Guide*, http://www.allmusic.com/; last visited 9 February 2004.

29. Quoted by Robert La Franco and Michael Schuman, "How Do You Say Rock 'n' Roll in Wolof?," *Forbes*, 17 July 1995, 30.

30. Mudrooroo Narogin, *Writing from the Fringe* (Melbourne: Hyland House, 1990), 64, as quoted by John Castles, "Tjungaringanyi: Aboriginal Rock," *From Pop to Punk to Postmodernism: Popular Music and Australian Culture from the 1960s to the 1990s*, ed. Philip Hayward (North Sydney: Allen and Unwin, 1992), 28.

31. For more on Yothu Yindi's positioning in the world music market see chapter 5.

32. For more on the question of world music and politics see my "Bad World Music" in *Bad Music: The Music We Love to Hate*, ed. Chris Washburne and Maiken Derno (New York: Routledge, 2004).

33. Frith, *Sound Effects*, 25.

34. Frith, *Sound Effects*, 24–27.

35. Ronnie Graham, *The Da Capo Guide to Contemporary African Music* (New York: Da Capo, 1988). There is a second volume: Ronnie Graham, *The World of African Music: Stern's Guide to Contemporary African Music*, vol. 2 (Boulder: Pluto, 1992).

36. See *Global Pop*.

37. poet, "Worldbeat."

38. Peterson, *Creating Country Music*, 4. See also Bill C. Malone, *Country Music USA*, rev. ed. (Austin: University of Texas Press, 1985), for a discussion of early white country musicians whose wide repertoires included blues songs.

39. See also Bill Ivey's contribution to the liner notes accompanying *From Where I Stand: The Black Experience in Country Music*, Warner Bros./Reprise 9 47428-2, 1998. And see George Lipsitz, "'Ain't Nobody Here But Us Chickens': The Class Origins of Rock and Roll," *Rainbow at Midnight: Labor and Culture in the 1940s* (Urbana: University of Illinois Press, 1994), for a discussion of black and white musical exchanges along class lines.

40. Phyllis Stark, "Trini Triggs Hopes to Break Barriers," *Billboard*, 28 February 1998, 40.

41. Timothy White, "'Stand' Up for Country Soul!," *Billboard*, 31 January 1998, 4.

42. Nat Hentoff, "Blues Brothers under the Skin," *Wall Street Journal*, 1 May 1998, § W, 12.

43. Robert Santelli, "The Neglected Soul of Country Music," *Rolling Stone*, 19 March 1998, 66.

44. Pierre Bourdieu, *Distinction: A Social Critique of the Judgement of Taste*, trans. Richard Nice (Cambridge: Harvard University Press, 1984), 18.

45. Richard Henderson, "What in the World Is It?," *Billboard*, 28 June 1997, 52.

46. Claudia Puig and Steve Hochman, "New Station Aims to Give Pop Fans a Choice," *Los Angeles Times*, 1 July 1994, § F, 24.

47. Quoted by Rick Mitchell, "American Tastes Move to World Beat," *Houston Chronicle*, 26 January 1992, 8.

48. Philip Spencer, *World Beat: A Listener's Guide to Contemporary World Music on CD* (Pennington, N.J.: A Cappella, 1992), 2–3.

49. Lash and Urry, *Economies of Signs and Space*, 260.

50. Richard A. Peterson and Paul DiMaggio, "From Region to Class, the Changing

Locus of Country Music: A Test of the Massification Hypothesis," *Social Forces* 53 (March 1975): 499. In making this argument, Peterson and DiMaggio draw on an article by Charles Seeger, "Music and Class Structure in the United States," *American Quarterly* 9 (fall 1957): 281–94, which is still well worth reading, not least for his history of the movement to make America musical, a movement that resulted in, among other things, the downgrading of "hillbilly" music that Peterson and DiMaggio recount.

51. See Broughton, Ellingham, Muddyman, and Trillo, eds., *World Music*.

52. Chuck Taylor, "Country Radio Leads in Listeners; Format Also Top in Demo Targets, Study Shows," *Billboard*, 24 May 1997, 93.

53. From Donna Petrozello, "Country Format Is Radio's Favorite," *Broadcasting and Cable*, 10 March 1997, 53–54.

54. Louise Witt, "Back to the Country," *American Demographics*, 1 November 2003, 9. See also Phyllis Stark, "Nashville Scene: Study Has Good News for Country Radio," *Billboard*, 31 July 2004.

55. Simon Broughton, personal communication, 6 November 1998, Maastricht.

56. See also my review of *Songlines, World of Music* 41 (1999): 181–83.

57. I would like to thank Jason Oakes for bringing this to my attention.

58. Jonathan Elias, *The Prayer Cycle*, Sony Classical SK 60569, 1999.

59. For more on Elias's *Prayer Cycle* see Lisa Leigh Parney, "Songs of 'Prayer Cycle' Seek Universal Themes," *Christian Science Monitor*, 23 April 1999, 20; Sony Classical's web site on Elias and this recording, http://www.sonyclassical.com/artists/elias/, last visited 18 August 2004; and my "World Music Revisited," 13th Internationaler Kongress der Gesellschaft für Musikforschung, Weimar, 20 September 2004.

60. Ching, "Acting Naturally," 233. See also Barbara Ching, *Wrong's What I Do Best: Hard Country Music and Contemporary Culture* (New York: Oxford University Press, 2001).

61. Ching, "Acting Naturally," 233.

62. I am indebted to Aaron Fox for this point.

63. Cheryl Heuton, "Country Fills the Airwaves," *Mediaweek*, 12 December 1994, 12.

64. Brian Mansfield, "Album Showcases Slack-Key Guitar Style," *USA Today*, 15 October 1997, § D, 4.

65. Chiori Santiago, "Ride 'Em, Paniolo!," *Rhythm Music*, March 1998, 27.

66. http://www.wbr.com/nashville/warnerwestern/cmp/paniolo.html [URL no longer active].

67. http://www.wbr.com/nashville/warnerwestern/cmp/paniolocds.html [URL no longer active].

68. http://www.wbr.com/nashville/warnerwestern/cmp/paniolo.html [URL no longer active].

69. Maureen Mahon, *Right to Rock: The Black Rock Coalition and the Cultural Politics of Race* (Durham: Duke University Press, 2004).

70. http://www.wbr.com/nashville/warnerwestern/ [URL no longer active].

71. Taylor, *Global Pop*.

72. Liner notes to *Songs of the Hawaiian Cowboy*, Warner Western 9 46561-2, 1997.

73. http://www.wbr.com/nashville/warnerwestern/cmp/paniolo.html [URL no longer active].

74. From alt.music.hawaiian. All quotations from Internet newsgroups are unedited unless otherwise indicated.

75. Ernie Cruz's song does not appear on Warner Western's collection.

76. Mansfield, "Album Showcases Slack-Key Guitar Style."

77. Rick Petreycik, review of *Songs of the Hawaiian Cowboy* and *New Country* (included in the press kit from Warner Western).

78. Santiago, "Ride 'Em, Paniolo!," 27.

79. Mansfield, "Album Showcases Slack-Key Guitar Style."

80. Mansfield, "Album Showcases Slack-Key Guitar Style."

81. Brian Mansfield, "Documentary, CD Round Up Hawaii's Cowboy Tradition," *USA Today*, 15 October 1997, § D, 4, and "Native Filmmaker Mines Some Unexpected History," *USA Today*, 15 October 1997, § D, 4.

82. See chapter 5.

83. See Charles Keil, " 'Ethnic' Music Traditions in the USA," *Popular Music* 13 (May 1994): 175–78, for a typically lucid argument on this point.

CHAPTER 7: WORLD MUSIC IN TELEVISION ADS

1. For more on the changing nature of television commercials in the 1990s see my "The Changing Shape of the Culture Industry; or, How Did Electronica Music Get into Television Commercials?," *Journal of Television and New Media*, forthcoming.

2. This practice goes back at least to the sixteenth century and probably much earlier. The use of nonsense syllables in this music was often used for parodic purposes, whether aimed at Moors in the *moresca* (sixteenth-century vocal works), at Jews, or at Turks (as in Jean-Baptiste Lully's *Le Bourgeois gentilhomme*, 1669–70). There were also works that poke fun at foreign accents and solecisms as well as "rustic" dialects of Italian and other European languages (Leeman Perkins, personal communication, 7 April 1999).

3. For a discussion of the gendered nature of travel and tourism see Eeva Jokinen and Soile Veijola, "The Disoriented Tourist: The Figuration of the Tourist in Contemporary Cultural Critique," *Touring Cultures: Transformations of Travel and Theory*, ed. Chris Rojek and John Urry (New York: Routledge, 1997).

4. Sherry B. Ortner, "Is Female to Male as Nature Is to Culture?," *Making Gender: The Politics and Erotics of Culture* (Boston: Beacon, 1996). See also her updated meditation on the same subject, "So, *Is* Female to Male as Nature Is to Culture?," *Making Gender*.

5. Danny Hulsizer, telephone interview with author, 16 March 1999.

6. Gabrielle Doré, telephone interview with author, 16 March 1999.

7. "Needledrop" is both a verb and a noun; as a noun, according to Linda M. Scott, it "refers to music that is prefabricated, multipurpose, and highly conventional. It

is, in that sense, the musical equivalent of stock photos, clip art, or canned copy." Linda M. Scott, "Understanding Jingles and Needledrop: A Rhetorical Approach to Music in Advertising," *Journal of Consumer Research* (September 1990), 223 n. 1.

8. Ann Haugen, telephone interview with author, 12 July 1999.

9. Brooke Sheffield Comer, "The Philosophy of Elias Associates," *Back Stage*, 29 April 1988, § B, 28.

10. David John Farinella, "Scoring in Dog Years: Elias Associates Fight On," *Mix*, May 1996, 162.

11. Farinella, "Scoring in Dog Years," 162, 164. Elias's interest in nonwestern, world music sounds is evident in his *The Prayer Cycle*, discussed in chapter 6, which is stylistically similar to many of these ads: a rather strange blend of classical, new age, and world music "styles," employing a number of "world voices," as Ann Haugen of Elias Associates described them (telephone interview with author, 19 February 1999).

12. Daniela Gilbert, "The Perfect Sample," *Shoot*, 21 October 1994, 20. Linda Tillery is an African American singer who specializes in African American folk and traditional musics.

13. Gilbert, "The Perfect Sample," 20.

14. Quoted by Greg Rule, "Jingles All the Way: Making Music for Commercials," *Keyboard*, March 1997, 72, 74.

15. Jeffrey P. Fisher, *How to Make Money Scoring Soundtracks and Jingles* (Emeryville, Calif.: Mix, 1997), 10.

16. Ann Haugen, telephone interview with author, 12 July 1999. This emphasis on "real" music is probably part of a more general trend in the larger music industry emphasizing "unplugged" sounds. These sounds are at the same time becoming increasingly differentiated from "electronica," that is, largely electronic techno musics, which are used increasingly in ads. See Frank Owen, "Electronica Arrives via Madison Ave.; Underground Techno Music Is a Hit in the Land of Jingles," *Washington Post*, 12 July 1998, § G, 1; and Simon Reynolds, "Electronica Goes Straight to Ubiquity," *New York Times*, 6 June 1999, § 2, 27.

17. However, some world music had been used in British ads before; see Philip Sweeney, "If It Sounds Familiar . . . ," *Independent* (London), 9 July 1992, 22.

18. Frances Fiorino, "Partners in Song," *Aviation Week and Space Technology*, 27 March 1995, 17. See also "Delta Air Lines Jingle Climbing European Charts," Associated Press, 15 April 1995.

19. Helen Nowicka, "Pride and Prejudice in Recording Business," *Guardian*, 10 November 1995, 5. See also Tan Ling Ai, "The Coming Together of Adiemus," *New Straits Times* (Malaysia), 31 March 1997, 4.

20. For the changing nature of classical music see for example Yahlin Chang, "Cross Over, Beethoven," *Newsweek*, 20 April 1998, 60–61; Robert Fink, "Elvis Everywhere: Musicology and Popular Music Studies at the Twilight of the Canon," *American Music* 16 (summer 1998): 135–79; Keith Goetzman, "An Orchestrated Push," *Utne Reader*, March–April 1998, 91–93; Allan Kozinn, "This Is the Golden Age," *New York Times*,

28 May 2006, § 2, 1; Norman Lebrecht, *Who Killed Classical Music? Maestros, Managers, and Corporate Politics* (Secaucus, N.J.: Birch Lane, 1997); Robert Levine, "Cross Over This," *Pulse!*, April 1998, 37–39; Kevin Loader, "A Mongrel of Dubious Pedigree: Classical Music Has Discovered Beat and Style," *New Statesman and Society*, 13 July 1990, 26; and my "Music and Musical Practices in Postmodernity," *Postmodern Music/Postmodern Thought*, ed. Joseph Auner and Judith Lochhead (New York: Routledge, 2002).

21. Boosey and Hawkes's edition features the cover photograph from the *Songs of Sanctuary Album*, with the following caption underneath: "As used in the TV Commercial: Delta Air Lines," complete with Delta's trademark symbol.

22. Quoted by Renee Kaplan, "Culture Vulture," *Newsday*, 20 July 1997, § C, 2.

23. Karl Jenkins, liner notes to Adiemus, *Songs of Sanctuary*, Virgin Records America 0170 67524 2 8, 1995.

24. Ai, "The Coming Together of Adiemus," 4.

25. Ai, "The Coming Together of Adiemus." According to Thomas B. Payne (personal communication, 15 July 1999), "adeamus" is probably the near-homonym here, though he says that there might be a medieval "barbarism" of the verb "eo" ("I go"), and that "adiemus" could certainly occur with the meaning suggested by Jenkins. I would like to thank Tom for his help with this word.

26. Rule, "Jingles All the Way," 72; emphasis in original.

27. http://www.sonymusicfinder.com.

28. For more on the musical standardization of mood for commercial purposes see Robert Fink, "Orchestral Corporate," *echo* 2 (2000), http://www.echo.ucla.edu/Volume2-Issue1/table-of-contents21.html.

29. Jenkins, liner notes to Adiemus, *Songs of Sanctuary*.

30. http://www.noahgrey.com/adiemus [URL no longer active].

31. "Chart Busters," *Shoot*, 18 July 1997, 30.

32. Erin Shoor, personal communication, 26 May 1999. Music has become so closely associated with some brands that some companies now sell recordings featuring music heard in their ads, or, in the case of Starbucks Coffee, in their coffee shops. See "Music to Their Brands' Ears," *Business and Industry*, May 1999, 35.

33. "Chart Busters," 30.

34. Quoted by Norman Lebrecht, "The Composer Who Sells a Million," *Daily Telegraph*, 22 July 1996, 17.

35. Telephone interview with Andrea Marcaccio, senior account executive at Bozell Worldwide, 9 March 1999.

36. See Jonathan Bellman's discussion of the drone in fifths in *The "Style Hongrois" in the Music of Western Europe* (Boston: Northeastern University Press, 1993).

37. For more on Mox see "Extracurricular Activities: Michael Boyd: Sittin' Pretty While Mox Rocks," *Creativity*, September 1998, 18; and Joel Selvin, "Ad Men Make Music as Mox," *San Francisco Chronicle*, 10 May 1998, 44.

38. "Chrysler Brand to Launch All-New 1998 Chrysler Concorde Ad Campaign,"

http://www.findarticles.com/cf_0/m4PRN/1998_Jan_15/20155797/p1/article
.jhtml, last visited 9 February 2004.

39. Telephone interview with Ann Haugen, 19 February 1999.

40. The drone on fifths is common in representations of nonwestern Others; see my "Korla Pandit: Music, Exoticism and Mysticism," *Widening the Horizon: Exoticism in Post-War Popular Music*, ed. Philip Hayward (Sydney: John Libbey / Perfect Beat Publications, 1999).

41. Quoted by Tom Peters, *Liberation Management: Necessary Disorganization for the Nano-second Nineties* (New York: Alfred A. Knopf, 1992), 46.

42. John Micklethwait and Adrian Wooldridge, *The Witch Doctors: Making Sense of the Management Gurus* (New York: Times Books, 1997), 227. I would like to thank Brad Garton for telling me about this book, as well as suggesting the management literature more generally.

43. Eliza G. C. Collins and Mary Anne Devanna, *The New Portable MBA* (New York: John Wiley and Sons, 1994), 406–7.

44. Peters, *Liberation Management*, 669.

45. Another term that has caught on is "glocalization," a word that originated in Japanese business in the late 1980s and was quickly picked up by American businesses. See Roland Robertson, "Globalisation or Glocalisation?," *Journal of International Communication* 1 (1994): 33–52. See also Roland Robertson, "Glocalization: Time-Space and Homogeneity-Heterogeneity," *Global Modernities*, ed. Mike Featherstone et al. (Thousand Oaks, Calif.: Sage, 1995); Paul Virilio, *Open Sky*, trans. Julie Rose (New York: Verso, 1997), also uses the term. For just two examples of the term in business discourse see Christopher Conte, "A Special News Report on People and Their Jobs in Offices, Fields and Factories," *Wall Street Journal*, 21 May 1991, § A, 1; and Martha H. Peak, "Developing an International Style of Management," *Management Review*, February 1991, 32–35. A recent scholarly article that considers the term is Marwan M. Kraidy, "The Global, the Local, and the Hybrid: A Native Ethnography of Glocalization," *Critical Studies in Mass Communication* 16 (December 1999): 456–76. For other uses of the term, as well as alternatives, see Philip Hayward, "Cultural Tectonics," *Convergence* 6 (spring 2000): 39–47. Finally, see my chapter "A Riddle Wrapped in a Mystery: Transnational Music Sampling and Enigma's 'Return to Innocence,'" *Strange Sounds: Music, Technology and Culture* (New York: Routledge, 2001), for a discussion of the term with respect to music.

46. See Castells, *Rise of the Network Society*, especially the chapter "The Informational Economy and the Process of Globalization."

47. Louis Althusser, "Ideology and Ideological State Apparatuses," *Lenin and Philosophy, and Other Essays*, trans. Ben Brewster (New York: Monthly Review Press, 1971).

48. "Music to Their Brands' Ears," 35.

49. Pierre Bourdieu, *Distinction: A Social Critique of the Judgement of Taste*, trans. Richard Nice (Cambridge: Harvard University Press, 1984), 18.

50. Bourdieu, *Distinction*.

51. Rosalind H. Williams, *Dream Worlds: Mass Consumption in Late Nineteenth-Century France* (Berkeley: University of California Press, 1982), 71.

52. Manuel Castells, *The Rise of the Network Society*, vol. 1 of *The Information Age: Economy, Society and Culture* (Cambridge, Mass.: Blackwell, 1996), 66; emphases in original.

53. Manuel Castells, *End of the Millennium*, vol. 3 of *The Information Age*, 346; emphasis in original.

54. Herbert S. Dordick, Helen G. Bradley, and Burt Nanus, *The Emerging Network Marketplace* (Norwood, N.J.: Ablex, 1988).

55. Leslie Sklair, *Sociology of the Global System*, 2d ed. (Baltimore: Johns Hopkins University Press, 1995), and *The Transnational Capitalist Class* (Malden, Mass.: Blackwell, 2001). See also Alessandro Aurigi and Stephen Graham, "The 'Crisis' in the Urban Public Realm," *Cyberspace Divide: Equality, Agency and Policy in the Information Society*, ed. Brian D. Loader (New York: Routledge, 1998).

56. The literature on cosmopolitanism is burgeoning. See Aijaz Ahmad, "The Politics of Literary Postcoloniality," *Race and Class* 36 (January–March 1995): 1–20; Homi K. Bhabha, "Unpacking My Library . . . Again," *The Post-Colonial Question: Common Skies, Divided Horizons*, ed. Iain Chambers and Lidia Curti (New York: Routledge, 1996); Timothy Brennan, *At Home in the World: Cosmopolitanism Now* (Cambridge: Harvard University Press, 1997); and Pheng Cheah and Bruce Robbins, eds., *Cosmopolitics: Thinking and Feeling beyond the Nation* (Minneapolis: University of Minnesota Press, 1998); Jonathan Friedman, "Global Crisis, the Struggle for Cultural Identity and Intellectual Porkbarrelling: Cosmopolitans versus Locals, Ethnics and Nationals in an Era of De-hegemonisation," *Debating Cultural Hybridity: Multi-Cultural Identities and the Politics of Anti-Racism*, ed. Pnina Werbner and Tariq Modood (New Jersey: Zed, 1997); Ulf Hannerz, *Transnational Connections: Culture, People, Places* (New York: Routledge, 1996); and Bruce Robbins, "Comparative Cosmopolitanism," *Social Text* 31–32 (1992): 169–86. For a treatment of the concept as it relates to music see Thomas Turino, *Nationalists, Cosmopolitans, and Popular Music in Zimbabwe* (Chicago: University of Chicago Press, 2000).

57. For a documentary history of this kind of social acceptance of communications technologies, see my "Music and the Rise of Radio in Twenties America: Technological Imperialism, Socialization, and the Transformation of Intimacy," *Wired for Sound: Engineering and Technology in Sonic Cultures*, ed. Thomas Porcello and Paul Greene (Middletown, Conn.: Wesleyan University Press, 2004); and Timothy D. Taylor, Mark Katz, and Anthony Grajeda, eds., *The Social Life of Early Sound Technologies: A History in Documents, 1880–1945* (Durham: Duke University Press, forthcoming).

58. Juliana Koranteng, "EAAA Awards; Abbott Mead Helps Delta Win Respect of Business Fliers," *Advertising Age*, 14 October 1996, § A, 6.

59. To Maxine Feifer the "post-tourist" knows that she's a tourist and is uninterested in the authentic. *Tourism in History: From Imperial Rome to the Present* (Briarcliff Manor, N.Y.: Stein and Day, 1986). See also John Urry's *The Tourist Gaze: Leisure and Travel in Contemporary Societies* (Thousand Oaks, Calif.: Sage, 1990).

60. Scott Lash and John Urry, *Economies of Signs and Space* (Thousand Oaks, Calif.: Sage, 1994), 259. "Disorganized capitalism" is the phase of capitalism that these authors theorized in *The End of Organized Capitalism* (Madison: University of Wisconsin Press, 1987).

61. Lash and Urry, *Economies of Signs and Space*, 260.

62. Celia Lury, "The Objects of Travel," *Touring Cultures*, ed. Rojek and Urry, 82.

63. The main writing I am referring to here is Baudrillard's *For a Critique of the Political Economy of the Sign*, collected in *Jean Baudrillard: Collected Writings*, ed. Mark Poster (Stanford: Stanford University Press, 1988). For a trenchant critique of Baudrillard and other contemporary writers on consumption see James G. Carrier and Josiah McC. Heyman, "Consumption and Political Economy," *Journal of the Royal Anthropological Institute* 3 (June 1997): 355–73.

64. Dick Hebdige, "Fax to the Future," *Marxism Today*, January 1990, 20.

CONCLUSION: SELVES/OTHERS, HISTORY, AND CULTURE

1. Anthony Giddens, *The Consequences of Modernity* (Stanford: Stanford University Press, 1990).

2. Clifford Geertz, Afterword, *Senses of Place*, ed. Steven Feld and Keith H. Basso (Santa Fe: School of American Research Press, 1996), 262.

3. I am borrowing the term "little cultures" from Grant McCracken, *Plenitude* (Toronto: Periph.: Fluide, 1997).

4. See chapter 1 of my *Strange Sounds: Music, Technology and Culture* (New York: Routledge, 2001).

Bibliography

MUSIC SCORES

Campra, André. *L'Europe galante*. Farnborough, Hants., England: Gregg, 1967.

Cowell, Henry. String quartet no. 4 (*United Quartet*). New York: C. F. Peters, 1966.

Doane, W. Howard, and E. H. Johnson, eds. *The Baptist Hymnal*. Philadelphia: American Baptist Publication Society, 1883.

Ives, Charles. *Piano Sonata no. 2: "Concord, Mass., 1840–1860"*. New York: Associated Music Publishers, 1947.

Jenkins, Karl. *Adiemus I: Songs of Sanctuary*. London: Boosey and Hawkes, 1994.

Lefkowitz, Murray, ed. *Trois Masques à la cour de Charles Ier d'Angleterre*. Paris: Centre National de la Recherche Scientifique, 1970.

Lully, Jean-Baptiste. *Le Bourgeois gentilhomme*. Paris: Éditions de la Revue musicale, 1930.

Mozart, Wolfgang Amadeus. *The Abduction from the Seraglio*. New York: Dover, 1989.

Rameau, Jean-Philippe. *Les Indes galantes*. Chefs-d'œuvre classiques de l'opéra français, 34. New York: Broude Bros., 1971.

Ravel, Maurice. *Chansons madécasses*. Paris: Durand, 1926.

———. *Shéhérazade*. Paris: Durand, 1911.

RECORDINGS

Adiemus. *Songs of Sanctuary*. Virgin Records America 0170 67524 2 8, 1995.

Aerosmith. *Nine Lives*. Sony/Columbia B000035X2Q, 1997.

Asian Dub Foundation. *Facts and Fictions*. Nation Records NAT 58, 1995.

Brook, Michael. *Hybrid*. EG Records/Opal EEGCD 41, 1985.

———. *Night Song*. Real World 2354, 1996.

Cash, Johnny. *Bitter Tears: Ballads of the American Indian*. Sony 66507, 1964.

Elias, Jonathan. *The Prayer Cycle*. Sony Classical SK 60569, 1999.

Eno, Brian, and David Byrne. *My Life in the Bush of Ghosts*. Sire/Warner Bros. 9 45374-2, 1981.

From Where I Stand: The Black Experience in Country Music. Warner Bros./Reprise 9 47428-2, 1998.

Gabriel, Peter. *Passion: Music for "The Last Temptation of Christ."* Geffen Records M5G 24206, 1989.

Jenkins, Karl. *Adiemus 2: Cantata Mundi.* Sony Classical 60282, 1997.

———. *Diamond Music.* Sony Classical 62276, 1997.

———. *Imagined Oceans.* Sony Classical 60668, 1998.

Khan, Nusrat Fateh Ali, and Michael Brook. *Night Song.* Real World 2354, 1996.

Kidjo, Angélique. *Ayé.* Mango/Antilles 1625 9934 4, 1994.

———. *Black Ivory Soul.* Columbia CK 85799, 2002.

———. *Oremi.* Island 314-524-521-2, 1998.

Linkin Park. *Hybrid Theory.* Warner Bros. 47755, 2000.

Madonna. *Ray of Light.* WEA/Warner Brothers B000002NJS, 1998.

Mox. *Mox.* RGB Records 505-2, 1998.

Mozart, Wolfgang Amadeus. *Die Entführung aus dem Serail.* L'Oiseau-Lyre, 430 339-2, 1991.

Newman, Randy. *Bad Love.* Fontana International 450115, 1999.

Passion: Sources. Realworld/Caroline 2301, 1989.

Rameau, Jean-Philippe. *Les Indes galantes.* Harmonia mundi 901367.69, 1991.

Sagoo, Bally. *Aaja Nachle.* Oriental Star/Sony Music 491982 2, 1998.

Simon, Paul. *Graceland.* Warner Bros. W2-25447, 1986.

———. *The Rhythm of the Saints.* Warner Bros. 9 26098-2, 1990.

Songs of the Hawaiian Cowboy / Na Mele O Paniolo. Warner Western 9 46561-2, 1997.

Turkish Military Band Music of Ottoman Empire. King Record Co., KICC 5101, 1987.

Wes. *Welenga.* Sony Music 48146-2, 1997.

What Is Bhangra? IRS Records 7243 8 29242 27, 1994.

Yothu Yindi. *Tribal Voice.* Hollywood Records HR-61288-2, 1992.

INTERVIEWS

Doré, Gabrielle. Telephone interview with author, 16 March 1999.

Haugen, Ann. Telephone interview with author, 19 February 1999.

———. Telephone interview with author, 12 July 1999.

Hulsizer, Danny. Telephone interview with author, 16 March 1999.

Marcaccio, Andrea. Telephone interview with author. March 9, 1999.

WEB SITES

http://mediasoftware.sonypictures.com/loop_libraries/showloop.asp?PID=628&ms=1.

http://mediasoftware.sonypictures.com/loop_libraries/showloop.asp?PID=634&ms=1.

http://mediasoftware.sonypictures.com/loop_libraries/showloop.asp?PID=636&ms=1.

http://www.cdnow.com/cgi-bin/mserver/SID=1261988902/pagename=/RP/CDN/
    FIND/album.html/ArtistID=SAGOO*BALLY/ITEMID=630225
http:///www.ishqrecords.com.
http://www.mallofamerica.com
http://www.noahgrey.com/adiemus/
http://www.sonyclassical.com/artists/elias/
http://www.sonymusicfinder.com
http://www.wbr.com/nashville/warnerwestern/
http://www.wbr.com/nashville/warnerwestern/cmp/paniolo.html
http://www.wbr.com/nashville/warnerwestern/cmp/paniolocds.html

INTERNET NEWSGROUPS

alt.music.hawaiian

FILMS

The Crowd. Directed by King Vidor. Metro-Goldwyn-Mayer, 1928.
The Mission. Directed by Roland Joffé. Warner Bros., 1986.

UNPUBLISHED MATERIALS

Allanbrook, Wye J. "The Secular Commedia: Comic Mimesis in Late Eighteenth-
    Century Music." Ernest Bloch Lectures, University of California, Berkeley, fall 1994.
Broughton, Simon. Personal communication, Maastricht, 6 November 1998.
Haig, Christine. "Our Music, Their Music: Identifying Meaning in Musical
    Experiences." Ph.D. diss., University of Otago, New Zealand, 2004.
Howard, Jean. "Gender on the Periphery." Feminist Interventions Series, Institute for
    Research on Women and Gender, Columbia University, 12 February 2001.
Kealy, Edward R. "The Real Rock Revolution: Sound Mixers, Social Inequality, and
    the Aesthetics of Popular Music Production." Ph.D. diss., Northwestern
    University, 1974.
Keenan, Elizabeth. "Ladies, Womyn, and Grrls: Policing the Borders of Gender and
    Generations at Women's Rock Music Festivals." Paper delivered at the annual
    meeting of the Society for Ethnomusicology, Atlanta, 19 November 2005.
Luker, Morgan. " 'Deconstructing Havana': Bill Laswell's *Imaginary Cuba* and the
    Critical Revision of Authenticity." Paper presented at the Society for
    Ethnomusicology, Estes Park, Colo., 27 October 2002.
Payne, Thomas. Personal communication, 15 July 1999.
Perkins, Leeman. Personal communication, 7 April 1999.
Seeger, Anthony. Personal communication, 7 June 2005.
Shoor, Erin. Personal communication, 26 May 1999.
Taylor, Timothy D. "The Commodification of Music at the Dawn of the Era of
    'Mechanical Music.' " In preparation.

————. "Old and New (Ethno)musicologies." Invited presentation, 11th International Seminar in Ethnomusicology, Intercultural Institute of Comparative Music Studies, Fondazione Giorgio Cini, Venice, 27 January 2005.

————. "World Music Revisited." 13th Internationaler Kongress der Gesellschaft für Musikforschung, Weimar, 20 September 2004.

Whaples, Miriam K. "Exoticism in Dramatic Music, 1600–1800." Ph.D. diss., Indiana University, 1958.

BOOKS AND ARTICLES

Abu-Lughod, Lila. "Writing against Culture." *Recapturing Anthropology: Working in the Present*, ed. Richard G. Fox. Santa Fe: School of American Research Press, 1991.

Adorno, Theodor. *Philosophy of Modern Music*, trans. Anne G. Mitchell and Wesley V. Blomster. London: Sheed and Ward, 1973.

————. *Quasi una Fantasia: Essays on Modern Music*, trans. Rodney Livingstone. New York: Verso, 1992.

Ahmad, Aijaz. "The Politics of Literary Postcoloniality." *Race and Class* 36 (January–March 1995): 1–20.

Albini, Steve. "Nemesis of Corporate Rock" [interview by Camran Afsari]. *Music Producers: Conversations with Today's Hottest Hitmakers*, ed. Barbara Schultz. Emeryville, Calif.: Mix, 2000.

————. "The Problem with Music." http://www.musicianassist.com/archive/article/ART/a-1098-1.htm.

Albright, Daniel. Introduction. *Modernism and Music: An Anthology of Sources*, ed. Daniel Albright. Chicago: University of Chicago Press, 2004.

Allen, Warren Dwight. *Philosophies of Music History: A Study of General Histories of Music, 1600–1900*. New York: Dover, 1962.

Alm, Irene. "Dances from the 'Four Corners of the Earth': Exoticism in Seventeenth-Century Venetian Opera." *Musica Franca: Essays in Honor of Frank A. D'Accone*, ed. Irene Alm, Alyson McLamore, and Colleen Reardon. Stuyvesant, N.Y.: Pendragon, 1996.

Althusser, Louis. "Ideology and Ideological State Apparatuses." *Lenin and Philosophy, and Other Essays*, trans. Ben Brewster. New York: Monthly Review, 1971.

Anderson, Emily, ed. and trans. *The Letters of Mozart and His Family*. London: Macmillan, 1985.

Anzaldúa, Gloria. *Borderlands: The New Mestiza*. San Francisco: Aunt Lute, 1991.

Appadurai, Arjun. *Modernity at Large: Cultural Dimensions of Globalization*. Minneapolis: University of Minnesota Press, 1996.

Arbeau, Thoinot. *Orchesography*, trans. Mary Stewart Evans. New York: Dover, 1967.

Armitage, David. *The Ideological Origins of the British Empire*. Cambridge: Cambridge University Press, 2000.

Arndt, Jürgen. *Der Einfluß der javanischen Gamelan-Musik auf Kompositionen von Claude Debussy*. Frankfurt: Lang, 1993.

Attali, Jacques. *Noise: The Political Economy of Music*, trans. Brian Massumi. Minneapolis: University of Minnesota Press, 1985.

Aurigi, Alessandro, and Stephen Graham. "The 'Crisis' in the Urban Public Realm." *Cyberspace Divide: Equality, Agency and Policy in the Information Society*, ed. Brian D. Loader. New York: Routledge, 1998.

Bakhtin, M. M. *The Dialogic Imagination*, ed. Michael Holquist, trans. Caryl Emerson and Michael Holquist. Austin: University of Texas Press, 1981.

———. *Rabelais and His World*, trans. Helene Iswolsky. Bloomington: Indiana University Press, 1981.

Balibar, Étienne. "Is There a 'Neo-Racism'?" *Race, Nation, Class: Ambiguous Identities*. New York: Verso, 1991.

Banerji, Sabita, and Gerd Baumann. "Bhangra 1984–8: Fusion and Professionalization in a Genre of South Asian Dance Music." *Black Music in Britain: Essays on the Afro-Asian Contribution to Popular Music*, ed. Paul Oliver. Buckingham: Open University Press, 1990.

Banerji, Sabita. "Ghazals of Bhangra in Great Britain." *Popular Music* 7 (May 1988): 207–13.

Barnett, Gregory. "Tonal Organization in Seventeenth-Century Music Theory." *The Cambridge History of Western Music Theory*, ed. Thomas Christensen. New York: Cambridge University Press, 2002.

Battersby, Christine. *Gender and Genius: Towards a Feminist Aesthetics*. Bloomington: Indiana University Press, 1989.

Baudrillard, Jean. *Jean Baudrillard: Collected Writings*, ed. Mark Poster. Stanford: Stanford University Press, 1988.

Bauman, Thomas. *W. A. Mozart: "Die Entführung aus dem Serail."* New York: Cambridge University Press, 1987.

Baumol, William J., and Hilda Baumol. "On the Economics of Musical Composition in Mozart's Vienna." *On Mozart*, ed. James M. Morris. Washington: Woodrow Wilson Center Press, 1994.

Beazley, C. Raymond. *The Dawn of Modern Geography*. New York: P. Smith, 1949.

Belk, Russell W. 1995. *Collecting in a Consumer Society*. New York: Routledge, 1995.

Bellman, Jonathan. *The "Style Hongrois" in the Music of Western Europe*. Boston: Northeastern University Press, 1993.

Bellman, Jonathan, ed. *The Exotic in Western Music*. Boston: Northeastern University Press, 1998.

Bentley, Jerry H. *Old World Encounters: Cross-Cultural Contacts and Exchanges in Pre-modern Times*. New York: Oxford University Press, 1993.

Berman, Marshall. *All That Is Solid Melts into Air: The Experience of Modernity*. New York: Penguin, 1988.

Berry, Colin. "The Sound of Silence: San Francisco's Ambient Music Labels Find Their Groove." *SF Weekly*, 17–23 May 1995, 16–18.

Besseler, Heinrich. *Bourdon und Fauxbourdon: Studien zur Ursprung der niederländischen Musik*, ed. and rev. Peter Gulke. Leipzig: Breitkopf and Härtel, 1974.

Bhabha, Homi K. *The Location of Culture*. London: Routledge, 1994.

————. "The Third Space: Interview with Homi Bhabha." *Identity: Community, Culture, Difference*, ed. Jonathan Rutherford. London: Lawrence and Wishart, 1990.

————. "Unpacking My Library . . . Again." *The Post-Colonial Question: Common Skies, Divided Horizons*, ed. Iain Chambers and Lidia Curti. New York: Routledge, 1996.

Bianconi, Lorenzo. *Music in the Seventeenth Century*, trans. David Bryant. New York: Cambridge University Press, 1987.

Bitterli, Urs. *Cultures in Conflict: Encounters between European and Non-European Cultures, 1492–1800*, trans. Ritchie Robinson. Stanford: Stanford University Press, 1989.

"Black History Month: Spirituals." *Orlando Sentinel*, 6 February 1998, § X, 1.

Bloechl, Olivia A. *Native American Song at the Frontiers of Early Modern Music*. Cambridge: Cambridge University Press, forthcoming.

————. "The Pedagogy of Polyphony in Gabriel Sagard's *Histoire du Canada*," *Journal of Musicology* 22 (summer 2005): 365–411.

————. "Protestant Imperialism and the Representation of Native American Song." *Musical Quarterly* 87 (2004): 44–86.

Boas, Franz. *Anthropology and Modern Life*. New York: Dover, 1986.

————. *The Mind of Primitive Man*. New York: Macmillan, 1911.

Born, Georgina, and David Hesmondhalgh, eds. *Western Music and Its Others: Difference, Representation, and Appropriation in Music*. Berkeley: University of California Press, 2000.

Borzillo, Carrie. "Deep Forest Growing in Popularity; 550's World Music-Dance Hybrid Climbs Charts." *Billboard*, 19 February 1994, 8.

————. "U.S. Ad Use Adds to Commercial Success of Deep Forest." *Billboard*, 11 June 1994, 44.

Bourdieu, Pierre. *Distinction: A Social Critique of the Judgement of Taste*, trans. Richard Nice. Cambridge: Harvard University Press, 1984.

Braunbehrens, Volkmar. *Mozart in Vienna, 1781–1791*, trans. Timothy Bell. New York: Grove Weidenfeld, 1990.

Breen, Marcus, ed. *Our Place, Our Music*. Australian Popular Music in Perspective, vol. 2. Canberra: Aboriginal Studies Press, 1989.

Brennan, Timothy. *At Home in the World: Cosmopolitanism Now*. Cambridge: Harvard University Press, 1997.

Brenner, Robert. *Merchants and Revolution: Commercial Change, Political Conflict, and London's Overseas Traders, 1550–1653*. Princeton: Princeton University Press, 1993.

Brett, Philip. "Eros and Orientalism in Britten's Operas." *Queering the Pitch: The New Gay and Lesbian Musicology*, ed. Philip Brett, Elizabeth Wood, and Gary C. Thomas. New York: Routledge, 1994.

Brofsky, Howard. "Rameau and the Indians: The Popularity of *Les Sauvages*." *Music in the Classic Period: Essays in Honor of Barry S. Brook*, ed. Allan W. Atlas. New York: Pendragon, 1985.

Brophy, Brigid. *Mozart the Dramatist: The Value of His Operas to Him, to His Age and to Us*. Rev. ed. New York: Da Capo, 1988.

Broughton, Simon, Mark Ellingham, and Richard Trillo, eds. *World Music: The Rough Guide*. Vol. 1, *Africa, Europe and the Middle East*. London: Rough Guides, 1999.

Broughton, Simon, and Mark Ellingham. *World Music: The Rough Guide*. Vol. 2, *Latin and North America, Caribbean, India, Asia and Pacific*. London: Rough Guides, 2000.

Broughton, Simon, Mark Ellingham, David Muddyman, and Richard Trillo, eds. *World Music: The Rough Guide*. London: Rough Guides, 1994.

Brown, Howard Mayer. *Sixteenth-Century Instrumentation: The Music for the Florentine Intermedii*. Musicological Studies and Documents 30 (1973).

Brunschwig, Henri. *French Colonialism, 1871–1914: Myths and Realities*, trans. William Glanville Brown. New York: Frederick A. Praeger, 1966.

Buell, Frederick. "National Postnationalism: Globalist Discourse in Contemporary American Culture." *American Quarterly* 50 (September 1998): 548–91.

Burckhardt, Jacob. *The Civilization of the Renaissance in Italy*, trans. S. G. C. Middlemore, 1860. Rep. Harmondsworth: Penguin, 1990.

Burkholder, J. Peter. *All Made of Tunes: Charles Ives and the Uses of Musical Borrowing*. New Haven: Yale University Press, 1995.

Campbell, Colin. *The Romantic Ethic and the Spirit of Modern Consumerism*. Cambridge, Mass.: Basil Blackwell, 1989.

Campbell, Mary B. *The Witness and the Other World: Exotic European Travel Writing, 400–1600*. Ithaca, N.Y.: Cornell University Press, 1988.

Canny, Nicholas, ed. *The Origins of Empire*. Vol. 1 of *The Oxford History of the British Empire*, ed. Wm. Roger Louis. New York: Oxford University Press, 1998–99.

Carrier, James G., and Josiah McC. Heyman. "Consumption and Political Economy." *Journal of the Royal Anthropological Institute* 3 (June 1997): 355–73.

Carroll, Rebecca. "Rodriguez Meets Byrne." *Mother Jones*, July–August 1991, 9.

Carter, Tim. "The Seventeenth Century." *The Oxford Illustrated History of Opera*, ed. Roger Parker. Oxford: Oxford University Press, 1994.

Cassirer, Ernst. *The Individual and the Cosmos in Renaissance Philosophy*, trans. Mario Domandi. New York: Barnes and Noble, 1963.

Castells, Manuel. *End of the Millennium*. Vol. 3 of *The Information Age: Economy, Society and Culture*. Cambridge, Mass.: Blackwell, 1998.

———. *The Rise of the Network Society*. Vol. 1 of *The Information Age: Economy, Society and Culture*. Cambridge, Mass.: Blackwell, 1996.

Castles, John. "Tjungaringanyi: Aboriginal Rock." *From Pop to Punk to Postmodernism: Popular Music and Australian Culture from the 1960s to the 1990s*, ed. Philip Hayward. North Sydney: Allen & Unwin, 1992.

Chafe, Eric. *Monteverdi's Tonal Language*. New York: Schirmer, 1992.

Chakrabarty, Dipesh. "Postcoloniality and the Artifice of History: Who Speaks for 'Indian' Pasts?" *Representations* 32 (winter 1992): 1–26.

Chan, Mary. *Music in the Theatre of Ben Jonson*. New York: Oxford University Press, 1980.

Chang, Yahlin. "Cross over, Beethoven." *Newsweek*, 20 April 1998, 60–61.

Chapme, Flavia Waters. *The Matachines Dance of the Upper Rio Grande: History, Music, and Choreography*. Lincoln: University of Nebraska Press, 1983.

"Chart Busters." *Shoot*, 18 July 1997, 30.

Cheah, Pheng, and Bruce Robbins, eds. *Cosmopolitics: Thinking and Feeling beyond the Nation*. Minneapolis: University of Minnesota Press, 1998.

Ching, Barbara. "Acting Naturally: Cultural Distinction and Critiques of Pure Country." *White Trash: Race and Class in America*, ed. Matt Wray and Annalee Newitz. New York: Routledge, 1997.

———. *Wrong's What I Do Best: Hard Country Music and Contemporary Culture*. New York: Oxford University Press, 2001.

Christensen, Thomas. *Rameau and Musical Thought in the Enlightenment*. Cambridge: Cambridge University Press, 1993.

———. "The Spanish Baroque Guitar and Seventeenth-Century Triadic Theory." *Journal of Music Theory* 36 (spring 1992): 1–42.

"Chrysler Brand to Launch All-New 1998 Chrysler Concorde Ad Campaign." http://www.findarticles.com/cf_0/m4PRN/1998_Jan_15/20155797/p1/article.jhtml.

Clifford, James. *Routes: Travel and Translation in the Late Twentieth Century*. Cambridge: Harvard University Press, 1997.

Coelho, Victor Anand. "Kapsberger's Apotheosis . . . of Francis Xavier (1622) and the Conquering of India." *The Work of Opera: Genre, Nationhood, and Sexual Difference*, ed. Richard Dellamora and Daniel Fischlin. New York: Columbia University Press, 1997.

Cohen, Lizabeth. *A Consumer's Republic: The Politics of Mass Consumption in Postwar America*. New York: Alfred A. Knopf, 2003.

Collins, Eliza G. C., and Mary Anne Devanna. *The New Portable MBA*. New York: John Wiley and Sons, 1994.

Comaroff, Jean, and John L. Comaroff. "Millenial Capitalism: First Thoughts on a Second Coming." *Millennial Capitalism and the Culture of Neoliberalism*. Durham: Duke University Press.

Comer, Brooke Sheffield. "The Philosophy of Elias Associates." *Back Stage*, 29 April, 1988, 28B.

Conte, Christopher. "A Special News Report on People and Their Jobs in Offices, Fields and Factories." *Wall Street Journal*, 21 May 1991, § A, 1.

Cooper, Frederick, and Ann L. Stoler. "Tensions of Empire: Colonial Control and Visions of Rule." *American Ethnologist* 16 (November 1989): 609–21.

Cooper, John Xiros. *Modernism and the Culture of Market Society*. New York: Cambridge University Press, 2004.

Corbett, John. "Experimental Oriental: New Music and Other Others." *Western Music and Its Others: Difference, Representation, and Appropriation in Music*, ed. Georgina Born and David Hesmondhalgh. Berkeley: University of California Press, 2000.

Cowell, Henry. "The Composer's World." *The Preservation of Traditional Forms of the Learned and Popular Music of the Orient and the Occident*, ed. William Kay Archer. Urbana: Center for Comparative Psycholinguistics, Institute of Communications Research, University of Illinois [1964].

———. "The Scientific Approach to Non-European Music." *Music Vanguard* 1 (summer 1935): 62–67.

———. "Towards Neo-Primitivism." *Modern Music* 10 (March–April 1933): 149–53.

"The Creatures." *Alternative Press*, November 1990. http://www.vamp.org/Siouxsie/Text/ap2.html.

Crocker, Richard. "Discant, Counterpoint, and Harmony." *Journal of the American Musicological Society* 15 (spring 1962): 1–21.

Cross, Gary. *An All-Consuming Century: Why Commercialism Won in Modern America*. New York: Columbia University Press, 2000.

Cunningham, Mark. *Good Vibrations: A History of Record Production*. Chessington, England: Castle, 1996.

Dahlhaus, Carl. *The Idea of Absolute Music*, trans. Roger Lustig. Chicago: University of Chicago Press, 1989.

———. *Studies on the Origin of Harmonic Tonality*, trans. Robert O. Gjerdingen. Princeton: Princeton University Press, 1990.

Davenant, Sir William. *The Shorter Poems, and Songs from the Plays and Masques*, ed. A. M. Gibbs. Oxford: Clarendon, 1972.

Davies, Hugh. "A History of Sampling." *Organised Sound* 1 (April 1996): 3–11.

Davies, Merryl Wyn, Ashis Nandy, and Ziauddin Sardar. *Barbaric Others: A Manifesto on Western Racism*. Boulder: Pluto, 1993.

de Certeau, Michel. *The Practice of Everyday Life*, trans. Steven Rendall. Berkeley: University of California Press, 1984.

"Delta Air Lines Jingle Climbing European Charts." Associated Press, 15 April 1995.

Denning, Michael. *Culture in the Age of Three Worlds*. New York: Verso, 2004.

Dent, Edward J. *Foundations of English Opera*. Cambridge: Cambridge University Press, 1928.

———. *Mozart's Operas: A Critical Study*. 2d ed. Oxford: Clarendon, 1947.

Diderot, Denis. "Supplement to Bougainville's 'Voyage.'" *The Enlightenment*, ed. Frank E. Manuel. Englewood Cliffs, N.J.: Prentice-Hall, 1965.

Dix, John. *Stranded in Paradise: New Zealand Rock and Roll, 1955–1985*. Wellington: Paradise, 1988.

DJ Jiten. Interview. http://www.streetsound.com/bhangra/intjiten83.html [URL no longer active].

Donington, Robert. *The Rise of Opera*. New York: Charles Scribner's Sons, 1981.

Dordick, Herbert S., Helen G. Bradley, and Burt Nanus. *The Emerging Network Marketplace*. Norwood, N.J.: Ablex, 1988.

Douglas, Mary. *Purity and Danger: An Analysis of Concepts of Pollution and Taboo*. Harmondsworth: Penguin, 1970.

Dussel, Enrique. "Eurocentrisim and Modernity (Introduction to the Frankfurt Lectures)." *boundary 2* 20 (autumn 1993): 65–76.

Eisenberg, Evan. *The Recording Angel: The Experience of Music from Aristotle to Zappa*. New York: Penguin, 1988.

Eliot, George. *Middlemarch*, ed. Gordon S. Haight. Boston: Houghton Mifflin, 1956.

Ellingson, Ter. *The Myth of the Noble Savage*. Berkeley: University of California Press, 2001.

Elliott, J. H. *The Old World and the New, 1492–1650*. New York: Cambridge University Press, 1970.

Emerson, Caryl. "Problems with Baxtin's Poetics." *Slavic and East European Journal* 32 (1988): 503–25.

Erlmann, Veit. *Music, Modernity, and the Global Imagination: South Africa and the West*. New York: Oxford University Press, 1999.

Evans, J. Martin. *America: The View from Europe*. San Francisco: San Francisco Book Company, 1976.

Everett, Yayoi Uno, and Frederick Lau, eds. *Locating East Asia in Western Art Music*. Middletown, Conn.: Wesleyan University Press, 2004.

"Extracurricular Activities: Michael Boyd: Sittin' Pretty While Mox Rocks." *Creativity*, September 1998, 18.

Fabian, Johannes. *Time and the Other: How Anthropology Makes Its Object*. New York: Columbia University Press, 1983.

Fagan, Brian. *Clash of Cultures*. New York: W. H. Freeman, 1984.

Farinella, David John. "Scoring in Dog Years: Elias Associates Fight On." *Mix*, May 1996, 157.

Farrell, Gerry. *Indian Music and the West*. Oxford: Clarendon, 1997.

Fauser, Annegret. *Musical Encounters at the 1889 Paris World's Fair*. Rochester, N.Y.: University of Rochester Press, 2005.

Feifer, Maxine. *Tourism in History: From Imperial Rome to the Present*. Briarcliff Manor, N.Y.: Stein and Day, 1986.

Feld, Steven. "From Schizophonia to Schismogenesis: On the Discourses and Commodification Practices of 'World Music' and 'World Beat.'" *Music Grooves: Essays and Dialogues*, by Charles Keil and Steven Feld. Chicago: University of Chicago Press, 1994.

———. "Notes on 'World Beat.'" *Music Grooves: Essays and Dialogues*, by Charles Keil and Steven Feld. Chicago: University of Chicago Press, 1994.

———. "pygmy POP: A Genealogy of Schizophonic Mimesis." *Yearbook for Traditional Music* 28 (1996): 1–35.

Fink, Robert. "Elvis Everywhere: Musicology and Popular Music Studies of the Twilight of the Canon." *American Music* 16 (summer 1998): 135–79.

———. "Orchestral Corporate." *echo* 2 (2000), http://www.echo.ucla.edu/Volume2-Issue1/table-of-contents21.html.

Fiorino, Frances. "Partners in Song." *Aviation Week and Space Technology*, 27 March 1995, 17.

Fisher, Jeffrey P. *How to Make Money Scoring Soundtracks and Jingles*. Emeryville, Calif.: Mix, 1997.

Flores, Juan. "'Que Assimilated, Brother, Yo Soy Asimilao': The Structuring of Puerto Rican Identity in the U.S." *Journal of Ethnic Studies* 13 (fall 1984): 1–16.

Foucault, Michel. *The Archaeology of Knowledge*, trans. A. M. Sheridan Smith. New York: Pantheon, 1972.

———. "Of Other Spaces." *Diacritics* 16 (1986): 22–27.

———. *The Order of Things: An Archaeology of the Human Sciences*. London: Tavistock, 1970.

Frank, Thomas. "Alternative to What?" *Sounding Off! Music as Subversion/Resistance/Revolution*, ed. Ron Sakolsky and Fred Wei-Han Ho. Brooklyn, N.Y.: Autonomedia, 1995.

———. *The Conquest of Cool: Business Culture, Counterculture, and the Rise of Hip Consumerism*. Chicago: University of Chicago Press, 1997.

Freud, Sigmund. *Dora: An Analysis of a Case of Hysteria*. New York: Touchstone, 1997.

Friedman, Jonathan. "Being in the World: Globalization and Localization." *Global Culture: Nationalism, Globalization and Modernity*, ed. Mike Featherstone. Newbury Park, Calif.: Sage, 1990.

———. "Global Crisis, the Struggle for Cultural Identity and Intellectual Porkbarrelling: Cosmopolitans versus Locals, Ethnics and Nationals in an Era of De-hegemonisation." *Debating Cultural Hybridity: Multi-Cultural Identities and the Politics of Anti-Racism*, ed. Pnina Werbner and Tariq Modood. Atlantic Highlands, N.J.: Zed, 1997.

Frith, Simon. "The Discourse of World Music." *Western Music and Its Others: Difference, Representation, and Appropriation in Music*, ed. Georgina Born and David Hesmondhalgh. Berkeley: University of California Press, 2000.

———. *Sound Effects: Youth, Leisure, Politics and Rock 'n' Roll*. London: Constable, 1983.

Fubini, Enrico. *Music and Culture in Eighteenth-Century Europe: A Source Book*. Chicago: University of Chicago Press, 1994.

Gandhi, Leela. *Postcolonial Theory: An Introduction*. New York: Columbia University Press, 1998.

Geertz, Clifford. Afterword. *Senses of Place*, ed. Steven Feld and Keith H. Basso. Santa Fe: School of American Research Press, 1996.

Giddens, Anthony. *Capitalism and Modern Social Theory: An Analysis of the Writings of Marx, Durkheim and Max Weber*. Cambridge: Cambridge University Press, 1971.

———. *The Consequences of Modernity*. Stanford: Stanford University Press, 1990.

Gilbert, Daniela. "The Perfect Sample." *Shoot*, 21 October 1994, 20.

Gillies, John. "Marlowe, the Timur Myth, and the Motives of Geography." *Playing the Globe: Genre and Geography in English Renaissance Drama*, ed. John Gillies and Virginia Mason Vaughan. Madison, N.J.: Fairleigh Dickinson University Press, 1998.

———. *Shakespeare and the Geography of Difference*. Cambridge: Cambridge University Press, 1994.

Gilsenan, Michael. *Imagined Cities of the East: An Inaugural Lecture Delivered before the University of Oxford on 27 May 1985*. Oxford: Clarendon Press, 1986.

Girdlestone, Cuthbert. *Jean-Philippe Rameau: His Life and Work*. 1957. Repr. New York: Dover, 1969.

Glazer, Nathan. *We Are All Multiculturalists Now*. Cambridge: Harvard University Press, 2000.

Goetzman, Keith. "An Orchestrated Push." *Utne Reader*, March–April 1998, 91–93.

Goldberg, Jonathan. *James I and the Politics of Literature: Jonson, Shakespeare, Donne, and Their Contemporaries*. Baltimore: Johns Hopkins University Press, 1983.

Golosinski, Matt. "Outer Bass: Bill Laswell Is a Deep-Groove Guerrilla Who's Not Afraid to Lay Down the Bottom Line." *Phoenix New Times*, 26 March 1998.

Gómez-Peña, Guillermo. "The New Global Culture: Somewhere between Corporate Multiculturalism and the Mainstream Bizarre (a Border Perspective)." *TDR* 45 (spring 2001): 7–30.

Gonzalez, Fernando. "Paul Simon's World Beat." *Boston Globe*, 14 October 1990, § B, 25.

Good, David P. *The Economic Rise of the Habsburg Empire, 1750–1914*. Berkeley: University of California Press, 1984.

Goodwin, Andrew. "Popular Music and Postmodern Theory." *Cultural Studies* 5 (May 1991): 174–90.

———. "Sample and Hold: Pop Music in the Digital Age of Reproduction." *On Record: Rock, Pop, and the Written Word*, ed. Simon Frith and Andrew Goodwin. New York: Pantheon, 1990.

Gopinath, Gayatri. "'Bombay, U.K., Yuba City': Bhangra Music and the Engendering of Diaspora." *Diaspora* 4 (winter 1995): 303–21.

Gordon, D. J. *The Renaissance Imagination: Essays and Lectures*, ed. Stephen Orgel. Berkeley: University of California Press, 1975.

Gossett, Susan. "Recent Studies in the English Masque." *English Renaissance* 26 (1996): 587–627.

Gottdiener, Mark. "The Consumption of Space and the Spaces of Consumption." *New Forms of Consumption: Consumers, Culture, and Commodification*, ed. Mark Gottdiener. Lanham, Md.: Rowan and Littlefield, 2000.

Gouk, Penelope. "The Role of Harmonics in the Scientific Revolution." *The Cambridge History of Western Music Theory*, ed. Thomas Christensen. New York: Cambridge University Press, 2002.

Graham, Ronnie. *The Da Capo Guide to Contemporary African Music*. New York: Da Capo, 1988.

———. *The World of African Music: Stern's Guide to Contemporary African Music*. Vol. 2. Boulder: Pluto, 1992.

Green, Nancy L., Laura Levine Frader, and Pierre Milza. "Paris: City of Light and Shadow." *Distant Magnets: Expectations and Realities in the Immigrant Experience, 1840–1930*, ed. Dirk Hoerder and Horst Rössler. New York: Holmes and Meier, 1992.

Greenblatt, Stephen. "Introduction: New World Encounters." *New World Encounters*, ed. Stephen Greenblatt. Berkeley: University of California Press, 1993.

———. *Marvelous Possessions: The Wonder of the New World*. Chicago: University of Chicago Press, 1991.

———. *Renaissance Self-Fashioning: From More to Shakespeare*. Chicago: University of Chicago Press, 1980.

————. "The Touch of the Real." *The Fate of Culture: Geertz and Beyond*, ed. Sherry B. Ortner. Berkeley: University of California Press, 1999.

Greene, Jack P. *The Intellectual Construction of America: Exceptionalism and Identity from 1492 to 1800*. Chapel Hill: University of North Carolina Press, 1993.

Grenier, Line. "From 'Diversity' to 'Difference.'" *New Formations* 9 (1989): 125–42.

Grenier, Line, and Jocelyne Guilbault. "Créolité and Francophonie in Music: Socio-Musical Repositioning Where It Matters." *Cultural Studies* 11 (May 1997): 207–34.

Grossberg, Lawrence. "Toward a Genealogy of the State of Cultural Studies: The Discipline of Communication and the Reception of Cultural Studies in the United States." *Disciplinarity and Dissent in Cultural Studies*, ed. Cary Nelson and Dilip P. Gaonkar. New York: Routledge, 1996.

Grout, Donald Jay, and Hermine Weigel Williams. *A Short History of Opera*. 3d ed. New York: Columbia University Press, 1988.

Guilbault, Jocelyne. *Zouk: World Music in the West Indies*. Chicago: University of Chicago Press, 1993.

Gupta, Akhil, and James Ferguson. "Beyond 'Culture': Space, Identity, and the Politics of Difference." *Cultural Anthropology* 7 (February 1992): 7–23.

Hale, J. R. *Renaissance Exploration*. New York: W. W. Norton, 1968.

Hall, Stuart. "Ethnicity: Identity and Difference." *Radical America* 23 (October–December 1989): 9–20.

Hannerz, Ulf. *Transnational Connections: Culture, People, Places*. New York: Routledge, 1996.

Hardt, Michael, and Antonio Negri. *Empire*. Cambridge: Harvard University Press, 2000.

Harrison, Frank. *Time, Place and Music: An Anthology of Ethnomusicological Observation c. 1550 to c. 1800*. Amsterdam: Frits Knuf, 1973.

Harvey, David. *The Condition of Postmodernity: An Enquiry into the Origins of Cultural Change*. Cambridge, Mass.: Basil Blackwell, 1989.

————. *Paris, Capital of Modernity*. New York: Routledge, 2003.

Hayward, Philip. "Cultural Tectonics." *Convergence* 6 (spring 2000): 39–47.

————. "Music Video, the Bicentenary (and After)." *From Pop to Punk to Postmodernism: Popular Music and Australian Culture from the 1960s to the 1990s*, ed. Philip Hayward. North Sydney: Allen and Unwin, 1992.

————. "Safe, Exotic and Somewhere Else: Yothu Yindi, Treaty, and the Mediation of Aboriginality." *Perfect Beat* 1 (January 1993): 33–42.

Hayward, Philip, and Karl Neuenfeldt. "Yothu Yindi: Context and Significance." *Sound Alliances: Indigenous Peoples, Cultural Politics and Popular Music in the Pacific*, ed. Philip Hayward. London: Cassell, 1998.

Hazard, Paul. *European Thought in the Eighteenth Century: From Montesquieu to Lessing*. Cleveland: World, 1969.

Heartfield, James. *The "Death of the Subject" Explained*. Sheffield: Sheffield Hallam University Press, 2002.

Hebdige, Dick. "Fax to the Future." *Marxism Today*, January 1990, 18–22.

Heer, Jatender S. "Revolutionizing Bhangra: Punjabi MC Gives Bhangra a Much Needed Jolt." *Welcome to Little India*, July 1998, 56.

Henderson, Richard. "What in the World Is It?" *Billboard*, 28 June 1997, 51–52.

Hentoff, Nat. "Blues Brothers under the Skin." *Wall Street Journal*, 1 May 1998, § W, 12.

Heuton, Cheryl. "Country Fills the Airwaves." *Mediaweek*, 12 December 1994, 12.

"Hindu Protest Forces Sony to Remake CD." *Hinduism Today*, July 1997, 47.

Hobsbawm, Eric. *The Age of Empire, 1870–1915*. New York: Pantheon, 1987.

Hodgen, Margaret T. *Early Anthropology in the Sixteenth and Seventeenth Centuries*. Philadelphia: University of Pennsylvania Press, 1964.

Holt, Douglas. "Postmodern Markets." *Do Americans Shop Too Much?* Boston: Beacon, 2000.

Hollinger, David A. *Postethnic America: Beyond Multiculturalism*. New York: Basic, 1995.

Horkheimer, Max, and Theodor Adorno. *Dialectic of Enlightenment*, trans. John Cumming. New York: Continuum, 1990.

Howard, Jean. *Theater of a City: Social Change and Generic Innovation on the Early Modern Stage*. Forthcoming.

Howard, Skiles. *The Politics of Courtly Dancing in Early Modern England*. Amherst: University of Massachusetts Press, 1998.

Howat, Roy. "Debussy and the Orient." *Recovering the Orient: Artists, Scholars, Appropriations*, ed. Andrew Gerstle and Anthony Milner. London: Harwood, 1995.

Hudson, Richard. "The Concept of Mode in Italian Guitar Music during the First Half of the 17th Century." *Acta Musicologica* 42 (1970): 163–83.

Hunter, Mary. "The *Alla Turca* Style in the Late Eighteenth Century: Race and Gender in the Symphony and the Seraglio." *The Exotic in Western Music*, ed. Jonathan Bellman. Boston: Northeastern University Press, 1998.

Hutnyk, John. "Adorno at Womad: South Asian Crossovers and the Limits of Hybridity-Talk." *Debating Cultural Hybridity: Multi-Cultural Identities and the Politics of Anti-Racism*, ed. Pnina Werbner and Tariq Modood. Atlantic Highlands, N.J.: Zed, 1997.

Huyssen, Andreas. "Mass Culture as Woman: Modernism's Other." *After the Great Divide: Modernism, Mass Culture, Postmodernism*. Bloomington: Indiana University Press, 1986.

Inda, Jonathan Xavier, and Renato Rosaldo. "Introduction: A World in Motion." *The Anthropology of Globalization: A Reader*. Malden, Mass.: Blackwell, 2002.

Ivey, Bill. Liner notes to *From Where I Stand: The Black Experience in Country Music*. Warner Bros./Reprise 9 47428-2, 1998.

Iwan, Christine. "Albion's Own Ace of Bass; Grammy-winning Bill Laswell Returns to His Hometown." *Enquirer* (Battle Creek), 16 June 2003.

Jacobson, Mark. "Playing the Synthesizer." *Natural History*, March 1996, 24–27.

James, Richard. "Ravel's *Chansons madécasses*: Ethnic Fantasy or Ethnic Borrowing?" *Musical Quarterly* 74 (1990): 360–85.

Jameson, Fredric. "Modernism and Imperialism." *Nationalism, Colonialism, and Literature*. Minneapolis: University of Minnesota Press, 1990.

Jenkins, Karl. Liner notes to Adiemus, *Songs of Sanctuary*. Virgin Records America 0170 67524 2 8, 1995.

John, Michael, and Albert Lichtblau. "Vienna around 1900: Images, Expectations, and Experiences of Labor Migrants." *Distant Magnets: Expectations and Realities in the Immigrant Experience, 1840–1930*, ed. Dirk Hoerder and Horst Rössler. New York: Holmes and Meier, 1992.

Johnson, Steven. "Henry Cowell, John Varian, and Halcyon," *American Music* 11 (spring 1993): 1–27.

Jokinen, Eeva, and Soile Veijola. "The Disoriented Tourist: The Figuration of the Tourist in Contemporary Cultural Critique." *Touring Cultures: Transformations of Travel and Theory*, ed. Chris Rojek and John Urry. New York: Routledge, 1997.

Judd, Cristle Collins, ed. *Tonal Structures in Early Music*. New York: Garland, 1998.

Kaminsky, Peter. "Vocal Music and the Lures of Exoticism and Irony." *The Cambridge Companion to Ravel*, ed. Deborah Mawer. New York: Cambridge University Press, 2000.

Kaplan, Renee. "Culture Vulture." *Newsday*, 20 July 1997, § C, 2.

Katz, Mark. *Capturing Sound: How Technology Has Changed Music*. Berkeley: University of California Press, 2004.

Katz, Ruth. *The Powers of Music: Aesthetic Theory and the Invention of Opera*. New Brunswick, N.J.: Transaction, 1994.

Kealy, Edward R. "From Craft to Art: The Case of Sound Mixers and Popular Music." *Sociology of Work and Occupations* 6 (1979): 3–29.

Keil, Charles. " 'Ethnic' Music Traditions in the USA." *Popular Music* 13 (May 1994): 175–78.

"Kidjo's 'Oremi' Is Heavenly." *Boston Herald*, September 1998, S25.

Klein, Naomi. *No Logo: Taking Aim at the Brand Bullies*. New York: Picador, 2000.

Klor de Alva, J. Jorge. "The Postcolonization of the (Latin) American Experience: A Reconsideration of 'Colonialism,' 'Postcolonialism,' and 'Mestizaje.' " *After Colonialism: Imperial Histories and Postcolonial Displacements*, ed. Gyan Prakash. Princeton: Princeton University Press, 1995.

Koranteng, Juliana. "EAAA Awards; Abbott Mead Helps Delta Win Respect of Business Fliers." *Advertising Age*, 14 October 1996, § A, 6.

Korten, David C. *When Corporations Rule the World*. West Hartford, Conn.: Kumarian, 1995.

Kozinn, Allan. "This Is the Golden Age." *New York Times*, 28 May 2006, § 2, 1.

Kraidy, Marwan. "The Global, the Local, and the Hybrid: A Native Ethnography of Glocalization." *Critical Studies in Mass Communication* 16 (December 1999): 456–76.

Kramer, Lawrence. "Consuming the Exotic: Ravel's *Daphnis and Chloe*." *Classical Music and Postmodern Knowledge*. Berkeley: University of California Press, 1995, 201–25.

La Franco, Robert, and Michael Schuman. "How Do You Say Rock 'n' Roll in Wolof?" *Forbes*, 17 July 1995, 103.

Lash, Scott, and John Urry. *Economies of Signs and Space*. Thousand Oaks, Calif.: Sage, 1994.

———. *The End of Organized Capitalism*. Madison: University of Wisconsin Press, 1987.

Laswell, Bill. "International Enigma" [interview by Bill Milkowski]. *Music Producers: Conversations with Today's Top Record Makers*, ed. Terri Stone. Emeryville, Calif.: Mix, 1992.

Lebrecht, Norman. "The Composer Who Sells a Million." *Daily Telegraph*, 22 July 1996, 17.

———. *Who Killed Classical Music? Maestros, Managers, and Corporate Politics*. Secaucus, N.J.: Birch Lane, 1997.

Lee, Martyn J. *Consumer Culture Reborn: The Cultural Politics of Consumption*. New York: Routledge, 1993.

Lefkowitz, Murray. "Lawes, William." *The New Grove Dictionary of Music and Musicians*, ed. Stanley Sadie. London: Macmillan, 1980.

———. *William Lawes*. London: Routledge and Kegan Paul, 1960.

Lester, Joel. *Between Modes and Keys: German Theory, 1592–1802*. Stuyvesant, N.Y.: Pendragon, 1989.

Leppert, Richard. "Social Order and the Domestic Consumption of Music: The Politics of Sound in the Policing of Gender Construction in Eighteenth-Century England." *The Consumption of Culture, 1600–1800: Image, Object, Text*, ed. Ann Bermingham and John Brewer. New York: Routledge, 1995.

Leppert, Richard, and Susan McClary, eds. *Music and Society: The Politics of Composition, Performance and Reception*. New York: Cambridge University Press, 1987.

Levine, Robert. "Cross over This." *Pulse!*, April 1998, 37–39.

Lichtheim, George. *Europe in the 20th Century*. London: Phoenix, 1972.

Lind, Michael. *The Next American Nation: The New Nationalism and the Fourth American Revolution*. New York: Free Press, 1995.

Lindley, David, ed. *The Court Masque*. Manchester: Manchester University Press, 1984.

Liner notes to *Songs of the Hawaiian Cowboy*. Warner Western 9 46561-2, 1997.

Liner notes to Wes, *Welenga*. Sony Music 48146-2, 1997.

Liner notes to *What Is Bhangra?* IRS Records, 7243 8 29242 27, 1994.

Lipp, Marty. "On the Record." *Newsday*, 11 June 2000, § D, 26.

Lipsitz, George. "'Ain't Nobody Here But Us Chickens': The Class Origins of Rock and Roll." *Rainbow at Midnight: Labor and Culture in the 1940s*. Urbana: University of Illinois Press, 1994.

———. "Consumer Spending as State Project: Yesterday's Solutions and Today's Problems." *Getting and Spending: European and American Consumer Societies in the Twentieth Century*, ed. Susan Strasser, Charles McGovern, and Matthias Judt. Cambridge: Cambridge University Press, 1998.

———. *Dangerous Crossroads: Popular Music, Postmodernism and the Poetics of Place*. New York: Verso, 1994.

Lister, David. "Mercury Prize." *Independent* (London), 26 July 2000, 7.

Loader, Kevin. "A Mongrel of Dubious Pedigree: Classical Music Has Discovered Beat and Style." *New Statesman and Society*, 13 July 1990, 26.

Locke, Ralph P. "Constructing the Oriental 'Other': Saint-Saëns's Samson et Dalila." *The Work of Opera: Genre, Nationhood, and Sexual Difference*, ed. Richard Dellamora and Daniel Fischlin. New York: Columbia University Press, 1997.

———. "Exoticism." *Grove Music Online*, ed. L. Macy (visited 22 August 2005), http://www.grovemusic.com.

———. "Exoticism and Orientalism in Music: Problems for the Worldly Critic." *Edward Said and the Work of the Critic: Speaking Truth to Power*, ed. Paul Bové. Durham: Duke University Press, 2000.

Lockspeiser, Edward. *Debussy: His Life and Mind*. New York: Cambridge University Press, 1978.

"The Lounge Fad." *Revolt in Style*. http://www.revoltinstyle.com/october/lounge/.

Lowe, Lisa. *Immigrant Acts: On Asian American Cultural Politics*. Durham: Duke University Press, 1996.

Lowinsky, Edward. "Musical Genius: Evolution and Origins of a Concept." *Musical Quarterly* 50 (July 1964): 321–40.

———. "Musical Genius: Evolution and Origins of a Concept, II." *Musical Quarterly* 50 (October 1964): 476–95.

———. *Tonality and Atonality in Sixteenth-Century Music*. Berkeley: University of California Press, 1961.

Lunt, Peter K., and Sonia M. Livingstone. *Mass Consumption and Personal Identity: Everyday Economic Experience*. Philadelphia: Open University Press, 1992.

Lury, Celia. "The Objects of Travel." *Touring Cultures: Transformations of Travel and Theory*, ed. Chris Rojek and John Urry. New York: Routledge, 1997.

Magdoff, Harry. *Imperialism in the Modern Phase*. Vol. 1. *Papers of the International Seminar on Imperialism, Independence and Social Transformation in the Contemporary World* [Delhi, 1972], ed. Baudhayan Chattopadhyay. New Delhi: People's Publishing House, 1974.

Magowan, Fiona. " 'The Land is Our Mäar (Essence), It Stays Forever': The Yothu-Yindi Relationship in Australian Aboriginal Traditional and Popular Musics." *Ethnicity, Identity and Music: The Musical Construction of Place*, ed. Martin Stokes. Providence, R.I.: Berg, 1994.

———. "Traditions of the Mind or the Music Video: Imagining the Imagination in Yothu Yindi's Tribal Voice." *Arena* 7 (1996): 99–111.

Mahon, Maureen. *Right to Rock: The Black Rock Coalition and the Cultural Politics of Race*. Durham: Duke University Press, 2004.

Maira, Sunaina Marr. *Desis in the House: Indian American Youth Culture in New York City*. Philadelphia: Temple University Press, 2002.

———. "Desis Reprazent: Bhangra Remix and Hip Hop in New York City." *Postcolonial Studies* 1 (November 1998): 357–70.

———. "Henna and Hip Hop: The Politics of Cultural Production and the Work of Cultural Studies." *Journal of Asian American Studies* 3 (October 2000): 239–69.

———. "Identity Dub: Second-Generation Indian Americans and Youth Culture."
   Cultural Anthropology 14 (February 1999): 29–60.

Malone, Bill C. *Country Music USA*. Rev. ed. Austin: University of Texas Press, 1985.

Mansfield, Brian. "Album Showcases Slack-Key Guitar Style." *USA Today*, 15 October
   1997, § D, 4.

———. "Documentary, CD Round Up Hawaii's Cowboy Tradition." *USA Today*,
   15 October 1997, § D, 4.

———. "Native Filmmaker Mines Some Unexpected History." *USA Today*, 15 October
   1997, § D, 4.

Martin, George. "Yesterday & Today" [interview by Mel Lambert]. *Music Producers:
   Conversations with Today's Hottest Hitmakers*, ed. Barbara Schultz. Emeryville, Calif.:
   Mix, 2000.

Martin, George, and John Burgess. "High Tea" [interview by Mr. Bonzai]. *Music
   Producers: Conversations with Today's Top Record Makers*, ed. Terri Stone. Emeryville,
   Calif.: Mix, 1992.

Mason, Peter. *Deconstructing America: Representations of the Other*. New York: Routledge,
   1990.

Masten, Jeffrey, and Wendy Wall, eds. *The Space of the Stage*. Renaissance Drama 28.
   Evanston: Northwestern University Press, 1999.

Mazzarella, William. "Culture, Globalization, Mediation." *Annual Review of Anthropology*
   (2004): 345–67.

McClary, Susan. "Constructions of Subjectivity in Schubert's Music." *Queering the Pitch:
   The New Gay and Lesbian Musicology*, ed. Philip Brett, Elizabeth Wood, and Gary C.
   Thomas. New York: Routledge, 1994.

———. *Conventional Wisdom: The Content of Musical Form*. Berkeley: University of
   California Press, 2000.

———. *Feminine Endings: Music, Gender, and Sexuality*. Minneapolis: University of
   Minnesota Press, 1991.

———. *Georges Bizet: "Carmen."* Cambridge: Cambridge University Press, 1992.

———. *Modal Subjectivities: Self-Fashioning in the Italian Madrigal*. Berkeley: University of
   California Press, 2004.

———. "Music, the Pythagoreans, and the Body." *Choreographing History*, ed. Susan
   Leigh Foster. Bloomington: Indiana University Press, 1995.

———. "Narrative Agendas in 'Absolute' Music: Identity and Difference in Brahms's
   Third Symphony." *Musicology and Difference: Gender and Sexuality in Music Scholarship*,
   ed. Ruth A. Solie. Berkeley: University of California Press, 1993.

McCormack, Neil. "At the Speed of Sound on Pop." *Daily Telegraph*, 15 February
   2001, 26.

McCracken, Grant. *Culture and Consumption: New Approaches to the Symbolic Character of
   Consumer Goods and Activities*. Bloomington: Indiana University Press, 1990.

———. *Plenitude*. Toronto: Periph.: Fluide, 1997.

McGovern, Charles. "Consumption and Citizenship in the United States, 1900–1940."

Getting and Spending: European and American Consumer Society in the Twentieth Century, ed. Susan Strasser, Charles McGovern, and Matthias Judt. Cambridge: Cambridge University Press, 1998.

McGrane, Bernard. *Beyond Anthropology: Society and the Other*. New York: Columbia University Press, 1989.

Meier, Bernhard. *The Modes of Classical Vocal Polyphony, Described According to the Sources*, trans. Ellen S. Beebe. New York: Broude Brothers, 1988.

Meintjes, Louise. "Paul Simon's Graceland, South Africa, and the Mediation of Musical Meaning." *Ethnomusicology* 34 (winter 1990): 37–73.

———. *Sound of Africa! Making Music Zulu in a South African Studio*. Durham: Duke University Press, 2003.

Melwani, Lavina. "Indian Chic: OM to the Music." *Little India*, April 1998, 20.

———. "It's a Party." *Welcome to Little India*, January 1997, 21.

Merli, John. "Country Riding High." *Broadcasting and Cable*, 2 March 1998, 30.

Messing, Scott. *Neoclassicism in Music: From the Genesis of the Concept through the Schoenberg/Stravinsky Polemic*. Ann Arbor: UMI Research Press, 1988.

Meyer, Eve R. "Turquerie and Eighteenth-Century Music." *Eighteenth-Century Studies* 7 (1973–74): 474–88.

Micallef, Ken. "Talvin Singh." *Rolling Stone*, 21 August 1997, 36.

Micklethwait, John, and Adrian Wooldridge. *The Witch Doctors: Making Sense of the Management Gurus*. New York: Times Books, 1997.

Mignolo, Walter D. *The Darker Side of the Renaissance: Literacy, Territoriality, and Colonization*. 2d ed. Ann Arbor: University of Michigan Press, 2003.

Mitchell, Rick. "American Tastes Move to World Beat." *Houston Chronicle*, 26 January 1992, 8.

Mitchell, Tony. *Popular Music and Local Identity: Rock, Pop and Rap in Europe and Oceania*. New York: Leicester University Press, 1997.

Montrose, Louis. "The Work of Gender in the Discourse of Discovery." *New World Encounters*, ed. Stephen Greenblatt. Berkeley: University of California Press, 1993.

Muecke, Stephen. *Textual Spaces: Aboriginality and Cultural Studies*. Kensington: New South Wales University Press, 1992.

Mueller, Richard. "Javanese Influence on Debussy's *Fantaisie* and Beyond." *Nineteenth-Century Music* 10 (autumn 1986–87): 157–86.

Muikku, Jari. "On the Role of the Tasks of a Record Producer." *Popular Music and Society* 14 (spring 1990): 25–34.

Mukhi, Sunita Sunder. *Doing the Desi Thing: Performing Indianness in New York City*. New York: Garland, 2000.

———. "Forging an Indian American Identity: Guess Who's Coming to Dinner?" *Little India*, May 1996, 49.

———. "Forging an Indian American Identity: Something to Dance About." *Little India*, April 1996, 53.

"Music to Their Brands' Ears." *Business and Industry*, May 1999, 35.

Nandy, Ashis. *The Intimate Enemy: Loss and Recovery of Self under Colonialism*. Delhi: Oxford University Press, 1983.

Nehring, Neil. *Flowers in the Dustbin: Culture, Anarchy, and Postwar England*. Ann Arbor: University of Michigan Press, 1993.

Nettl, Paul. "Die Moresca." *Archiv für Musikwissenchaft* 14 (1957): 165–74.

Neuenfeldt, Karl. "Yothu Yindi: Agendas and Aspirations." *Sound Alliances: Indigenous Peoples, Cultural Politics and Popular Music in the Pacific*, ed. Philip Hayward. London: Cassell, 1998.

———. "Yothu Yindi and Ganma: The Cultural Transposition of Aboriginal Agenda through Metaphor and Music." *Journal of Australian Studies* 38 (September 1993): 1–11.

Nicholls, David. "Cowell, Henry." *Grove Music Online*, ed. L. Macy. http://www .grovemusic.com.

———. "Henry Cowell's *United Quartet*." *American Music* 13 (summer 1995): 195–217.

———. "Transethnicism and the American Experimental Tradition." *Musical Quarterly* 80 (winter 1996): 659–94.

Nichols, Roger. *Debussy*. London: Oxford University Press, 1973.

Nicol, Lisa. "Culture, Custom and Collaboration: The Production of Yothu Yindi's Treaty Videos." *Perfect Beat* 1 (January 1993): 23–32.

Norton, Richard. *Tonality in Western Culture: A Critical and Historical Perspective*. University Park: Pennsylvania State University Press, 1984.

Nowicka, Helen. "Pride and Prejudice in Recording Business." *Guardian*, 10 November 1995, 5.

Obelkevich, Mary Rowen. "Turkish Affect in the Land of the Sun King." *Musical Quarterly* 63 (July 1977): 367–89.

Oja, Carol. *Making Music Modern: New York in the 1920s*. New York: Oxford University Press, 2000.

Okoye, Felix N. *The American Image of Africa: Myth and Reality*. Buffalo: Black Academy Press, 1964.

Orgel, Stephen. *The Jonsonian Masque*. 2d ed. New York: Columbia University Press, 1981.

———. *The Illusion of Power: Political Theater in the English Renaissance*. Berkeley: University of California Press, 1975.

Orledge, Robert. "Evocations of Exoticism." *The Cambridge Companion to Ravel*, ed. Deborah Mawer. New York: Cambridge University Press, 2000.

Ortner, Sherry B. "Is Female to Male as Nature Is to Culture?" *Making Gender: The Politics and Erotics of Culture*. Boston: Beacon, 1996.

———. "Resistance and the Problem of Ethnographic Refusal." *Comparative Studies in Society and History* 37 (January 1995): 173–93.

———. "So, *Is* Female to Male as Nature Is to Culture?" *Making Gender: The Politics and Erotics of Culture*. Boston: Beacon, 1996.

Oumano, Elena. "Island Targets R&B Market with New Album from Kidjo." *Billboard*, 23 May 1998, 1.

Outram, Dorinda. *The Enlightenment*. Cambridge: Cambridge University Press, 1995.

Owen, Frank. "Electronica Arrives via Madison Ave.; Underground Techno Music Is a Hit in the Land of Jingles." *Washington Post*, 12 July 1998, § G, 1.

Pagden, Anthony. *European Encounters with the New World: From Renaissance to Romanticism*. New Haven: Yale University Press, 1993.

———. *Peoples and Empires: A Short History of European Migration, Exploration, and Conquest, from Greece to the Present*. New York: Modern Library, 2001.

Parkin, David. "Nemi in the Modern World: Return of the Exotic?" *Man* 28 (March 1993): 79–99.

Parney, Lisa Leigh. "Songs of 'Prayer Cycle' Seek Universal Themes." *Christian Science Monitor*, 23 April 1999, 20.

Parry, J. H. *The Age of Reconnaissance*. Berkeley: University of California Press, 1981.

———. *The Establishment of the European Hegemony, 1415–1715: Trade and Exploration in the Age of the Renaissance*. New York: Harper and Row, 1966.

Peak, Martha H. "Developing an International Style of Management." *Management Review*, February 1991, 32–35.

Perlis, Vivian. *Charles Ives Remembered: An Oral History*. New York: W. W. Norton, 1974.

Pestelli, Giorgio. *The Age of Mozart and Beethoven*, trans. Eric Cross. New York: Cambridge University Press, 1984.

Peters, Tom. *Liberation Management: Necessary Disorganization for the Nanosecond Nineties*. New York: Alfred A. Knopf, 1992.

Peterson, Richard A. *Creating Country Music: Fabricating Authenticity*. Chicago: University of Chicago Press, 1997.

Peterson, Richard A., and Paul DiMaggio. "From Region to Class, the Changing Locus of Country Music: A Test of the Massification Hypothesis." *Social Forces* 53 (March 1975): 497–506.

Petreycik, Rick. n.d. Review of *Songs of the Hawaiian Cowboy, New Country* (included in press kit from Warner Western).

Petrozello, Donna. "Country Format Is Radio's Favorite." *Broadcasting and Cable*, 10 March 1997, 53–54.

Petzoldt, Richard. "The Economic Conditions of the 18th-Century Musician." *The Social Status of the Professional Musician from the Middle Ages to the 19th Century*, ed. Walter Salmen, trans. Herbert Kaufman and Barbara Reisner. New York: Pendragon, 1983.

Pieterse, Jan Nederveen. *White on Black: Images of Africa and Blacks in Western Popular Culture*. New Haven: Yale University Press, 1992.

Platt, Peter. *Reason Diminished: Shakespeare and the Marvelous*. Omaha: University of Nebraska Press, 1997.

poet, j. "Worldbeat." All-Music Guide, http://www.allmusic.com/, n.d.

Potoker, John. "Doing What Feels Right" [interview by Nick Vallelonga]. *Music Producers: Conversations with Today's Top Record Makers*, ed. Terri Stone. Emeryville, Calif.: Mix, 1992.

Powers, Harold. "Is Mode Real?: Pietro Aron, the Octenary System, and Polyphony." *Basler Jahrbuch für historische Musikpraxis* 16 (1992): 9–52.

Prasad, Anil. "Extending Energy and Experimentation" [interview with Bill Laswell, 27 April 1999], http://www.innerviews.org/inner/laswell.html.

Pratt, Mary Louise. *Imperial Eyes: Travel Writing and Transculturation*. New York: Routledge, 1992.

Preibisch, Walter. "Quellenstudien zu Mozart's 'Entführung aus dem Serail': Ein Beitrag zu der Geschichte der Türkenoper." *Sammelbände der Internationalen Musik-Gesellschaft* 10 (1908–9): 430–76.

Puig, Claudia, and Steve Hochman. "New Station Aims to Give Pop Fans a Choice." *Los Angeles Times*, 1 July 1994, § F, 24.

Rabinow, Paul. *French Modern: Norms and Forms of the Social Environment*. Chicago: University of Chicago Press, 1995.

Radano, Ronald. *Lying Up a Nation: Race and Black Music*. Chicago: University of Chicago Press, 2003.

Ramjug, Peter. "Robert Palmer Has a Little Bit of Everything in His Music." Reuters, 22 December 1998.

Randel, Don. "Emerging Triadic Tonality in the Fifteenth Century." *Musical Quarterly* 57 (1971): 73–86.

Rao, Nancy. "American Compositional Theory in the 1930s: Scale and Exoticism in 'The Nature of Melody' by Henry Cowell." *Musical Quarterly* 85 (2001): 595–640.

Reck, David. "The Neon Electric Sarswati." *Contributions to Asian Studies* 12 (1978): 3–19.

Reynolds, Simon. "Electronica Goes Straight to Ubiquity." *New York Times*, 6 June 1999, § 2, 27.

Rieff, David. "Multiculturalism's Silent Partner." *Harper's*, August 1993, 62–71.

Ritzer, George. *Enchanting a Disenchanted World: Revolutionizing the Means of Consumption*. Thousand Oaks, Calif.: Pine Forge, 1999.

Rivera, Benito. "Harmonic Theory in Musical Treatises of the Late Fifteenth and Early Sixteenth Centuries." *Music Theory Spectrum* 1 (1979): 80–95.

Robbins, Bruce. "Comparative Cosmopolitanism." *Social Text* 31–32 (1992): 169–86.

Robertson, Carol. "Introduction: The Dance of Conquest." *Musical Repercussions of 1492: Encounters in Text and Performance*, ed. Carol Robertson. Washington: Smithsonian Institution Press, 1992.

Robertson, Roland. "Globalisation or Glocalisation?" *Journal of International Communication* 1 (1994): 33–52.

———. "Glocalization: Time-Space and Homogeneity-Heterogeneity." *Global Modernities*, ed. Mike Featherstone et al. Thousand Oaks, Calif.: Sage, 1995.

Robicheau, Paul. "Listening to History." *Boston Globe*, 25 September 1998, § S, 25.

Robinson, Michael F. *Opera before Mozart*. New York: William Morrow, 1966.

Robinson, Paul. "Is *Aida* an Orientalist Opera?" *Cambridge Opera Journal* 5 (July 1993): 133–40.

Romero, D. James. "His Drum-and-Bass Is Served with Some Spice." *Los Angeles Times*, 20 July 1997, 56.

Rosand, Ellen. *Opera in Seventeenth-Century Venice: The Creation of a Genre*. Berkeley: University of California Press, 1991.

Ross, Andrew. Review of *Deep Forest*. *Artforum*, December 1993, 11.

Rouse, Roger. "Thinking through Transnationalism: Notes on the Cultural Politics of Class Relations in the Contemporary United States." *Public Culture* 7 (spring 1995): 353–402.

Rousseau, Jean Jacques. "Sonate." *Dictionnaire de Musique*. Hildesheim: Georg Olms Verlagsbuchhandlung, 1969.

Rule, Greg. "Jingles All the Way: Making Music for Commercials." *Keyboard*, March 1997, 8.

Rushdie, Salman. *Imaginary Homelands*. London: Granta, 1991.

Russ, Martin. *Sound Synthesis and Sampling*. Oxford: Focal Press, 1996.

Rygg, Kristin. *Masqued Mysteries Unmasked: Early Modern Music Theater and Its Pythagorean Subtext*. Hillsdale, N.Y.: Pendragon, 2000.

Sachs, Curt. *World History of the Dance*, trans. Bessie Schönberg. New York: W. W. Norton, 1963.

Sadie, Stanley. *The New Grove Mozart*. New York: W. W. Norton, 1983.

Said, Edward W. *Culture and Imperialism*. New York: Alfred A. Knopf, 1993.

————. *Orientalism*. New York: Vintage, 1979.

Sale, Kirkpatrick. *The Conquest of Paradise: The Columbian Legacy*. New York: Alfred A. Knopf, 1990.

Santelli, Robert. "The Neglected Soul of Country Music." *Rolling Stone*, 19 March 1998, 66.

Santiago, Chiori. "Ride 'Em, Paniolo!" *Rhythm Music*, March 1998, 27.

Sartre, Jean-Paul. *Search for a Method*, trans. Hazel E. Barnes. New York: Alfred A. Knopf, 1967.

Satie, Erik. *A Mammal's Notebook: Collected Writings of Erik Satie*, ed. Ornella Volta, trans. Antony Melville. London: Atlas, 2002.

Savage, Roger. "Rameau's American Dancers." *Early Music* 11 (October 1983): 441–52.

Sayers, Dorothy L. *Have His Carcase*. New York: Harper Paperbacks, 1995.

Schoenberg, Arnold. *Style and Idea: Selected Writings of Arnold Schoenberg*, ed. Leonard Stein, trans. Leo Black. Berkeley: University of California Press, 1985.

Schor, Juliet. *Do Americans Shop Too Much?* Boston: Beacon, 2000.

Schorske, Carl E. *Fin-de-Siècle Vienna: Politics and Culture*. New York: Vintage, 1981.

Schubart, Christian Friedrich Daniel. "On the Human Voice and the Characteristics of the Musical Keys," trans. Ted DuBois. *New England Review* 25 (winter–spring 2004): 166–71.

Scott, Derek B. "Orientalism and Musical Style." *Critical Musicology Journal*, http://www.leeds.ac.uk/music/info/critmus/articles/1997/02/01.html.

Scott, Linda M. "Understanding Jingles and Needledrop: A Rhetorical Approach to Music in Advertising." *Journal of Consumer Research* (September 1990): 223–36.

Seeger, Charles. "Music and Class Structure in the United States." *American Quarterly* 9 (fall 1957): 281–94.

Selvin, Joel. "Ad Men Make Music as Mox." *San Francisco Chronicle*, 10 May 1998, 44.

Sengupta, Somini. "To Be Young, Indian and Hip." *New York Times*, 30 July 1996, § 13, 11.

Shannon, Christopher. *A World Made Safe for Differences: Cold War Intellectuals and the Politics of Identity*. Lanham, Md.: Rowan and Littlefield, 2001.

Sharma, Ashwani. " 'Sounds Oriental': The (Im)Possibility of Theorizing Asian Musical Cultures." *Dis-Orienting Rhythms: The Politics of the New Asian Dance Music*, ed. Sanjay Sharma, John Hutnyk, and Ashwani Sharma. Atlantic Highlands, N.J.: Zed, 1996.

Sharp, Cecil, and Herbert C. MacIlwaine. *The Morris Book: A History of Morris Dancing, with a Description of Eleven Dances as Performed by the Morrismen of England*. Rev. ed. London: Novello, 1912–24.

Shepherd, John. *Music as Social Text*. Cambridge: Polity, 1991.

Sherrard, Geoffrey. "The Illustrious Industrious Bill Laswell." http://www.glowmag .com/laswell/laswell.html, n.d.

Shin, Paul H. B. "Hot New Music Has Some Very Old Roots." *Daily News* (New York), 18 February 1998, 3.

Shoemaker, Adam. "The Politics of Yothu Yindi." Working Papers in Australian Studies 88–96, ed. Kate Darian-Smith. [London:] Sir Robert Menzies Centre for Australian Studies, Institute of Commonwealth Studies, University of London, 1994.

———. "Selling Yothu Yindi." *Republica: All Same as Family in a Big 'Ouse*, ed. George Papaellinas. Sydney: Angus and Robertson, 1994.

Sklair, Leslie. *Sociology of the Global System*. 2d ed. Baltimore: Johns Hopkins University Press, 1995.

———. *The Transnational Capitalist Class*. Malden, Mass.: Blackwell, 2001.

Slater, Don. *Consumer Culture and Modernity*. Malden, Mass.: Polity, 1997.

Sly, Leslie. "Bill Laswell: World Music Mixes from a Material Guy." *Keyboard*, June 1994, 10–11.

Smith, Adam. *Essays on Philosophical Subjects*, ed. W. P. D. Wightman and J. C. Bryce. Oxford: Clarendon, 1980.

Snowden, Frank M. *Before Color Prejudice: The Ancient View of the Blacks*. Cambridge: Harvard University Press, 1983.

Sonneck, O. G. *Miscellaneous Studies in the History of Music*. New York: Macmillan, 1921.

Spencer, Neil. "Kaftans Are Back but Singh Wants No Part of Any Indian Summer." *Observer* (London), 16 February 1997, 10.

Spencer, Philip. *World Beat: A Listener's Guide to Contemporary World Music on CD*. Pennington, N.J.: A Cappella, 1992.

Spurr, David. *The Rhetoric of Empire: Colonial Discourse in Journalism, Travel Writing, and Imperial Administration*. Durham: Duke University Press, 1993.

Stallybrass, Peter, and Allon White. *The Politics and Poetics of Transgression*. Ithaca: Cornell University Press, 1986.

Stark, Phyllis. "Nashville Scene: Study Has Good News for Country Radio." *Billboard*, 31 July 2004.

————. "Trini Triggs Hopes to Break Barriers." *Billboard*, 28 February 1998, 40.

Steblin, Rita. *A History of Key Characteristics in the Eighteenth and Early Nineteenth Centuries*. Ann Arbor: University of Michigan Press, 1983.

Stepan, Nancy. *The Idea of Race in Science: Great Britain, 1800–1900*. London: Macmillan, 1982.

Sterne, Jonathan. *The Audible Past: Cultural Origins of Sound Reproduction*. Durham: Duke University Press, 2003.

Sternfeld, F. W. *The Birth of Opera*. Oxford: Clarendon, 1993.

Stocking, George W., Jr. *Race, Culture, and Evolution: Essays in the History of Anthropology*. New York: Free Press, 1968.

Stokes, Martin. "Music and the Global Order." *Annual Review of Anthropology*, 2004, 47–72.

Stoler, Ann Laura. "Carnal Knowledge and Imperial Power: Gender, Race, and Morality in Colonial Asia." *Gender at the Crossroads of Knowledge: Feminist Anthropology in the Postmodern Era*, ed. Micaela di Leonardo. Berkeley: University of California Press, 1991.

————. "Rethinking Colonial Categories: European Communities and the Boundaries of Rule." *Comparative Studies in Society and History* 31 (January 1989): 134–61.

————. "Sexual Affronts and Racial Frontiers: European Identities and the Cultural Politics of Exclusion in Colonial Southeast Asia." *Tensions of Empire: Colonial Cultures in a Bourgeois World*, ed. Frederick Cooper and Ann Laura Stoler. Berkeley: University of California Press, 1997.

Storper, Michael. "Lived Effects of the Contemporary Economy: Globalization, Inequality, and Consumer Society." *Millennial Capitalism and the Culture of Neoliberalism*, ed. Jean and John L. Comaroff. Durham: Duke University Press, 2001.

Stravinsky, Igor. *An Autobiography*. 1936. Repr. New York: W. W. Norton, 1962.

————. "Some Ideas about My Octuor." *Stravinsky: The Composer and His Works*, by Eric Walter White. 2d ed. Berkeley: University of California Press, 1979.

Straw, Will. "Sizing Up Record Collections: Gender and Connoisseurship in Rock Music Culture." *Sexing the Groove: Popular Music and Gender*, ed. Sheila Whiteley. New York: Routledge, 1997.

Strohm, Reinhard. *The Rise of European Music, 1380–1500*. Cambridge: Cambridge University Press, 1993.

Strong, Roy. *Art and Power: Renaissance Festivals, 1450–1650*. Berkeley: University of California Press, 1984.

Stubington, Jill, and Peter Dunbar-Hall. "Yothu Yindi's 'Treaty': Ganma in Music." *Popular Music* 13 (October 1994): 243–59.

Subotnik, Rose Rosengard. *Developing Variations: Style and Ideology in Western Music*. Minneapolis: University of Minnesota Press, 1991.

Sulzer, Johann Georg. *Allgemeine Theorie der schönen Künste, in einzelnen, nach alphabetischer*

Ordnung der Künstwörter aufeinanderfolgenden Artikeln abgehandelt. Excerpted in *Music and Aesthetics in the Eighteenth and Early-Nineteenth Centuries,* ed. Peter le Huray and James Day. Abridged ed. Cambridge: Cambridge University Press, 1988.

Susman, Warren. *Culture as History: The Transformation of American Society in the Twentieth Century.* New York: Pantheon, 1984.

Sweeney, Philip. "If It Sounds Familiar. . . ." *Independent* (London), 9 July 1992, 22.

————. *The Virgin Directory of World Music.* London: Virgin, 1991.

Szabolcsi, Bence. "Exoticisms in Mozart." *Music and Letters* 37 (October 1956): 323–32.

Tamm, Eric. *Brian Eno: His Music and the Vertical Color of Sound.* Boston: Faber and Faber, 1989.

Tan Ling Ai. "The Coming Together of Adiemus." *New Straits Times* (Malaysia), 31 March 1997, 4.

Taruskin, Richard. "Of Kings and Divas." *New Republic,* 13 December 1993, 31–44.

Taylor, Charles. *Multiculturalism: Examining the Politics of Recognition,* ed. Amy Gutmann. Princeton: Princeton University Press, 1994.

Taylor, Chuck. "Country Radio Leads in Listeners; Format Also Top in Demo Targets, Study Shows." *Billboard,* 24 May 1997, 93.

Taylor, Timothy D. "Aesthetic and Cultural Issues in Schumann's *Kinderszenen.*" *International Review of the Aesthetics and Sociology of Music* 21 (December 1990): 161–78.

————. "Bad World Music." *Bad Music: The Music We Love to Hate,* ed. Chris Washburne and Maiken Derno. New York: Routledge, 2004.

————. "The Changing Shape of the Culture Industry; or, How Did Electronica Music Get into Television Commercials?" *Journal of Television and New Media,* forthcoming.

————. *Global Pop: World Music, World Markets.* New York: Routledge, 1997.

————. "Korla Pandit: Music, Exoticism and Mysticism" *Widening the Horizon: Exoticism in Post-War Popular Music,* ed. Philip Hayward. Sydney: John Libbey / Perfect Beat, 1999.

————. "Music and Musical Practices in Postmodernity." *Postmodern Music/Postmodern Thought,* ed. Joseph Auner and Judith Lochhead. New York: Routledge, 2002.

————. "Music and the Rise of Radio in Twenties America: Technological Imperialism, Socialization, and the Transformation of Intimacy." *Wired for Sound: Engineering and Technology in Sonic Cultures,* ed. Thomas Porcello and Paul Greene. Middletown, Conn.: Wesleyan University Press, 2004.

————. Review of *Songlines. World of Music* 41 (1999): 181–83.

————. "Sampling and Consumption." *Sound Unbound: Music, Multimedia, and Contemporary Sound Art: An Anthology of Writings on Contemporary Culture,* ed. Paul D. Miller. Cambridge: MIT Press, forthcoming.

————. *Strange Sounds: Music, Technology and Culture.* New York: Routledge, 2001.

Taylor, Timothy D., Mark Katz, and Anthony Grajeda, eds. *The Social Life of Early Sound Technologies: A History in Documents, 1880–1945.* Durham: Duke University Press, forthcoming.

Thomas, Nicholas. *Colonialism's Culture: Anthropology, Travel, and Government*. Princeton: Princeton University Press, 1994.

Thompson, Craig J. "A New Puritanism?" *Do Americans Shop Too Much?* Boston: Beacon, 2000.

Thompson, Emily. *The Soundscape of Modernity: Architectural Acoustics and the Culture of Listening in America, 1900–1933*. Cambridge: MIT Press, 2002.

Till, Nicholas. *Mozart and the Enlightenment: Truth, Virtue and Beauty in Mozart's Operas*. New York: W. W. Norton, 1992.

Todorov, Tzvetan. *On Human Diversity: Nationalism, Racism, and Exoticism in French Thought*, trans. Catherine Porter. Cambridge: Harvard University Press, 1995.

Tomlinson, John. *Globalization and Culture*. Chicago: University of Chicago Press, 1999.

Tooley, R. V. *Maps and Map-Makers*. 7th ed. London: B. T. Batsford, 1987.

Toop, David. *Exotica*. New York: Serpent's Tail, 1999.

Trouillot, Michel-Rolph. "Anthropology and the Savage Slot: The Poetics and Politics of Otherness." *Recapturing Anthropology: Working in the Present*, ed. Richard G. Fox. Santa Fe: School of American Research Press, 1991.

Tsering, Lisa. "Bally Gets Busy with Bhangra, Film Projects." *India West*, August 1998, http://members.tripod.com/~LisaTsering/index-8.html [URL no longer active].

Turino, Thomas. *Nationalists, Cosmopolitans, and Popular Music in Zimbabwe*. Chicago: University of Chicago Press, 2000.

Turner, Graeme. *Making It National: Nationalism and Australian Popular Culture*. St. Leonards: Allen and Unwin, 1994.

Twitchell, James B. *Lead Us into Temptation: The Triumph of American Materialism*. New York: Columbia University Press, 1999.

Urry, John. *The Tourist Gaze: Leisure and Travel in Contemporary Societies*. Thousand Oaks, Calif.: Sage, 1990.

Virilio, Paul. *Open Sky*, trans. Julie Rose. New York: Verso, 1997.

Wallerstein, Immanuel. *Historical Capitalism*, pubd. with *Capitalist Civilization*. New York: Verso 1983.

———. *The Modern World-System: Capitalist Agriculture and the Origins of the European World-Economy in the Sixteenth Century*. New York: Academic, 1974.

Walls, Peter. *Music in the English Courtly Masque, 1604–1640*. Oxford: Clarendon, 1996.

Walser, Robert. *Running with the Devil: Power, Gender, and Madness in Heavy Metal Music*. Middletown, Conn.: Wesleyan University Press, 1993.

Waters, Malcolm. *Globalization*. New York: Routledge, 1995.

Watkins, Glenn. *Pyramids at the Louvre: Music, Culture, and Collage from Stravinsky to the Postmodernists*. Cambridge: Belknap Press of Harvard University Press, 1994.

———. *Soundings: Music in the Twentieth Century*. New York: Schirmer, 1995.

Watson, C. W. *Multiculturalism*. Philadelphia: Open University Press, 2000.

Weininger, Otto. *Sex and Character: An Investigation of Fundamental Principles*, ed. Daniel Steuer and Laura Marcus, trans. Ladislaus Löb. Bloomington: Indiana University Press, 2005.

Weisel, Al. "Deep Forest's Lush Lullaby." *Rolling Stone*, 21 April 1994, 26.

Welsford, Enid. *The Court Masque: A Study in the Relationship between Poetry and the Revels*. Cambridge: Cambridge University Press, 1927.

Wentz, Brooke. "No Kid Stuff." *Beat*, 1993, 42–45.

———. "Youssou N'Dour: Is He Shaking the Tree or Cutting It Down?" *Rhythm Music*, May–June 1994, 38.

Werblin, Cathy. "Vietnamese Full Moon Celebration Planned." *Los Angeles Times* (Orange County Edition), 28 September 1996, § B, 2.

Whaples, Miriam K. "Early Exoticism Revisited." *The Exotic in Western Music*, ed. Jonathan Bellman. Boston: Northeastern University Press, 1998.

Wheeler, Roxann. *The Complexion of Race: Categories of Difference in Eighteenth-Century British Culture*. Philadelphia: University of Pennsylvania Press, 2000.

Wheelock, Gretchen. "Schwarze Gredel and the Engendered Minor Mode in Mozart's Operas." *Musicology and Difference: Gender and Sexuality in Music Scholarship*, ed. Ruth A. Solie. Berkeley: University of California Press, 1993.

White, Timothy. " 'Stand' Up for Country Soul!" *Billboard*, 31 January 1998, 4.

Wieviorka, Michel. "Is Multiculturalism the Solution?" *Ethnic and Racial Studies* 21 (September 1998): 881–910.

Williams, Raymond. "Base and Superstructure in Marxist Cultural Theory." *Problems in Materialism and Culture*. London: Verso, 1980.

———. *Culture*. Glasgow: William Collins Sons, 1981.

———. *Keywords: A Vocabulary of Culture and Society*. London: Fontana, 1976.

———. *Marxism and Literature*. New York: Oxford University Press, 1977.

———. "Metropolitan Perceptions and the Emergence of Modernism." *The Politics of Modernism: Against the New Conformists*. New York: Verso, 1989.

Williams, Rosalind H. *Dream Worlds: Mass Consumption in Late Nineteenth-Century France*. Berkeley: University of California Press, 1982.

Williams, Steven. "State of 'Graceland.' " *Los Angeles Times*, 24 August 1986, 92.

Wilson, W. Daniel. "Turks on the Eighteenth-Century Operatic Stage and European Political, Military, and Cultural History." *Eighteenth-Century Life* 2 (1985): 79–92.

Witt, Louise. "Back to the Country." *American Demographics*, 1 November 2003, 9.

Wolff, Janet. "The Ideology of Autonomous Art." *Music and Society: The Politics of Composition, Performance and Reception*, ed. Richard Leppert and Susan McClary. New York: Cambridge University Press, 1987.

Yergin, Daniel, and Joseph Stanislaw. *The Commanding Heights: The Battle for the World Economy*. New York: Simon and Schuster, 1998.

Young, Robert. *Colonial Desire: Hybridity in Theory, Culture and Race*. New York: Routledge, 1995.

Yunupingu, Mandawuy. "Yothu Yindi: Finding Balance." *Race and Class* 35 (April–June 1994): 113–20.

Zemp, Hugo. "The/An Ethnomusicologist and the Record Business." *Yearbook for Traditional Music* 28 (1996): 36–56.

Zerzan, John. "Tonality and the Totality." *Future Primitive and Other Essays*. Brooklyn, N.Y.: Autonomedia, 1994.

Zuberi, Nabeel. *Sounds English: Transnational Popular Music*. Urbana: University of Illinois Press, 2001.

Zukin, Sharon. *Landscapes of Power: From Detroit to Disney World*. Berkeley: University of California Press, 1991.

Index

Dufay, Guillaume, 227 n. 43

Dun, Tan, 194

"Durch Zärtlichket und Schmeilcheln"
(Mozart), 63–64

Dussel, Enrique, 17

Dvořák, Antonín, 74

Dylan, Bob, 2

Ecclesie militantis/Sanctorum arbitorio (Dufay),
227 n. 43

Economies of Signs and Space (Lash and Urry),
136–37

"Egyptians" (advertising spot), 199

"electronica" music, 255 n. 16

Elements of Geology (Lyell), 74

Elias, Jonathan, 175, 187, 255 n. 11

Elias Associates, 185–90, 198–200

Eliot, George, 43

Elizabeth I (Queen), 22–23, 57

Elliott, J. H., 21, 50, 216 n. 8

EMI Entertainment Properties, 202

Enlightenment: aesthetic ideology and,
99–102; cartography in, 26; Mozart's
operas influenced by, 64–72, 230 n. 77;
musical representation in, 48–51; otherness in, 43–48

Eno, Brian, 133, 141, 243 n. 34

Entführung aus dem Serail, Die (Mozart), 11,
51, 57–72; minor keys in, 62–66

Enya, 186

Erikson, Erik H., 119

Erlmann, Veit, 7

Erwartung (Schoenberg), 85

ethnicity: commercialization of world
music and, 190–91; culture and, 123–26;
identity and, 119–21

ethnomusicology, 2, 7–10

European culture: colonialism and, 17–42;
exoticism in music of, 49–51; gender roles and, 22–23; imperialism and
changes in, 78–83; tonality's emergence
in, 24–42

Europe galante, L' (Campra), 52

evolutionism, 11; Boas's critique of, 107–8

Evora, Cesaria, 144

exoticism: consumption and, 90–99;
Cowell and, 106; ethnomusicology and,
8–10; in European music, 32–35, 49–51;
global information capital and, 202–4;
imperialism and, 78; limitations to concept of, 209–13; in musicology, 2, 9,
49–51; post-tourism and, 205–8

Fair Maid of the West, The (Heywood), 54

Falstaff (Verdi), 60

Fantaisie (Debussy), 86

fantasy, 95

Feifer, Maxine, 205

Feind, Barthold, 32–35

Feld, Steven, 87

Feminine Endings (McClary), 5

feminism, 121

Ferry, Jules, 98–99

fifth (interval), 199, 257 n. 40

"First Date" (advertising spot), 199

Fisher, Jeffrey P., 188, 199

"Fling" (advertising spot), 198–200

folk music: bhangra remix and, 152–55;
Hawai'ian cowboy music as, 176–83;
Romantic music influenced by, 73–74;
Ives's use of, 103–4; Mozart's use of,
62–63, 230 n. 74; Stravinsky's use of,
104

Foucault, Michel, 5, 8; exoticism and, 5, 8,
209–13; on similarity, 20; on spatialization, 25

four-stages theory of culture, 44–48

Fox, Richard G., 164

Franco-Prussian War, 98

Frank, Thomas, 166–67, 169, 175

Franz Joseph (Emperor), 80

French music, 89–99

Freud, Sigmund, 79, 82

Frith, Simon, 5, 168–69

From Where I Stand: The Black Experience in Country Music (recording), 170

Gabriel, Peter, 127, 148, 160, 199
Galilei, Galileo, 27–29, 31
gamelan, 187
gamma philosophy, 157–58
Gates, Henry Louis, Jr., 202
Gatinella, Roy, 202
Gedanken von der Opera (Feind), 32
Geertz, Clifford, 4–5, 210
gender: European colonialism and, 22–23, 42; imperialism and, 79–83; mass culture and, 81–82; otherness in Mozart's operas and, 66–72
genius, 3
geographical margins: commercialization of world music and erasure of, 190–91; in country music, 166–67; culture and, 70–72
Gibbs, A. M., 223 n. 96
Giddens, Anthony, 209–13
globalization: collaboration in culture and, 126–29; consumption and, 115–18; contemporary popular music production and, 129–39; as cultural system, 113–21; defined, 114–15; faux world music and, 201–8; informational capital and social élites in, 202–4; multiculturalism and, 119–21, 123–26; musicology and, 11–12; self-identity and, 118–21; world music categorization and, 167
Global Pop (Taylor), 11, 114–15, 126, 163, 170–71, 182–83, 210
"glocalization," 257 n. 45
Gluck, Christoph Willibald von, 60
Goldsmith, Oliver, 48
Goman, Stanley, 167
Gómez-Peña, Guillermo, 126
Gopinath, Gayatri, 147
Graceland (Simon), 127–29, 134, 246 n. 12
Graham, Ronnie, 169

Gramophone, 174
Grass Roots (Panjabi MC), 149
gravity, tonality and, 27–29
Grazzini, Antonfrancesco, 221 n. 92
Great Works, 3–4. *See also* classical music ideology
Greenblatt, Stephen, 4–5, 20–21, 24, 52
Greene, Jack P., 220 n. 61
"grotesque realism," 33–34
Guilbault, Jocelyne, 144
Gupta, Akhil, 164

Habsburg Empire, 80, 86
Haddad, Bob, 171
Haig, Christine, 76
Hall, Stuart, 9, 72, 79
Hans Raj Hans, 151
Hardt, Michael, 24, 146
Harrison, George, 166
Harrison, Lou, 106
Haugen, Ann, 186–88, 255 n. 16
Hawai'ian music, 176–83
Heart of Darkness (Conrad), 88
Hearts of Space, 164
Hebdige, Dick, 208
Heinichen, Johann David, 27
Hesmondhalgh, David, 6–7
hexatonic scale, 94
Heywood, Thomas, 54
High Bird (band), 141
Hindi remix music, 146–55
history: musicology and role of, 2–4, 8; self-identity and, 209–13
History of Sir Francis Drake, The (opera), 37
History of the Earth and Animated Nature (Goldsmith), 48
Hobsbawm, Eric, 75, 78, 86, 90
Hodgen, Margaret T., 47
Holt, Douglas, 117, 240 n. 22
"Homme armé, L'," 228 n. 43
homosexuality, 82–83
Hudson, Richard, 40

Potoker, Joe, 133

power, 1–2

Powers, Harold, 25, 219 n. 39

Prayer Cycle, The (Elias), 175, 255 n. 11

"Premier Tambourin" (Rameau), 56–57

Prichard, John, 74

Pride, Charley, 169–70

"primitives," 43–48

Principles of Geology (Lyell), 74

production of music: globalization and, 130–39, 242 n. 28, 243 nn. 29–30; hybridity discourses in, 141–46

project concept, 120–21

Publicis (advertising agency), 199

Pulcinella (Stravinsky), 104

Punjabi music, 146–55, 247 n. 26

Purity and Danger (Douglas), 71

Qawwali music, 148

race: categorization of world music and, 164–65; commercialization of world music and, 190–200; culture and, 123–26; Enlightenment concepts of, 44–48; European colonialism and views of, 19–20, 98–99; history of, 9, 215 n. 18; hybridity in music and, 143–44, 245 n. 12; identity and, 119–21; nineteenth-century attitudes toward, 74–75; otherness and, 72; politics in music and, 167–68; popular music and, 166

Racine, Jean, 219 n. 45

Radano, Ronald, 7

Ralegh, Walter, 22–23

Rameau, Jean-Philippe, 11, 27–28, 51–57, 60, 71–72, 226 n. 41

Rao, Nancy, 105–6, 108, 236 n. 97

Ravel, Maurice, 11, 83, 86–87; French modernism and, 89–99

Ray of Light (Madonna), 152, 248 n. 40

Reagan, Ronald, 118, 240 n. 26

Real World (record label), 148

rebelliousness, 165–66

Reformation: European colonialism and, 22, 217 n. 25; history of opera and, 31–35

representational modalities: in eighteenth-century European music, 49–72; global information capital and, 202–4; history and culture and, 210–13; imperialism and, 75–83, 97–99; in Ravel's music, 97–99

Rhythm of the Saints (Simon), 128

Rieff, David, 124–26

Riney, Hal, 199

Rising from the East (Sagoo), 148

"Ritournelle" (Rameau), 228 n. 55

rock music: categorization of, 163; commodification of, 166–70; country music vs., 168–69, 175–76; politics and, 165–70; as world music, 167–70

Rodgers, Jimmie, 170

"Romans" (advertising spot), 199

Roots of Bhangra (recording), 150

Rosand, Ellen, 30–31

Rousseau, Jean-Jacques, 100, 225 n. 18

Rowbotham, John Frederick, 76–77

Royal Caribbean Cruise Lines, 198–200, 208

Rudhyar, Dane, 106

Running with the Devil (Walser), 5

Ruskin, John, 100

Ryan, Rosie, 156

Saatchi and Saatchi, 188, 195–96, 204

Sacre du printemps, Le (Stravinsky), 104

Sagoo, Bally, 148, 150–52

Said, Edward: on imperialism, 87–88; orientalism of, 34–35, 51; on otherness in Mozart, 72, 75, 226 n. 34

Saint-Saëns, Camille, 86

Salmacida Spolia (Davenant), 37

Salome (Strauss), 82, 233 n. 37

Salome (Wilde), 82

Salonen, Esa-Pekka, 194

Sanchez, Michael, 142–43

Timothy D. Taylor is a professor of ethnomusicology and musicology at the University of California, Los Angeles.

Library of Congress Cataloging-in-Publication Data
Taylor, Timothy Dean.
Beyond exoticism : western music and the world / Timothy D. Taylor.
p. cm. — (Refiguring American music)
Includes bibliographical references (p.   ) and index.
ISBN-13: 978-0-8223-3957-1 (cloth : alk. paper)
ISBN-13: 978-0-8223-3968-7 (pbk. : alk. paper)
1. Music—Social aspects. 2. Exoticism in music. 3. Music and globalization. I. Title.
ML3916.T39 2007
780.9—dc22   2006027818